ALL · IN · ONE

CCSK™

Certificate of Cloud Security Knowledge

EXAM GUIDE

ABOUT THE AUTHOR

Graham Thompson is the founder of Intrinsec Security, a cloud security consulting and training organization that serves enterprises and governments across North America. He is a security professional with more than 25 years of experience in areas such as systems engineering, technical architecture, vulnerability assessment, and a variety of management roles. He has built successful multimillion-dollar security solutions for leading enterprises and government agencies.

Since 2010, Graham has dedicated himself to cloud security. He has architected and assessed cloud security solutions for government agencies and Fortune 500 financial, telecom, and retail companies across North America. He is a Cloud Security Alliance and (ISC)² authorized trainer of CCSK, CISSP, and CCSP, a course he helped develop as a subject matter expert.

In addition to his CSA and (ISC)² certifications, Graham has obtained multiple certifications, including Amazon, ISACA (CISA), Microsoft (MCSE), Cisco, Symantec, Fortinet, SANS, and others. He attended McGill University in Montreal and has been an adjunct professor for multiple security courses at Algonquin College in Ottawa.

About the Technical Editors

Ryan Bergsma, CCSK, is a dedicated cybersecurity professional who endeavors to promote best practices in cybersecurity in general and cloud security in particular. As the Training Program Director for the Cloud Security Alliance, he is constantly looking for ways to turn the most recent best practices documentation into training products that can help to fill the cybersecurity skills gap and develop individuals who can create a more secure cyber ecosystem. Ryan comes from a sales and business background and holds a bachelor's degree in computer information system security.

Daniele Catteddu is a security and risk management practitioner and a privacy evangelist. He worked in senior roles in both the private and public sectors. Currently, he is the CTO at Cloud Security Alliance, where he is responsible for driving the adoption of the organization technology strategy. He is the co-founder of the CSA STAR Program and a member of the Italian Standard National delegation at ISO/IEC SC27. He is a lecturer at the Maastricht University Centre on Privacy & Cybersecurity, a member of the European Privacy Association Scientific Committee, and a member of the Advisory Board of the Kent University CyberSecurity. In the past, he worked at ENISA, the European Union Agency for Cybersecurity, as an expert in the areas of critical information infrastructure protection and emerging and future risks. Before joining ENISA, he worked as an information security consultant in the banking and financial sector. He holds a master's degree in business administration and economics from the University of Parma (Italy). He is a frequent keynote speaker at leading security conferences and the author of several papers on cybersecurity and privacy.

Dr. Peter van Eijk, CCSK, CCSP, is a highly accomplished information technology professional with more than 40 years of experience in many fields of information and communications technology as well as computer science. He is a practitioner, a researcher, and a teacher. His experience includes teaching and researching computer networks, managing many projects and groups on digital infrastructure projects, and acting as the technical director of an Internet service provider. In his consulting career, his practical experience includes IT shared services cost and risk assessments, client-service architectures, IT strategy, collaborative architectures, and shared services implementations. He has also been active in ISO standardization activities, on government committees on critical network infrastructures, and as a volunteer for CSA activities. He authored and delivered several cloud-training programs, including the first version of what is now known as CompTIA Cloud Essentials. He is currently working as an independent CCSK trainer and as an associate professor of cybersecurity and the cloud at Hogeschool Utrecht. He holds a master's degree in mathematics and computer science from the University of Groningen and a PhD from Twente University.

CCSK™
Certificate of Cloud Security Knowledge
EXAM GUIDE

Graham Thompson

New York   Chicago   San Francisco
Athens   London   Madrid   Mexico City
Milan   New Delhi   Singapore   Sydney   Toronto

CCSK™ Certificate of Cloud Security Knowledge All-in-One Exam Guide

4 5 6 7 8 9   LCR   24 23 22 21

Library of Congress Control Number: 2019954757

ISBN   978-1-260-46008-7
MHID   1-260-46008-8

Sponsoring Editor
Wendy Rinaldi

Editorial Supervisor
Janet Walden

Project Manager
Anupriya Tyagi,
   Cenveo® Publisher Services

Acquisitions Coordinator
Emily Walters

Technical Editors
Ryan Bergsma, Daniele Catteddu,
   Peter van Eijk

Copy Editor
Lisa Theobald

Proofreader
Lisa McCoy

Indexer
Claire Splan

Production Supervisor
Lynn M. Messina

Composition
Cenveo Publisher Services

Illustration
Cenveo Publisher Services

Art Director, Cover
Jeff Weeks

This book is dedicated to you, the reader. My wish is that you use the knowledge in this book to secure your potential. Knowing that you may benefit by my efforts drove me to the finish line. Here's to your future success.

CONTENTS AT A GLANCE

CONTENTS

FOREWORD

Technology today can seem like a dizzying carnival ride. It moves fast, changes directions without notice, and if you aren't thinking about security, you can get hurt. Cloud computing is undoubtedly one of our most important and pervasive technologies. The cloud, in many ways, is the backbone of our global economy; it is used by consumers, businesses, and governments every day and has supplanted traditional, on-premises IT to a large degree. The idea of consuming compute as an on-demand service is compelling for organizations of all sizes and will only grow.

Securing the cloud is one of the most important mandates of the broader cybersecurity industry. The Cloud Security Alliance was formed in 2009 to address this issue and to create fundamental security best practices and educational programs to achieve this goal. CSA has grown into one of the most important security organizations worldwide, with more than 100 chapters and offices on five continents. CSA developed the Certificate of Cloud Security Knowledge (CCSK) to provide a competency benchmark for IT and security professionals to assure that they have the right set of skills to take all of the appropriate actions to secure the cloud computing they interact with. The CCSK is highly lauded, has won numerous awards, and is often a requirement for many positions.

Today, we are facing a critical skills gap in cybersecurity. Many studies have shown that the global gap in cybersecurity professionals literally runs into the millions. Of the professionals who are employed in our industry, a large number need to upgrade their skills from traditional on-premises IT security to the dynamic world of cloud computing. The CCSK is one of the keys to a better, more lucrative career.

Why is cloud security knowledge unique? Because cloud computing changes constantly and has a unique shared responsibility model, and the security best practices that must be employed have a great deal of nuance compared to those required for a computer that an administrator has complete control over. For example, performing vulnerability scans on traditional systems must be carefully coordinated to ensure that results are accurate and that other production systems are not impacted. On the other hand, the cloud has a tremendous number of new automation capabilities that can make many existing problems, such as patch management, much easier to address at scale. DevSecOps is a term describing a radical new approach to coordinated security with these new tools. It is important for you to understand the security differences in the cloud for operations, risk management, and, ultimately, for compliance with the plethora of security and privacy requirements.

To help meet these challenges, I am delighted to endorse this McGraw-Hill publication, the *CCSK Certificate of Cloud Security Knowledge All-in-One Exam Guide*, authored by CCSK trainer Graham Thompson. The CSA team has worked closely with McGraw-Hill to ensure that this book is a comprehensive guide to version 4 of the CCSK. Readers will be introduced to a diverse set of topics that make up the full body of knowledge that is the CCSK. Readers will be provided with everything needed to attempt and pass the examination for the CCSK. They will even receive a discount code to take the test at a reduced price!

For Cloud Security Alliance, a not-for-profit association with deep roots in the cybersecurity industry, raising the bar in how we protect the world's information is more than a vocation—it is a passion. We truly believe that a few experts reading this tome may play an outsized role in saving our digital world. Thank you for choosing this book, and good luck in achieving the Certificate of Cloud Security Knowledge.

Jim Reavis
CEO, Cloud Security Alliance

ACKNOWLEDGMENTS

I first want to thank my Princess and our four boys, Graham Jr., Nathan, Ryan, and Tristan. You've all put up with so much while I have been in an endless pursuit of building a career and self-validation. You all have given me a life that I can only wish for others. Maybe someday I'll believe in myself as much as you all do.

This book wouldn't have been possible without the incredible efforts by Ryan Bergsma, Daniele Catteddu, and Peter van Eijk of the Cloud Security Alliance. Their technical reviews and contributions helped immensely in making this book what it is. Because of their input, this book not only prepares you for the CCSK exam, but it will make you a better security professional overall. At least that's my hope.

I would also like to sincerely thank Jim Reavis, founder and CEO of the Cloud Security Alliance, for everything he has done for me since the initial launch of the CCSK. Without him, none of this would have been possible. My family and I will always be appreciative of your kindness and support.

To Wendy and the team at McGraw-Hill, thanks for all of your patience during the process and for answering all of my beginner questions. Before this project began, I honestly never appreciated all of the individuals and effort that goes into making a book with a top publisher. I promise I will never look at a bookstore the same way.

From a professional and career perspective, I want to thank everyone that I have had the pleasure of working with over these past decades. A special nod goes to the whole team at CTP. It has been an honor working with all of you. I never believed that a company could ever feel like a family, especially when you're a consultant. Thanks for allowing me to help build that boat. By the way, Liz, the orchid is still alive and holds a very special place in our home.

Finally, I want to thank my mother, Florence Thompson (nee Kingan). She was such a strong woman and a true inspiration. A single parent trying her best to raise a wild-child son (that's me!). How I wish you were here with us now to see how everything has worked out.

INTRODUCTION

When the present iteration of cloud computing became generally available circa 2007, there was much confusion in the market regarding what the cloud was and how it was different from virtualization, mainframes, grid computing, and other technologies. To add to the general confusion regarding this technology, companies didn't understand how to properly secure data being stored and processed in a cloud environment. To aid companies in the secure adoption of cloud services, the Cloud Security Alliance (CSA) created the industry's first guide to addressing cloud security with the creation of the inaugural Security Guidance for Critical Areas of Focus in Cloud Computing in 2009 (I'll just call this the Guidance document from now on).

Since its creation, the Guidance has been updated multiple times (now at version 4) and continues to serve countless enterprises looking to securely adopt cloud services. The Guidance itself is the basis of the Certificate of Cloud Computing Knowledge (CCSK) designation. This book is written to help you understand the various domains of knowledge covered by the CSA Guidance as well as the companion document (ENISA) so you can pass your CCSK exam and be a professional who helps companies address appropriate security for cloud environments of all types.

Why Get Certified?

Companies of all sizes are adopting cloud services. These companies have come to the realization that secure implementation and management of the cloud aren't the same as traditional computing and that dedicated professionals need to be in place to secure this new era of computing. The CCSK was the first cloud security designation available in the industry. More than a decade later, it is still widely regarded as an industry-leading certification that demonstrates holders have both the qualification and competency to tackle cloud security across a wide range of disciplines. Obtaining your CCSK demonstrates to employers that you possess the knowledge required to address security controls properly in any cloud environment.

How to Get Certified

You take the CCSK exam online; it is not a proctored exam. You can attempt the exam from any Internet-accessible machine at a time of your choosing. There is no experience requirement for you to take the exam, but experience in general IT security is beneficial to your probability of success. At the time of writing, the exam itself comprises 60 questions and takes 90 minutes, and you need 80 percent or higher to pass. The exam is open book, but—make no mistake—it is a very tough exam.

In preparation for your exam, I recommend that you understand the concepts covered in this book and have reviewed the main documents the exam itself is built from. These are the CSA Guidance (v4) and ENISA Cloud Computing Benefits, Risks, and

Recommendations for Information Security. These documents are freely available on the Cloud Security Alliance web site. I strongly encourage you to have these documents available when you take the exam. I also recommend that you have two monitors available if possible. One is for the exam itself and the other is for the Guidance and ENISA documents, as well as the latest copy of the Cloud Controls Matrix.

Three notes about this exam: First, like all technical exams, you can expect the question writer to try to "trick" you. You need to understand what the question is really asking. The second note is not to get lulled into a false sense of security because the exam is open book. You have 1 minute 30 seconds per question in the CCSK exam (60 questions in 90 minutes). Do not think you can look up every question, and please do not open Google. They are testing you on your knowledge of CSA best practices, not what someone on the Internet says.

Finally, trust what you've learned from this book and answer questions with your instincts. Everything in this book has been written to prepare you fully for anything you may be asked in the CCSK. Unless you are proven wrong in a later question, never change your mind. Nine times out of ten, you'll overthink the answer and change it to a wrong answer. Understand the question, trust your gut, and move on to the next question.

Once you pass the exam, you are a CCSK holder for life. The exam version is updated when the CSA Guidance is updated. For example, the current version of the Guidance and the CCSK are both version 4. There are no Continuing Professional Education (CPEs) to file, no annual maintenance fees (AMFs) to pay, and the CSA does not "retire" your certification if you don't pay for another exam in a short time period (here's looking at you, every vendor certification ever). As you can imagine, you'd be wise to update your certification to the current level in the future, but let's get the certificate first before looking down that road.

CCSK Domains

The knowledge that you will be tested on is rather immense and covers a wide range of domains. This is what makes the CCSK exam difficult to pass and valuable as a result. This isn't an "I can configure a security group" type of exam. It is a vendor-neutral exam that addresses a wide range of topics, from governance, risk, and compliance (GRC), all the way through to understanding the proper security controls surrounding new technologies such as big data, serverless computing, and containers. The following is an overview of the 14 domains of the CSA Guidance and the ENISA document that is also covered in the CCSK exam.

Domain 1: Cloud Computing Concepts and Architectures

This domain sets the foundational knowledge of cloud security standards, including references to standards publications from organizations such as NIST and ISO. Key topics delivered in the domain consist of essential characteristics, service models, deployment models, and logical models. A critical takeaway from this domain is the logical model. Understanding this model is critical to your truly understanding the shared responsibility your company inherits when it adopts cloud computing of any type.

Domain 2: Governance and Enterprise Risk Management

Governance and risk management are incredibly broad topics. This domain focuses on the changes to governance, risk management (both enterprise and information), and information security functions as a result of using cloud services. This is where due diligence comes into play. If you are storing regulated data with a cloud service provider (CSP) that in turn leverages a discount storage emporium in some far-off land with zero security controls in place, you are ultimately accountable. Sure, the CSP is the one who chose to use a discount storage offering, but you will face the consequences of their actions in courts of law and with regulators. In other words, you can never outsource accountability, so do yourself a favor and perform due diligence.

Domain 3: Legal Issues, Contracts, and Electronic Discovery

Following up on governance, this domain addresses legal implications associated with adopting and delivering cloud services. It deals with legal issues (such as jurisdictional requirements and e-discovery), third-party contracts, and third-party access to data stored in a cloud environment. When thinking of the legal impacts that are possible with the cloud, you should keep a couple of things in mind. First, the laws are being drawn up as you read this. There's very little in the way of precedence for lawyers to use to help guide executives, and this is true around the globe. Second, unless you are engaged as counsel for your firm, you really have no business instructing your company on legal implications associated with the cloud and the various jurisdictional landmines that may arise. Your goal here is to understand that there are potential issues as a result of the cloud and that you need legal input in some situations.

Domain 4: Compliance and Audit Management

Compliance is a function that ensures policies are being followed. Audit is a key function of ensuring that your people are following guidance (proving or disproving that compliance is met). Pretty simple, right? There's good news delivered in this domain. Most of what you do in traditional IT will remain similar to what you're doing in the cloud. The bad news? Your cloud implementations probably don't follow your security policies, because nobody has been watching. Why is nobody watching? Great question. To answer that, you have to consider who is educating business owners about the risks of the cloud (hint: vendors). This domain discusses the things to look for when you're adding the cloud to your existing compliance and audit programs.

Domain 5: Information Governance

When you think of governance and information security, what do you think they are in place to protect? Are they there to protect systems, or are they in place to protect the information stored in those systems? What will cause a company to mess up so badly that they end up on the front page of a national newspaper? A disclosure of consumer information is the answer. Now consider this data in the cloud. What is the data classification level? Where is it stored? How is it protected? Who can access the data? These are some of the questions that need to be addressed when you're considering governance and protection of data being stored in the cloud. This domain covers them all and then some.

Domain 6: Management Plane and Business Continuity

The management plane is how everything is built and managed in a cloud environment. You can consider it the human interface into the inner workings of a cloud implementation. Securing this human interface is the single most critical aspect of a secure cloud environment, regardless of the service model used. Want to click a box to encrypt Software as a Service (SaaS) data? Management plane. Want to build a new server instance in Infrastructure as a Service (IaaS)? Management plane. Want to set up a failover region and copy data or images across the country or around the globe nightly to support disaster recovery and business continuity requirements? You guessed it, management plane. Regarding business continuity and disaster recovery in IaaS, how are you going to architect and plan for that? If you're thinking of a multicloud approach, you really need to understand what you're getting into before you do it (TLDR—usually not a great idea).

Domain 7: Infrastructure Security

Workloads in a cloud environment are so much more than just virtual machines. Today's cloud infrastructure uses software defined networking, containers, immutable instances, serverless computing, and other technologies that are covered in this module. How is this virtual infrastructure protected? How are detection and response performed? Where are your log files being stored? Are they protected in the event of an account compromise? If your plan for protection is an agent, and vulnerability assessments in a cloud are limited to running a scanner against an IP address, you need to rethink your options in this new environment.

Domain 8: Virtualization and Containers

Virtualization is a core technology in the cloud, and it's not just virtual machines. Virtualization is how compute, network, and storage pools resources are created and is the driving force behind the multitenancy aspect of cloud services. In this domain, we look at the responsibility split for securing various virtualized technologies—what to look for from the provider and what you need to do as the consumer. You'll learn that even the virtualized networking technology that we are accustomed to as IT professionals is antiquated in this new environment. The second part of this domain covers the various components involved with containers and approaches to securing them.

Domain 9: Incident Response

As the old saying goes, failing to plan is planning to fail. Unless you have gone through the exercise of planning and continuously testing your incident response capability in a cloud environment, your company is guaranteed to be surprised when an incident occurs and your incident response team's first question is, "Who do we call to disconnect the server from the network?" Does your incident response team have the virtual tools required for this new virtual environment? Have your incident response processes been completely changed for cloud services? Many things can remain as they were before the cloud, but incident response is not one of them. Having new processes to take advantage of cloud services is the difference between minutes and hours of downtime.

Domain 10: Application Security

Application security of migrated applications doesn't change as a result of running them in a cloud. Cloud-native applications are a completely different story. These cloud-native apps could be using permanent (such as access keys) or temporary (such as role inheritance) credentials to begin with. If they are using permanent credentials, how are these credentials rotated in accordance with policy? If temporary credentials are being used, how are these checked for least privilege (developers are going to develop, after all)? What happens if this new cloud-native app has a series of dependencies on other CSP services, and some of them are prohibited from use in your company because they have not been assessed by an independent third party?

Domain 11: Data Security and Encryption

A lot of what is considered "adequate" encryption in the cloud is based on the classification of data. When encryption is required (because of regulatory or policy requirements), you have three things to consider: the location of the data, the location of the encryption engine, and key location. Your company's risk tolerance is unique. Some company policies may require localized key management, and others may be OK with checking a box (literally). This domain explores the trade-offs associated with various encryption-at-rest services such as provider-managed and customer-managed keys.

Domain 12: Identity, Entitlement, and Access Management

When implementing or assessing cloud services, your primary check is, and will always be, access controls. Like traditional IT, least privilege is always the best approach to granting individuals access to what they need to do their jobs, and nothing more. Is this basic? Absolutely. So is not granting everyone in the world access to personally identifiable information (PII) data on millions of clients stored in S3, yet that has happened on numerous occasions. What is not basic? Permissions that are granted via JSON scripts that need to be validated as part of any assessment or audit of IaaS. You need to know how these entitlements are processed and their resultant permissions set.

Domain 13: Security as a Service

Security as a Service (SecaaS) enables you to protect your cloud and traditional assets via a cloud offering. When thinking of SecaaS, think of *Security Software as a Service*. There are many benefits associated with this type of deployment, such as the ability to use someone else's infrastructure, that will enforce your corporate policy. A vast number of security services are available, ranging from identity management to vulnerability assessments. Even if you are not using a vendor's cloud offering, your company is still impacted by the systemic shift in the industry. This is because vendor stakeholders are demanding a recurring revenue model that the cloud brings. Research and development are being poured into the cloud version and not the traditional offering.

Domain 14: Related Technologies

The final domain of the CSA Guidance deals with security of technologies that are not exclusive to the cloud, but that are generally deployed in a cloud because of the elasticity and broad network access characteristics of cloud computing. There are four technologies covered by the CSA: big data, Internet of Things, mobile devices, and serverless computing. Of these, most of the focus is on big data. Securing big data can be exceptionally challenging, because it is often a collection of technologies, each with its own security and process requirements. The main components of a big data system that are common are distributed data collection, distributed storage, and distributed processing.

ENISA Cloud Computing: Benefits, Risks, and Recommendations for Information Security

This document, which contains information included in the CCSK exam, covers the security benefits, associated risks, vulnerabilities, and recommendations for cloud computing. Although written by the ENISA in 2009, this document is still an important source of key risks surrounding cloud services, and it remains timely. Although much of this document is covered as part of the CSA Guidance document, it covers the vulnerabilities and associated organizational, technical, legal, and general risks associated with cloud computing.

The Differences Between Traditional and Cloud Security

Security principles don't change as a result of moving to the cloud. You still have a requirement to grant people the permissions they need to do what they need to do, and nothing more. The "Security CIA (Confidentiality, Integrity, Availability) Triad" still exists, as does the requirement for controls surrounding prevention, detection, and response capabilities. What mostly changes is "who" is responsible for the controls and "how" they are implemented. Take an SaaS system that is used for PII data, for instance. If the provider you are using doesn't perform encryption of data at rest and that data is compromised, you will be accountable to your clients and any regulatory body. Is telling your clients, "We assumed the provider encrypted the data, but we were wrong," a valid defense? In some cases, the responsibility for implementation of a security control may be transferred to a CSP, but make no mistake, your company always remains accountable for security and privacy, no matter which party implements the controls.

Corporate governance and policies need not change as a result of moving to the cloud, but they need to be extended to cover cloud services. When you're adopting public cloud services, always remember that you are building a cyber supply chain based on third parties that you have little to no control over. Take, for example, a McAfee study published in 2017 that stated that 52 percent of companies surveyed indicated that they had definitively tracked a malware infection to an SaaS application. This is just one example of why you need to perform due diligence on any provider that you will rely upon to store or process data securely. At this time, there seems to be a disconnect across all industries as to what a CSP is expected to do for customers and what they actually do, or even make available for customers to meet policies. Many business owners expect an SaaS vendor to take care of everything for them. Ask yourself this question: "How can you meet a policy that states credential revocation upon termination if nobody in your firm has been tasked with maintaining the identity and access management (IAM) offered by the provider?"

 NOTE To read about the study, "Building Trust in a Cloudy Sky," visit https://www.mcafee.com/enterprise/en-us/assets/executive-summaries/ es-building-trust-cloudy-sky.pdf.

Now that the basics have been covered, cloud security seems pretty straightforward, doesn't it? Perform your due diligence, assign someone to manage the security settings offered by the provider, and everything will be awesome. Well, that was SaaS. IaaS is a completely different story.

It may sound repetitive, but IaaS really is what you make of it. If you migrate a "legacy" application from your data center to an IaaS provider, your security at the application (applistructure) and data (infostructure) levels doesn't change at all. The operating system security stays the same, as do the security controls in the application itself. Your people already know how to configure and secure these things, right? What is completely different, however, is the virtual environment (metastructure) in which this application is running, and, of course, the physical (infrastructure) environment that belongs to a third party in a public cloud deployment, to which you likely have no access. Much of this book addresses the security controls for prevention, detection, and response capabilities at the metastructure layer.

On the other hand, building a cloud-native application thrusts your company into a brand-new world where security controls may be supplied by the vendor, may be limited, or may even be nonexistent. Serverless applications are calling unknown services and have unknown dependencies that may have both security and licensing issues. Even if your applications are using approved services, you must consider the level of privilege associated with access to said services. Are your developers using permanent or temporary credentials?

And then there are the free cloud offerings. You would expect the CSP to deliver complete transparency to customers, but do you really expect a "freemium" provider to advertise that usage of their "free" product grants them ownership of all data stored in their environment? I mean, how else do you expect them to grow a client base?

When looking at cloud security in its totality, we can see the old 80/20 rule comes into play yet once again—that is, 80 percent of everything you've always done as a security professional in IT remains the same, and 20 percent more changes the game entirely.

Hopefully I've gotten your attention and you're excited to get your cloud security certification journey underway. Let's get started securing your potential. You got this!

Cloud Computing Concepts and Architectures

This chapter covers the following topics from Domain 1 of the CSA Guidance:

- Cloud Logical Model
- Definitions of Cloud Computing
- Cloud Service Models
- Cloud Deployment Models
- Reference and Architecture Models
- Cloud Security, Compliance Scope, and the Shared Responsibility Model
- Areas of Critical Focus in Cloud Security

The beginning is the most important part of the work.

—Plato

As Plato said, the most important part of the work is at the beginning, which should start with laying a strong foundation. This chapter serves as the foundation for the chapters that follow and includes concepts that you need to understand to be a successful CSA Certificate of Cloud Security Knowledge (CCSK) candidate. It describes and defines cloud computing, establishes baseline terminology, and details the overall logical and architectural frameworks such as the International Standards Organization/International Electrotechnical Commission (ISO/IEC) 17789 standard and the National Institute of Standards and Technology (NIST) 800-145 and 500-292 standards, which are discussed throughout the book.

EXAM TIP   You'll be seeing quite a few references to standards by NIST and other organizations in this book. Don't jump away from this book and start studying these documents. The CCSK exam is about cloud security according to the CSA; it's not about NIST standards. The exam is open-book, so if you're facing a question about a Special Publication number (the number, not the content within), you can quickly look it up in the CSA Guidance document. As for the content of the CSA Guidance document itself, this book covers everything you need to know (and then some!) for your exam.

Although cloud services are presented to the consumer in a user-friendly format, the implementation required to support upwards of 1 million customers behind the scenes is quite different from what even the most seasoned IT professionals are accustomed to. The cloud service provider (CSP) creates and manages an offering that consists of pools of resources (Compute, Network, Storage) that are accessed via controllers that communicate using application programming interfaces (APIs). It is through these pools and API access that several essential characteristics of the cloud (such as self-service, elasticity, and resource pooling) are possible. A very high-level diagram shown in Figure 1-1 demonstrates how the controller is key to serving resources in an abstracted (you don't access the hardware directly) and orchestrated (coordinates the processes) manner. In a nutshell, you basically request something (Compute, Network, Storage) from the controller, and the controller takes care of the rest for you.

 NOTE Generally, RESTful APIs (REST stands for Representational State Transfer) are used because the APIs are considered lightweight (inexpensive) calls in comparison to the alternative Simple Object Access Protocol (SOAP) API calls. SOAP API calls have the benefit of security services being part of all calls, but the associated overhead makes them larger (more expensive) in comparison. I'll discuss RESTful and SOAP APIs in greater detail in Chapter 6.

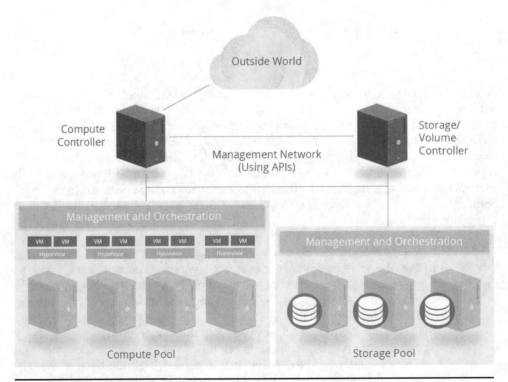

Figure 1-1 Cloud controllers and pools of resources. (Used with permission of Cloud Security Alliance.)

When most people think of the cloud, they think of how "cheap" it is in comparison to the traditional information technology (IT) structure. While cloud computing can be (but is not always) cheaper because of economies of scale at the provider's side, cloud consumers must appreciate that the provider cannot be everything to everyone (that is, the CSP cannot meet everyone's security policies). As a result, you need to be very aware of the shared responsibilities that come with any potential cost savings. The provider will supply you with some security controls, but you will be responsible for implementing other controls. The bottom line here is this: the idea that a CSP takes care of everything for you is a fallacy that really needs to die. Although the shared responsibilities are primarily based on the service model consumed (Software as a Service [SaaS], Platform as a Service [PaaS], or Infrastructure as a Service [IaaS]), the deployment model also comes into play when determining what a consumer must do to secure a cloud environment properly.

 NOTE   Refer to the "Glossary" at the end of this book for definitions and explanations of all the cloud acronyms.

Cloud computing offers tremendous potential benefits in agility, resiliency, and economy. As a result, organizations can move faster (no hardware purchases and racking/stacking servers), reduce downtime (if architected to take advantage of elasticity and other cloud characteristics), and save money (no capital expenses, and operational expenditures can be reduced by right-sizing server specs and quantity on the fly to meet actual demand). As for security at the provider level, the CSP business model requires that extremely strong controls be in place if the provider is to remain in business. (Would you do business with a cloud provider that was successfully hacked three times in the past year?) I'm not saying that providers must create some sort of impenetrable security through breakthrough research on the security capabilities of dilithium crystals—but they can, and generally will, spend appropriate time and money to make certain that security is very well architected into everything they do. In fact, I'm kind of jealous of the security function in provider environments. I mean, there aren't too many companies out there that will spend months making sure that security is fully addressed before going live with a product. In most organizations, the security group is given the heads-up on Wednesday that a new application is being deployed on Saturday and that it's a top priority, so security will have to be addressed in the next version.

The cloud is really what you make of it. You can simply migrate a server in a "like-for-like" fashion by performing a physical-to-virtual (P2V) migration to create that very same system running in a cloud environment. You might think this would be the easiest way to adopt cloud services, but the thing is, all you've really done is take a server that you have physical control over and make a virtual image of it, so that now you are running a single point of failure in someone else's physical environment over which you have no control.

The real power of the cloud is manifested when you understand and adopt cloud-native models and adjust your architectures and controls to align with the features and capabilities of cloud platforms. If architected properly, servers can be treated as cattle, not pets. (This expression is often used to describe a pattern where servers are viewed as easily replaceable commodities, not "long-standing" resources, as they are in a traditional environment.) The focus of workload management moves from "we need X servers" to "we need this application to serve X concurrent connections." In fact, you may not even have servers to manage if you are leveraging serverless computing (aka functions). Although I haven't covered serverless computing yet (that happens in Chapter 7), I'm using this opportunity to emphasize that security in a cloud environment can drastically change based on how you use it, up to and including having to secure something that never existed in the past.

What follows in this chapter builds a foundation for the rest of the book, provides a common language and understanding of cloud computing for security professionals, begins highlighting the differences between cloud and traditional computing, and helps guide security professionals toward adopting cloud-native approaches that result in better security (and other benefits), instead of creating more risks.

Cloud Logical Model

The cloud *logical model* is a CSA creation that clearly defines four layers of functionality and applicable security requirements that exist in both traditional and cloud environments:

- **Infrastructure layer**   Infrastructure security
- **Metastructure layer**   Virtual environment security
- **Infostructure layer**   Data security
- **Applistructure layer**   Application and operating system security

 EXAM TIP   Understand these layers of the logical model! These layers are key to understanding cloud security responsibility shifts and passing your CCSK exam.

The following sections describe the layers of the logical model as covered by the CSA.

Infrastructure

The servers, networking, and storage pools exist at this layer. Security at this layer involves properly securing the physical world. Do you run a private cloud that you own? You own this layer. Have a public cloud? This layer is owned and operated by someone else. In other words, it's the provider's world, and you're just working in it.

Metastructure

This layer is the game-changing aspect of cloud. In this layer, you both configure and manage a cloud deployment of any type. The single biggest thing you need to understand immediately about the difference between the cloud and traditional IT is the metastructure

The Importance of Metastructure Security

Here's an example that will help you understand why metastructure security is so important.

Question: Why does this employee we fired six months ago still have access to the payroll database?

Answer: Metastructure security.

Question: How did we wind up on the front page of a national newspaper for leaking information on millions of customers?

Answer: Metastructure security.

The following table provides the results of some insecure metastructure configurations—"misconfigurations"—that actually occurred with Amazon Simple Storage Service (Amazon S3). All of these issues occurred because someone granted everyone in the world read access to these files. This is so basic, yet still so misunderstood. Is this misconfiguration or incompetence? I'll let you decide. The basics still matter, folks.

Discovery Date	No. of Records Compromised	Information Exposed
June 2017	198 million	Voter records containing personally identifiable information (PII), including names, birthdates, addresses, and more
July 2017	6 million	PII, account details, and PINs used by a company to validate customers
December 2017	123 million	Census and credit rating data for nearly every US household
April 2019	540 million	Facebook account data, including users, likes, comments, and more

In case you're thinking to yourself, "What's the big deal? That's not even a billion records!" Let's move from S3 leaks to a company that is the poster child (thus far) for the importance of building and maintaining a secure metastructure: Code Spaces. Don't bother going to the Code Spaces web site, because the company went out of business in 2014.

Although I've seen some variations to the story, the main gist behind it all is that a bad actor gained access to the console (metastructure), attempted to extort the company, and destroyed everything when the company tried to regain control. Pick your poison here—leaking millions of records or a company going bankrupt as a result of metastructure security. Either way, you can appreciate how important metastructure security is.

Oh, just one more thing about this story: Before Code Spaces was compromised, the company displayed the following on its web site: "Backing up data is one thing, but it is meaningless without a recovery plan, not only that a recovery plan—and one that is well-practiced and proven to work time and time again. Code Spaces has a full recovery plan that has been proven to work and is, in fact, practiced." Uh-huh. That's right up there with a company stating, "Security and privacy are very important to us" after a breach or "The check is in the mail."

METASTRUCTURE

in your data center. It is within the metastructure logical layer that you build the virtual tools required for a virtual world (the cloud).

You'll perform configuration in the *management plane* through a graphical user interface (GUI), a command-line interface (CLI), or an API, depending on what the provider offers to interact with its infrastructure. Right about now, I like to call out the need for virtual tools for a virtual world. Want to add a new user for SaaS? You do it here. Want to set up a zero-trust network in IaaS? This is the place to do it.

If your team knows nothing about the metastructure, they know nothing about securely configuring, managing, or responding to incidents in the cloud. Make no mistake: *you* are in charge of configuring and managing this layer. Configuration and management mistakes in this layer are why so many companies have been burned in the past when using cloud services (and will likely continue to be burned for the rest of time).

> **EXAM TIP** Remember that the management plane is part of the metastructure.

Infostructure

This is where the information and data reside. This could be file storage, databases—whatever. Security in this layer doesn't really change; how you secure things may change, but the principles of data security remain the same.

Applistructure

Applications and all of the services used to build and support them reside here. Your applications could be running on a Microsoft or Linux server of your own, or they could be running in a wide variety of new technologies such as containers, microservices, or serverless networks (I cover these technologies later). If you take an image of a running system and migrate it into the cloud, nothing changes from a security perspective. In this scenario, operating systems will always need patches, and application security still applies as it always has. As you start to build "cloud-native" applications to take advantage of the new technologies the cloud offers, your security is likely to change dramatically. I'll cover these changes in Chapter 10.

> **TIP** If you are reassessing an application that has been migrated in a "like-for-like" fashion from your data center to the cloud, nothing about your assessment of the application itself changes. The controls at the operating system are the same, as are the application security controls. Focus your efforts on the metastructure layer.

Cloud Computing Definitions

You'll find many definitions for "the cloud" out in the marketplace. For the CCSK exam, you really need to care about only two organizations and how they describe what a cloud comprises. Both NIST and CSA state that there are five essential characteristics, three

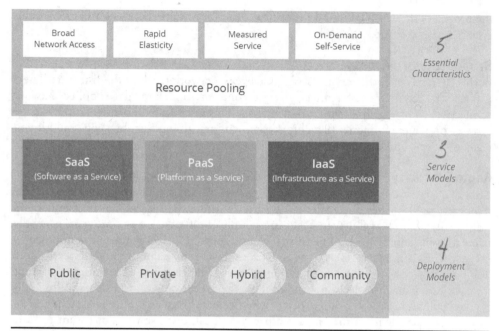

Figure 1-2 A cloud comprises five essential characteristics, three service models, and four deployment models. (Used with permission of Cloud Security Alliance.)

service models, and four deployment models. You will need to memorize these for the CCSK exam. Figure 1-2 gives a graphical view of these items.

NOTE ISO/IEC 17788 refers to multitenancy as a sixth essential characteristic.

Essential Characteristics

Simply stated, the following essential characteristics determine whether an offering is really a cloud service or not. If an organization is trying to sell you its "cloud service" and it doesn't have the five characteristics discussed here, you're getting "cloudwashed" (a term for trying to sell a non-cloud service as a cloud service) and not really getting the value that the cloud can bring to your company.

Resource Pooling

Resources (Compute, Network, Storage) are the most fundamental characteristic of the cloud. Resources are pooled, and consumers are granted access. A consumer's access to the pools is tightly isolated from that of other consumers, typically based on policies at the provider's side. NIST 800-145 specifically calls out multitenancy as an aspect of this essential characteristic.

Broad Network Access

In this characteristic, the service is available over a network (such as the Internet). There is no special requirement for direct physical connectivity or provider-supplied network connectivity. For example, you could manage an entire IaaS implementation via the browser on your cell phone. (I highly recommend not doing this, but you could if you really want to ruin your eyesight!)

Rapid Elasticity

This characteristic is the most powerful aspect of cloud. It enables consumers to scale resources based on demand, often automatically (note that access can be manual and scaling still applies). Scaling can occur in a couple of different ways. *Scaling up* generally refers to using more powerful servers (such as a four-CPU configuration as opposed to two), whereas *scaling out* refers to adding more servers (for example, adding servers to a web farm to service requests). Depending on the application and architecture, you want to make sure your provider supports scaling either up or out to meet demand. In addition to having the ability to add capacity when demand increases, you need to be able to *scale down* when demand drops. This aspect is critical, because you don't want to scale up to respond to a temporary increase in demand—you'd stay there in perpetuity and be surprised when the provider's bill is suddenly three times what it was the month before!

Measured Service

The measured service essential characteristic makes the cloud a pay-as-you-go model of computing: you're simply charged for what you use. Another term used in the CSA Guidance is "utility computing," which is akin to how you consume electricity or water from a utility.

On-Demand Self-Service

You have the ability to provision resources on your own without human intervention at the provider's side. Put another way, if your provider tells you that your ticket for a new server instance is very important to them and they will act on it in 48 to 72 hours, you're being cloudwashed. In Chapter 10, you'll see how this self-service characteristic can be used to automate security response capability using APIs through the implementation of event-driven security.

 EXAM TIP Here's a reminder about the essential characteristics, and it's a big one for your exam. The five characteristics are from NIST (SP800-145). ISO/IEC 17788 calls out multitenancy as an additional essential characteristic. NIST includes multitenancy as part of resource pooling, and CSA states that clouds are multitenant by nature. Just remember that all three organizations see the cloud as a multitenant environment, but only ISO/IEC lists multitenancy separately.

Cloud Service Models

The service model is a portion of the cloud reference architectures from ISO/IEC 17789 and NIST 500-292 documentation (CSA research uses the NIST model). The service model is presented as a stack to gain a high-level understanding of what is performed by a cloud service provider. This stack may be referred to as the "SPI" (SaaS, PaaS, IaaS) stack or SPI tiers. Figure 1-3 depicts the service models and how they are built on top of each other to form the SPI stack.

Unfortunately, the marketing folks took notice of the "as a service" part and went pretty wild with it. As a result, there are all kinds of "as a service" categories such as

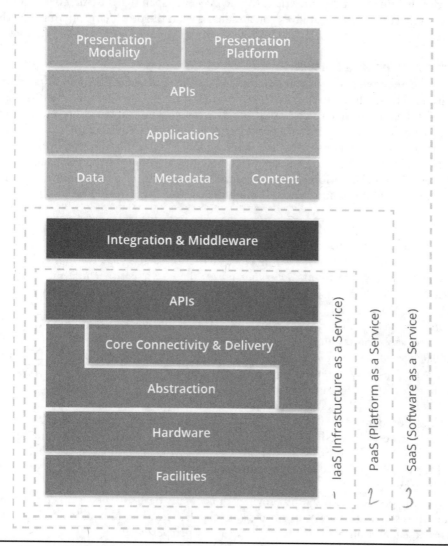

Figure 1-3   Service models are arranged on an SPI stack. (Used with permission of Cloud Security Alliance.)

Identity as a Service (IDaaS), Function as a Service (FaaS), and anything else that sounds "cool." The reality, as far as your exam is concerned, is that three service models form the SPI stack (or tiers).

 NOTE You'll see in Chapter 13 that CSA does call out Security as a Service as an additional service model, but as far as the current discussion goes, you can think of it as Security *Software* as a Service.

A final note about the SPI stack: Not every available category of service fits in nicely and cleanly into one of the three tiers. (Some may even span tiers!) Remember that this is merely a descriptive tool that gives you an idea of what the provider is offering regarding the responsibility shift associated with the offering. It is by no means a rigid framework.

Infrastructure as a Service

IaaS is the underlying foundation that consists of the physical facilities and infrastructure hardware. The hardware itself may be customized, proprietary, or standard off the shelf, but it's still hardware, like you'll find in any data center. The difference, however, is in the resource pooling, abstraction, automation, and orchestration. Abstraction is usually based on virtualization of servers, networks, and/or storage. It is this abstraction that allows for the pools of resources to be created (for example, a group of hypervisors all working together). The orchestration enables a controller to request resources from the pools of resources, and all this is automated through the use of APIs (mostly RESTful APIs).

About Hypervisors

The most commonly known form of virtualization is a *virtual machine*, which is generally synonymous with *hypervisor* (also called a virtual machine monitor, or VMM) technology. Essentially, the hypervisor acts as the host and allows a single hardware server to host many virtual machines that are referred to as "guests." The hypervisor is tasked with "tricking" the guest machines into thinking they are directly accessing the underlying hardware, but in reality they are operating in an isolated virtual environment with their own virtual hardware resources. (Put in a more polished way, the hypervisor is an abstraction layer that decouples the physical hardware from the guest operating system.)

There are two types of hypervisors of note: Type 1 hypervisors are installed directly onto the physical server (such as VMware ESXi, Xen, or KVM), and Type 2 hypervisors are installed on top of the operating system already running on a server (such as VMware Workstation, VMware Workstation Player, or Oracle VM VirtualBox). I can't imagine any cloud service provider using anything other than a Type 1 hypervisor.

The hypervisor used by the provider can actually have an impact on consumers and thus should be known in advance of provider selection. Not all hypervisors are created equal from performance and capability perspectives.

EXAM TIP It's important to remember that an IaaS system can be summarized as consisting of facilities (physical data center), hardware (proprietary or standard), abstraction (virtualization), and orchestration (APIs).

Let's look at a scenario that ties this all together. Say you want to create an Ubuntu Server instance with two CPUs, 12GB of RAM, 2TB of storage, and two network cards. Here's what happens behind the scenes at the provider side (shown in Figure 1-4):

1. The cloud controller contacts the compute controller to request that a new server with two CPUs and 12GB of RAM be created.

2. The cloud controller contacts the storage controller to allocate 2TB of storage. This storage is connected to the new server instance through a storage network.

3. The cloud controller requests two virtual network interface cards from the network controller.

After all of this is performed, the cloud controller takes the requested Ubuntu Server image, copies it to the newly created virtual server, boots it, and configures it. Once this is done (measured in seconds or minutes), the controller makes the connection information available to the consumer.

The IaaS service can usually be accessed via multiple methods—web, CLI, or API. These interfaces are created and made available by the provider for customers to manage their virtual environment, hence the term *cloud management plane* (and is part of the metastructure logical model covered earlier in this chapter). In fact, the display of a web interface is mainly for human convenience. The provider will take actions performed graphically and convert them to API calls that are then executed. As a cloud consumer,

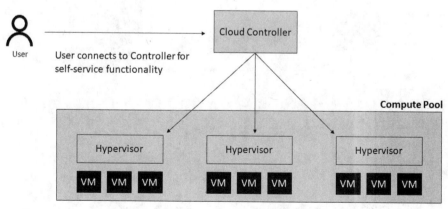

Cloud Controller orchestrates access to underlying pool of resources using APIs

Figure 1-4 Automation and orchestration of cloud components

anything you can do via the web interface can be done via the API calls that are exposed. More mature cloud implementations by consumers are programmatically driven through accessing APIs. In fact, this programmatic-driven virtual infrastructure (referred to as a *software defined infrastructure*, which is covered in Chapter 6) is something that every cloud consumer should strive for. The less human intervention through a web browser, the better, because there will be less human error and a much higher level of agility.

Platform as a Service

Of the three service models, PaaS is the blurriest of all of them. By CSA definition, PaaS adds a layer of integration with application development frameworks; middleware capabilities; and functions such as databases, messaging, and queuing. Figure 1-5 demonstrates a PaaS offering built on top of IaaS that creates a shared platform on which applications are run.

In the PaaS service model, the provider builds the infrastructure (or leverages IaaS from another provider), creates a shared platform that customers will leverage, and may expose security controls they believe customers want control over. The main benefit of using

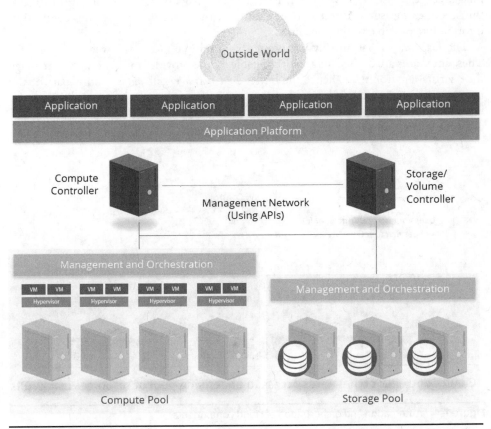

Figure 1-5   PaaS offering built on top of IaaS. (Used with permission of Cloud Security Alliance.)

PaaS is that it removes the overhead associated with building and maintaining servers and shifts that responsibility over to the provider (the service becomes somewhat of a black box). Customers in turn leverage this multitenant platform that is fully managed by the provider.

You can think of PaaS as a development platform that you can use to gain quick access to an environment to build things on, or to leverage for functionality. Take a "Database as a Service" PaaS offering, for example. Rather than launching an instance, configuring the operating system, and then installing and configuring your chosen SQL software, you simply choose the SQL platform you want and answer a few questions, and your database is available within minutes.

The downside to PaaS, as far as security is concerned, is that controls exposed to the customer are restricted compared to those possible in IaaS. Consider this example scenario: A major provider's SQL PaaS offering enforces an eight-character password for the master SQL account. It's embedded within the service and isn't even part of the provider's integrated access management (IAM) offering. There's no password complexity enforcement, no rotation, and no way to check to see whether the password meets policy. This isn't to say PaaS is inherently insecure; it may, in fact, be more secure than a compliant application built in IaaS or in your own data center. But compliance isn't security, and vice versa.

 NOTE I was on an engagement once where a client who was considering using a SQL PaaS changed direction because they were unable to configure the Network Time Protocol (NTP) to use an internal NTP server as required by policy. Depending on your company, you may have to use an IaaS offering and build everything yourself just to meet corporate policy.

Change management is another issue you can run into with the PaaS provider owning and managing the platform. The provider can, and will, change what platforms will be supported and which ones will be deprecated over time. It is on you not only to be advised of these changes but also to identify potential issues and fix them before your provider makes the change. For example, if you are running application code in a development platform, you may eventually get an e-mail from your vendor announcing the introduction of a change to the platform that will break your application if your code has a dependency on functionality that is being deprecated. In a way, your provider is now dictating part of your change management. The provider may give you weeks, or they may give you months. It's up to them, not you, because they own the platform.

Software as a Service

The SaaS model can be simply defined as "renting a turnkey application from a provider." All SaaS applications are considered multitenant in nature and support access by web browsers and mobile applications. In many cases, SaaS applications also support access via API calls. The type of API supported (REST versus SOAP) and capabilities offered via the API are dependent on the provider in question.

The architecture of an SaaS application behind the scenes can range from a single server running both web and SQL services (read: single point of failure), or it can be an extremely complex system that consists of load balancers, redundant server farms, serverless components, and anything else imaginable. There are no rules or regulations as to what an SaaS (or any service model) provider must or must not do.

 NOTE "We're ten guys, we're all really smart, and we do the right thing; there's our security program." This is a quote told to me by an auditor of a multibillion-dollar company, who was interviewing the CTO of a potential SaaS provider as part of their due diligence. Needless to say, the provider didn't get the company's business. Always remember there are no rules or regulations as to what any CSP must do. This is especially true for SaaS, where the startup costs are trivial when compared to IaaS.

From a security and due diligence perspective, an important aspect of SaaS services is that the SaaS provider may use a separate provider for IaaS or PaaS purposes. The biggest issue here has to do with salespeople exaggerating the security of their application because it's being run in a different provider network. To be honest, I can't say if this happens because of ignorance or because they have no problem lying to prospective clients. As you already know, the cloud is a shared responsibility, and the SaaS vendor is just another client to the IaaS provider. If the application you are consuming has security issues at the applistructure layer (such as privilege escalation), that is 100 percent on the SaaS vendor. Along the same lines, the SaaS vendor who says their application is PCI- or HIPAA-compliant because it's being run in a compliant infrastructure is equally guilty of ignorance or worse. I'll cover the concept of compliance inheritance in greater detail in Chapter 4.

Cloud Deployment Models

Both NIST and ISO/IEC call out four deployment models, which refer to how the technologies are owned and how they are consumed. Deployment models are separate from the service models; with deployment models, you can have a private PaaS, for example. The main item to remember for your CCSK exam is the level of trust of other tenants who also use the service.

Public Cloud

This one is pretty simple. Anyone in the world with a credit card (stolen or not) can sign up to use the service. The infrastructure is owned and managed by a third party and is located off premises—somewhere other than your location.

Private Cloud

A private cloud is built for a single organization. Period. Full stop. Notice that unlike what I did with the public cloud, I'm not saying who owns or manages the infrastructure, and I didn't state whether it was on or off premises. That's because it can be any combination. You can have your own team install and manage a cloud infrastructure in your data center, or you can call a private cloud supplier and they could spin one up for you in their data center. The important fact is that only trusted people (well, people within your organization at least) will be accessing the cloud. Another trick in understanding what constitutes a private cloud is that it is really nothing more than controller software that automates and orchestrates access to pools of resources.

 NOTE A private cloud is also multitenant. An example of a tenant in a private cloud would be the groups in your company. Take HR and Finance groups, for example. These are two separate tenants as far as private cloud is concerned, because the HR group shouldn't have the same access to Finance's resources, and vice versa. The difference is that a private cloud tenant is trusted.

Community Cloud

A community cloud is generally built for multiple trusted organizations with similar concerns (such as a risk profile). The community cloud is much like a private cloud in that it can be built and managed by your company, or it can be outsourced. The co-tenants are also contractually bound. The key difference between a private and a community cloud is that the financial risk is shared across multiple contractually trusted organizations in the community cloud.

 TIP Don't get too hung up on the nuances between private and community clouds. Consider a franchise model, as an example. The "ACME Burger Joint" mega-corp builds a cloud and charges the franchisees a set fee to build and manage the community cloud that they all use to store financials, marketing materials, ordering data, and so on. Your particular corporate structure will dictate what terms you will use. At the end of the day, everyone has shared concerns, and that's what really matters.

Hybrid Cloud

A hybrid cloud is an interesting model with regard to how its definition has changed over the years. A hybrid cloud has historically been referred to as the connection of two different clouds (such as a public and private cloud) that are bound together by standardized or proprietary technologies that enabled data and application portability. In the past few years, however, this term has been extended to include a non-cloud data center being connected, or bridged, to a cloud provider.

The most important capabilities that are associated with the hybrid deployment model are portability and cloud bursting. *Portability* is the ability to shift where a workload is executed—for example, creating a P2V image of a physical server and moving that to a cloud environment. The connectivity between your data center and the cloud environment (hybrid) makes this possible. *Cloud bursting* means leveraging a cloud provider to supply additional resources to meet additional load. In this scenario, you could have a load balancer that will direct incoming web traffic either to internal or to cloud-based systems depending on current load.

EXAM TIP Don't get lost in applistructure thoughts when you're considering the cloud bursting example! How your web application handles things like state transfer and other application-level issues is out of scope for this discussion. For the exam, just recall the example of having a load balancer that will send incoming traffic to a web server that can be in your data center or a cloud-hosted system, depending on current load.

Cloud Security Scope and the Shared Responsibility Model

When looking at securing or assessing a cloud environment, you should keep in mind that the CSP is always responsible for implementing and configuring some aspects of the computing environment, and you are responsible for other aspects of the environment. This split is referred to as the *shared responsibility model* of the cloud. This shared responsibility model will determine the scope of each party's cloud security efforts.

Shared Responsibility Model

You know that the cloud has a security responsibility shift. You also know that this responsibility shift is based on the metastructure, because it includes the management plane. All traditional security principles and domains remain the same. The differentiator with the cloud is that the nature of risks, roles and responsibilities, and implementation of controls changes, often dramatically.

When thinking of the responsibility shifts, you should try to remember that the provider is going to supply customers with security that will satisfy most requirements, but you can't expect miracles. The provider will never know that you recently fired an employee and that the employee's access should be revoked. That's on you!

From a risk-tolerance perspective, every company, even the function in every company, will be different, and it's impossible for the provider to address every risk that every customer may need addressed, even for items the provider is responsible for. For all the models, you have general risk approaches: accept the risk, mitigate the risk by deploying a control to minimize the impact or likelihood, or avoid the risk.

NOTE Here's an extreme example of having to accept the risk the provider accepts: At a place I once worked, all devices were required to go through an X-ray process before they could be attached to the network. If the provider doesn't require something like this but your organization requires it, you're really limited to two options: accept the risk or avoid it by not using that provider's service.

For your exam, you should know that security responsibility maps to the degree of control any given actor has over the architecture stack. This is dictated primarily by the service model being consumed.

Responsibility	On-Premises	IaaS	PaaS	SaaS
Data governance	Customer	Customer	Customer	Customer
Client access endpoints	Customer	Customer	Customer	Customer
Identity and access management	Customer	Customer	Customer	Customer
Application security	Customer	Customer	Shared	Provider
Network security	Customer	Customer	Shared	Provider
Operating system security	Customer	Customer	Provider	Provider
Physical security	Customer	Provider	Provider	Provider

Table 1-1   Security Responsibility for Different Service Models

Table 1-1 shows a high-level breakdown of the security responsibility shift that comes with each service model in the SPI stack and how it compares to a traditional (on-premises) data center.

Notice in the table that in all the models, the customer is never outsourcing everything to the provider. You will always maintain a degree of responsibility, no matter what service model is used.

Let's take a look at a few examples of each service model to help you better understand Table 1-1:

- **SaaS**   You're renting access to a turnkey application. The provider is responsible for the application itself and everything that supports it, down to the physical security. As the customer, you're limited to what is exposed to you as a configurable item. For example, the provider could enable you to create a new user and assign certain permissions to that account, or it may allow for only one type of user; it's up to them to create it, and it's up to you to determine whether it's acceptable based on your risk tolerance.

- **PaaS**   In this example, we see a shared responsibility for the application security as well as the network security entries. Consider a scenario where you're using PaaS to run a custom application that you created. All the security surrounding the application code is on you—it's your application after all! But why is it shared? It's shared because the provider is responsible for the platform you're using to run the application on. As for the network security portion, the provider maintains the network and supplies standard security controls (such as firewalls and intrusion prevention systems), but what if you want certain IP addresses blocked? That part would be on you to integrate into your code, or you could use a web application firewall, for example.

- **IaaS**   This one is pretty simple, right? You're involved in everything aside from the facilities, physical hardware, and hypervisor. For instance, the provider may offer you operating system images that have all the latest patches installed, but once you launch an image to make your own instance, you're responsible for patching and securing everything to meet your security policies. As far as the network security entry, this is where things get interesting. You are responsible for using the network controls the provider makes available (such as a virtual firewall service like a security group). The provider creates the virtual firewall service and exposes that security control to customers so they can configure it according to their requirements. It's not the provider's responsibility to configure those for you.

Figure 1-6 shows how the security responsibility shifts based on the service model. The most important security consideration is knowing who is responsible for particular controls in any given cloud workload. In other words, you can't just assume a provider uses a particular control because they are providing a particular service model (SaaS, PaaS, IaaS). As already mentioned, the service models provide a description; it's not a firm framework. To get to the bottom of who is responsible for doing what, you should ask the following questions for every project:

- What does the provider do?
- What does the consumer need to do?
- Does the cloud provider enable customers to do what they need to do?
- What is included in the documentation the provider gives to customers?
- What is guaranteed in the contract and service level agreements?

 EXAM TIP The CCSK exam will likely test you on the shared responsibility between providers and customers. Take note of the following high-level recommendations for providers and customers: First, providers should properly design and implement controls. They should clearly document internal security controls and customer security features so the cloud user can make an informed decision. Second, customers should build a responsibilities matrix to document who is implementing which controls and how. This should be done on a per-workload basis. Selected controls should align with any necessary compliance standards.

Figure 1-6 Security responsibility shifts based on service model. (Used with permission of Cloud Security Alliance.)

Cloud Security Alliance Tools

OK, so you know there's a shared responsibility, you know that at a high level, customers are responsible for determining what controls need to be in place according to compliance standards, and you know that providers should implement security and be transparent about this—but wouldn't it be awesome if you had some kind of control model or framework to follow when investigating a provider security capability? Good news! The CSA has tools that you can use to assess security controls in a cloud environment in the Cloud Controls Matrix (CCM) and the Consensus Assessments Initiative Questionnaire (CAIQ). CSA even offers a freely available repository of provider-completed CAIQ responses, called the Security Trust Assurance and Risk (STAR) registry. We'll cover these tools at an appropriate level for the CCSK exam.

 EXAM TIP Don't waste your time memorizing all of the controls checked by the CSA tools! Download the most recent version of the CCM and the CAIQ, understand the format of each document and its purpose, and have it open when you take your CCSK exam. Remember, the exam is open-book.

Cloud Controls Matrix

The CCM tool contains more than 130 cloud security controls across 16 domains and maps them to multiple security and compliance standards. CCM version 3.0.1 is tested as part of the CCSK v4 exam. The nice thing about the CCM is that it can be used to document the security responsibilities of both the provider security controls and your own implementation of systems in a cloud environment.

If you haven't done so already, take a moment to access the CCM by downloading it from the CSA web site (cloudsecurityalliance.org). You should probably download the CAIQ at the same time, because I'm covering that one next. Because I can't go through every single entry (nor do you want to!), I'm going to use the first control in the CCM as a guide to understanding the structure of the spreadsheet.

The structure of the CCM itself is broken down into the following portions:

- **Control Domain and Control** This section lists the control domain and an individual control. For example, the first entry in the CCM is the "Application and Interface Security" domain, and "Application Security" is the individual control.

- **Control ID** This is a simple identification code for the control in question. Using the first entry as a reference, this is called AIS-01.

- **Updated Control Specification** This statement specifies the control objective. The wording for AIS-01 states, "Applications and programming interfaces (APIs) shall be designed, developed, deployed, and tested in accordance with leading industry standards (e.g., OWASP for web applications) and adhere to applicable legal, statutory, or regulatory compliance obligations."

- **Architectural Relevance** This section states the areas that may be impacted by a control. Using AIS-01 as our example, this control is applicable to compute, storage, application, and data. It is not applicable to the physical or network components of a system.

- **Corporate Governance Relevance** Is this a governance item, or is it a technical issue? AIS-01 states it is not a governance item.

- **Cloud Service Delivery Model Applicability** What service model does this apply to (SaaS, PaaS, IaaS)? AIS-01 applies to all of the service models.

- **Supplier Relationship** Who is responsible to implement this control? Is it the provider, the customer, or both? In the AIS-01 example, this is listed as a provider responsibility.

- **Scope Applicability** This section maps the control to a wide variety of standards such as NIST, PCI, COBIT, ISO, and more. Using PCI 3.0 as an example (because it's easiest), we see a mapping between CCM AIS-01 and PCI DSS v3.0 control 6.5.

So now that you understand the basic structure of the document, I want to highlight a couple of items about this document. For your exam, you should know that the biggest reason the CCM is widely followed by companies of all sizes as part of cloud assessments is because of the information covered in the "Scope Applicability" section. The CSA knows this, so you should expect an exam question on it. Don't bother memorizing all of the mapping possibilities. Second, this is a framework to follow. Just like any other standard out there, the scope is going to require tailoring (or tuning). In other words, the CCM is a great starting point to create assessment checklists based on your compliance requirements, but it is no means complete for every company in every possible scenario.

 EXAM TIP Remember that the CCM is an excellent starting point to build a cloud assessment program based on your existing compliance requirements, but it will need to be tailored to meet your needs.

Consensus Assessments Initiative Questionnaire

Cloud providers can use the CAIQ template to document their security and compliance controls. The structure itself is very close to the CCM with one main difference: the CAIQ contains questions that are very direct and less ambiguous than the control specifications found in the CCM. Take, for example, our AIS-01 control. Here's the CCM Control Specification wording: "Applications and programming interfaces (APIs) shall be designed, developed, deployed, and tested in accordance with leading industry standards (e.g., OWASP for web applications) and adhere to applicable legal, statutory, or regulatory compliance obligations."

The CAIQ includes the CCM specification, but it also asks the following four direct questions in a yes-or-no format (there's also a Notes field that providers often use to expand beyond a simple yes-or-no response):

- Do you use industry standards (Building Security in Maturity Model [BSIMM] benchmarks, Open Group ACS Trusted Technology Provider Framework, NIST, and so on) to build in security for your systems/software development lifecycle (SDLC)?

- Do you use an automated source code analysis tool to detect security defects in code prior to production?

- Do you use manual source code analysis to detect security defects in code prior to production?

- Do you verify that all of your software suppliers adhere to industry standards for systems/software development lifecycle (SDLC) security?

NOTE "That's where they get them!" This was the reaction from a CISO when I presented him with the CAIQ as a means to inform clients of how their SaaS had been secured. Turns out he was asked the CAIQ questions (there's 295 of them!) from prospective clients on a weekly basis. We quickly moved on to discuss the STAR registry.

STAR Registry

The highlight of the STAR registry is its collection of filled-out CAIQ responses from vendors. This repository is freely available, and you can use it to perform a "stealth" inspection of a provider's security controls before even engaging the provider.

EXAM TIP You should be aware of a couple of things about the whole STAR program. The CAIQ entries are considered "self assessments." Each self assessment is referred to as a "Level 1" STAR entry.

In the following list, I purposefully omitted a few items from the registry because they are out of scope for your CCSK exam. In fact, even the Level 2 discussion is out of scope, but knowing about it is valuable for you as you work with cloud vendors, so I include it here. You will find a few different levels in the STAR registry.

- **STAR Level 1: Self Assessment** There is no oversight or third-party inspection regarding what is listed here and what is actually the truth. That said, I like to think that no vendor would be careless enough to list "mistruths" in their STAR entry, because this would eventually be discovered and the vendor would likely suffer tremendous reputational damage. Still, just be aware that it's called "Self Assessment" for a reason. If you want a third party to sign off on statements, you need to look for the Level 2 STAR entry.

- **STAR Level 2: Third-Party Certification**   There are actually two ways providers can be listed as having achieved STAR Level 2: STAR Certification or STAR Attestation. The STAR Certification requires that ISO 27001 requirements are followed in a cloud environment being consumed. The STAR Attestation requires that Service Organization Control 2 (SOC 2) criteria are followed. Both require an independent third party having assessed the provider's environment.
- **STAR Level 3: Continuous Auditing**   This level is a placeholder for future continuous audit. At this time, it is unavailable to any providers because the standard is still being developed.

 EXAM TIP   Remember that the STAR Registry contains CAIQ entries that are filled out by vendors and uploaded to the Cloud Security Alliance without any third-party review or assessment.

Cloud Reference and Architecture Models

Models are tools that you can use to help guide security decisions. The CSA divides these models into four distinct items, or tools, that you can use:

- **Conceptual Models**   These can include visualizations and descriptions that explain concepts and principles. The logical model (infostructure, applistructure, metastructure, and infrastructure) with what exists at each level is an example of a conceptual model.
- **Controls Models**   This categorizes and details specific cloud security controls and/or categories of controls. The CCM and ISO 27017 are examples of controls models recommended by the CSA.
- **Reference Architectures**   Ask ten people what a "reference architecture" is and you'll get ten different answers. According to the CSA, reference architectures can be anything from a very abstract, high-level concept, to a very detailed concept, down to specific controls and functions. NIST 500-299 (an example architecture diagram shown in Figure 1-7) and the CSA Enterprise Architecture (shown in Figure 1-8) are examples of reference architectures recommended by the CSA.
- **Design Patterns**   These are considered reusable solutions to particular problems. Take, for example, log management in an IaaS environment. You can implement the log management system once and leverage it as part of other systems that are built. Like the reference architecture, a design pattern can be abstract (a box on a diagram) or specific to particular platforms.

Cloud Security Process Model

The following steps are recommended by the CSA as a means to identify a high-level process for managing cloud security. Note that details, controls, and processes are omitted, as this discussion intends to list the activities that should be performed. How you perform them is based on the particular workload. Figure 1-9 graphically shows these steps.

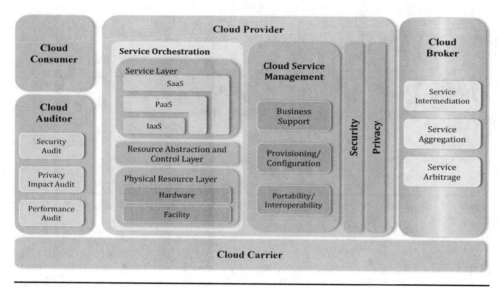

Figure 1-7   NIST 500-292 reference architecture example. (Source: NIST 500-292.)

 TIP   Prior to any of these steps being performed, you need to address one item—classification of data. Without classification of data, you can't determine the value and importance of data, so you can't determine any required security and compliance controls, right? So after you finish your classification, you can proceed with the steps.

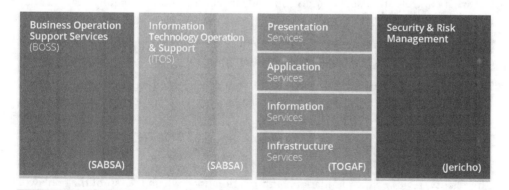

Figure 1-8   CSA Enterprise reference architecture example. (Used with permission of Cloud Security Alliance.)

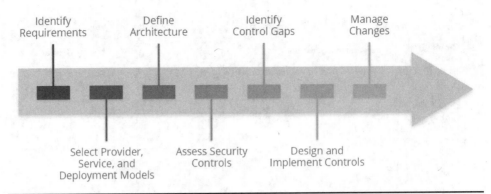

Figure 1-9 Cloud security process model. (Used with permission of Cloud Security Alliance.)

Step 1   Identify required security and compliance controls that must be in place to meet compliance requirements. These requirements will exist no matter where the system is run.

Step 2   Select the cloud service provider, the service model, and the deployment model used. This will assist you in understanding the shared responsibilities.

Step 3   Define the architecture. What components and services will the system use? How can you secure something if you don't know what it does and what other systems or components it interacts with?

Step 4   Assess security controls. Remember the responsibility of implementing security could be that of the provider, or it may be your responsibility.

Step 5   Identify control gaps. You know what's required per compliance requirements and what controls are available. Can you find any controls that are required that are not implemented or exposed to you?

Step 6   Design and implement controls to fill the gaps. If the provider doesn't offer a control that you need, you're going to have to implement a control to address the gap.

Step 7   Manage changes over time. Security (especially cloud security) is never a one-and-done approach. You have to keep up to date with all changes at the provider side and address any security gaps should they arise.

Chapter Review

This chapter reviewed the foundational information upon which the rest of the book will build from. For your CCSK exam, you must be completely clear on the logical model and, most importantly, the metastructure layer where you will configure and manage a new virtual world through the management plane. Other topics that you can expect to be tested on include the following:

- Understand the differences between cloud computing and traditional infrastructure or virtualization, and how abstraction and automation impacts security.
- Know the definitions of cloud computing such as service and deployment models and their associated attributes, inside-out.
- Become familiar with the NIST model for cloud computing and the CSA reference architecture and how they impact the shared security responsibility model of the cloud.
- Know how to use the CSA Consensus Assessments Initiative Questionnaire (CAIQ) to evaluate and compare cloud providers.
- Know how to use the CSA Cloud Controls Matrix to assess and document cloud project security and compliance requirements and controls, as well as who is responsible for each.
- Use a cloud security process model to select providers, design architectures, identify control gaps, and implement security and compliance controls.

Questions

1. Which document type is stored in the STAR registry for Level 1 entries?
   A. CCM
   B. CAIQ
   C. Vendor statements of compliance
   D. Government-issued authority to operate letter

2. Which service model has the provider assuming the most responsibility?
   A. SaaS
   B. PaaS
   C. IaaS
   D. They are all the same as far as responsibility shifts are concerned.

3. Which logical model holds the management plane that is exposed to customers?
   A. Infostructure
   B. Applistructure
   C. Metastructure
   D. Infrastructure

4. You are running a web server in an IaaS environment. You get a call from a customer saying the server appears to have been compromised. Which logical model has been impacted?

   A. Infostructure

   B. Applistructure

   C. Metastructure

   D. Infrastructure

5. Which of the following is NOT an essential characteristic of cloud as per NIST?

   A. Elasticity

   B. Multitenancy

   C. Resource pooling

   D. On-demand self-service

6. In which logical model would you implement a virtual firewall?

   A. Infostructure

   B. Applistructure

   C. Metastructure

   D. Infrastructure

7. How is one consumer's access tightly isolated from other consumers in a public cloud environment?

   A. Strong passwords

   B. RBAC

   C. Policies at the provider side

   D. Policies at the customer side

8. Orchestration enables a controller to request resources from a pool of resources. How is this done?

   A. Ticketing system prioritizes clients based on support level

   B. Through the use of REST APIs

   C. Through the use of RPC

   D. Via network calls

9. You are instructed to build a server with eight CPUs and 8GB of RAM. Which service model would you use?

   A. SaaS

   B. PaaS

   C. IaaS

   D. No cloud provider supports a machine with 8 CPUs

10. Your company is using a PaaS provider to host a Python 2.7–based application. One day, the provider sends you an e-mail stating they will no longer support the Python 2.7 platform and all applications must be upgraded to use Python 3.6 within two weeks. What is the first action you should take?

    A. Test the application in Python 3.6.

    B. Tell the provider you can't meet this timeline.

    C. Providers are restricted by law from doing this.

    D. Launch a lawsuit against the provider for pain and suffering.

Answers

1. **B.** Providers will upload copies of filled-out CAIQ responses. Although ISO and/or SOC can be used as part of a Level 2 STAR entry, Level 1 entries use the CAIQ, not the CCM.

2. **A.** The SaaS service model has the provider assuming responsibility for most (not all) controls.

3. **C.** The management plane is part of the metastructure logical model.

4. **B.** The web server is part of the applistructure. The controls surrounding the web server would be implemented at the metastructure level, but the web server itself is at the applistructure level (and data is at the infostructure layer).

5. **C.** NIST doesn't call out multitenancy as an essential characteristic. ISO, however, does call out multitenancy as part of the resource-pooling essential characteristics.

6. **C.** All controls in the virtual environment are performed at the metastructure layer. If the question asked about installing a firewall agent, that would occur at the applistructure layer.

7. **C.** Tenants are protected by policies at the provider side. Consider, for example, network sniffing. One tenant will never see network traffic destined for another tenant. As a general rule, one tenant should never know that another tenant even exists. Although consumers will also have their own policies in place, the provider must ensure that there is strong isolation of workloads and tenants. This makes C the best answer.

8. **B.** Orchestration generally uses REST API calls. Although orchestration is, of course, performed across a network, the best answer is REST API calls. This is an example of the tricks that test writers like to pull on candidates.

9. **C.** This is a prime example of why you would use IaaS—access to core foundational computing.

10. **A.** When a platform is deprecated (no longer supported), the provider will generally give you access to a test environment where you can test your application using the new platform. As for the time provided in the question, it's a bit extreme based on what I've experienced, but there is no law stopping a provider from giving you hours to migrate, let alone weeks.

Governance and Enterprise Risk Management

This chapter covers the following topics from Domain 2 of the CSA Guidance:
- Tools of Cloud Governance
- Enterprise Risk Management in the Cloud
- Effects of Various Service and Deployment Models
- Cloud Risk Trade-offs and Tools

The buck stops here.

—President Harry S. Truman

Although cloud computing didn't exist when President Truman was in office, his statement is something to remember about your accountability when you outsource to the cloud. You can choose the third-party provider to which you will outsource the building and operational responsibilities of a cloud environment, but you can never outsource accountability. This is why proper governance is critical to your firm at the highest levels.

Although the title implies that there are two areas of focus in this domain, there are really four areas, or roles, that play a part in a strong governance and risk management program. The roles involved are governance, enterprise risk management, information risk management, and information security. The following provides a high-level understanding of these roles:

- **Governance** Includes the policy, process, and internal controls that direct how an organization is run; it includes everything from structures and policies to leadership and other mechanisms for management. You can consider governance as assigning directive controls. The policies to be implemented will often be built from the corporate mission statement and will address the laws, regulations, and standards faced by a company that must be followed in order to continue operations. Governance relies on the compliance function to ensure that directives are being followed throughout the enterprise.

- **Enterprise risk management** Includes managing overall risk for the organization, aligned with the organization's governance and risk tolerance. Enterprise risk management (ERM) includes all areas of risk, not merely those concerned with technology.

- **Information risk management** Addresses managing risk to information, including information technology (IT). Organizations face all sorts of risks, from financial to physical, and information is only one of multiple assets an organization needs to manage. If you work in IT, you are likely most acquainted with this area of risk management.

- **Information security** Includes the tools and practices used to manage risk to information. Information security isn't the be-all and end-all of managing information risks; policies, contracts, insurance, and other mechanisms also have roles to play (including physical security for nondigital information). However, a—if not *the*—primary role of information security is to provide the processes and controls required to protect electronic information and the systems we use to access it.

In a simplified hierarchy, information security is a tool of information risk management, which is a tool of enterprise risk management, which is a tool of governance. The four are all closely related but require individual focus, processes, and tools.

NOTE The CSA calls out the following governance standards, but you don't need to know these standards to prepare for your exam. I've listed them here so you can do some additional reading if you are seeking a cure for insomnia. The CSA will test you on the impact of the cloud on these roles, not on these popular standards of governance.
—ISO/IEC 38500:2015 - Information Technology - Governance of IT for the Organization
—COBIT - A Business Framework for the Governance and Management of Enterprise IT
—ISO/IEC 27014:2013 - Information Technology - Security Techniques - Governance of Information Security

Governance

This section is divided into two main areas: first, a governance backgrounder that describes the role of corporate governance and governance changes that result from adopting cloud services and, second, the areas of importance to focus on regarding cloud governance issues.

NOTE The backgrounder sections throughout this book are intended to address any knowledge gaps on a subject you may have before a full discussion of the impact of the cloud. Backgrounders do not contain information that you will be tested on in the CCSK exam.

Governance Backgrounder

Ever heard the expression, "it starts at the top"? Well, that's enterprise governance in any company of any size. The governance function is centered at the board or the executive level in an organization. There are many aspects of governance, ranging from corporate governance to IT governance, but the important thing to remember is that all governance has a singular goal of enabling the organization to achieve its goals. This is why at a high level, governance can be directly connected all the way back to the corporate mission statement, and at an even higher level, governance can be connected back to the definition of what leadership considers the actual purpose of the company.

The components that make up corporate governance can vary widely. Figure 2-1 shows a high-level view of some of the more generally accepted components of corporate governance.

For years, the "Anglo-American model" of governance has always stated that a company exists for the benefit of its shareholders, and its main goal in that pursuit is maximizing profits. In August 2019, the Business Roundtable, a group of nearly 200 chief executive officers from leading US companies, redefined the purposes of an American company: to invest in employees, deliver value to customers, deal ethically with suppliers, support local communities, embrace sustainable practices to protect the environment, and generate long-term value for shareholders. This statement is incredibly powerful, because it defines specific goals of a company, which will drive the governance function to meet these goals in addition to laws, regulations, standards, and other requirements the company faces.

Figure 2-1 Corporate governance framework

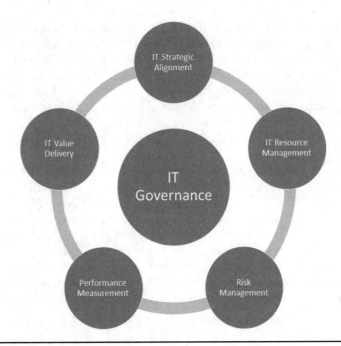

Figure 2-2 Components of IT governance

Following corporate governance is IT governance. IT governance can be defined as the processes that ensure the effective and efficient use of IT in enabling an organization to achieve its goals. Figure 2-2 shows a high-level view of the various components of IT governance. This is, of course, a very simple view of the IT governance function. For example, the latest version of the COBIT Core Model includes 40 governance and management objectives for establishing IT governance. You won't be tested on these as part of the CCSK exam, but knowing the aspects of IT governance isn't a bad thing.

This concludes the backgrounder section of governance. Now let's look at how governance changes as a result of adopting cloud services.

Cloud Governance

Because cloud computing likely introduces a third party into the company mix, a company now has a form of indirect control based on contracts. Where a customer's ability to define, enforce, and monitor adherence to company policies may be dictated by the cloud provider, corporate governance is impacted by the cloud. Additionally, key information related to service management of the cloud environment is (hopefully) produced by the cloud providers, not by the customers themselves. In fact, the only time that governance won't be altered as a result of using the cloud is a scenario in which your own people have implemented automation and orchestration software in your own data center and your company fully manages it like any other system in your data center today.

(Recall from Chapter 1 that a private cloud serves one organization only and doesn't dictate the location or management.)

The primary issue to remember about governing cloud computing is that although an organization can outsource responsibility (authority over actions) for governance, a company can never outsource liability, even when using external providers. As such, the organization will always retain accountability (liability for actions, or lack of actions) if anything goes wrong. This is always true, with or without the cloud, but it is useful to keep in mind when you're navigating cloud computing's concepts of shared responsibility models.

With some cloud providers having more than a million customers, it is simply impossible for providers to give every customer everything they need from contract, service level agreement, and security control perspectives. As such, providers will supply customers with extremely standardized services (including contracts and service level agreements) that are consistent for all customers. Governance models cannot necessarily treat cloud providers the same way they'd treat dedicated external service providers, such as co-location or web hosting providers, which typically customize their offerings, including custom contracts, background screening of employees, and legal agreements, for each client.

The contract between the customer and the provider will identify the responsibilities and mechanisms for governance; the customer needs to understand both and identify any process gaps. If a gap is identified, the customer needs to adjust their own processes to close the gap or accept the associated risks.

 TIP Governance gaps don't necessarily exclude using the provider. If you excluded every provider that didn't completely address everything you needed, you'd find yourself unable to use any provider. Identifying gaps and addressing them is the CSA way to address governance challenges.

Tools of Cloud Governance

Here's some great news! Your company likely already has contracts in place with cloud providers, so you know what needs to be done when onboarding a third party. Unfortunately, though, the cloud provider contract is different from, say, a co-location provider contract, because with a co-location provider, you are outsourcing everything—the hardware, staff, management, operations, and so on. That said, you need to be aware of several tools and how they change with the cloud compared to other forms of outsourcing. These are covered in the next few sections.

Contracts The contract is the number one tool of governance. The legally binding contract agreement is your only "guarantee" of any level of service or commitment. Simply put, if it's not in the contract, it doesn't exist. Notice the quotes around the term "guarantee." If the provider breaks the terms of the contract or doesn't fulfill the terms of a service level agreement, you're looking at a legal dispute. (Watch the guarantee scene from the movie *Tommy Boy* for further information on the value of some guarantees.)

The term "contract" is actually a little misleading, because it seems to imply that a single document is involved; however, the contract will often refer to other documents as well. Consider the following example from the first sentence of the Microsoft Azure Agreement:

> This Microsoft Azure Agreement is between you or the entity you represent, or, if no such entity is designated by you in connection with a Subscription purchase or renewal, you individually ("you") and Microsoft Corporation ("Microsoft", "we", "us", or "our") and consists of the below terms and conditions, as well as the Acceptable Use Policy, the Services Terms, the SLAs, and the Offer Details for your Subscription, or renewal (together, the "Agreement").

So, basically, a contract includes the following legally binding documents:

- **Terms and Conditions** This is the main document that describes aspects of the service, how customer data will be used, termination clauses, warranties, applicable laws, and other fascinating items written by the provider's lawyers to protect them as much as the law will allow.

- **Acceptable Use Policy** This states what you can and cannot do when consuming the service.

- **Services Terms** This contains service-specific contractual agreements by the provider.

- **Service Level Agreements** This details items such as availability uptime commitments and penalties for not meeting those commitments. Quite often, the penalties to the provider for failing to meet monthly service level agreements (such as 99.9 percent availability) take the form of extra service credits—and the customer usually needs to submit a claim and show evidence of unavailability.

- **Clauses Based on Your Subscription and/or Renewal** These would be specific legal agreements based on your particular subscription. With cloud services, the commitments from a provider to the customer are largely based on the customer's subscription level. Consider an extreme example: a free version of a product may have clauses that state that the provider can access your usage data, while the paid version doesn't allow the provider to access your data. Make sure that you understand the subscription level and review that specific documentation.

 EXAM TIP For the exam, remember that contracts define the relationship between providers and customers, and they are the primary tool for customers to extend governance to their suppliers.

Cloud Provider Assessments Assessment is part of the due diligence a customer must perform in advance of using a cloud provider. The assessment should leverage all available information, ranging from contract reviews to provider-supplied audit reports and reviews of technical documentation of the system. Technical assessments may be limited by the provider (for example, no physical access because of security concerns). How the provider supplies technical documentation is up to them: they may post detailed information online, or they may make it available only in-person at their offices for your review.

Aside from a technology perspective, most supplier assessments are performed as part of a cloud provider's assessment. Assessed items generally include financial viability, history, feature offerings, third-party attestations, feedback from peers, and so on.

Compliance Reporting   Two simple words summarize this governance tool—*standards* and *scope*. Leading cloud providers will spend vast sums of money to ensure that they can promote compliance with a wide multitude of standards. They go through the time and expense of obtaining these certifications and reports in order to attract clients that are subject to particular laws and regulations. All of the standards have one issue in common, however—the scope of the engagement. Take International Standards Organization /International Electrotechnical Commission (ISO/IEC) certification, for example. The scope of the ISO/IEC audit could be only the IT department. Where does that leave you if you're looking for a cloud provider with the ISO/IEC certification that you want to use to make your provider selection decisions? It leads you to understand that merely being "certified" doesn't mean anything if the service you are consuming is not within the scope of the audit.

Popular standards that providers often promote include the following:

- **NIST 800-53**   This control set is part of the bigger NIST Risk Management Framework. If you work for a government agency, this is likely the control set that you are most familiar with. More than 600 controls in 800-53 cover low, moderate, and high classification systems.

- **FedRAMP**   The Federal Risk and Authorization Management Program tailors the NIST 800-53 control set for cloud services. Providers must be FedRAMP authorized (known as an Authority to Operate, or ATO) to offer their services to the US government.

- **ISO/IEC 27017**   The "code of practice for information security controls based on ISO/IEC 27002 for cloud services" standard is essentially the control set from ISO 27002, tailored for cloud services.

- **COBIT**   The Control Objectives for Information and Related Technology (yeesh!) is a governance and risk management framework owned by ISACA. It is not a set of controls like Cloud Controls Matrix (CCM), FedRAMP, or ISO 27017. Rather, its focus is on enterprise governance and management of IT, not just security. You won't likely see any provider promoting this as compliance, but it's brought up in the guidance and it's a mapping in the CCM.

- **PCI**   The good old Payment Card Industry and its Data Security Standard (DSS) is a very popular industry standard because of penalties associated with noncompliance. Just a note on this one: A provider being "PCI compliant" does not mean your applications are automagically "PCI compliant." This is a perfect example of the shared responsibility of all cloud models, and you will need to assess your applications if they are part of the PCI cardholder data environment.

- **HIPAA**   The Health Insurance Portability and Accountability Act is US public law that requires data privacy and security provisions for safeguarding medical information. It is not cloud specific, but it does apply to the cloud if medical information is stored in a cloud environment.

Thankfully, the CSA Guidance doesn't go into detail about *all* the standards out there, but there is *one* that you need to be aware of: System and Organization Controls (SOC, pronounced "sock"). The SOC (formerly known as Service Organization Control) by the American Institute of Certified Public Accountants (AICPA) is used by the vast majority of service providers to report on controls at a service organization. The SOC report is generated by an independent CPA and is available from the provider via a nondisclosure agreement (NDA). Although multiple report types are available (SOC 1, SOC 2, SOC 3), these reports are based on the AICPA Statements on Standards for Attestation Engagements 18 (SSAE 18) (previously SSAE 16) standard. Here's a breakdown of the three SOC levels:

- **SOC 1**   This SOC report is used for Internal Control over Financial Reporting (ICFR) and is used for entities that audit financial statements.

- **SOC 2**   This SOC report is titled "Report on Controls at a Service Organization Relevant to Security, Availability, Processing Integrity, Confidentiality, or Privacy." It deals with ensuring that controls at an organization are relevant for security, availability, and processing integrity of systems.

- **SOC 3**   This publicly available high-level SOC report contains a statement from an independent CPA that a SOC engagement was performed, plus the high-level result of the assessment (for example, it could indicate that the vendor statement of security controls in place is accurate).

 NOTE   You'll read more about the ISO/IEC standards and SOC report contents in Chapter 4.

Now if that's not quite confusing enough for you, the AICPA thought it would be a great idea to have different types of report levels as well:

- **Type 1**   A point-in-time look at the design of the controls
- **Type 2**   An inspection of the operating effectiveness of the controls

As you can see, you'll probably want to receive and review the Type 2 report because it actually tests the controls in question. The bottom line here is that as a security professional, you want to get access to a provider's SOC 2, Type 2, report. It will offer great detail into the security controls in place, tests performed, and test results.

CAUTION Do not assume that a provider simply having a SOC report is sufficient to prove the provider's due diligence. Even a legitimate SOC report can refer to practices and assessments that you perceive as unacceptable risks. You always need to review the SOC report.

Of course, providers aren't forced to use a standard like SOC reporting or ISO to supply third-party assessment of controls. They could offer you a self-assessment they created that is based on a standard such as the CCM and CAIQ, covered in Chapter 1, or they may even allow potential clients to perform their own audits—but this is rare.

 CAUTION Not all audit firms (or auditors) are created equal, and the experience, history, and qualifications of the firm should be included in your governance decisions. Additionally, consider the auditors themselves. If they do not have knowledge of cloud environments, this can lead to false findings and all kinds of issues, especially in cloud-native applications that can implement controls that would be completely foreign to an auditor who is unfamiliar with new control approaches in a serverless environment, for example. The CSA recommends that you work with auditors who possess knowledge of the cloud—and there's no better way for an auditor to demonstrate knowledge of the cloud than by holding a CCSK designation!

Risk Management

As mentioned earlier, enterprise risk management (ERM) is the overall management of risk for an organization, and information risk management (IRM) is focused on information and information systems. Both of these functions are related to the governance function, as governance ultimately determines acceptable risk to the organization as a whole. Recall from the previous governance section that the contract defines the roles and responsibilities for risk management between a cloud provider and a cloud customer. The contract, along with other documentation supplied by the provider, can be used to determine where potential for untreated risk exists. You also know that you can never outsource your overall responsibility and accountability for risk management to an external provider, so proper risk management is critically important for your organization. A review of the provider's documentation, assessments, and audits will provide much more information to help with an effective risk decision.

Risk Management Backgrounder

Before discussing the changes to risk management as a result of the cloud, I think it's important to discuss risk management basics for those who may not be familiar with this function. This backgrounder section cannot cover every aspect of risk management, as the topic is incredibly broad and frankly not applicable for your CCSK exam. If you are highly interested in the subject of risk management, I recommend you access the NIST

800-39 document that I used as the basis of this overview. If you are already very comfortable with the principles of risk management, feel free to jump to the next section.

ISACA defines risk management as "the process of identifying vulnerabilities and threats to the information resources used by an organization in achieving business objectives, and deciding what countermeasures, if any, to take in reducing risk to an acceptable level, based on the value of the information resource to the organization." According to the "Managing Information Security Risk" publication by NIST (SP 800-39), risk management consists of four core activities. Following is a list of the activities, or steps, and a brief description of each.

Step 1: Risk Framing   In this step, the company creates a risk management strategy that details how it assesses, responds to, and monitors risk. It takes into account the laws, regulations, and standards that shape the organization's approach to managing risk. Most importantly for this discussion, it determines risk tolerance, which can be used to determine acceptable versus unacceptable risk. It is the basis upon which the company makes all risk decisions, from investments to operational decisions. This initial step demonstrates the need for strong collaboration between governance and risk management functions.

Step 2: Assessing Risk   In this step, not surprisingly, risk assessment is used to identify, prioritize, and estimate risk to corporate assets (among other items). In this step, the company identifies potential threats and vulnerabilities and tries to determine the likelihood and impact of threats being realized by an exploited vulnerability. This assessment calculation is the very definition of risk. There are two main means of risk assessment: First, in *qualitative risk assessment*, a subjective ranking is applied (such as low, moderate, high) to the impact as well as the probability of a threat occurring, to drive a final risk ranking. Second, the *quantitative risk assessment* applies financial figures to assets. At the end of this exercise, the company can apply a value to each risk to determine whether it is acceptable or not based on the risk tolerance derived from the risk framing step (step 1).

Step 3: Responding to Risk   In this step, a determination is made regarding the course of action required to respond to a perceived risk. Several response options are available: accept the risk and don't apply any measures to reduce the impact of a threat being realized; avoid the risk by not proceeding with the operation; mitigate the risk by implementing controls to reduce the likelihood or impact of a threat being realized; share the risk by engaging in an activity with other parties or groups; and, finally, transfer the risk to another party by purchasing insurance (such as cyberinsurance), for example. In general, risk is mitigated by deploying a control to reduce the likelihood or impact of a risk being realized to an acceptable level. The risk that remains is called *residual risk*. In a cloud environment, there are, of course, two parties involved, and the provider may be the one that is deploying controls to mitigate risk. The residual risk will be considered either acceptable or unacceptable. If your company determines that it is an unacceptable risk, you need to deploy additional controls and further mitigate the risk, or avoid the risk by not using the service.

TIP Perhaps you find yourself in a situation with identified risk, and you want to transfer that risk to another party. Cyberinsurance is often used in this case. Here's the trick with insurance, though: it covers only primary damages, not secondary damages such as loss of reputation. You need to understand the limits with insurance, because even the primary costs of dealing with an attack can be astronomical and reputational damages may cost your organization even more.

As for what is considered an acceptable risk and what is not, it all comes down to the customer company's risk tolerance. Customers shouldn't have a blanket clause as to what is considered acceptable risk for anything that occurs. Take a marketing "cats with hats" application versus an internal financial report application. Do both have the same security concerns? Of course they don't. Your risk acceptance should align with the value and requirements of the assets involved. The goal over time for your company is to have an understanding of the cloud services that are consumed and the types of assets that can be used in each service.

Step 4: Monitoring Risk The final phase of risk management involves verifying the ongoing effectiveness of risk response measures and maintenance of compliance (audit and compliance subjects are covered in Chapter 4). Beyond this, though, identifying any changes made that may impact risk to an organization and ensuring that risk treatments remain appropriate are also important. Identification can be performed through manual processes such as threat assessments or automated processes such as configuration management, vulnerability assessments, and so on. In this step, process improvement activities can be identified and implemented.

Cloud Risk Management

Risk management is risk management, regardless of where your systems and information are stored. Risk still needs to be framed, assessed, responded to, and monitored. Risk management in a cloud environment must include the service models and deployment models, because these impact the shared responsibilities inherent to cloud services. The following sections address the changes that the cloud can effect on your current risk management.

 NOTE Remember that moving to the cloud doesn't change your risk tolerance; it just changes how risk is managed.

The Effects of Service and Deployment Models

As the cloud is a shared responsibility model, we have to look at who is generally responsible for managing components from both service model and deployment model perspectives. We will start by looking at the impact of the service models, and then we'll look at the impact of deployment models on governance and risk management.

Service Model Effects

As you may recall from Chapter 1, the service model will give you a high-level view of shared responsibilities. The more functionality the supplier provides, the more they will be responsible for all facets of information security.

Software as a Service   SaaS is essentially renting access to a turnkey application that is supplied by the provider. Providers in the SaaS space range in size from very small to very large. Given the wide spectrum of vendors, it is critical that you ensure that a potential SaaS vendor is a proper fit for your company, because you are essentially outsourcing everything from the facilities up to the application itself, which places most responsibility for security on the provider.

Another consideration is that your SaaS provider may very well in turn be outsourcing to a Platform as a Service (PaaS) or an Infrastructure as a Service (IaaS) vendor. This establishes not just a third party, but fourth and possibly fifth parties as part of your outsourcing chain. If this is the case, you will need to determine which vendors are involved and assess those environments as well.

Platform as a Service   The responsibility shift tilts more toward the customer with PaaS compared to SaaS. You have more capability to configure security within the product you are building on top of a shared platform that the provider fully manages. An example of this would be implementing encryption within an application built on a shared PaaS platform. In this scenario, information risk management and information security are focused primarily on the platform being procured and, of course, the application itself. Given that PaaS is breaking up the IT stack in novel ways, it is important that you review in detail how the contract provisions map to required controls and control opportunities.

 NOTE   According to the CSA Guidance, the likelihood of a fully negotiated contract is lower with PaaS than with either of the other service models. That's because the core driver for most PaaS providers is to deliver a single capability with very high efficiency.

Infrastructure as a Service   You already know that of all the three service models, IaaS is the closest to a traditional data center. As such, this service model results in the customer having the most responsibility to configure controls, be they supplied by the provider (such as logging) or implemented by the customer (such as host-based firewalls in an instance). The issue with governance and risk management lies in the orchestration and management layers supplied by the provider. As most IaaS is built on virtualization technology, the provider's selection and configuration of the hypervisor and its subsequent ability to isolate workloads properly is completely out of your control. The only thing you can do about addressing potential isolation failure is to understand how the provider mitigates against this possibility and make an informed decision in advance of using that provider. As you will likely have no access to audit these controls yourself, this becomes a document review exercise, assuming the provider is transparent with their processes.

Deployment Model Effects

The deployment model is based on ownership and management of the infrastructure as well as the trust level of other tenants. So it makes sense that changes in governance and risk management will result. Let's look at the various deployment models in public, private (both hosted and on-premises), community, and hybrid clouds to determine how they change governance and risk management.

Public Cloud   This model is very straightforward. A third party owns and manages the infrastructure, and the facilities are located outside of your data center. Employees of the provider and possibly unknown subcontractors they engage manage everything. Fellow tenants are untrusted, as anyone with a credit card and a dream can run workloads alongside your workloads, possibly on the same hardware.

NOTE   Remember that the provider (such as PaaS and SaaS) you have a contract with may be outsourcing some facilities to yet another party.

Negotiated contracts that address controls and other technical issues are unlikely in a public cloud because of the volume of customers and the natural multitenancy of public cloud offerings. As such, you will have to assess the controls implemented by the provider, perform a gap assessment, and fill in the gaps yourself. Or you will have to accept the risk (which again should always be done on a per-asset basis given its particular value).

NOTE   Inflexible contracts are a natural property of multitenancy.

Private Cloud   Governance in a private cloud boils down to one very simple question: which party owns and manages the private cloud? You could call a provider and have them spin up and manage a private cloud for you, or you could have your people install the private cloud automation and orchestration software to turn your data center into a "private cloud." In the event that your company owns and operates the private cloud, nothing changes. If, on the other hand, you have outsourced the build and management of your private cloud, you have a *hosted private cloud*, and you have to treat the relationship as you would any other third-party relationship. It will, however, be different from governance of a public cloud, because you are dealing with a one-to-one type of relationship. Just as you would with any other supplier contract, you have to make sure your provider is contractually obligated to do everything you want in advance. If you request something and the provider is not obligated to supply that service, you will likely face the dreaded "change order" charges as you would with any other supplier today.

EXAM TIP If you are asked a question about governance in a private cloud, pay attention to who owns and manages the infrastructure. An outsourced private cloud can incur much more change than insourced.

Hybrid and Community Cloud   With the hybrid and community cloud deployment models, you have two areas of focus for governance activities: internal and the cloud. With hybrid clouds, the governance strategy must consider the minimum common set of controls that make up the cloud service provider's contract and the organization's internal governance agreements. In both hybrid and community models, the cloud user is either connecting two cloud environments or a cloud environment and a data center.

For community clouds specifically, governance extends to the relationships with those organizations that are part of the community that shares the cloud, not just the provider and the customer. This includes community membership relations and financial relationships, as well as how to respond when a member leaves the community.

Cloud Risk Management Trade-Offs

There are advantages and disadvantages to managing enterprise risk for the cloud deployment models presented in this chapter. These factors are, as you would expect, more pronounced for a public cloud and a hosted private cloud:

- You have less physical control over assets and their controls and processes. You don't physically control the infrastructure or the provider's internal processes.

- You have a greater reliance on contracts, audits, and assessments, as you lack day-to-day visibility or management.

- You lack direct control. This creates an increased requirement for proactive management of the relationship and adherence to contracts, which extends beyond the initial contract signing and audits. Cloud providers also constantly evolve their products and services to remain competitive, and these ongoing innovations may exceed, strain, or not be covered by existing agreements and assessments.

- Cloud customers have a reduced need (and an associated reduction in costs) to manage risks that the cloud provider addresses under the shared responsibility model. You haven't outsourced accountability for managing the risk, but you can certainly outsource the management of some risks.

 NOTE   Governance of the relationship with the provider, especially changes introduced by the provider (such as new services), *must* be an ongoing effort.

Assessing Cloud Service Providers

You are dealing with two types of risk management when you assess the cloud: the risk associated with use of third-party cloud service providers and the risk associated with the implementation of your systems in the cloud. The fundamental aspects of risk management (covered earlier in the chapter) don't change as a result of the cloud. The framework, processes, and tools for all aspects of governance, risk, and compliance (GRC) that you use today can and should be applied to a cloud environment. The biggest change to your GRC program as a result of adopting cloud services will rest in your initial and continued assessment of service providers.

 NOTE The European Network and Information Security Agency (ENISA) has published a "Cloud Computing Risk Assessment" document to assist with assessment of risks in a cloud environment. This document is discussed in Chapter 15.

Supplier Assessments

The initial supplier assessment sets the groundwork for the cloud risk management program. The following steps and a graphical view of these steps (Figure 2-3) show what you should follow as part of a supplier assessment:

1. Request or acquire documentation.

2. Review the provider's security program and documentation.

3. Review any legal, regulatory, contractual, and jurisdictional requirements for both the provider and your organization.

4. Evaluate the contracted service in the context of your information assets.

5. Separately evaluate the overall provider, such as its finances/stability, reputation, and outsourcers.

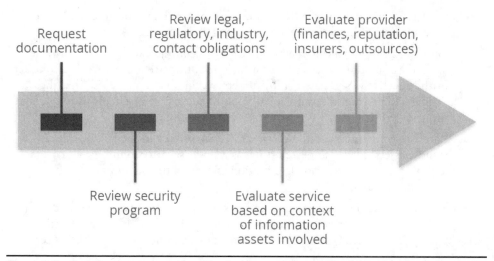

Figure 2-3 Supplier assessment steps. (Used with permission of Cloud Security Alliance.)

Because you know that governance and risk management of a cloud provider is never a one-and-done approach, you need to stay on top of the relationship. To that end, consider the following recommendations for vendor risk management:

- Don't assume all services from a particular provider meet the same audit/assessment standards. You will have to assess the latest audit/assessment reports and determine whether a service you are considering was in scope and tested or not.
- Periodic assessments should be scheduled and automated if possible.

 NOTE Automation of assessments is possible if the provider exposes APIs to customers.

Chapter Review

This chapter reviewed the recommendations by the Cloud Security Alliance surrounding the elements of governance and risk management changes that are associated with cloud consumption. The CCSK exam will not test you on the various standards out there that can be leveraged for traditional IT consumption. Your goal is to understand the differences that occur with governance and risk management as a result of consuming cloud services. To that end, make sure you fully understand the following points, which were all covered in this chapter:

- Identify the shared responsibilities of security and risk management based on the chosen cloud deployment and service models. Develop a cloud governance framework/model as per relevant industry best practices, global standards, and regulations such as CSA CCM, COBIT, NIST RMF, ISO/IEC 27017, HIPAA, PCI DSS, EU GDPR, and so on.
- Understand how a contract affects your governance framework/model. You're introducing a supply chain when consuming cloud services.
- Don't assume that you can effectively negotiate contracts with a cloud provider—but this also shouldn't necessarily stop you from using that provider. If a contract can't be effectively negotiated and you perceive an unacceptable risk that the provider accepts, consider implementation of alternative mechanisms to manage (mitigate) that risk (such as monitoring or encryption).
- Align risk requirements to the specific assets involved and the risk tolerance for those assets. There is no such thing as a single security solution that covers everything. Asset values and classification are very different and need to be addressed separately.
- Create a specific risk management and risk acceptance/mitigation methodology to assess the risks of every solution in the space. The Cloud Controls Matrix (covered in Chapter 1) can be an excellent starting point to create this process,

but the process will need to be tailored based on your company's specific risk tolerance for specific assets.

- Use controls to manage residual risks. If you cannot deploy controls to manage risk that the provider accepts, you have two choices: accept or avoid the risks.

- Use tooling to track approved providers based on asset type (for example, linked to data classification), cloud usage, and management. This tooling can be anything from a spreadsheet to an advanced supplier tracking tool.

- Like Ferris Bueller said, life moves pretty fast. If you don't stop and look around once in a while, you could miss it. Cloud provider reassessments should occur on a scheduled basis and be automated to the extent possible.

- Develop a process for cloud provider assessments. This should include the following:

  - Contract review

  - Self-reported compliance review

  - Documentation and policies

  - Available audits and assessments

  - Service reviews adapting to the customer's requirements

  - Strong change-management policies to monitor changes in the organization's use of the cloud services

Questions

1. Chris is looking to procure a new CRM SaaS solution for his organization's business unit. What is the first step Chris should take as part of performing a risk assessment of a potential vendor?

   A. Determine monthly costs.

   B. Ask reference clients about their satisfaction with the product.

   C. Determine the level of sensitivity of data that will be stored in the application.

   D. Obtain and review supplier documentation.

2. Pat is looking for an industry standard set of controls that are cloud specific. What can Pat select controls from to create a baseline risk assessment process?

   A. ISO 27001

   B. NIST RMF

   C. COBIT

   D. CCM

3. Your IaaS vendor assures you that your applications will be PCI compliant if you use their cloud offering. What is wrong with this statement?

   A. The vendor has no idea what they are talking about.

   B. The vendor is lying to you.

   C. The vendor doesn't understand the shared responsibility model of cloud.

   D. All of the above are true.

4. How often should risk assessments be performed against a cloud service provider?

   A. Upon initial assessment prior to on-boarding

   B. Upon initial assessment and on an ongoing basis

   C. Providers don't allow customers to perform risk assessments

   D. There are no risks associated with cloud services

5. Which service model is most congruent with existing governance and risk management processes?

   A. SaaS

   B. PaaS

   C. IaaS

   D. Internally managed private cloud

6. When you're assessing a provider, which of the following SOC reports should be sought from a vendor when assessing security controls?

   A. SOC 1, Type 1

   B. SOC 1, Type 2

   C. SOC 2, Type 1

   D. SOC 3

7. What is a natural property of multitenancy?

   A. Inflexible contracts

   B. Being hacked by co-tenants

   C. Economies of scale

   D. Shared responsibility

8. What risk must be mitigated by a customer?

   A. Any risk

   B. Risks associated with the service model

   C. Risks accepted by the provider

   D. Risks listed in the Cloud Controls Matrix

9. What is the number one tool of governance in a cloud?

   A. Reviewing vendor certifications

   B. Training your people on cloud security

   C. Working with auditors with cloud experience

   D. Contract reviews

10. What must be first understood when considering governance of a private cloud?

    A. Who owns and manages the private cloud

    B. The automation and orchestration software used

    C. The credentials of the people managing the private cloud

    D. Contract clauses in place with the private cloud vendor

Answers

1. **D.** The first step in performing a risk assessment is requesting documentation.

2. **D.** The CCM has a series of controls that are cloud specific. None of the other answers are applicable.

3. **D.** All of the statements are applicable.

4. **B.** Risk assessments should be performed prior to and throughout the use of a provider's offering.

5. **C.** IaaS is the service model most congruent with traditional governance and risk management. The private cloud is a deployment model, not a service model. Note: Watch out for trick answers like this on any technical exam!

6. **C.** The best answer listed is SOC 2, Type 1. SOC 1 deals with financial reporting controls. A SOC 3 report doesn't contain any tests performed or their results. A SOC 2, Type 2, report is the best to use when reviewing a provider from a security perspective, but since it's not listed as a potential answer, SOC 2, Type 1, is the best possible answer.

7. **A.** Inflexible contracts are a natural characteristic of multitenancy because the provider cannot afford or manage a million-plus custom contracts.

8. **C.** The best answer is that a customer must mitigate any risk accepted by the provider, except for any risk the customer determines unacceptable. This must be based on the value of a particular system and cannot be a blanket approach.

9. **D.** Contract reviews are the primary tool associated with governance in a cloud.

10. **A.** The first item that must be understood when you're dealing with a private cloud is who owns and manages the cloud infrastructure. If the infrastructure is internally owned and managed, little changes. If it's outsourced, governance changes to reflect the fact that the supplier is in control.

Legal Issues, Contracts, and Electronic Discovery

This chapter covers the following topics from Domain 3 of the CSA Guidance:
- Legal Frameworks Governing Data Protection and Privacy
- Cross-Border Data Transfer
- Regional Considerations
- Contracts and Provider Selection
- Due Diligence
- Third-Party Audits and Attestations
- Electronic Discovery
- Data Custody
- Data Preservation
- Data Collection
- Response to Subpoenas or Search Warrants

The power of the lawyer is in the uncertainty of the law.

—Jeremy Bentham

This quote by Mr. Bentham perfectly sums up the legal issues surrounding cloud computing. The legal aspect of the cloud is a two-pronged issue for your firm. On one hand, governments can take years to create laws that always seem to play catch-up with technology. On the other hand, and more importantly from a CCSK exam perspective, all jurisdictions move at different speeds, and quite often laws in one country can be markedly different from laws in other jurisdictions.

This chapter covers primary legal issues raised by moving data to the cloud, dealing with contracts with cloud service providers (CSPs), and electronic discovery. Be forewarned that you will not be a legal expert after reading this chapter. The goal of this chapter is to deliver an understanding as to the importance of having your company's legal counsel involved in procuring cloud services, especially when dealing with cloud providers (or even customers) across multiple jurisdictions. In addition, be aware that laws and regulations change frequently, so you should verify the relevancy of information contained in this domain before relying on it. This domain focuses on the legal implications of public and third-party–hosted private clouds. A private cloud owned and operated by a company is more of a technical issue than a legal one, as an on-premises private cloud is really just the automation and orchestration of corporately owned and managed computing assets.

Legal Frameworks Governing Data Protection and Privacy

Many countries have their own legal frameworks requiring appropriate safeguards to protect the privacy of personal data and the security of information and computer systems. In the European Union, for example, most of these privacy laws have been around since the late 1960s and 1970s. These were ultimately the basis for the Organization for Economic Cooperation and Development (OECD) Privacy Guidelines, which were adopted in 1980. This then fed the formation of the Data Protection Directive, aka Directive 95/46/EC, which superseded the General Data Protection Regulation (GDPR, covered later in this chapter). The main point is this: These privacy laws aren't new. They have been built over years and are only now being rigorously enforced.

 EXAM TIP You don't need to do a deep dive into the various EU standards, the differences between them, and release dates for the CCSK exam. They're highlighted in this introduction because GDPR is a huge deal these days.

From a legal perspective, three entities are involved when cloud services are consumed (shown in Figure 3-1), and all have different requirements from a legal perspective.

 EXAM TIP Of the three models, you should get your head around the role of the controller/custodian and remember that jurisdiction is very important to determine applicable laws.

- **Provider/Processor** This one is straightforward. This is the cloud service provider. The provider must operate in accordance with the laws in the jurisdictions in which they operate.
- **Custodian/Controller** This is the entity that holds end-user data. The naming of this role is dependent on the location you're in. In the United States, it's called

Figure 3-1
Legal entities involved with storing end-user data in cloud

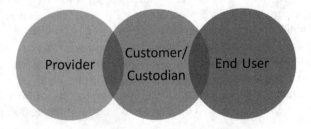

the "data custodian"; in Europe, it's called the "data controller." Either way, this entity is legally accountable for properly securing end-user data. As an example of a data custodian/controller, if your company uses an Infrastructure as a Service (IaaS) provider to store your customer data, you are the data custodian/controller of that end-user data. The custodian/controller must operate in accordance with the laws of the jurisdiction in which the company operates.

- **End User/Data Subject** This entity (such as you and I) has their data being held by a controller/custodian.

 NOTE Although I am using both the European and North American terms (such as custodian/controller), there are fine distinctions between the two types. I present them this way out of simplicity to help you understand the roles without diving into the legal minutiae across jurisdictions.

These privacy laws define numerous obligations, such as confidentiality and security obligations that a custodian/controller and provider/processor must abide by. The data custodian/controller is prohibited from collecting and processing personal data unless certain criteria are met. For example, the data custodian/controller is limited to what the end user has consented to regarding the collection and proposed uses of the end user's data, according to the consent agreement. When using a data processor (such as a CSP) to process data on its behalf, a data custodian/controller remains responsible (accountable by law) for the collection and processing of that data. As the data custodian/controller, you are required to ensure that your provider/processor takes adequate technical and organizational security measures to safeguard the data. This, of course, requires that you perform proper due diligence with regard to the provider.

 CAUTION The legal requirement on the data custodian/controller is no joke. Being labelled the data custodian has very real legal ramifications. If your company holds end-user data and is found to be negligent in privacy or security as required by laws (or even prudent practice) in your company's jurisdiction, your company is open to being sued.

Despite common themes among countries on all continents, each has developed data protection regimes that may conflict with another's regime. As a result, cloud providers and cloud users operating in multiple regions struggle to meet compliance requirements. In many cases, the laws of different countries may apply according to the following criteria:

- The location of the cloud provider
- The location of the data custodian/controller
- The location of the end user
- The location of the servers

- The legal jurisdiction of the contract between parties, which may be different from the locations of any of the parties involved

- Any treaties or other legal frameworks between those various locations

 TIP If your company has global operations, you can expect to run into conflicting legal requirements. This conflict constitutes a legal risk, which should be treated seriously or formally accepted.

Now do you see why the CSA Guidance covers the legal aspects of cloud services? Figuring out all these issues and how they interact on a global scale must be done by your company's legal counsel, but as a CCSK holder, you'll need to know when to call legal in. After all, only legal counsel has any authority to advise executives on the legal risks involved with anything your company does, right? The bottom line is this: the location where an entity operates is critical knowledge that plays an important role in determining due diligence requirements and legal obligations. Figure 3-2 shows the various legal issues that exist in every jurisdiction around the world.

Required Security Measures

Many countries have adopted privacy laws that are either *omnibus* (covers all categories of personal data) or *sectoral* (covers specific categories of personal data). These laws often require that appropriate security measures be in place to ensure that privacy-related data

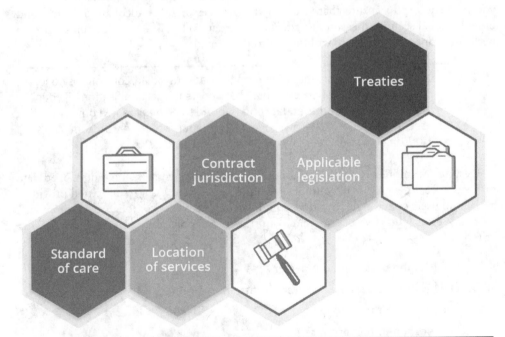

Figure 3-2 Legal aspects involved with the use of cloud services. (Used with permission from CSA.)

is properly protected. These security measures may require companies to adopt technical, physical, and administrative measures. These measures may of course be used to protect more than just personal information; they will likely be leveraged to protect other sensitive data sets such as financial data and trade secrets, for example.

Treaties

A *treaty* is an agreement between two political authorities. There are two treaties worthy of discussion to help you prepare for the CCSK exam. You may have heard of the *International Safe Harbor Privacy Principles*, otherwise known as the Safe Harbor agreement, between the United States and the European Union. This treaty basically allowed companies to commit voluntarily to protecting EU citizens' data stored in the United States the same way that it would protect the data if it were held in the European Union. This agreement was terminated in 2015, however, and was replaced shortly afterward with a new agreement, the *EU-US Privacy Shield*. Privacy Shield operates in much the same way as Safe Harbor, in that Privacy Shield allows for personal data transfer and storage between the European Union and the United States. Companies self-certify as having appropriate privacy measures in place, and Privacy Shield serves as a data transfer mechanism under the EU GDPR.

 NOTE I will address GDPR highlights later in this chapter.

Restrictions to Cross-Border Data Transfers

Barring a treaty such as the Privacy Shield in place, which establishes an adequate level of protection, many countries prohibit data being stored outside of their boundaries. If no treaty is in place, however, it is still possible to store data in a foreign country, although it requires a more complex solution. In this scenario, the data importer and exporter may sign a contract ensuring privacy rights for end users. The complexity may come from some cases requiring prior permission from a data protection commissioner before data can be transferred into or out of the country.

In the CSA Guidance, two examples are cited as countries that prohibit data from being exported—Russia and China. These countries' data localization laws require that data pertaining to individuals residing in their countries be stored within the individual's home country. Make no mistake; there are other countries and even Canadian provinces that have the same laws, but the CSA Guidance addresses only these two countries (which are covered more in depth later in this chapter).

CLOUD Act

The Clarifying Lawful Overseas Use of Data Act (CLOUD Act) was introduced in the United States in 2018. Its purpose is to finalize some legal issues surrounding the US government's ability to issue subpoenas or warrants to access client data stored by an American provider, regardless of where that data is physically stored.

A great example of the importance of the CLOUD Act is a court case between Microsoft and the US Department of Justice (DOJ). The DOJ wanted access to data stored in an Irish data center. Microsoft defended its client (which a CSP should always do!) by refusing DOJ access because the data itself was held outside of the United States. A court battle ensued and went all the way to the Supreme Court. During this time, the CLOUD Act was passed, and the Supreme Court declared the case moot because the CLOUD Act gave the DOJ access to the data because Microsoft is an American company.

 TIP A CSP should always defend clients from over-reaching access requests by any authorities. Customers should look for this language in contracts.

Regional Examples

As mentioned earlier in this chapter, many countries around the world have their own laws that address privacy and security requirements. We will be addressing some examples from the CSA Guidance as part of this section.

 NOTE To add to the complexity involved with these laws across jurisdictions is the language of the laws themselves. In multiple cases, jurisdictions (such as Japan or Germany) will release English versions of the laws, but only the local-language version of the legal text is considered to be the authoritative version, and there are no guarantees as to the appropriateness of the offered translated version.

Asia Pacific Region

The Asia Pacific region covered in the CSA Guidance consists of Australia, China, Japan, and Russia.

(Used with permission from CSA.)

Australia

In Australia, the Privacy Act of 1988 (Privacy Act) and the Australian Consumer Law (ACL) of 2010 serve to protect end users. The Privacy Act includes 13 Australian Privacy Principles (APPs), which apply to all private-sector and not-for-profit organizations with revenues greater than AUD $3 million, all private health service providers, and some small businesses. The Privacy Act can apply to (protect) any Australian customer even if the CSP is based outside of Australia and even if other laws are stated in a contract.

Australia amended its 1988 Privacy Act in February 2017 to require companies to notify affected Australian residents and the Australian Information Commissioner in the event of a security breach. A breach of security must be reported under two conditions: if there is unauthorized access or disclosure of personal information that would be likely to result in serious harm, or if personal information is lost in circumstances where unauthorized access or disclosure is likely to occur—and if it did occur, it would be likely to result in serious harm to any of the individuals to whom the information relates.

NOTE Australia is not alone in its clause that only lost data deemed to likely result in serious harm should be reported. Canada's Personal Information Protection and Electronic Documents Act (PIPEDA) includes the same type of clause. Like Australia, it is up to the entity that lost the data to determine whether or not there is a serious risk of harm as a result of lost data.

China

Over the past few years, China has implemented legal structures to address the privacy and security of personal and company information. Its 2017 Cyber Security Law (2018 updates are covered later) governs the operations of network operators and critical information infrastructure operators. The 2017 law requires these operators to implement a series of security requirements, including the design and adoption of information security measures; the formulation of cybersecurity emergency response plans; and assistance and support to investigative authorities, where necessary, for protecting national security and investigating crimes. The law requires providers of network products and services to inform users about known security defects and bugs and to report such defects and bugs to relevant authorities.

In addition, the law includes a data localization provision, which requires that personal information and other important data be stored within the territories of the People's Republic of China. (What constitutes "important data" in the 2017 Cyber Security Law is extremely vague and subject to great debate in the legal community.)

The 2018 update of the Cyber Security Law gave more power to China's Ministry of Public Security (MSP). Additional powers effectively allow the MSP to perform penetration testing of systems (on-site or remote), check for prohibited content, and copy any user information and share any information with other state agencies. In the event of an on-site visit, two members of the People's Armed Police are allowed to be present to ensure that procedures are followed.

EXAM TIP The 2018 update to this law is not covered as part of the CSA Guidance and therefore not likely to be part of the CCSK exam. However, from a real-life perspective, if you operate outside of the Chinese market but want to do business in China, it is highly advisable that you discuss both localization and governmental access to data stored in China with your legal counsel.

Japan

Like many countries, Japan's Act on the Protection of Personal Information (APPI) requires the private sector to protect personal information and data securely. There are several other national laws, such as the Law on the Protection of Personal Information Held by Administrative Organs (not a typo), and sector-specific laws, such as the healthcare industry that requires registered health professionals to maintain the confidentiality of patient information.

Japan also limits the ability to transfer personal data to third parties (such as cloud providers). The prior consent of the data subject is required in order to transfer data to a third party. This consent is not required if the country of destination has an established framework for the protection of personal information that meets the standard specified by the Personal Information Protection Commission. Such a framework between Japan and the EU was ratified in 2018, around the same time the GDPR came into effect.

Russia

The Russian data protection laws state that citizen data must be localized. In other words, like China, Russian citizen data must be stored within Russia. Roskomnadzor, the Russian Data Protection regulator, is responsible for enforcement of the law and has already blocked access to multiple web sites based on the fact that they may store Russian citizen data but do not do so within Russia. Essentially, if you see that a web site isn't available in Russia, it's because the web site owners don't operate and store such data within Russia.

NOTE Multiple web sites track companies that are blocked in Russia and/or China as a result of their localization laws.

European Union and European Economic Area

The EU adopted the GDPR in 2016 (which became enforceable in May 2018), which is binding on all EU member states, as well as members of the European Economic Area (EEA). It replaced Directive 95/46/EC on the Protection of Personal Data, which had been the legal basis of data protection laws of all EU and EEA member states.

(Used with permission from CSA.)

NOTE The EEA consists of the EU countries plus Iceland, Lichtenstein, and Norway.

Another document you should know about that governs protection of personal data in the EU/EEA is Directive 2002/58/EC on Privacy and Electronic Communications. This directive is being phased out and is expected to be replaced with the new E-Privacy Regulation, but this new regulation has been delayed for years, and these delays are likely to continue for the foreseeable future.

Of course, privacy isn't possible to implement without some form of security. The Network Information Security Directive (NIS Directive) addresses these security requirements. Adopted alongside the GDPR in 2016, the NIS Directive was implemented in May 2018. This saw EU/EEA member states implementing new information security laws for the protection of critical infrastructure and essential services. The next two sections address both GDPR and the NIS Directive.

General Data Protection Regulation

The GDPR applies to any legal entity engaged in economic activity (both organizations and individuals) that processes data associated with EU citizens, and it will be adjudicated (a legal term for making an official decision) by the data supervisory authorities or the courts of the member states that have the closest relationship with the individuals or the entities on both sides of the dispute. The following list covers the GDPR's basic points:

- **Applicability** The GDPR applies to the processing of personal data in the context of the activities of a controller or processor in the EU/EEA, regardless of whether or not the processing takes place in the EU/EEA. It also applies to the processing of personal data of data subjects who are in the EU/EEA by a controller or a processor not established in the EU/EEA if the processing relates to the offering of goods or services (paid or not) or the monitoring of the behavior of a data subject when the behavior takes place within the EU/EEA.

- **Lawfulness** Processing personal data is permitted only if the data subject has freely given specific, informed, and unambiguous consent to the processing of their personal data, or the processing is authorized by a statutory provision.

- **Accountability obligations** The GDPR has created numerous obligations for companies, including requiring that companies retain records of their processing activities. A data protection impact assessment must always be conducted when the processing could "result in a high risk to the rights and freedoms of natural persons." Companies are expected to develop and operate their products and services in accordance with "privacy by design" and "privacy by default" principles.

- **Data subjects' rights** Data subjects have rights regarding the processing of their data. The big ones are the right to object to use of their personal data, the right to be forgotten, and the right to have corrections made to their data.

- **Cross-border data transfer restrictions** Personal data cannot be transferred outside the EU/EEA to a processor or custodian/controller that is located in a country that does similar protection of personal data and privacy rights. A company can prove that it will be offering the "adequate level of protection" required by executing Standard Contractual Clauses (SCC), signing up to the EU-US Privacy Shield, obtaining certification of Binding Corporate Rules (BCRs), or complying with an approved industry code of conduct or approved certification mechanism. In rare cases, the transfer may be allowed with the explicit, informed consent of the data subject, or if other exceptions apply.

- **Breaches of security** The GDPR requires that data controllers report security breaches within 72 hours of detection. The reporting requirements are risk-based, and there are different requirements for reporting the breach to the Supervisory Authority and to the affected data subjects.

- **Discrepancies among member states** The GDPR allows member states to implement additional requirements above and beyond the GDPR baseline. For example, Germany (one of the leading countries when it comes to privacy regulations prior to GDPR) requires that a data protection officer be appointed if the company has more than nine employees.

- **Sanctions** Violations of the GDPR expose a company to significant sanctions. These sanctions may reach up to 4 percent of the company's global gross income, or up to EUR 20 million, whichever is greater.

NOTE To touch on enforcement of GDPR fines and sanctions, consider that it took the German government five days after the GDPR came into effect to use the GDPR in a decision (ICANN vs. EPAG, over the collection of WHOIS data). Then, in July 2019, the UK Independent Commissioner's Office (ICO) was the first member state to announce an intention to issue game-changing fines against British Airways and Marriott. The fines combined are approximately £280,000,000 (roughly US$350 million). It's safe to assume that these cases will be rigorously fought by the two companies and will probably be in the courts for years, but the message is clear—the GDPR has real teeth, and companies need to invest in security and privacy as a result.

Network Information Security Directive

The NIS Directive required each EU/EEA member state to implement the directive into its national legislation by May 2018 and identify Operators of Essential Services (OES), such as energy, transport, banking, financial market infrastructures, health, drinking water supply, and distribution, by November 2018. In addition to these OES, the NIS directive addresses (albeit to a less stringent regime) digital service providers (DSPs). The specific types of companies considered to qualify as a DSP include cloud service providers, online marketplaces, and search engines. DSPs should be aware that the NIS Directive also applies to companies based outside of the European Union whose services are available within the European Union. These companies are obliged to assign an EU-based representative to act on their behalf in ensuring NIS Directive compliance.

The NIS Directive establishes a framework to enable networks and information systems to resist, at a given level of confidence, actions that compromise the availability, authenticity, integrity, or confidentiality of stored, transmitted, or processed data, or the related services that are offered by or accessible through those networks and information systems.

NOTE Regarding "authenticity" versus "integrity": *Integrity* can be defined as assurance of the accuracy and reliability of information and systems from its original state (called a "reference version"). *Authenticity* is defined as assurance that the "reference version" data has not been altered from what it was when another party was in control of it. It's a fine detail and not applicable for your CCSK exam, but the NIS Directive uses the term "authenticity" in addition to the "CIA Triad" (Confidentiality, Integrity, and Availability) of information security that most people are familiar with, so I just wanted to address the difference here.

The requirements to be implemented into national laws include the following:

- Each member state must create a computer security incident response team (CSIRT). These CSIRTs will work in cooperation with CSIRTs across all EU/EEA members as part of a cohesive EU-wide network.

- Those organizations who qualify as DSPs under the Directive's criteria must implement a range of risk management measures, both technical and operational. DSP organizations must comply with the Directive's incident reporting protocol, which requires that organizations notify "without undue delay" CSIRTs and other relevant bodies about any significant security incidents encountered.

- Each member must provide evidence of the effective implementation of security policies, such as the results of a security audit.

- Each member must take technical and organizational measures to manage risks posed to the security of networks and information systems used in their operations.

- Each member must take appropriate measures to prevent and minimize the impact of incidents affecting the security of the networks and information systems used for the provision of such essential services, to facilitate the continuation of those services.

- Each member must provide information necessary to assess the security of their networks and information systems.

- Each member must notify the competent authority without undue delay of any incident having a substantial impact on the provision of a service.

The NIS Directive states that the responsibility to determine penalties for noncompliance rests with the individual member states and not the European Union. The Directive does, however, state that penalties must be "effective, proportionate, and dissuasive."

EXAM TIP Remember that the NIS Directive applies to companies outside of the EU/EEA whose services are available in the European Union and that an EU-based representative must be established to ensure NIS Directive compliance.

The Americas

As with all other jurisdictions previously covered, all the various jurisdictions across the Americas have differing laws and regulations that companies must abide by. Most important, however, are the US laws and regulations. This importance is not just from a CCSK exam perspective, as the exam is global in nature. It is important that you remember that CSPs

(Used with permission from CSA.)

must follow laws and regulations in their own jurisdictions. I believe it is fair to assume that you will be consuming cloud services from at least one American provider, regardless of where you or your company are physically located.

US Federal Laws

There are a few examples of US laws and regulations that apply to organizations in the United States. These include financial regulations in the Gramm-Leach-Bliley Act (GLBA), the Health Insurance Portability and Accountability Act of 1996 (HIPAA), and the Children's Online Privacy Protection Act of 1998 (COPPA). All these regulations contain provisions that pertain to the privacy and the adoption of reasonable security measures surrounding processing of personal information.

Most of these laws require companies to take precautions when hiring subcontractors and service providers (including CSPs). They may also hold organizations responsible for the acts of their subcontractors. For example, both GLBA and HIPAA require that covered organizations use written contract clauses requiring third parties to use reasonable security measures and comply with data privacy provisions.

US State Laws

Most security and privacy laws and regulations in the United States are driven at a state level. These laws apply to any entity that collects or processes personal information (as narrowly defined in the applicable law) of individuals who reside in that state, regardless of where in the United States the data is stored.

State laws differ widely across the United States, down to the most basic element of what is considered "protected information." For example, California declares that a username and a password are considered protected data. Meanwhile, across the street in Arizona, a username and password are not considered protected data. When it comes to playing it safe and ensuring that you are compliant with all standards, you're going to want legal counsel involved to determine the "hardest" state-level privacy requirements and follow those.

EXAM TIP Remember that many states have laws and regulations that require organizations to ensure that service providers provide adequate privacy protections and security measures for personal data.

Security Breach Disclosure Laws

Several federal and state security and privacy laws or rules require entities that have suffered a breach of security that compromised specified categories of data, such as personally identifiable information (PII) and especially patient health information (PHI), to notify affected individuals promptly, and in many cases, notify state or federal agencies of the occurrence of the breach of security.

For a state breach disclosure law, I like to point out Washington State's Breach Notification Law (enacted in 2015). This law states that any breach that is reasonably expected to impact more than 500 Washington State residents must be reported to the Washington State attorney general within 45 days following discovery. All breach notifications are published on the Washington State Attorney General web site. Contrast this law with the breach notification law in Alabama, which was the final state to implement a breach notification law in June 2018. Alabama requires notification to individuals within 45 days if lost data is "deemed to cause substantial harm." Notification to consumer reporting agencies and the state attorney general must be performed if more than 1000 Alabama citizens are impacted. All states have wildly different requirements regarding what data constitutes a breach, notification times, damages, and so forth.

Understanding these laws is critical for both cloud customers and cloud providers, because breaches of security are resulting in larger fines than ever before. As a result of a breach of PII data, Equifax is currently facing a cost of $700 million in fines and litigation alone. This is above and beyond any costs the company incurred to fix security issues, reputational damage, and all other "standard" costs associated with a breach.

Federal and State Agencies

Cloud providers and consumers should also be aware that laws don't live in a vacuum; they continuously change. US government agencies, such as the Federal Trade Commission (FTC), and the state attorneys general have used their power under federal or state "unfair and deceptive practices" acts to fine companies whose privacy or security practices are inconsistent with their claims, thus making their practices unfair or deceptive. From a privacy and security enforcement perspective, the FTC has the ability to issue fines and consent orders that outline FTC findings and how a company will address any issues (and generally includes a requirement of 20 years of FTC oversight). Both consent orders and fines can be used by legal counsel to update or modify security and privacy statements based on the new precedents they provide.

The FTC has the ability to impose significant fines on companies found to be in violation of a consent order. In July 2019, for example, the FTC fined Facebook $5 billion for violations of a consent order the company agreed to in 2011.

 EXAM TIP   Remember that the FTC has taken the charge from a federal perspective on consumer privacy rights. State attorneys general deal with consumer privacy rights at a state level.

Central and South America

Central and South American countries are adopting data protection laws at a rapid pace. Argentina, Chile, Colombia, Mexico, Peru, and Uruguay have passed data protection laws inspired mainly by the EU Directive 95/46/EC and may include references to the Asia-Pacific Economic Cooperation (APEC) Privacy Framework. These laws include security requirements and assign the data custodian/controller the burden of ensuring the protection and security of personal data wherever the data is located, and especially when data is being transferred to a third party, such as a cloud provider.

Contracts and Provider Selection

In addition to the various laws and regulations you may face as a cloud customer, you will likely have contractual obligations that require you to protect the personal information of your own clients, contacts, or employees (aka stakeholders) to ensure that data is not used for any reason other than its original intent and is not shared with third parties. These clauses are usually found in the terms and conditions and/or privacy statement that a company posts on its web site, or from written contracts. For example, a Software as a Service (SaaS) cloud provider (data processor) may be bound by the terms of its service agreement to process personal data only for certain purposes.

The main thing to remember when it comes to contracts and provider selection is that you must do what you say you do, and this is true whether you state it in a contract or in a privacy statement on your web site. This is also true when you're outsourcing data processing or storage to a cloud provider. If you tell end users that their data will be secure in your hands (such as data encrypted at rest), you must make sure this is possible in a cloud environment. You must admit it would be fairly ridiculous to tell customers their data will be protected in a certain fashion as long as that data is in your own data center, but if it happens to be moved to a cloud environment, then this statement doesn't apply.

If the privacy notice follows the GDPR (which most legal counsel will insist upon as a general precaution) and allows individual data subjects to have access to their personal data and to have this information modified or deleted, the CSP must also allow these access, modification, and deletion rights to be exercised to the same extent as it would in a non-cloud relationship.

The terms and conditions and privacy statements tell your end users how you will handle their data, period. As the data custodian/controller, your company is legally responsible and accountable for making sure those protections are in place. Know the old saying, "ignorance is no excuse"? What do you think would happen if one of your clients sued you for loss of data and you told the judge you didn't know the provider didn't secure data once you moved it? You need a full understanding of what the provider does (external due diligence) and what you must do to support your claims and capabilities to do so (internal due diligence), and you must get everything in writing. If the provider lied to you (in writing) and you get sued by your end users, you at least have an ability to launch a lawsuit against the provider. Who wins in this situation? Probably the lawyers and nobody else.

The laws, regulations, standards, and related best practices discussed earlier also require data custodians/controllers to ensure that these obligations will be fulfilled by conducting due diligence (before execution of the contract) and security audits (during performance of the contract).

Internal Due Diligence

As you know, as the data custodian/controller, you face legal repercussions if you do not meet a potential global mix of requirements imposed on safeguarding end-user data entrusted to your organization. Even then, you may be restricted from transferring your client data to a third party because of contract obligations.

NOTE I have experienced these restrictions first-hand. A company that was looking at procuring cloud services instead of building a new data center had to postpone using the cloud because some clients had a "no third-party" processing clause in their contracts and others did not. Rather than making an attempt to determine which workloads and systems could be put in the cloud, they made the decision to remove that clause from all client contracts as they came up for renewal.

Both cloud providers and customers must consider their own respective practices, needs, and restrictions to identify relevant legal and compliance requirements. As part of internal due diligence, a cloud customer should determine whether its business model allows for the use of cloud computing services in the first place and under which conditions. For example, you may be restricted by law from relinquishing control of company data if you work in a critical infrastructure capacity. Alternatively, a cloud vendor may find it prudent to evaluate in advance the cost of compliance in jurisdictional areas that may be subject to legal requirements with which the vendor is unfamiliar.

NOTE For an example of the cost of compliance, it can cost a cloud provider more than US$1 million to obtain an Authority to Operate (ATO) before they are authorized to sell their product to US federal agencies.

At all times, you must consider the "cloud friendliness" of data that will be migrated to a cloud environment. If the data processed by the company is so sensitive or confidential that its disclosure would lead to a disastrous scenario for your company, you might want to reconsider transferring it to a cloud service or take significant precautions for its transfer and storage. Just remember that not all data has the same value and/or regulations surrounding it. You always need to take a risk-based approach. Financial reports for a publicly traded company have Sarbanes-Oxley (SOX) requirements and need to be tightly controlled, but the latest marketing blog content for the same organization likely doesn't have the same security requirements.

Monitoring, Testing, and Updating

The cloud environment is very dynamic. As such, any cloud customer needs to be fully aware of any changes being made by the provider. This will likely force the customer to adapt to a rate of change that may be unfamiliar. You may have developers using new services or entirely new ways of computing if a change is left unchecked. Periodic monitoring, testing, and evaluation of cloud services are recommended to ensure that required privacy and security measures are followed. Without periodic testing of both cloud services and your use of cloud services, you may be taking on unacceptable risk without even knowing it.

NOTE Many providers may restrict you from testing their systems, platforms, and applications. This restriction may force you into more of a paper exercise, where you are reliant on such providers supplying you with documentation of tests performed by third parties. Either way, you have to keep up with changes!

New security threats, laws, and compliance requirements need be addressed promptly. Both cloud clients and cloud providers must keep abreast of relevant legal, regulatory, contractual, and other requirements, and both must ensure that security controls continue to evolve as new technologies emerge.

EXAM TIP The concept of periodic monitoring, testing, and evaluation of your requirements and the vendor relationship is applicable for basically every subject in the CSA Guidance. You need to be aware of any changes— technical and legal!

External Due Diligence

Due diligence of prospective CSPs must be performed prior to your using their services. This requires that you request and review all relevant documentation from the provider, such as security documentation, contracts, terms and conditions, and acceptable use policies. The goal here is not just to assess the overall service provider but to investigate the actual services you are consuming! After all, what's the sense of inspecting a service that you won't be using?

TIP Remember that the Cloud Security Alliance's STAR registry (covered in Chapter 1) is an excellent source of information about security of a provider's services.

Everything you do from a due diligence perspective must be risk-based. Does it make sense to spend the same amount of effort assessing a service, whether the workload is a payroll system or the latest "cats with hats" marketing program? Of course it doesn't. The criticality of the workload should always be considered when performing due diligence of a service.

Sources of information need not be limited to documentation supplied by the vendor. You may find a treasure trove of information from sources such as other customers, online searches about the vendor's reputation, and reviews of any reports of litigation filed against the provider. These sources may highlight the quality or stability of a service and support capabilities, for example.

Contract Negotiations

Once your due diligence is performed and you decide that you are comfortable using a particular provider and service, the next step is ensuring that you and/or your legal team have fully read and understood the conditions included in the contract. After all, a contract is intended to describe accurately the understanding of all parties. As the nature of cloud computing is based on economies of scale, it is highly likely that you will find many contract clauses to be non-negotiable. This isn't to say that all providers will have non-negotiable clauses (or entire contracts for that matter). You may be able to negotiate contract terms with smaller providers if you are willing to be a reference client for them, for example. If a provider isn't open to changing contract clauses, it doesn't mean you need to abandon them as a service provider. It means that you need to understand your requirements, what the provider is contractually obligated to deliver, and fill any potential gaps by implementing appropriate controls. Alternatively, risk acceptance is always an option. Your organization's risk tolerance will determine the appropriate course of action.

NOTE   You know those "I agree to the terms and conditions" checkboxes that nobody reads before clicking them and using a service? Those are legally binding agreements. This is what is often called a "click-through" or "click-wrap" agreement. Ignorance is never a defense, and telling a judge, "In my defense, nobody actually reads that stuff," is not a great legal strategy.

Third-Party Audits and Attestations

Most large providers will not allow your company to perform an audit of their data centers. The reality is that you will be reliant on third-party audits and attestations to serve as assurance of compliance with aspects of the provider's infrastructure. This transparency is critical for the provider to have available to prospective and current customers. It is the customer's responsibility to evaluate the most recently available audit or attestation, its scope, and the features and services included in the assessment. You will want to also take into consideration the date of the documentation you are reviewing. Does it reflect the way things are today, or is the report you're relying on five years old, with little applicability to the current environment?

TIP   Remember that you always need to consider the services being consumed and whether those services are part of the scope of an assessment.

Electronic Discovery

The laws surrounding discovery and collection of evidence in a lawsuit are not limited to the United States. The CSA Guidance points out many American laws as part of e-discovery, but the general concepts are the same in many jurisdictions in which you may be operating. Of course, consulting with your legal counsel is the best way to understand and identify any e-discovery differences between jurisdictions.

In the United States, the Federal Rules of Civil Procedure (FRCP) govern the procedure in all civil actions and proceedings in US district courts. Of all the rules contained in the FRCP, we are most concerned with Rule 26: Duty to Disclose; General Provisions Governing Discovery. The rule requires that a party make disclosures based on information reasonably available and must also disclose any witnesses who will present evidence at trial.

Evidence can either be used in support of your case or against it. You might think of e-discovery as a requirement in the case of a judge's request for a litigation hold, or a hold order (which asserts that documents relevant to a case may not be destroyed), but the reality is that data can also be used to support a case. Many litigants have lost cases as a result of not having supporting documentation because they deleted, lost, or modified data that would have been instrumental in their court case. On the flipside, if a judge deems data was purposefully deleted or otherwise destroyed, he or she may issue an instruction of "adverse inference" to the jury. This means the jury must consider the data as being purposefully deleted and will assume it contained worst-case damaging evidence.

From a cloud perspective, the cloud provider may be required to collect electronically stored information (ESI). As the consumer, you must work with the provider to plan how you will identify all documents that may pertain to a particular e-discovery request. The following sections address the requirements associated with the FRCP in a cloud environment that should be addressed in advance of engaging a provider.

Possession, Custody, and Control

This is a simple requirement. If you can produce data (electronic or not), you are legally obligated to produce it. It doesn't matter where the data is stored—it could be in your system; it could be in a provider's system. What does matter is that you, as the customer, may not be able to produce the evidence, and the provider must be engaged. For example, say there's a case where an originating IP address is in question. You won't have this data in the case of an SaaS provider, so the provider must be able to produce that evidence for the court.

 NOTE The CSA Guidance says that "hosting data via a third party does not obviate a party's obligation to produce data." ("Obviate" sounds more official than "remove," "avoid," or "prevent.")

Relevant Cloud Applications and Environment

There may be a question as to what a particular application does or how data is processed within the system. In this scenario, the CSP will be subpoenaed by a judge directly.

Searchability and E-Discovery Tools

The tools you use today for e-discovery may not be applicable in a scenario in which you are using a provider to store or process data. The lack of tools may increase the amount of time (and therefore expense) required to produce any relevant data. The capabilities and costs of a provider to assist or minimize efforts associated with a customer's requirement to address discovery should be negotiated in advance. If it's not negotiated in advance, "surprises" such as a provider's inability to assist or astronomical bills may result, and nobody likes bad surprises.

Preservation

As mentioned earlier in this book, e-discovery and data preservation laws are not unique to the United States and the FRCP. The European Union governs this under Directive 2006/24/EC. Japan, South Korea, and Singapore have similar laws, as do South American countries Brazil (Azeredo Bill) and Argentina (Data Retention Law of 2014).

Data Retention Laws and Recordkeeping Obligations

A myriad of laws deal with data retention periods. All of these must be addressed by your company, which can lead to additional costs related to storage of data that can be reasonably expected to be requested in the event of a court case. The CSA Guidance lists the following questions customers should consider before migrating data to the cloud:

- What are the ramifications of retaining data under the service level agreement (SLA)?
- What happens if the preservation requirements outlast the terms of the SLA?
- If the client preserves the data in place, who pays for the extended storage, and at what cost?
- Does the client have the storage capacity under its SLA?
- Can the client effectively download the data in a forensically sound manner so it can be preserved offline or nearline?

 TIP Data retention services may be available, but at an additional cost. Make sure that you understand whether multiple parties will be involved (such as an SaaS provider using IaaS) and how that may impact you.

Another important aspect of data retention is the scope of preservation. Legal requests must be very specific as to the data requested. However, if a customer is unable to retain specific information sets with the necessary granularity, they may be in a situation where they have to "over-preserve." This can lead to increased costs, as someone (such as a client-paid attorney's staff) has to sift through all this information to determine what is actually required by the courts. This is called a *document review* or *privilege review*.

With all of the new technologies associated with the cloud, e-discovery is becoming increasingly complex in a world where storage is more dynamic than ever. For example, take an SaaS cloud environment that programmatically modifies or purges data when uploaded by a client, or one in which the data is shared with people or other systems that are unaware of the need to preserve. The trick is to realize what data may realistically be required in a court of law and to work with the provider to understand the best way to preserve such data.

Data Collection

Cloud services (especially SaaS) may not give you the same level of access that you are accustomed to. Collection of data may be impacted, ranging from being unable to retrieve data yourself, to a dramatic increase in the effort required to access data because of a potential lack of transparency of how data is stored and/or processed within a cloud service. This lack of transparency may lead to issues with validating that any data found is complete and accurate. Additional challenges may arise as a result of the functionality of the application storing the data. For instance, although five years' worth of data may be stored in a provider's service, if the provider limits the data exported to a month's worth at a time, it means that additional effort and expense will be associated with collection of that data.

Other issues regarding collection of data from a cloud service that generally isn't experienced within a data center is the bandwidth available for exporting data from a cloud environment and ensuring that the export is done in a forensically sound manner (with all reasonably relevant metadata preserved) and that it follows appropriate chain-of-custody requirements. As the old saying goes, never underestimate the bandwidth of a station wagon full of tapes hurtling down the highway.

Finally, it is important to note that the FRCP does include a clause, 26(b)(2)(B), that excuses a litigant from presenting data that is truly not reasonably accessible. The mere complaint that additional effort is required to retrieve data does not fall into this category, however, and you will be responsible for the extra time and cost associated with such data collection.

Forensics

I'll sum up this topic with a common saying I use for the cloud: you need virtual tools for a virtual world. You will not be able to take a hard drive, make a bit-by-bit image of it, and perform your investigations using this exact replica. You will be forced to use virtual tools to perform forensics on cloud workloads. In fact, not being able to present a bit-by-bit copy of a drive serves as a great example of the FRCP 26(b)(2)(B) clause that excuses presentation of data if it's not reasonably accessible. In reality, this type of forensic analysis is rarely warranted in cloud computing, because of the nature of storage (virtualized) that doesn't provide significant additional relevant information.

NOTE You'll learn more about forensics in Chapter 9 of this book.

Reasonable Integrity

In order for evidence to be considered admissible in a court of law, it must be considered accurate and authenticated. This is true regardless of where such evidence is held. "Authenticated" is the key word. This legal term means the data is considered genuine. This is where a chain of custody comes into play. If data cannot be authenticated, it cannot be considered admissible evidence in a court of law (barring any extenuating circumstances). The cloud does change how chain of custody is ensured. Take an example of a cloud provider that may allow you to export data, but any metadata is stripped as part of the process. But the metadata may be required to validate that the data is indeed genuine and therefore admissible in a court of law.

Direct Access

Direct access may be impossible from both the customer and the SaaS provider (for example) you have a contract with if the provider, in turn, is using a third-party IaaS to store and process data. After all, the SaaS provider in this example is just another customer of the IaaS provider and may not have any access to the hardware or facilities. As such, in this example, a requesting party may need to negotiate directly with the IaaS provider for any access.

Native Production

When digital evidence is requested, it is expected to be produced in standard formats such as PDF or CSV. If a cloud provider can export data from their highly proprietary system in a proprietary format only, this data may not be admissible as evidence in a court of law. The only circumstance that may require the export of data in a proprietary format is if relevant metadata would be lost if converted to a standard format.

Authentication

As discussed earlier, authentication in a legal sense means evidence is considered genuine and has nothing to do with identity management (we cover that in Chapter 12). The mere notion of storing data in a cloud has nothing to do with its authentication. The issue is the integrity of the data and that it wasn't altered or modified since creation (chain of custody), just as it would be if it were stored on a server in your own data center.

Cooperation Between Provider and Client in E-Discovery

When multiple parties are involved in storing data, all parties should reasonably expect to be involved in producing ESI, especially when proprietary systems are used by the provider. The issues surrounding e-discovery covered in this chapter should be accounted for in SLAs between the provider and the customer. Providers should also consider creating systems with "discovery by design" to attract clients. (Discovery by design essentially means the provider has planned for discovery requests being an expected occurrence and that extreme measures, such as limiting other tenants from updating their data in the event of a litigation hold, do not need to be performed.)

Response to a Subpoena or Search Warrant

A general best practice for providers is to have their customers' best interests in mind at all times, and this includes responding to subpoenas and search warrants for access to customer data. Providers should fight overbroad or otherwise problematic demands for information when possible. As the customer, you cannot reasonably expect a provider to break the law to protect your data from being handed over to a government agency, as the provider may be compelled by law to do so based on the jurisdiction in which they are operating.

Chapter Review

This chapter discussed the legal issues surrounding the use of cloud services, the importance of performing both internal and external due diligence, and some aspects of e-discovery and the admissibility of electronically stored information (ESI).

NOTE Although you may be full of legal mumbo-jumbo at this point, you can check out the Sedona Conference web site (https://thesedonaconference.org/) for more information surrounding the handling of ESI if you're hungry for more on this topic.

From an exam perspective, you'll want to be comfortable with the following:

- Cloud customers should understand the relevant legal and regulatory frameworks, contractual requirements, and restrictions that apply to the handling of their data or data in their custody, and the conduct of their operations before moving systems and data to the cloud.

- Cloud providers should clearly and conspicuously disclose their policies, requirements, and capabilities, including all terms and conditions that apply to the services they provide.

- Cloud customers should conduct a comprehensive evaluation of a proposed cloud service provider before signing a contract, and they should regularly update this evaluation and monitor the scope, nature, and consistency of the services they purchase.

- Cloud providers should publish their policies, requirements, and capabilities to meet legal obligations for customers, such as electronic discovery.

- Cloud customers should understand the legal implications of using particular cloud providers and match those to their legal requirements.

- Cloud customers should understand the legal implications of where the cloud provider physically operates and stores information.

- Cloud customers should decide whether to choose where their data will be hosted, if the option is available, to comply with their own jurisdictional requirements.

- Cloud customers and providers should have a clear understanding of the legal and technical requirements to meet any electronic discovery requests.

- Cloud customers should understand that click-through legal agreements are legally binding.

Questions

1. What does "authentication" mean in a trial?

   A. Evidence is considered genuine.

   B. This is the stage at which a judge is assigned and known to both parties.

   C. A witness is approved as an expert and their testimony will be considered.

   D. Both parties involved in a lawsuit are declared.

2. Which organization deals with privacy rights at a federal level in the United States?

   A. Federal Communications Commission (FCC)

   B. Federal Trade Commission (FTC)

   C. Federal Office of the Attorney General

   D. Homeland Security

3. GDPR replaced which Data Protection Directive?

   A. PIPEDA

   B. FRCP

   C. Directive 95/46/EC

   D. NIS

4. When is a party excused from presenting evidence in a court of law?

   A. When it doesn't exist

   B. When it is too expensive to retrieve

   C. Never; a party must always present data when it's requested by a judge

   D. When it is not reasonably accessible

5. What format should be used when presenting electronically stored information (ESI) in a court of law?

   A. PDF

   B. CSV

   C. Standard format

   D. Native format

6. Which of the following may lead to issues with validating that any data found is complete and accurate when stored in a cloud environment?

   A. Transparency

   B. Use of unknown hardware at provider location

   C. There are no issues with validating data stored in the cloud

   D. Lack of metadata in cloud environments

7. Which of the following is the minimum retention period for any data that may be required in a court of law?

   A. 1 year

   B. 5 years

   C. Any data that may be considered evidence must be retained in perpetuity.

   D. There is no general minimum retention period of data.

8. What is the most important item to consider when reviewing third-party audits and attestations?

   A. The firm that performed the audit

   B. The services being consumed by the customer

   C. The location of services

   D. The service provider certification

9. What should a customer do when dealing with a non-negotiable contract where controls may be lacking?

   A. Do not use the service provider.

   B. Identify any gaps and fill them with appropriate controls.

   C. Purchase cyberinsurance to mitigate the associated risk.

   D. Accept the risk the provider accepts.

10. The Australian Privacy Act requires that a breach disclosure be performed in which scenario?

    A. When any data pertaining to a citizen is disclosed

    B. When personally identifiable information is disclosed

    C. When disclosure would be likely to cause serious harm to the individual

    D. The Australian Privacy Act does not address breach notification requirements

Answers

1. A. "Authentication" means that the data evidence is considered genuine and is therefore admissible in a court of law.

2. B. The FTC is the federal organization responsible for consumer protection and privacy rights. The state attorney general performs the same activity at the state level.

3. C. GDPR replaced the Data Protection Directive 95/46/EC. PIPEDA is a Canadian data protection law. FRCP is the set of rules governing civil law. NIS is the EU-wide cybersecurity legislation.

4. D. FRCP clause 26(b)(2)(B) permits data not being presented as evidence when it is not reasonably accessible. This may be applicable, for instance, when a bit-level copy of a drive is required when the data is stored in a cloud environment.

5. C. The best answer is that evidence is most useful if it is presented in a standard format. Although both PDF and CSV can be considered standard formats, neither is the best answer here, because standard format is more accurate as a response. Presentation of native format may be required if metadata isn't properly preserved as part of an export routine.

6. A. Transparency issues may cause issues with validating that any data found is complete and accurate. Any issues must be identified as part of due diligence of the provider environment.

7. D. There are no mandated retention periods that are generically applied to all data sets. Different retention periods will be applied by laws or other means (such as standards, continued value to the company, and so on) based on the type of data. Although data that can be reasonably expected to serve as evidence in a court case should be preserved by an organization, there is no retention period mandated for these data sets.

8. B. The services being consumed by the customer is the most important item to consider when reviewing third-party audits and attestations. Although all of the other options are certainly valid, they are of little value if the services consumed are not part of the scope of the audit being reviewed.

9. **B.** The best answer is to identify potential gaps and implement controls to address perceived risk. Although risk response may include avoiding the risk by not using the provider, accepting the risk, and mitigating financial damages by purchasing cyberinsurance, the best answer is to identify the controls the provider is contractually required to supply, determine your requirements, and address gaps by deploying controls.

10. **C.** The Australian Privacy Act requires that a breach of security must be reported when personal information that may lead to serious harm is disclosed.

Compliance and Audit Management

This chapter covers the following topics from Domain 4 of the CSA Guidance:
- Impact of the Cloud on Contracts
- Compliance Scope
- Compliance Analysis Requirements
- How the Cloud Changes Audits
- Right to Audit
- Audit Scope
- Auditor Requirements

Trust, but verify.

—Russian proverb

You may recall this quote from President Ronald Reagan (during nuclear disarmament discussions with the Soviet Union), but this Russian proverb is truer today than ever with regard to cloud services. Providers will supply you with all sorts of documentation to build trust in an offering, but how are the security statements within these documents verified to ensure that you remain compliant with regulations that affect your company? The reality is that you're likely dealing with third-party audits with regard to the *verify* portion of this proverb.

 EXAM TIP Remember that audits are a key tool to prove or disprove compliance.

The virtualized and distributed nature of the cloud forces customers to understand and appreciate jurisdictional differences and their implications on existing compliance and audit standards, processes, and practices that aren't faced in the traditional data center environment.

Auditors need to adjust to the virtual world that is cloud computing. Regulations aren't written specifically to address cloud environments, just as they aren't written specifically for a particular programming language or operating system to run applications that fall under regulatory focus. Regulatory bodies such as NIST and ISO have created cloud-specific guidance and/or control frameworks to try to fill the gap between traditional and cloud deployments. Your understanding of the compliance challenges in a cloud environment is paramount, and these challenges need consideration when you're developing a cloud strategy.

Following are some compliance items that you should consider as part of your cloud implementation:

- **Jurisdictional issues**   Your company may face regulations that forbid the export of data to foreign jurisdictions.

- **Shared responsibility model inherent with all types of cloud services**   Remember that shared responsibility will be highly dependent on the service model being consumed (Software as a Service [SaaS], Platform as a Service [PaaS], or Infrastructure as a Service [IaaS]).

- **Compliance inheritance**   Consider PCI, for example. The IaaS provider you use to host a credit card processing system may be Payment Card Industry (PCI) Level 1 certified, but your application must meet all other PCI requirements as well.

- **Supply chain complexity**   Consider the complexity of the supply chain. For example, many SaaS providers of all sizes may themselves use an outsourced IaaS solution to store customer data, or SaaS providers that leverage multiple PaaS providers may in turn use different IaaS providers.

- **Artifacts of compliance from the provider**   All the artifacts of compliance (such as system logs) that you require for traditional systems will still be required in a cloud environment. The real question is whether you can obtain these artifacts and do so in a timely manner.

- **Scope relevance**   Are the features and services of a cloud provider within the scope of your previously performed audits and assessments?

- **Compliance management**   How does the provider manage compliance and audits—not just now, but over time as well?

- **Audit performance**   How are audits of cloud computing performed compared to those in a traditional data center environment?

- **Provider experience**   Does the provider have experience working with regulatory bodies?

 EXAM TIP   Earning a CCSK is a great way for auditors to demonstrate their knowledge of cloud services. Remember that customers should work with auditors who have knowledge of the differences between traditional IT and the cloud.

This chapter covers two related subjects: compliance and audits. Each section contains backgrounder information on the subject material, since not all readers will have an appreciation of these functions. This information sets the stage for a discussion on how these functions change as a result of cloud technologies.

EXAM TIP You won't see any general questions in the CCSK exam on either compliance or auditing basics, but do expect to see questions on cloud-specific changes to compliance and audits.

Compliance Backgrounder

Compliance generally means conformance to regulations, laws, policies, standards, best practices, and contracts. It is an important part of GRC (governance, risk, and compliance) that enables proper oversight of computing—and cloud computing is no different. A compliance framework is the set of policies, procedures, processes, and technologies implemented by an organization to identify and adhere to applicable requirements based on laws, regulations, and standards. Compliance also involves an assessment of the costs of noncompliance and can act to prioritize and fund compliance initiatives. Compliance is both expensive and mandatory, but the costs associated with noncompliance could be devastating to a company, and executives in a company charged with noncompliance could face jail time as a result.

As mentioned, compliance works in conjunction with governance and risk management to create GRC. To help you understand how compliance fits in, I'm going to stick with the following flow: *Governance* considers the corporate obligations (from laws and regulations, to protecting the interests of stakeholders and shareholders, corporate ethics, and social responsibilities) that determine how a company operates. Governance helps the company form and manage its risk tolerance. This then feeds *risk* management to implement the required controls to address both regulations and risk tolerance. *Compliance* then uses audits to ensure that appropriate controls are indeed in place.

I like to use the *Deming cycle*—Plan, Do, Check, Act (PDCA)—to show relationships within the risk management spectrum. (This well-known "continuous quality improvement model" was developed by W. Edwards Deming in the 1950s.) Here is a simplified list of these phases in GRC terms:

- **Plan** Determine what regulations are in scope and what controls need to be addressed as a result.
- **Do** Implement the required controls.
- **Check** Perform audits to ensure that required controls meet the requirements.
- **Act** Fix any deficiencies and provide feedback to future improvements.

NOTE Compliance does not always equal security, and security does not always equal compliance. Still, if your company's cloud deployments are determined to be noncompliant, changes will need to be made.

The concepts of compliance and associated auditing don't change as a result of using cloud services. After all, a cloud service provider (CSP) is just another third party, and you most likely have some form of a third-party oversight program in place. There are, however, specific compliance items that you need to consider for cloud implementations, which are covered in the following sections.

Impact of the Cloud on Contracts

When examining contracts and service agreements between your organization and cloud service providers, you should focus on the following items:

- **Security service level agreements** The importance of security SLAs is often overlooked when reviewing CSP contracts. Following is a nonexhaustive list of the key items you should look for as part of a security SLA with a cloud provider:
  - Specific written compliance commitments for standards that apply to your organization
  - Service level commitments and liability terms for a data breach
  - Exposure of detailed security monitoring for your organization's implementation
  - Explicit descriptions of security implementations and commitment to compliance

- **Ownership of data** Believe it or not, some cloud providers have clauses in their contracts that transfer ownership of any data uploaded by a customer to the provider. In turn, the customer gets unlimited access to this data, but the provider is allowed to do whatever they please with said data, including retaining it upon contract termination and/or selling it to others. This is more common with "free" versions of SaaS products.

- **Right to audit** You may see this referred to as a "first-party audit." Essentially, this is a contractual clause that allows the customer to examine the supplier's premises and systems upon reasonable notice. You may see this clause in an SLA if the provider sees a reason to take extreme measures to get your business. The reality is that big providers almost never grant this ability to customers.

- **Third-party audits** This clause requires the provider to undergo appropriate and regular audits. Reports from these audits should be made available to customers upon request. The reports should also include remediation plans for any significant issues identified in the reports.

- **Conformance to security policies** You need to understand the security policies in place at the cloud provider and understand how they meet your particular policy requirements. In the likely event that a service provider contract does not fully address your policies, you need to fill the gaps with your own controls.

- **Compliance with laws and regulations** Contract clauses should clearly state that the service provider conforms to all relevant laws and regulations that are important to your organization. For example, if you are looking to store healthcare information in a particular provider's environment, you must ensure that the provider is contractually bound to remain compliant with HIPAA regulations.

- **Incident notification**   You should understand how incidents are declared and how customers are notified by the provider (and vice versa) of incidents. Notifications could be required for service changes, interruptions, and, of course, security incidents. Specific time periods should be stated in the contract for these notifications.

- **Liabilities**   Liabilities clauses should clearly state which parties are liable for which actions and activities. Available remedies should also be listed should either party fail to perform adequately.

- **Termination terms**   The contract should contain provisions that describe the actions a CSP will perform if the business relationship is terminated. For example, how will customer data be deleted when a customer leaves, and in what time frame?

In addition to these items, you should investigate a couple of other items that are not cloud specific:

- **Service levels**   Understand the CSP's acceptable service levels and the processes that are followed in the event of service interruptions. Is there an escalation path for notifications, or does the provider supply clients with a status update web site? In the event of a widespread outage, a CSP will likely use a status update page to update customers on outages or system-wide issues. Another aspect you need to understand is that many cloud providers will give customers only "service credits" as a form of penalty if unavailability is in excess of stated availability agreements (generally 99.9 percent uptime). And some providers will issue these credits only if the customer makes a claim for credits and shows the provider evidence of the outage.

- **Quality levels**   What remedies are in place if quality standards, such as following best practices and quality control procedures, are not met by the provider? You need to remember that operational procedures performed by the cloud provider in a cloud environment have a direct impact on your company's ability to operate in that environment.

How the Cloud Changes Compliance

The two biggest terms to remember about compliance in a cloud environment are "compliance inheritance" and "continuous." The following sections discuss both topics.

Compliance Inheritance

Going back to the logical model from Chapter 1, infrastructure in particular, you already know that this is completely under the control of the public cloud provider, and you most likely won't have access to audit that environment. So what's a company to do to prove compliance?

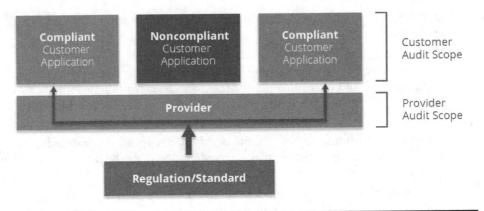

Figure 4-1   Compliance inheritance. (Used with permission of Cloud Security Alliance.)

Use of third-party audit results (such as those discussed in Chapter 2 and later in this chapter), called "pass-through audits" by the CSA, is a form of compliance inheritance. In this case, you basically confirm that a provider is compliant with the areas for which they are responsible via vendor-supplied audit results or certifications, and then you ensure that your systems running in the cloud environment are also compliant. This is the core of the shared responsibility model discussed in previous chapters.

Consider an example, such as that shown in Figure 4-1, in which you build a credit card processing application on top of a Windows server that doesn't have any form of malware inspection. (Congratulations! You just failed to meet PCI DSS 5.3!) The provider gave you a "PCI DSS Level 1" environment in which to operate your application, and yet you still blew it. This is the shared responsibility model in action. The provider is responsible for the facilities and the hardware, and your organization is responsible for configuring the server instance, the application, and any required logical security controls.

 CAUTION   If your SaaS provider claims they are PCI compliant just because they are using a PCI-compliant IaaS provider, there's only one thing you should do—RUN. That screams to me that they have no idea of proper security or compliance.

Continuous Compliance

I want to take a moment to make a distinction here between *continuous monitoring* and *continuous auditing*. Although they are often considered joint activities (some refer to it as CM/CA), they really aren't the same thing. One commonality they share is that "continuous" doesn't necessarily mean *real-time analysis*. NIST defines Information Security Continuous Monitoring (ISCM) thusly: "Security controls and organizational risks are assessed and analyzed at a frequency sufficient to support risk-based security decisions to adequately protect organization information." On the other hand, ISACA (formerly known as Information Systems Audit and Control Association) calls out the distinction between a "traditional" and a "continuous" audit as a short time lapse between the facts to be audited, the collection of evidence, and audit reporting. Techniques to perform continuous auditing are referred to as *computer-assisted audit techniques*. The bottom line is that "continuous" does not mean real-time 24×7×365. It addresses performing something at an appropriate frequency, and that is up to the system owner.

 NOTE Check out NIST 800-137 for everything you ever wanted to know about continuous monitoring, but were afraid to ask! It's great stuff, but not cloud specific, so don't go overboard when prepping for your CCSK exam.

Now that I have addressed the term "continuous" and what it means according to organizations such as NIST and ISACA, let's turn our focus to the cloud and see what the CSA has to say on the subject. The guidance itself is fairly limited in coverage, as the only reference to continuous compliance, audit, and assurance is the following:

> Compliance, audit, and assurance should be continuous. They should not be seen as merely point-in-time activities, and many standards and regulations are moving more towards this model. This is especially true in cloud computing, where both the provider and customer tend to be in more-constant flux and are rarely ever in a static state.

In other words, there's a requirement to be up-to-date continuously with any changes made at the provider's side (in addition to your changes, of course) that may impact compliance. So, for example, if your provider moves its data center jurisdiction and your data is now noncompliant with a government regulation, you need to know about this as soon as realistically possible.

Beyond the guidance, however, the CSA has done a lot of work on its continuous compliance assessment program and has made it part of the STAR registry, which was covered back in Chapter 1. The goal of the STAR Continuous is to address the security posture of cloud providers between point-in-time audits. When you adopt STAR's continuous auditing with an increased audit frequency, the chances of deviation of the provider's security posture become lower, and customers can have better validation of a provider with an "always up-to-date" compliance status.

That's great and all, but how do providers address this continuous compliance initiative? *Automation*, that's how! Remember that cloud environments are automated environments to begin with, so why can't testing of the environment be automated as well and be executed by the provider at an expected testing frequency between the point-in-time audits they currently provide to customers? Of course, not everything can be automated, so additional manual activities will have to be performed as well, but through the use of this STAR Continuous approach, customers will be able to have greater confidence in the security controls in the provider's environment.

NOTE Check out the CSA web site if you are interested in learning more about the STAR Continuous program. Just be aware that you will *not* be asked any questions on your CCSK exam about that particular program, because it is not covered as part of the CSA Guidance. The EU Security Certification (EU-SEC) project also offers a white paper, "Continuous Auditing Certification," that you may want to check out for further information.

Finally, the cloud may also change compliance by the introduction of a global network at your disposal. As you know, all jurisdictions have their own laws and regulations that may cause regulatory issues for your firm if sensitive data is accidentally placed in, or moved to, a different jurisdiction. Additional compliance challenges may arise because not all services and regions offered by a provider may have undergone the same audits and attestations.

Audit Backgrounder

In *CISA Certified Information Systems Auditor All-in-One Exam Guide, Fourth Edition* (McGraw-Hill, 2020), author Peter Gregory defines *audit* as "a systematic and repeatable process where a competent and independent professional evaluates one or more controls, interviews personnel, obtains and analyzes evidence, and develops a written opinion on the effectiveness of controls." Alternatively, ISO 19011:2018 defines *audit* as a "systematic, independent and documented process for obtaining audit evidence [records, statements of fact, or other information that is relevant and verifiable] and evaluating it objectively to determine the extent to which the audit criteria [a set of policies, procedures, or requirements] are fulfilled." As you can see, there is commonality across multiple organizations as to how an audit is defined. Some key takeaways need to be mentioned:

- First are the terms "systematic" and "repeatable." This requires that a methodology/standard be followed. This will be driven as part of the audit management function. I discuss audit management in the next section of the chapter.

- Second, a key term regarding audits is "independent." Audits must be independently conducted and should be robustly designed to reflect best practices, appropriate resources, and tested protocols and standards. Naturally, you may have concerns regarding the true independence of an auditor, or the firm itself if they are being paid by the cloud provider. In this case, you need to place your trust in the audit firm as being a true independent source.

Audits generally include some form of testing. The two types of testing are *compliance testing* and *substantive testing*. Compliance testing is used to determine whether controls have been properly designed and implemented. This type of testing would also include tests to determine whether the controls are operating properly. Substantive testing, on the other hand, looks at the accuracy and integrity of transactions that go through processes and information systems. In general, you'll likely be relying on previously performed audits that have used compliance testing.

Audit Management in the Cloud

Most organizations are subject to a mix of internal and external audits and assessments to assure compliance with internal and external requirements. Audit reports include a compliance determination as well as a list of identified issues, and they may contain remediation recommendations. Information security audits and assessments typically focus on evaluating the effectiveness of security management and controls.

Audit management ensures that audit directives are implemented properly. This function includes determining appropriate requirements, scope, scheduling, and responsibilities. Audit management uses compliance requirements and risk data to scope, plan, and prioritize audit engagements.

> **NOTE**   Since this is a cloud-specific book, I will include cloud-related information throughout the planning steps where it makes sense to do so.

Audits are planned events, and planning audits is part of the audit management function. Audit planning includes several stages. It is very important for you to note that audits of both a CSP's and your company's usage of the cloud will be required. Much of the auditing of a CSP will consist of third-party audit reviews that won't require the same planning as regular audits, as you will be consuming audit reports, not creating them. However, from the perspective of an internal use of a cloud audit, general audit management principles will remain, but you will require highly specialized resources who understand the new cloud-specific technologies (such as containers and serverless technologies) that may be associated with your deployments.

For audit planning, consider the following when creating audit schedules and assigning resources for audits of cloud environments:

- **Purpose**   What is the goal of the audit? Is it to determine compliance with a particular law, standard, contractual obligation, or internal requirement that has been introduced or changed? It is an initial audit of a service provider to determine appropriateness of use, or is it intended to determine whether a previously discovered deficiency has been remediated?

- **Scope**   This is the most critical aspect when consuming cloud services. All certifications and audit results supplied by a provider will have a specific scope. Scope can be based on specific services, geography, technology, business processes, or even a segment of the organization. You must understand the scope of an audit report and compare it to what you are actually consuming.

- **Risk analysis**   This is another area that is directly related to cloud services. What cloud services pose the highest level of risk to your organization based on the criticality of the data being stored in a particular environment? This will ultimately determine the frequency and depth of audits that need to be performed against the wide array of cloud services your company is presently using or will be using in the future. Always remember that this isn't just a provider issue. You will need to audit your implementation as well in the shared responsibility model of the cloud.

- **Audit procedures**   The procedures are the rules and processes defined in the audit methodology and/or standard. Compliance audits may determine the procedures that should be followed and the qualifications of the auditor. Audits of cloud environments should be performed by auditors with knowledge of cloud environments.

- **Resources**   The resources that need to be identified include the time that should be allocated for performance of the audit and the tools that will be required to execute the audit. For a cloud environment that exposes a programmatic interface such as CLIs or APIs, the tools may be developed so they are highly repeatable.

- **Schedule**   An audit schedule should be developed that gives the auditor an appropriate amount of time to perform interviews, collect and analyze data, and generate audit reports. The time it takes to perform the audit will depend on multiple factors, such as the size of the scope, the applicable controls (ISO calls this the "Statement of Applicability"), and the complexity of the environment. This can be accelerated for the cloud because your auditors will likely be reviewing third-party audits. Alternatively, determining how often point-in-time audits should be performed can also be considered a function of audit management.

SOC Reports and ISO Certifications Backgrounder

Most CSPs will use two primary audit standards to demonstrate that appropriate security is in place for their cloud services: Service Organization Control (SOC) and International Standards Organization (ISO) standards. I'm covering these to increase your understanding of the standards themselves. You won't be tested on the contents of either SOC reports or ISO certifications as part of your CCSK exam, but if you're going to be working in a cloud environment, you should know what the standards are and how they differ.

 NOTE   Honestly, you will not be tested on the following backgrounder information. If you're not interested in information that's not about the CCSK exam, feel free to jump to the next section.

SOC Backgrounder

Although I covered the SOC report levels and types in Chapter 2 (quick reminder: SOC 1 is for financial reporting, SOC 2 is for security controls, Type 1 is a point-in-time look at control design, and Type 2 looks at operating effectiveness of controls over a period of time), you should understand a few more items before reviewing the SOC 2 reports supplied by your providers. The areas covered here include the definitions of terms associated with a system, the various Trust Services Criteria (TSC, formerly known as Trust Services Principles and Criteria), and some associated control categories.

Let's begin with definitions of terms used to describe a system. According to the AICPA, a system comprises the following components:

- **Infrastructure**   The physical structures, IT, and other hardware such as facilities, computers, equipment, and networks.

- **Software**   The application programs and system software, including operating systems, middleware, and utilities.

- **People**   All personnel involved in the governance, operation, and use of a system. Examples include developers, operators, users, vendor personnel, and managers.

- **Processes**   Both automatic and manual processes. All processes are included as part of the engagement report.

- **Data**   The information used or processed by a system.

These terms are all included as part of the attestation engagement report standard by the AICPA and cannot be selected by the management of the CSP when they want to have a particular system undergo an SOC report process.

Next up are what the AICPA defines as the five *Trust Services Criteria*. Management of the CSP can select the trust services they will attest to. Some providers may include only the security trust service criteria examined by an auditor, while others may include all five in their reports. The trust services and their associated goals from the AICPA are as follows:

- **Security**   The system is protected against unauthorized access, use, or modification.

- **Availability**   The system is available for operation and use as committed or agreed to.

- **Confidentiality**   Information designated as confidential is protected as committed or agreed to.

- **Processing Integrity**   System processing is complete, valid, accurate, timely, and authorized.

- **Privacy**   A system's collection, use, retention, disclosure, and disposal of personal information is in conformance with privacy notices.

Each of these trust services has associated categories and controls (basically defining what a system must do). All of the trust services leverage what the AICPA calls the *Common Criteria*. Essentially, the Common Criteria consists of seven categories and the control objectives within each category that must be checked. These categories and high-level descriptions are as follows:

- **Organization and Management**   How the organization is structured and the processes the organization has implemented to manage and support people within its operating units.

- **Communications**   How the organization communicates its policies, processes, procedures, commitments, and requirements to authorized users and other parties of the system, and the obligations of those parties and users to the effective operation of the system.

- **Risk Management and Design and Implementation of Controls**   How the entity identifies potential risks that would affect the entity's ability to achieve its objectives, analyzes those risks, develops responses to those risks including the design and implementation of controls and other risk mitigating actions, and conducts ongoing monitoring of risks and the risk management process.

- **Monitoring of Controls**   How the entity monitors the system, including the suitability and design and operating effectiveness of the controls, and how the organization takes action to address identified deficiencies.

- **Logical and Physical Access Controls**   How the organization restricts logical and physical access to the system, provides and removes that access, and prevents unauthorized access to meet the criteria for the trust services addressed in the engagement.

- **Systems Operations**   How the organization manages the execution of system procedures and detects and mitigates processing deviations, including logical and physical security deviations, to meet the objectives of the trust services addressed in the engagement.

- **Change Management**   How the organization identifies the need for changes to the system, makes the changes following a controlled change management process, and prevents unauthorized changes from being made to meet the criteria for the trust services addressed in the engagement.

The final thing I think is important for you to know about SOC reports is the concept of *Complementary User Entity Controls* (CUEC). They're important because they also drive home the concept of the shared responsibility model of the cloud. These CUECs are contained within the SOC report supplied to customers by the provider to advise customers that certain controls must be in place by the customer to support the SOC report. Some of the more important items to note that will likely be applicable to all cloud services involve logical security. This includes items such as establishing administrators, ensuring that accounts in the system are appropriate and checked on a regular basis, and ensuring that accounts are removed once they are no longer required.

ISO Backgrounder

Now that you understand the structure of the SOC reporting standard and you have a good idea of what you should be looking for when you're reviewing these reports, let's move on to the ISO/IEC standards you may encounter when assessing providers.

 NOTE   I am not covering all the ISO standards—not even close. There are literally more than 20,000 ISO standards for everything from quality control (such as ISO 9001) to information security (27000 series).

Following are a few pertinent cybersecurity-related standards that may be promoted by CSPs:

- **ISO/IEC 27001**   This standard defines the requirements for an information security management system (ISMS). Note that the entire organization is not necessarily affected by the standard, because it all depends on the scope of the ISMS. The scope could be limited by the provider to one group within an organization, and there is no guarantee that any group outside of the scope has appropriate ISMSs in place. It is up to the auditor to verify that the scope of the engagement is "fit for purpose." As the customer, you are responsible for determining whether the scope of the certification is relevant for your purposes.

- **ISO/IEC 27002**   This standard is a code of practice and serves as a control catalog used in an ISMS. Where the ISO/IEC 27001 standard has an appendix with a list of controls, the ISO/IEC 27002 documentation lists the controls and includes implementation guidance that serve as best practice recommendations. More than 130 controls are included in the 27002 documentation.

- **ISO/IEC 27005**   This is the ISO information security risk management guidelines document. This standard is used by organizations to implement information security risk management effectively in compliance with the ISO/IEC 27001 standard.

- **ISO/IEC 27017**   This is the set of security controls from ISO/IEC 27002, modified for cloud services, and it adds cloud-specific controls the ISO calls a "cloud service extended control set" that must be addressed. Essentially, this documentation takes all the controls found in ISO/IEC 27002 and adds implementation guidance for both cloud customers and providers.

- **ISO/IEC 27018**   This is the code of practice for protection of personal data in the cloud computing environment. Like ISO/IEC 27107, it adds implementation guidance from ISO/IEC 27002 controls applicable to protecting personally identifiable information (PII).

 NOTE   Other ISO/IEC standards also come into play regarding auditing, such as ISO/IEC 17021, 27006, and 19011.

ISO/IEC 27002 controls that support ISMS address security concerns across a wide variety of domains. Although this book doesn't cover every single control, it includes the areas of focus (security control clauses) that ISO/IEC 27002 does cover, so you can get an idea of the areas checked as part of an ISO certification:

- Security Policies
- Organizing Information Security
- Asset Management
- Human Resources Security

- Physical and Environmental Security
- Communications and Operations Management
- Access Control
- Information Systems Acquisition, Development, and Maintenance
- Information Security Incident Management
- Business Continuity Management
- Compliance

The following table breaks down the differences between SOC 2 and ISO/IEC 27001.

Area of Focus	SOC 2	ISO/IEC 27001
General Purpose	Used by service organizations to demonstrate to customers that it meets established security criteria to state the system in scope is protected against unauthorized physical and logical access	Certification that demonstrates that an ISMS is in place that meets specified requirements
Applicability	Systems in scope of engagement report are tested against one or more principles	ISMS is in place within scope of audit (determined by company)
Report	Contains auditor opinion, management assertion, description of controls, tests of controls, and results.	Single-page certification (some providers may make audit reports available)

How the Cloud Changes Audits

Let's shift focus to attestations and certifications used when dealing with cloud providers, because you will be reliant mostly on third-party audits. An *attestation* is a declaration that something exists or is true. *Certification* is an official document attesting to a status or level of achievement. Both attestations and certifications are based on audit findings. A SOC 2 report is a primary example of an attestation that's widely used by CSPs. Primary examples of certifications used by CSPs are ISO/IEC 27001 and ISO/IEC 27017 (among others).

Auditing changes dramatically in a cloud environment, because you will most likely be consuming these aforementioned third-party attestations and certifications rather than performing your own audits (remember these will be viewed as a security issue by the provider). In many instances, these attestation reports will be available only under a nondisclosure agreement (NDA). This is the case with SOC 2 reports, for example. This is a condition of the AICPA itself, not the provider.

As you are relying on third-party audits and related attestations and certifications, ensuring the scope of the audit and when the audit was performed are more important than ever. Scope issues you'll want to address include the data centers, services, and, of course, the controls assessed. All audits and assessments are point-in-time activities. As they say in the financial world, past performance may not be indicative of future results.

You always want to obtain the latest attestation or audit report. These reports aren't released continuously throughout the year, nor are they made available immediately. Don't be surprised to see that the latest report is actually a few months old. What you are consuming is the result of an audit that was performed during a certain period of time. If you recall from the continuous compliance discussion earlier in this chapter, it is the time gap between audits that CSA STAR attempts to address.

Finally, you know there's a shared responsibility model at play with the cloud and that it's not just all about auditing the provider. You will need to collect your own *artifacts of compliance* to address your organizational compliance requirements. These artifacts of compliance (see the examples shown in Figure 4-2) don't change as a result of moving to the cloud. What does change is where these artifacts are stored, and how they are controlled may also change. You always want to identify required artifacts and how they can be either generated by your systems or made available by a provider.

Right to Audit

With regard to audits of outsourcing providers, it is generally impossible to audit providers unless they have contractually agreed to allow your organization to audit them. This contract clause is known as the *right-to-audit clause* (aka first-party audit). Without a right-to-audit clause, you will be reliant on published reports such as SOC and ISO/IEC (aka third-party audit). As a CCSK candidate, you must remember that a provider may see auditors in their data center as a security risk. I always imagine thousands of auditors standing in a line that stretches around the outside of the data center, all waiting their turn for access. Now consider the provider with a million customers—would every single one of them have the right to audit? I'm sure you can determine that the result would be mayhem, and that's why providers generally don't allow such audits.

Audit Scope

Audit scope takes on a dual intent with concern to cloud services. You have the scope of a third-party audit when dealing with onboarding and maintaining a CSP, and then you have the audit of your usage of a particular cloud service. You need to address a few

Figure 4-2
Artifacts of compliance remain the same in the cloud. (Used with permission of Cloud Security Alliance.)

questions as part of the audit scope when you're assessing providers. Some of the bigger questions are listed here:

- **What certifications does the cloud service provider have?** A SOC 2, Type 2, attestation engagement report will contain detailed information on the system, the tests that were performed, any findings, and management response. On the other hand, an ISO/IEC 27001 certification will generally be a single certification page signed off by the ISO auditor, stating that a part of the organization or the whole organization has obtained its ISO certification for its ISMS and will be good for a period of three years.
- **What services is your company consuming, and are they addressed in the report you have access to?**
- **Are there any subservice organizations used by the provider?** For example, if you are researching an SaaS that uses an IaaS provider for storing customer data, you need to examine the IaaS provider as well.

Above and beyond the auditing of the service provider, you must also consider the auditing of your organization's use of cloud services. A good place to start with this is the CUECs discussed earlier in this chapter (in the "SOC Backgrounder" section). These will be focused mainly on metastructure settings, but your audit scope doesn't end there. Don't forget compliance inheritance and shared responsibilities that were also covered in this chapter, and remember that artifacts of compliance don't change; what changes is that the provider may need to produce these artifacts, or may need to allow you to maintain these artifacts. The bottom line for auditing your usage of the cloud is this: you must maintain compliance regardless of where the systems and/or data is held, and this requires you to inspect all facets of your implementations, ranging from the metastructure all the way up to the infostructure layer.

Auditor Requirements

Your company should engage only auditors who have cloud knowledge, such as those who have earned their CCSK. With so many new approaches to implementation in cloud services, the audit function requires an auditor who understands the possibilities available with cloud deployments. For example, consider the concept of immutable servers (covered in Chapter 7), which states that you don't patch servers; rather, you update an image and replace the vulnerable running server instance with the newly patched server image. An auditor who doesn't understand this concept may be confused and mark this down as a finding, while in reality, there are many arguments in favor of this approach from a security perspective.

Chapter Review

This chapter addressed compliance and audit management when working with a cloud environment. From a CCSK exam perspective, remember that everything regarding the basics of compliance and audits and why they are performed remains the same in every situation.

What changes is who is performing these audits, and that it's likely to be an independent third-party auditor. Providers will supply customers with third-party (or pass-through) audits, and you need to review these to understand the scope of the engagement and therefore the applicability to your usage of the provider's offering.

Other items that you should remember for your CCSK exam are as follows:

- Remember that compliance, audit, and assurance should be continuous, not point-in-time activities. This applies for both customers and providers.

- Cloud providers should always be as transparent as possible. They should clearly communicate their audit results, certifications, and attestations.

- Customers should always review audit results provided by providers with particular attention to the services and jurisdictions in the audit scope.

- Cloud providers must maintain their certifications/attestations over time and proactively communicate any changes in status. Customers must ensure that they are aware of any changes made by the provider that may impact them.

- Providers should supply customers with commonly needed evidence and artifacts of compliance, such as logs of administrative activity that the customer cannot otherwise collect on their own.

- Cloud customers should evaluate a provider's third-party attestations and certifications to support compliance obligations.

- To avoid potential misunderstanding, customers and providers should engage auditors with experience in cloud computing.

- When a provider's artifacts of compliance are insufficient, customers should create and collect their own artifacts. An example of this is adding logging into an application running in a PaaS that doesn't offer appropriate logging capabilities.

- Customers should keep a register of cloud providers used, relevant compliance requirements, and current statuses. The CSA Cloud Controls Matrix (see Chapter 1) can support this activity.

Questions

1. How must audits be conducted?

    A. Always by your company

    B. Always by the provider

    C. Always by an independent auditor

    D. Always by a federal regulator

2. A pass-through audit is a form of what?

   A. Compliance inheritance

   B. Demonstration of adherence by the provider to industry standards

   C. A physical assessment that has taken place as part of the audit

   D. A term used for all services being in scope for the audit engagement

3. How do audits work with compliance?

   A. Audits are the technical means to assess systems.

   B. Audits are the processes and procedures used to assess systems.

   C. Audits are a key tool for proving or disproving compliance.

   D. Audits are required for proper governance of cloud systems.

4. What is true about an attestation?

   A. Attestation is another term for an audit.

   B. Attestation is a legal statement from a third party.

   C. Attestation is testimony in a court of law.

   D. Attestations can be performed only by a CPA.

5. What is the purpose of audit management?

   A. Manages the frequency of audits

   B. Manages the auditors and their awareness of systems

   C. Manages the scope of audits

   D. Ensures that audit directives are implemented properly

6. What should you pay particular attention to when reviewing previously performed audit reports given to you by a provider?

   A. The services and jurisdictions in the audit scope

   B. The firm that performed the audit

   C. The date of the audit report

   D. The auditor's stated opinion

7. What should a customer do when they cannot collect evidence of compliance on their own?

   A. Tailor the scope of reporting to reflect lack of evidence.

   B. Accept the risk of not demonstrating compliance to regulators.

   C. Evidence not made available to a cloud customer is removed from regulatory oversight.

   D. Such data should be supplied to the customer by the provider.

8. What is the benefit of continuous compliance to a customer of cloud services?

   A. The customer is supplied with real-time updates to changes in a provider's environment.

   B. Any changes made to the provider's environment are supplied within one week.

   C. There are no benefits because customers should only be concerned with a provider being ISO certified.

   D. An increased audit frequency lowers the chance of unknown deviation of security posture in the provider's environment.

9. What should a customer do if a provider's artifacts of compliance are insufficient?

   A. File for a scoping exclusion request.

   B. Create and collect their own artifacts.

   C. Don't use the provider.

   D. Do nothing.

10. What can be done to avoid potential confusion when auditing a cloud service provider?

   A. Work with auditors who have their CCSK certification.

   B. Work with auditors supplied by providers.

   C. Work with CPAs.

   D. Work with auditors certified by the Institute of Certified Auditors.

Answers

1. **C.** The key concept for audits is that they are performed by an independent auditor. This is true for all audits. Although you may want to conduct an audit of a provider yourself, the provider may view giving you access to a data center as a security issue, for example.

2. **A.** Pass-through audits are a form of compliance inheritance. The audit does not speak to the completeness of the audit scope itself. Rather, it certifies that the controls implemented and managed by the provider are compliant. Your organization is required to meet compliance for your systems and data in the provider's environment.

3. **C.** The most accurate and therefore the best answer is that audits are used to prove or disprove compliance with corporate governance.

4. **B.** Attestations are legal statements from a third party. They are used as a key tool when customers evaluate and work with cloud providers, because customers often are not allowed to perform their own assessments. Attestations differ from audits in that audits are generally performed to collect data and information, whereas an attestation checks the validity of this data and information to an agreed-upon

procedure engagement (such as SOC). Attestations can be performed by certified public accountants (CPAs), but this answer doesn't properly address the question.

5. **D.** Audit management ensures that audit directives are implemented properly. All the other possible answers form part of this activity, but the best answer is that all of these directives are implemented properly.

6. **A.** Although all the answers are not necessarily incorrect, CSA best practice recommends that particular attention be paid to the services and jurisdictions that are part of the audit scope, so this is the best answer.

7. **D.** Providers should supply customers with evidence of compliance and artifacts when customers cannot generate these themselves. All the other answers are just plain wrong.

8. **D.** An increased audit frequency lowers the chance of unknown deviation of the security posture in the provider's environment. *Continuous* doesn't mean *real-time*, and it does not imply any set schedule. It means that any changes or findings are discovered between certification cycles, usually through the use of automation.

9. **B.** If a provider's artifacts of compliance are insufficient, customers should collect their own. There's no such thing as a scoping exclusion request.

10. **A.** When selecting auditors, you always want to work with auditors that have knowledge of cloud computing. The CCSK certification validates an auditor's understanding of cloud services.

Information Governance

This chapter covers the following topics from Domain 5 of the CSA Guidance:

- Governance Domains
- Six Phases of the Data Security Lifecycle and Their Key Elements
- Data Security Functions, Actors, and Controls

Data is the new gold.

—Mark Cuban

Over the years, I've seen "IT Security" morph from a focus on physical security, to operating system security in the late '90s, and then network security in the mid 2000s. Now, with a new name—*cybersecurity*—much of the focus is (finally) turning to the applications and the data processed and stored by these systems. This is, if you will, the next frontier in IT security.

The primary goal of information security is to grant only those permissions required by someone to do their job, and nothing more. This is the concept of *least privilege*. As companies move data to the cloud, multitenancy, shared responsibilities, new services, abstracted controls, and new ways of processing data using provider services all need to be addressed by security with management, operational, and technical controls that address not only preventative but also detection and corrective (or response) capabilities. In a nutshell, what needs to be addressed when protecting data remains the same, but how you do it can vary dramatically in a cloud environment.

 NOTE "Data" and "information" are used interchangeably in the CSA Guidance and in this book, but there is a difference between the two. Having a bunch of data is cool and all, but it is useless until it's processed and understood. Once understood, it becomes valuable information. The CCSK exam won't test you on this difference, but it's something I thought needed to be addressed before proceeding.

Of course, you can't have appropriate controls deployed to protect information if you don't have proper information/data governance. To understand information and data governance, we'll look at two definitions—the first from CSA, and the second from NIST:

- CSA defines data/information governance as "Ensuring the use of data and information complies with organizational policies, standards and strategy—including regulatory, contractual, and business objectives."

- NIST defines data governance as "A set of processes that ensures that data assets are formally managed throughout the enterprise. A data governance model establishes authority and management and decision making parameters related to the data produced or managed by the enterprise."

I would say these two definitions can work together, because the NIST definition is more granular in what data governance is, while the CSA definition describes why it's performed. Notice that the words "data" and "information" can be used interchangeably. That said, if I use the term "data" instead of "information," or vice versa, you'll know the same subject is being covered.

 TIP Moving to the cloud creates a greenfield opportunity to reexamine how you manage information and find ways to improve things. Don't lift and shift existing problems.

This rest of this chapter covers the different facets of information governance and introduces the *data security lifecycle* that can be used as a framework to identify required controls to implement least privilege for accessing and otherwise working with data.

Cloud Information Governance Domains

As covered in the NIST definition, information governance consists of a series of processes to manage data formally throughout the enterprise. The processes involved are broken down into the following domains of information governance, all of which must be in place to ensure that data is secured appropriately:

- **Ownership and custodianship**   Your company is always legally accountable if anything happens to data that you are in control of.

- **Information classification**   Classification can serve as decision criteria as to where data can and should be stored and processed. From a cloud perspective, this classification may determine whether or not the information can be stored in the cloud. You may not have used information classification systems in the past, but this is the basis upon which all future cloud-based information governance decisions should depend. This topic is covered in more depth later in this chapter.

- **Information management policies**   This directive control states how data and information should be managed. As available controls can widely vary based on SPI tiers (SaaS, PaaS, IaaS) and the providers themselves, acceptable service models and controls made available by the provider for the different classifications used in your organization should be considered. For instance, if you require encryption of data at rest and your SaaS provider doesn't offer it, you should find a different provider for such data.

- **Location and jurisdiction policies**   As you know, the cloud can be global, and different jurisdictions have different requirements. Any geographical considerations must be part of your information governance. This can be addressed as part of your information management policies or as a stand-alone policy, but it is critical that acceptable locations and jurisdictions be addressed by your organization.

- **Authorizations**   This covers who is allowed to access certain information and/or data and how the concepts of least privilege and segregation of duties are addressed. The concept of authorizations doesn't change for cloud-based systems compared to traditional data centers, but the importance of authorizations is much greater in a cloud environment, because, in some cases, authorizations may be the only control exposed to you by a provider and you will not be able to rely on physical controls as a form of compensating control (for example, for data accessible only from inside the building).

- **Contractual controls**   These are your company's only legal tools to ensure that appropriate governance requirements are implemented and followed by the cloud provider.

- **Security controls**   These tools are required to implement data governance. Controls exposed to customers, and how these controls are configured, will vary based on the provider and potentially the service you are consuming.

Migrating to the cloud can offer your company an opportunity to assess and fix any issues with your current governance program. You have a greenfield opportunity when first moving to the cloud, so why not use this opportunity to address outstanding issues and get it right from day one? Take information classification, for example. You may not be using classification today, but doing so is critical to determine which data sets are appropriate for the cloud (aka cloud-friendly).

Information Classification Backgrounder

In its simplest form for learning purposes, *data classification* can be described as the process of grouping data into categories through evaluation and labelling for the purpose of identifying appropriate security controls. Of course, there are numerous examples of how classification of information can benefit non-security issues, but this being a security book, I'll focus on how data classification is the foundational step in risk management and information governance.

NOTE   As with all backgrounders in this book, you will not be tested on this information as part of the CCSK exam. I have provided it in case you are unfamiliar with the topic.

To demonstrate the importance of information classification, I like to use the US government as an example (because it is a huge organization and, more importantly, all the documentation it uses is the most detailed in the industry and is copyright free). The American government uses a security lifecycle called the NIST Risk Management Framework (RMF), which is detailed in NIST SP 800-37. The first step in the RMF is the categorization of systems (see the sidebar "Classification vs. Categorization").

Two primary documents deal with information and system categorization in the US government. These are the Federal Information Processing Standard (FIPS) Standards for Security Categorization of Federal Information and Information Systems (known as FIPS 199) and NIST 800-60 (which is based on FIPS 199). The US government uses these guides to determine required controls based on impact due to loss of confidentiality, integrity, or availability. Figure 5-1 shows the different levels based on impact. Ignoring classification isn't an option for the US government, and it shouldn't be an option for your organization either, especially when it comes to cloud services.

Security Objective	POTENTIAL IMPACT		
	LOW	MODERATE	HIGH
Confidentiality Preserving authorized restrictions on information access and disclosure, including means for protecting personal privacy and proprietary information. [44 U.S.C., SEC. 3542]	The unauthorized disclosure of information could be expected to have a **limited** adverse effect on organizational operations, organizational assets, or individuals.	The unauthorized disclosure of information could be expected to have a **serious** adverse effect on organizational operations, organizational assets, or individuals.	The unauthorized disclosure of information could be expected to have a **severe or catastrophic** adverse effect on organizational operations, organizational assets, or individuals.
Integrity Guarding against improper information modification or destruction, and includes ensuring information non-repudiation and authenticity. [44 U.S.C., SEC. 3542]	The unauthorized modification or destruction of information could be expected to have a **limited** adverse effect on organizational operations, organizational assets, or individuals.	The unauthorized modification or destruction of information could be expected to have a **serious** adverse effect on organizational operations, organizational assets, or individuals.	The unauthorized modification or destruction of information could be expected to have a **severe or catastrophic** adverse effect on organizational operations, organizational assets, or individuals.
Availability Ensuring timely and reliable access to and use of information. [44 U.S.C., SEC. 3542]	The disruption of access to or use of information or an information system could be expected to have a **limited** adverse effect on organizational operations, organizational assets, or individuals.	The disruption of access to or use of information or an information system could be expected to have a **serious** adverse effect on organizational operations, organizational assets, or individuals.	The disruption of access to or use of information or an information system could be expected to have a **severe or catastrophic** adverse effect on organizational operations, organizational assets, or individuals.

Figure 5-1 FIPS 199 Categorization Grid. (Source: FIPS Publication 199 Standards for Security Categorization of Federal Information and Information Systems.)

Classification vs. Categorization

You may have worked in environments where the term "categorization" was used instead of "classification," especially if you have worked with government organizations in the past. The US government is a little different from normal organizations because it uses document classifications such as Classified, Secret, and Top Secret based on the impact of loss of confidentiality. The government categorizes information and systems into three groups (low, moderate, high) to determine appropriate controls based on the impact due to loss of confidentiality, integrity, and availability. The CSA uses only the term "classification," so unless the discussion is specific to US government documentation, I'll be lumping them together under the term "classification."

Your organization will need to determine the various classifications to be used in your environment. Many organizations use three levels, and these could be as simple as public, private, and restricted. Again, these classifications are generally based on the impact of a loss of confidentiality, integrity, and availability. It is up to your organization to determine whether it will use an average value, a weighted value, or a high-water mark (the highest value) to determine classification. For example, FIPS 199 calls for use of high-water implementation, so if the impact to confidentiality is high but the impact to integrity and availability is low, the data classification is considered to be high.

TIP Keep your classification levels as simple as possible. Start with three levels and expand only as absolutely required.

Most organizations place the responsibility of data classification on the data owners themselves, because they are the ones best positioned to understand the value and criticality of their own data. With that said, users need to understand how classification works and why it is important. If you ask someone in your company's finance group, for example, if confidentiality of a particular data set should be rated low, medium, or high, you'll likely be met with a blank stare. To address this and make things easier for everyone, you could make a list of questions that users will be able to work with easily. Some organizations label these questions a "Statement of Sensitivity." The goal here is to make human-readable questions that can be answered in a simple yes/no format. Here are some examples:

- Does the data contain personally identifiable information?
- Does the data contain health record information?
- Does the data contain information that, if compromised, would jeopardize an individual's safety?

- Does the data contain information that, if compromised, would embarrass an individual?
- Does the data contain trade secrets or company intellectual property?
- Does the data contain information that is, or is expected to be, publicly available?

As you can see from these simple questions, you can determine whether the data in question is subject to regulations such as the General Data Protection Regulation (GDPR) and/or the Health Insurance Portability and Accountability Act (HIPAA), or if the data contains sensitive corporate data that would benefit from a higher classification.

Information classification must be an ongoing activity, not a one-and-done approach. There are many reasons why this activity should be ongoing, ranging from information suddenly increasing or decreasing in value to an organization (for example, financial reports being publicly released changes the classification from high to public), to external forces such as new regulations or laws. For example, the GDPR (covered in Chapter 3) has had a significant impact on data classification requirements for companies, in that data about customers and other data subjects now has a substantial impact associated with it, as loss of confidentiality can result in damaging fines.

Data classification will often rely on metadata (data about the data) such as tags and labels that define the classification level of the data and how it should be handled and controlled. There are three types of data classification approaches out there today:

- **User-based**   Data owners are expected to select the appropriate classification for a particular data set. For example, a user sending an e-mail would be required to select a classification level in a pull-down menu in Microsoft Outlook prior to it being sent.
- **Content-based**   This classification approach inspects and interprets data looking for known sensitive data. In this scenario, the classification program will scan a document, looking for keywords. Classification is automatically applied based on the content of the document.
- **Context-based**   This classification approach looks at application, storage location, or the creator of the data as an indicator of sensitive information. For example, a file created by the chief financial officer using a financial reporting application may be automatically considered highly sensitive.

Both the content- and context-based classification systems can be automated with data classification tools that are available from many vendors and that will automatically determine an appropriate classification level and apply appropriate labels and/or tags. User-based classification enables users to select the appropriate classification level, and the classification system will apply the appropriate labels and/or tags to the data. This approach will, of course, require that users understand your corporate classification structure and which classifications should be applied.

Data classification is the basis of data security. Systems such as data loss prevention (DLP), electronic discovery, cloud access security brokers (covered in Chapter 11), and even encryption tools can work with data classification to protect both data within your company and data sent out of your company via everything from e-mail to cloud-based storage and SaaS applications. Once classification levels are established in your organization, you can use them to determine acceptable use of the cloud through creation of an acceptable cloud usage policy (covered later in this chapter).

Information Management Backgrounder

I'll bet you didn't know that there are more than 30 zettabytes (that's 30 billion terabytes by the way!) of data in the digital world today, and it's expected to grow to 175ZB by 2025. If you find that number too large to comprehend, just consider that more than 188 million e-mails are sent every minute of every day (to be honest, I'm not sure if that's any better). Your company currently stores nothing close to a zettabyte of data, but if you work for a large firm, dozens of petabytes of data consisting of millions of files, e-mails, and more isn't out of the question. Your company is generating and capturing more data than ever before, and this will only accelerate. Now consider how much of that data is actually valuable. Data and information that has value is the lifeblood of many companies, and it needs to be appropriately managed. What should be kept, how long should it be kept, and what should be discarded? The information management (IM) function attempts to address these and additional items.

IM details how an organization plans, identifies, creates, collects, receives, governs, secures, uses, exchanges, maintains, and disposes of information. In simpler terms, IM makes information available to the right person in the right format at the right time. The principles of IM, listed next, can help your organization with efficient use of information and can make it easier to find and ensure its protection and preservation in accordance with legal and regulatory requirements:

- Avoid collecting duplicate information.
- Share and reuse information with respect to legal and regulatory restrictions.
- Ensure that information is complete, accurate, relevant, and understandable.
- Safeguard information against unlawful access, loss, and damage.
- Preserve information in accordance with its operational, legal, financial, and historical value.

Information Management Lifecycle

The IM lifecycle involves managing the flow of data as it passes through various phases while in your possession. There are a multitude of different IM lifecycles out there, ranging from three to seven phases, with various phases either combined or broken out—but, generally, the lifecycle looks something like the one shown in Figure 5-2.

I'm purposefully using an illustration that matches the phases of the data security lifecycle covered in the next section. The fact is, each of the phases of the lifecycle can be used to determine how data can be addressed to maximize value to your organization.

Figure 5-2
Information man-
agement lifecycle

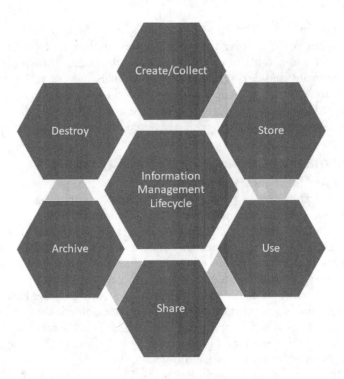

(I'm deliberately ignoring security in the following phase descriptions because these will
be covered in the next section.)

- **Phase 1: Create/Collect**   Data of any type and from multiple sources is either
  created or collected by your organization in some fashion. When existing data is
  modified, it is considered created data.

- **Phase 2: Store**   In this phase, data is stored in some fashion. This is where
  you need to determine a means to minimize storage requirements through
  compression, de-duplication, and other means.

- **Phase 3: Use**   Data is viewed, processed, or otherwise used in some way to
  create valuable information your company can use in decision-making, for
  example.

- **Phase 4: Share**   Data is made available to other parties.

- **Phase 5: Archive**   At this stage, the data has little or no value to the company,
  but it may be kept for many reasons, such as to generate historical analytics or
  address regulatory or legal requirements.

- **Phase 6: Destroy**   Data is no longer needed but is taking up space, and it faces
  no legal or regulatory requirements for retention, so the data is deleted from
  storage. Failure to destroy data leads to increased storage costs.

Now that I have covered the background information on IM and classification, let's move on to the IM policies that will inform stakeholders of the expectations your company has surrounding the information your company holds.

Information Management Policy

The purpose of an IM policy is to advise all stakeholders of IM requirements. Like any other policy document, an IM policy document may range from a few pages to dozens of pages. More lengthy IM policies will also clearly define roles involved in IM and their particular responsibilities. The following sections present example policies that address the key items that should be included as part of any general IM policy.

Purpose This policy and its related practices address the management of corporate information from its creation or acquisition through to its use, modification, distribution, storage, accessibility, communication, and disposition or destruction. The company is committed to the management and protection of its corporate information. Information in any medium, including electronic and paper-based, is deemed a valuable corporate asset.

Scope Corporate information includes records that document company business transactions, decisions, and activities. Records provide evidence of adherence to company policies, controls, and standards, as well as the operational, contractual, statutory, and regulatory requirements for all areas in which the company conducts its business. The company recognizes that processes, information systems, and infrastructure for capturing, sharing, reporting, and storing relevant corporate information enables the organization to conduct its business efficiently, effectively, and securely.

Policy Statements Corporate information, including intellectual property, developed by or for the company is to be treated as company property. The organization must also protect the privacy and property rights of others. Corporate information obtained and used by staff under confidentiality or license agreements must be handled according to the terms of the appropriate agreement.

All staff and service providers are required to do the following:

- Manage and protect corporate information in accordance with this policy and related practices, including statutory and regulatory requirements.

- Maintain accountability for appropriate security, access, and retention of any specific corporate information entrusted to them.

- Understand the implications of corporate information mismanagement and misuse, including the potential costs and risks to the company, its staff, and its business associates.

- Report incidents and assist in investigations relating to corporate information mismanagement and misuse.

Compliance and Enforcement   Violations of this policy include, but are not limited to, the following:

- Unsanctioned activities that disrupt or prevent access to, or control of, the company's corporate information

- Failure to handle and protect corporate information and records properly

- Using or disclosing corporate information in a manner that damages the company's reputation or business

- Attempts to circumvent this policy and related practices, controls, and standards

- Failure to comply with applicable laws, contractual obligations, or statutory and regulatory requirements

- Failure to comply with acceptable use of corporate information as outlined within the code of business conduct and ethics

Disciplinary action, up to and including termination of employment or service contracts, will be taken against anyone who violates the policy and its related practices.

Acceptable Use Policy for Cloud Services

Now that I have addressed both information classification and the IM function itself, let's look at how these are relevant to a cloud environment. One way that many organizations address IM risks is through implementation of an acceptable use policy for cloud services.

Generally, organizations will consider their existing information classifications and determine what is an acceptable cloud service in which to store various categories of data based on the impact to confidentiality, integrity, and availability (as you saw with FIPS 199). Your acceptable use policy for the cloud will depend on your existing governance. Do you allow users to procure their own cloud services, or must every cloud service used by your organization be authorized by management (such as the CIO, for example)? Perhaps you have a hybrid approach based on the classification of the data, where high and moderate classified data can be stored and processed only in authorized cloud environments, but public data can be stored by users in any cloud service.

One critical aspect to remember when considering a cloud acceptable use policy is compliance. I'll use HIPAA as an example to cover the importance of regulated data being stored in a cloud and what could happen if you allow your users to choose providers themselves. I covered compliance inheritance in Chapter 4, so you know that both the service provider and the customer must maintain compliance. Regarding HIPAA specifically, companies that work with protected health information (PHI) such as healthcare providers and insurance companies (referred to as covered entities) can use only providers that are "business associates" with which they have a written business associate agreement. What are the potential damages for a covered entity storing data with a provider without having a signed business associate agreement in place? Here's an example: In 2016, North Memorial Health Care in Minnesota was slapped with a $1.55 million fine for not having a business associate agreement in place with a provider.

If you don't have an acceptable usage policy in place at your firm, how are your employees to know what data sets can be stored in specific environments? You may be best served by creating a cloud governance program and having that group deal with all the contracts and other governance items on your users' behalf.

The Data Security Lifecycle

The data security lifecycle is a CSA modeling tool that is based on the common IM lifecycle, but the CSA tool focuses on security aspects and locations throughout the various stages of creation through the ultimate disposal of the lifecycle.

It is critical that you understand that this lifecycle is meant to be a high-level framework. The goal here is to use the lifecycle to understand controls that should be implemented to stop a possible security breach from happening. It is not meant to be applied to every bit of data throughout your organization, because, quite frankly, that would drive everyone off the deep end.

There are six stages in the data security lifecycle:

- **Create**   Data is created or existing content is modified.
- **Store**   Data is committed to some form of storage repository.
- **Use**   Data is viewed, processed, or otherwise used in some way. This doesn't include data modification, because that's jumping back to the creation of a new file.
- **Share**   Data is made available to other parties.
- **Archive**   The data's useful life is over, but it may be kept to address regulatory or legal requirements, for example.
- **Destroy**   Data is deleted from storage.

Data (be it structured or unstructured) doesn't go through all the phases in order, nor does it need to go through all the stages. For example, you can create a document and share it with others, who make changes. After the changes have been made, a new file has basically been created. Using this example, you can easily see how data can jump back and forth between the stages.

Table 5-1 lists the phases of the lifecycle and some potential controls that can be inserted regarding who or what can be done with data at each phase. A multitude of controls are possible, of course, and technology is continuously evolving, so please don't consider the table to be exhaustive.

The one control that I would like to spend a moment on is this concept of *crypto shredding*. It is essentially impossible to be certain that data in a cloud is actually deleted when you press the DELETE key. If your risk tolerance requires that you have certainty that data can never be retrieved once deleted, you have two choices at your disposal: you can hire Tom Cruise to break into the data center *Mission Impossible*–style to physically destroy all the drives and tapes that have ever been used to store your data, or you can implement crypto shredding. To be honest, at this point in time it might be easier to hire Tom Cruise.

Table 5-1

Information
Management
Lifecycle and
Potential
Controls

Lifecycle Phase	Potential Controls
Create	Classification labels Entitlements
Store	Encryption at rest Access controls Rights management Content discovery
Use	Access control lists Application security Activity monitoring Logical controls
Share	Encryption in transit Data loss prevention Logical controls Application security
Archive	Encryption Asset management
Destroy	Content discovery Crypto shredding

In theory, crypto shredding is the process of storing encrypted data with an encryption key and then simply deleting the data and the encryption key that was used to encrypt the data in the first place. I'm sure you can see the complexity involved with all of these data keys being generated, tracked, and destroyed. It's great in theory, but basically impossible in real life.

To that end, you're going to have to look at the provider's documentation to understand how a cloud service provider sanitizes data once it's deleted (aka disk wiping). In most cases, you'll find they may "zeroize" the data, meaning they overwrite the bits that were used with a bunch of zeros before it is released back into the storage resource pool. The number of times they do this (called passes) however, is likely limited and may not meet your organization's media sanitization policy. (If you want to learn more about media sanitization, you can check out NIST SP 800-81r1, but don't expect any CCSK test questions on that material.)

Beyond the technical items just covered, you would be well served to seek a guarantee from your provider that no disks will leave their data center without being wiped first. Many providers treat their data centers like "Hotel California," where disks can enter the data center but can never leave. In this case, drives that are no longer used to store customer data are physically shredded in the data center. Again, though, there are no rules or regulations as to what the provider must or must not do.

Locations and Entitlements

Locations, in the context of the data security lifecycle, can be tricky. When considering locations, you must think not only about where the data resides (in the cloud or in a traditional data center) but also where the access device is located (local or remote). As you can easily imagine, data stored in a cloud environment can be easily created and used from anywhere in the world if there are no controls in place to stop this from happening. Data stored in a data center today might be in a cloud environment tomorrow, and vice versa.

Perhaps you have a requirement stating that all data held in the cloud must be encrypted at rest, but data in your own data center doesn't have that requirement. Take that initial requirement a step further: Does this now mean that data should not be used in the cloud as well? After all, data needs to be unencrypted to be processed (until homomorphic encryption becomes a viable technology). This means that you now have different controls based on the location of the data, which means you have multiple data security lifecycles. Now see what I mean about needing to keep the discussion at a high level?

"Entitlements" is a word the CSA chose to use instead of "permissions" or "rights." You can safely translate it to "permissions" if you want, but the CCSK exam will likely use the term "entitlements" all the same. You simply have two things to consider regarding these entitlements: Who is accessing the data, and how do they access it? If you don't want someone or something (an actor) to do something (a function) with data, you need to apply a control to stop it from happening. Pretty simple, right? Let's look more into that topic in the next section.

Functions, Actors, and Controls

Now that you know what actors, functions, and controls are, you need to understand what functions are possible in this data security lifecycle—what the actors are allowed to do, what they're not allowed to do (their entitlements), and the possible controls to stop disallowed functions from happening.

For functions, we know we have various phases of the lifecycle in create, store, use, share, archive, and destroy. Well, there are super high-level functions these can map to. Actors are generally considered to be accessing (reading) the data, processing (using) the data, or storing the data. Now what do each of those functions mean?

- **Accessing the data** You need to access a data set in order to read, update, use, share, archive, and destroy data.

- **Processing the data** This involves being able to transact, or work with, the data—for example, updating a client record or performing a business transaction.

- **Storing the data** Finally, you need the ability to store data if you're going to commit it to storage.

Table 5-2 shows how these functions are connected to the phases of the lifecycle.

Table 5-2		Create	Store	Use	Share	Archive	Destroy
Information Lifecycle Functions and Phases	**Access**	X	X	X	X	X	X
	Process	X		X			
	Store		X			X	

	Create	Store	Use	Share	Archive	Destroy
Jano	Allowed	Allowed	Allowed	Allowed	Allowed	Allowed
Isabelle	Allowed	Allowed	Allowed	Allowed	Control Required	Control Required
Jacob	Allowed	Allowed	Allowed	Control Required	Control Required	Control Required

Table 5-3 Example Lifecycle Phase Entitlements for Driveline Solutions System–On Premises

Now, of course, these three basic functions (access, process, and store) don't really work when it comes to identifying appropriate controls in place to stop specific actors from doing specific activities. Let's take a hypothetical example of a company called Driveline Solutions and their inventory system to see this concept of entitlements in action.

There are three main actors involved with tracking, fulfilling, and delivering orders in this scenario: Jano Benyamin (company owner), Isabelle Roy (inventory manager), and Jacob Richler (shop foreman). As the owner of Driveline, Jano wants full control of any data his company owns. Isabelle doesn't need as many entitlements to the data because her job is to create new work orders and share these work orders with Jacob, who will then update the system to say the job is completed and ready to ship. Let's see what entitlements can be implemented to grant least privilege for these actors involved, as listed in Table 5-3.

Now let's say Driveline Solutions adopts a business continuity plan that includes running a replica of the inventory system in the cloud. They have determined that the backup system should be read-only, having data copied to it from the on-premises inventory system on a nightly basis. The replica system in the cloud is used only in the case of an outage of the "master" inventory system that is on premises and should never be used to create new records. In that case, the entitlements will drastically change based on the location of the data, as shown in Table 5-4.

In this scenario, we took the same data and changed the location. As a result of the location change, the business decision was made that data would be available to anyone only as read-only access and would not be updatable. Same data, different location, which leads us to having multiple data security lifecycles.

	Create	Store	Use	Share	Archive	Destroy
Jano	Control Required	Control Required	Allowed	Control Required	Control Required	Control Required
Isabelle	Control Required	Control Required	Allowed	Control Required	Control Required	Control Required
Jacob	Control Required	Control Required	Allowed	Control Required	Control Required	Control Required

Table 5-4 Example Lifecycle Phase Entitlements for Driveline Solutions System–Cloud Hosted

EXAM TIP The main goal of the data security lifecycle as far as the CCSK exam goes is not to know every possible control to limit every possible action by any possible actor on every possible data set (or the validity of doing so!). The goal for the exam is to understand that you have basic functions that map to phases of the data lifecycle. Based on the location of the data or the access device (that's the key for the exam!), you may have different data security lifecycles.

Chapter Review

This chapter addressed the need for information governance and the processes involved. It then reviewed the data security lifecycle that can be used to identify where controls are required to support information governance for different activities and different locations, from where the data is held (traditional on premises or cloud) to device access (internal or external access).

In preparation for your CCSK exam, you should be comfortable with the following items in particular:

- Understand your information governance requirements (legal, regulatory, and so on) as part of planning to move data to the cloud.

- Remember that extending information governance to include cloud services requires both contractual and security controls.

- Use the data security lifecycle to identify controls to limit the functions that actors can perform. As different locations may require different controls, you will have multiple data security lifecycles.

- Migrating to the cloud can serve as an excellent opportunity to identify and address current information governance issues.

Questions

1. The data security lifecycle considers which of the following?

    A. Location

    B. How to configure security controls

    C. Who can access data

    D. Service models

2. Which of the following can be used to determine whether or not information should be held in a cloud?

    A. Privacy policy

    B. Information classification

    C. Data security lifecycle

    D. Acceptable use policy

3. Which of the following locations are considered part of the data security lifecycle?

    A. Location of data

    B. Location of access device

    C. Location of the data center

    D. A and B

4. What is the goal of information governance (select the best answer)?

    A. Ensure that appropriate personnel have access to required data.

    B. Ensure that data is stored in approved locations.

    C. Formally manage data throughout the enterprise.

    D. Create and manage information security policies.

5. Which of the following is considered a tool to implement data governance?

    A. Security policies

    B. Security controls

    C. Information classification

    D. All of the above

6. What is a legal tool to ensure that appropriate governance requirements are implemented and followed by the cloud provider?

    A. Security controls

    B. Contractual controls

    C. Strong change management

    D. Entitlements

7. What can be used to determine what actors are allowed to do and what they're not allowed to do?

    A. Entitlements

    B. Information classification

    C. Information governance

    D. Contractual controls

8. Moving to the cloud creates a greenfield opportunity to reexamine what?

    A. How you manage information and find ways to improve things

    B. Existing security policies

    C. Existing security controls

    D. Existing information classification capabilities

9. Extending information governance to include cloud services requires:

   A. Security controls

   B. Contractual controls

   C. Both contractual and security controls

   D. Provider supplying a written business associate agreement

10. What does an authorization determine?

   A. The legally accountable party for security of end-user data

   B. Whether data can be stored in a cloud environment

   C. Permitted cloud service providers based on classification of data

   D. Who is allowed to access certain information and/or data

Answers

1. **A.** The data security lifecycle differs from the information management lifecycle in that it takes location into account. As a result, multiple locations can lead to your managing multiple data security lifecycles. Although the data security lifecycle does address security controls at each stage, it does not dictate how these are to be created or who should be allowed to access what data. Entitlements are used to determine who should have access to particular data. The data security lifecycle doesn't address the service models at all.

2. **B.** The best answer is information classification. An acceptable use policy may make the determination of what data classification level is allowed to be stored, but this relies on having classification to begin with. The data security lifecycle can be used to determine what controls should be applied based on the stage of the lifecycle, so C is not the best answer for this particular question. As with the acceptable use policy, the privacy policy may state how data is to be handled, and as such there may be restrictions in place over PII being stored in a cloud—but, again, the information classification is the best answer for this question.

3. **D.** I'm sorry for the trick question. The data security lifecycle considers the locations of the data and the access device. Now does that mean the location of the data center is implied as a result? Maybe, maybe not. One could argue the location of the data center would determine the jurisdiction and therefore dictate what controls need to be applied, but there's nobody to argue with when you're taking your exam.

4. **C.** The best answer is that information governance exists to formally manage data throughout the enterprise. The other answers are true statements, but information governance deals with more than just those individual statements. Therefore, the best answer is C.

5. B. Security controls are considered a tool to implement data governance. Policies themselves don't do anything to implement data governance. Yes, they are absolutely needed, but they are statements (directive controls), not actual preventative controls to stop someone from doing something. Classification is also required for strong governance, but again, classification itself isn't going to stop an actor from performing a function.

6. B. The only legal tool to ensure that appropriate governance requirements are implemented and followed by the cloud provider is contractual controls. None of the other options are legal tools.

7. A. Entitlements determine what actors are allowed to do and what they're not allowed to do. Contractual controls are a legal tool, and information governance is much larger than determining what actors can and cannot do, so B and C are not the best answers. Classification of data may assist control selection, but, again, it is not the best answer.

8. A. Moving to the cloud gives you the opportunity to look at how you manage information and find ways to improve things. This can include all the other answers as well, but since the first answer covers all the other options, it is the best answer.

9. C. The best answer is that both security and contractual controls are required to extend information governance to the cloud. The business associate agreement is applicable only for HIPAA-regulated data, and it would be covered as a contractual control.

10. D. Authorizations determine who is allowed to access certain information and/or data and are part of information governance. The customer always retains legal accountability in the event of end-user data being compromised. Although we want to have information management assist in the selection of appropriate cloud providers and determine data classifications, these are not authorizations.

Management Plane and Business Continuity

This chapter covers the following topics from Domain 6 of the CSA Guidance:
- Management Plane Security
- Business Continuity and Disaster Recovery in the Cloud
- Architect for Failure

When you are thirsty, it's too late to think about digging a well.

—Japanese proverb

Preparation is important if you want your business to survive: you need to be one step ahead—to act before you suffer any consequences of inaction. This chapter is all about thinking ahead and implementing security before things go sideways. The chapter marks somewhat of a transition in this book—from the business side of the cloud to the technical aspects associated with cloud computing. It begins with coverage of securing the management plane and then moves on to business continuity and disaster recovery in a cloud environment.

In the logical model, as covered in Chapter 1, you learned that the *metastructure* is the virtual world for which you need virtual tools. The *management plane* is the area where the virtual infrastructure of your cloud is built, configured, and destroyed. Remember that the management plane is a part of the metastructure. The management plane is your single interface to view, implement, and configure all of your resources in this virtual world.

The concept of a management plane isn't anything new. In fact, the term "management plane" has been used in networking for years to describe the interface used to configure, control, and monitor networking devices. Unlike other environments, in which you could configure a particular port to be a management interface and that required direct physical access to the management plane, you (or anyone) can connect to the management plane supplied by a cloud provider across the Internet using APIs or web browsers.

The management plane is also where you implement most disaster recovery (DR) and business continuity planning (BCP) options. Many providers, especially Infrastructure as a Service (IaaS) providers, will make multiple data centers and multiple regions available to you. It is up to your company to determine an appropriate strategy and to execute that strategy by using those options. This involves an understanding of concepts such as *recovery time* and *recovery point objectives* (see the upcoming "BCP/DR Backgrounder" section if you're unfamiliar with these terms) and choosing the best approach to meet these business requirements.

The bottom line is that saying "the provider does everything for me" is likely a fallacy. Sure, your Software as a Service (SaaS) provider may have dynamic failover from one region to another and you don't need to do anything to have BCP/DR in place, but what about exporting data held in that SaaS? Does the provider do that for you automatically, or do you have to enable that export of data? What format is the exported data in? Can it be accessed only using a provider's system? If so, where does that leave you if your provider goes bankrupt, is hacked and their system is destroyed, or is a victim of ransomware and all client data (including yours) is encrypted and the provider refuses to pay?

As the opening quote suggests, when you can't access your data, it's too late to think about recovery options.

Management Plane

The management plane is the most important area that you need to secure tightly—and it is solely your responsibility to secure access to it. Anyone with full access to the management plane quite simply has the power to build or destroy anything in your virtual world. Proper implementation and management of restricting access to the management plane is job number 1 as far as securing any cloud implementation. After you ensure that the management plane is secured, you can worry about securing your assets in a cloud environment. After all, an attacker may not be able to log on directly to a virtual server through the management plane and steal your data, but they could use the management plane to make copies of volumes and export them, or they could blow away any running instances and all backups. Simply stated, if someone has access to the management plane, they could find all kinds of inventive ways to gain access to your servers and other assets in the cloud.

Think about someone using your resources for bitcoin mining and sticking your organization with the bill. Want a super-inventive example? How about someone gaining access to the management plane in an IaaS environment and then using that access to add a script that will execute on one or all of your servers the next time they're rebooted. Oh—and that script will install a back door and will succeed, because the script will run as the root user in Linux or the system account in Windows. I don't want to muddy the waters and the difference between the metastructure and the applistructure, but I do want to give you an example of the unforeseen damage a malicious actor can cause if they have access to the management plane.

As you know, the cloud is a shared responsibility model, and this applies to the management plane as well. The provider is responsible for building a secure management plane for you to access, and you are responsible for ensuring that only appropriate people have appropriate qualifications to manage your virtual world and that every user has least privileges, and nothing more, to do only what they need to do.

NOTE   The concept of least privilege is more important than ever when considering security of the management plane.

Application Programming Interface Backgrounder

An application programming interface (API) is a programmatic interface to a system that enables services to communicate without having to understand how a system is implemented. APIs are used behind the scenes (as discussed in Chapter 1), and it is very common for cloud providers to expose APIs to customers for programmatic access. This section covers APIs themselves, the leading API "standards" used in the cloud, and how customers can use these APIs to do remarkable things in a cloud environment.

Before we get to the use of publicly available open APIs as a customer in a cloud environment, let's look at how a company used internal APIs to transform its business completely. In around 2002, Amazon was struggling with a computing environment that had become quite unmanageable. As a result of the challenges, CEO Jeff Bezos issued his now famous "API Mandate" that required every business group throughout Amazon to expose an internal API for everything they did. Want HR information? There's an API for that. Need marketing information? There's an API for that. Here are a few of the highlights from the API Mandate:

- All teams will expose their data and functionality through service interfaces.
- Teams must communicate with one another through these interfaces.
- There will be no other form of interprocess communication allowed: no direct linking, no direct reads of another team's data store, no shared-memory model, and no back doors whatsoever. The only communication allowed is via service interface calls over the network.
- It doesn't matter what technology you use.
- All service interfaces, without exception, must be designed from the ground up to be externalize-able. In other words, the team must plan and design to be able to expose the interface to developers in the outside world. No exceptions.
- Anyone who doesn't do this will be fired.

I believe Mr. Bezos was dead serious about this transformation to APIs because he really felt Amazon could scale to meet increased demand only if the company took a highly modular approach to everything. By imposing these interfaces, the company could remove system-specific dependencies and therefore improve agility, efficiency, and speed as a result.

That was an example of *internal APIs*. But there are also *external APIs* that are exposed to the outside world. APIs that are meant to be consumed by others (such as customers and partners) are generally referred to as *open APIs*. You could also have *private APIs*, where access to the API is restricted.

Let's look at a use case of externally available private APIs. Suppose you created an awesome new application with a proprietary algorithm that predicted neighborhood home price values ten years into the future. You could try to convince potential home buyers to pay for access themselves, or you could charge real estate brokers for access and make that valuable data available only under contract. Many companies in this scenario would likely go the private API route, because it's probably a much cheaper way to enter the market as opposed to spending millions on marketing to the general public. In this scenario, APIs are critical to the success of the company from a revenue perspective, not just with regard to agility and other benefits of internal APIs.

Finally, and most importantly for our subject, we turn our attention to open APIs on the Web. These are the APIs that a web site (such as Twitter, Facebook, and so on) exposes to customers, but more importantly for this subject, these are the APIs that a cloud provider would expose so their customers can programmatically access resources. Most, if not all, cloud providers in every service model will expose both an API and a web interface for customers. The functionality of these exposed APIs will, of course, be vendor-dependent. Some IaaS providers may offer all functionality through their APIs, while an SaaS provider may allow you to create a new record, but not modify a record, for example. This leads us to another interesting Amazon-related observation. When Amazon created Amazon Web Services, only API access was available for consumer access; there was no web interface. I think this is the exact opposite of what you would expect to come first when a company launches a product for mass consumption. But when you think about it, it shows just how valuable Amazon considers APIs for itself and for everyone else.

Now that you know about the different API deployments, let's move on to the different "standards" that are popular for open APIs. The two dominant ones are REST and SOAP. I'll cover each one separately, giving appropriate consideration for both.

First up is Representational State Transfer (REST). REST isn't actually a standard; it's considered an architectural style, and that's why I put quotes around the word "standards." You'll never see a "REST 2.0," for example. REST is *stateless* (meaning it doesn't retain session information) and depends on other standards (such as HTTP, URI, JSON, and XML) to do its job. Every REST call uses an HTTP method. The following table lists the methods and a high-level overview of what each does:

HTTP Method	Purpose
GET	Retrieves resources
POST	Creates a new resource
PUT	Updates an existing resource by replacing the original resource
DELETE	Deletes a resource
PATCH	Performs a partial update of an existing resource; does not replace the original resource

So what does REST look like in action? The following examples show how you would get a list of your server instances from three major IaaS providers.

NOTE   These examples don't address the authentication or authorization processes that will need to be performed. API authentication is discussed later in this chapter.

AWS Example:

```
GET https://ec2.amazonaws.com/?Action=DescribeInstances
```

Microsoft Azure Example:

```
GET https://management.azure.com/subscriptions/{subscriptionId}/providers/
Microsoft.Compute/virtualMachines?api-version=2018-06-01
```

Google Cloud Example:

```
GET https://www.googleapis.com/compute/v1/projects/{project}/zones/{zone}/instances
```

You have probably noticed something here—they're all different! You have to consult the API reference guide for any provider you want to work with. Each will expose functionality differently.

NOTE   For all the details you could ever want to know about web APIs and REST, look up Roy Fielding's dissertation, "Architectural Styles and the Design of Network-based Software Architectures." I'm just highlighting key facts about APIs as background information.

Now how about terminating (deleting) an instance? Here are some examples.

AWS Example:

```
DELETE
https://ec2.amazonaws.com/?Action=TerminateInstances
&InstanceId.1=i-1234567890abcdef0
```

Microsoft Azure Example:

```
DELETE https://management.azure.com/subscriptions/{subscriptionId}/
resourceGroups/{resourceGroupName}/providers/Microsoft.Compute/
virtualMachines/{vmName}?api-version=2018-06-01
```

Google Cloud Example:

```
DELETE https://www.googleapis.com/compute/beta/projects/{project}/zones/
{zone}/instances/{resourceId}
```

Now that you have an idea of how easy it is to execute commands in the REST API, I hope you have an appreciation for how easy it would be for anyone with administrative control of the management plane to programmatically destroy everything in your environment within seconds. They would just need to create a simple script that lists all instances and then issue a terminate command for each one listed. One last thing before we move on: Do you notice how all of the API requests are using HTTPS? This is the thing about REST.

It uses other standards. If you want your requests to be secure, you need to use HTTPS, because security isn't baked into REST. This is very different from the SOAP API.

Simple Object Access Protocol (SOAP) is a standard *and* a protocol. It's often said that REST is like a postcard and SOAP is like an envelope. Unlike REST, SOAP has security included inside it, as well as other features, but there is more overhead associated with SOAP than with REST as a result. As such, the use cases for SOAP are more for internal enterprise purposes with high security requirements. Cloud providers often won't expose a SOAP API to customers, and any that did likely don't anymore. For example, Amazon Web Services (AWS) used to have a SOAP API for Elastic Compute Cloud (EC2), but the company deprecated (removed) it back in 2015. At the end of the day, you're most likely going to run into REST APIs if you're dealing with anything web-related.

Quite often, APIs can be used in a programming language of your choice. For example, if you want to make a Python script that would create an instance in AWS, you can use the AWS Boto3 Software Development Kit (SDK). The following offers an example of such a script:

```
import boto3
ec2 = boto3.resource('ec2')
instance = ec2.create_instances(
    ImageId = 'ami-1234567891234',
    MinCount = 1,
    MaxCount = 1,
    InstanceType = 't2.micro',
    KeyName = 'tester',
    SubnetId = 'subnet-1234567891234')
print (instance[0].id)
```

 TIP Using a vendor's API is always best if you really want to understand how a particular provider works. The web interface usually hides a lot of functionality.

I would like to conclude this backgrounder with the concept of an *API gateway*. The API gateway serves as the single interface with which a requesting machine will connect to one or multiple APIs behind it and will deliver a seamless experience for customers. The API gateway is beneficial from a security perspective because it can inspect incoming requests for threat protection (such as denial of service, code injection attacks, and so on) and can be used to support authentication and authorization services. This is particularly true with delegated authorization with microservices (covered in Chapter 12).

Accessing the Management Plane

The management plane is often accessible via multiple methods. In general, you can expect to have access to command-line interface (CLI) tools, a web interface, or APIs. Think of the API as being the engine that runs everything. Whether you use the web interface, the CLI, or any SDK, you're likely having your request translated to the provider API, and that, in turn, is executed at the provider.

As mentioned earlier, if you really want to see under the hood regarding what a provider allows, using the API will often show what you're looking for. You can generally consider that anything available via the web console will also be available via the API.

If something is exposed via an API, it can be accessed programmatically. And if it can be accessed programmatically, it can be automated. A provider may offer some functionality to either method first, but these encounters should be rare with any established provider. I would take it as a safe bet that "beta" functionality will be exposed via the API first, but, personally, I'm not a big fan of using anything "beta" in a production environment.

When you're considering these different access methods from a security perspective, be aware that quite often different credentials will be involved. For example, when you're connecting via the web browser, standard credentials such as a username and password are generally used. These credential sets can be stored within the cloud provider's environment, or you can use identity federation to keep the credentials on your side and not on the provider's side. (Federation is covered in Chapter 12.)

Aside from the web browser access, accessing via the API generally uses either HTTP request signing or the OAuth protocol (discussed in Chapter 12). Some providers will use an access key and secret access key as the credentials as part of authenticating and signing REST requests. The access key itself acts like your username, and the secret access key is like your password. Behind the scenes, the secret access key is used to sign the request.

The *key* (see what I did there?) is that you understand that the management plane can be accessed by a variety of means and will likely use different methods to authenticate access. How are these credentials being used and secured? Let's move on to that part.

Securing the Management Plane

When you first register or sign up with a cloud provider, you will create an initial account that is considered the *master account* (some providers may call this the root account, which is a terrible name considering UNIX has been using it for decades). This account needs to be tightly locked down and used only to establish proper identity and access management. Here is some guidance regarding the creation and securing of this initial master account:

1. Create the account using a unique *corporate* e-mail address (for example, c-dbs45er@acme.com). This e-mail address will be the user ID for the master account and may serve as the way your provider will engage with your company. This account should *never* be created by someone using their personal e-mail address, or even their own corporate e-mail address.

2. Set up a distribution list for this master account e-mail. This will prevent several problems (for example, the original creator leaves the company and all e-mails wind up in /dev/null [a UNIX term for a garbage bin], or someone vital doesn't see an urgent message from the provider).

3. Establish a strong password that meets your security policy at the very least, and establish multifactor authentication (MFA) for this account based on a hardware MFA device. How you do this will vary based on the provider you are working with, but many, if not all, providers will support the *time-based one-time password* (TOTP), a temporary passcode generated by an algorithm that uses the current time of day as one of its authentication factors. Other providers may support a newer MFA method, Universal 2nd Factor (U2F), which is considered by many to be a safer MFA method than TOTP.

NOTE You can also use a "virtual" TOTP such as Google Authenticator, but given the fact that you're going to be storing the MFA device for safekeeping, a virtual MFA device may not make the most sense in an enterprise scenario.

Once the account, password, and MFA for the master account are set, you need to set up a new super-admin account you can use to access the management plane. Once that's done, you should write down the master account logon ID and password, put them in an envelope along with the MFA device, and lock these in a safe. From this point forward, the master account should be used only in emergencies, and all activity performed should use appropriate accounts.

NOTE There are three possible "factors" involved in MFA: something you know (such as a password), something you have (such as a smart card), and something you are (biometrics such as fingerprints or retina scans).

To secure the management plane properly, you need two things: a solid plan of who is allowed to do what (entitlements) and a provider that has a robust identity and access management (IAM) system that supports identification, authentication, and authorization with appropriate granularity. This granularity will enable you to implement a *least-privilege approach* to restrict who is permitted to perform specific actions in your cloud environment.

NOTE IAM is discussed further in Chapter 12, but don't bother jumping there just yet.

The Importance of Least Privilege and MFA

It's really important that you take a least-privilege approach regarding who can access and manage the cloud environment. This doesn't apply only to user accounts; it also applies to IAM roles. Why do I focus on least privileges? Consider the following example: A major bank was compromised by essentially allowing a role to list the contents of an object storage bucket (covered in Chapter 11). Huh? Yes...it's true. A role having access to list the contents of an object storage bucket led to an attacker being able to identify files that he accessed and downloaded. These files contained personally identifiable information (PII) data on millions of clients. Had the role's permissions been to *read* a known filename but not *list* the filename contents, the bank's data may not have been compromised—or, at the very least, it would have been a whole lot harder for the attacker to find the PII data.

EXAM TIP   Seriously, implement least privileges. If you are asked about appropriate permissions, the answer will always be related to the principle of least privilege.

This is an extreme example, but at a basic framework level, what does your organization do to handle access within its internal network? Does everyone have an administrator account that they use on a day-to-day basis? If they do, put down this book and get that fixed right away! That's not likely the case, however. In most organizations, users are given only the appropriate permissions to do their jobs and nothing more. Storage administrators should have access to manage and configure storage, and server admins may be granted the ability to create instances but not terminate them. You can't go wrong by always assuming a credential will be compromised and locking it down to minimize potential impact (which is, of course, a control to minimize risk).

You will encounter two main sets of credentials in cloud environments of all types: usernames and passwords for web console logins, and access keys for programmatic access. Access keys are considered a "permanent credential." I have two warnings about using access keys in a cloud environment:

- *Access keys (and secret keys) should never be included in any script.* These are, after all, clear-text credentials. I'm sure you don't use hard-coded clear-text passwords in scripts, so why would it be alright to do it with a different kind of credential? If the access key is kept in a script and that script is pushed to a public software repository such as GitHub, it can take minutes for a malicious actor to discover those credentials.

- *Access keys should be avoided if at all possible in favor of "temporary credentials."* Temporary credentials use what some providers call "IAM roles." In the temporary credential model, cloud user accounts are given minimal credentials, and role inheritance is used to elevate privileges so programs can execute successfully.

In addition to establishing accounts with least privilege as a paramount factor, you need to strongly consider the use of MFA for all accounts, not just the master account. The use of MFA (especially U2F) has demonstrable success in thwarting account takeovers. For example, Google implemented U2F with security keys internally in 2017. Guess how many of their 85,000 employees have been successfully phished since? Zero. Nada. Zilch. I think that's pretty impressive. Consider that this is an internal network and not a publicly available management plane—do you think the use of MFA for all management plane access would improve security across the board? I do. MFA should be implemented in any cloud environment; it's just as important for SaaS as it is for Platform as a Service (PaaS) and IaaS.

Management Plane Security When Building or Providing a Cloud Service

So far we have been looking at what the customer can do to secure their use of the management plane. What should the provider focus on when building the management plane, and what should customers be inspecting prior to using a provider? The following offers some considerations:

- **Perimeter security** How has the provider implemented controls to protect its network from attacks, both lower-level network defenses and the application stack, for both web consoles and API gateways?

- **Customer authentication** Does the provider allow use of MFA? What types of MFA are supported, and what systems in the provider's environment can use MFA? Does the provider support cryptographically secure methods of authentication such as OAuth or HTTP request signing?

- **Internal authentication and credential passing** How does the provider allow for access within the environment? Do they support temporary credentials through the implementation of IAM roles, for example?

- **Authorization and entitlements** How granular are the permissions that customers can use to support least privilege? Does the provider simply grant anyone logging on with administrative privileges? If so, you won't be able to create job-specific permissions, and that's not a good thing because any account compromise can be devastating.

- **Logging, monitoring, and alerting** This is a critical consideration. How can you collect artifacts of compliance if you have no ability to log failed and successful logins, or to log what actions are taken by particular IAM accounts? The ability to log actions can lead to discovery of malicious actions, and if appropriate orchestration is possible in the environment, this can be used to support event-driven security (covered in Chapter 10) to lower response times to seconds instead of hours thanks to automated response capabilities.

Business Continuity and Disaster Recovery in the Cloud

BCP/DR in a cloud environment differs from BCP/DR in a traditional IT world, because the cloud environment offers a pay-as-you-go model. Every decision you make has an associated cost and likely additional complexity. Let's consider an IaaS example: Implementing BCP/DR in a single region is often easier and less costly than implementing BCP/DR in multiple regions. Providers may charge additional fees to copy data from one region to another, and you may need to create region-specific scripts to reflect changes in asset IDs. Then there are the jurisdictional challenges, as discussed in previous chapters, and how they may impact BCP/DR legally.

BCP/DR Backgrounder

Business continuity planning and disaster recovery are often considered one and the same, but they really aren't the same things. They do, however, work together in support of a company's *recovery and resiliency planning* (commonly used for BCP/DR in many companies). This backgrounder covers some of the more important aspects of both.

 NOTE Recovery of a system doesn't necessarily mean 100 percent recovery. It could mean getting the system back up to 60 percent capacity, or it could involve creating a brand new system (or a new normal, if you will).

BCP is about continuing business operations, even if the organization is in a crippled state while DR steps are undertaken. BCP is not just focused on the IT systems in a company; it includes determining which systems are critical to operations, determining acceptable downtimes or losses, and applying appropriate mechanisms to meet those targets. DR is a part of a recovery and resiliency function that focuses on recovering from an incident, and it is generally IT-system focused. I like to differentiate the two by saying that BCP is about the people and operations, while DR is about technology. The two work together as part of a recovery and resiliency plan for your company, which needs appropriate policies, procedures, measurements, and, of course, testing to ensure that the plan addresses business requirements.

 NOTE Consider a Sony example to demonstrate the difference between BCP and DR. When the company was completely compromised in 2014, business continuity consisted of using a phone tree, where executives would use cell phones to call one another down the chain to communicate status updates; using Gmail for e-mail; using manual machines to cut paychecks; and using repurposed Blackberry smartphones that were stored in a closet somewhere. These BCP stopgaps kept the business operating while it restored systems as part of its DR. Disaster recovery, in the meantime, consisted of rebuilding all the systems compromised during the attack.

Before doing anything BCP/DR related, you must first identify the critical systems that need to be addressed. Not all systems have the same value to the organization, right? If your payroll system goes down, do you really expect employees to work for free until the system can be recovered? Or consider the loss of a graphics program used for new promotions. Is that program as important as payroll? Determining critical systems requires analyses, including business impact analysis (BIA), threat analysis, and impact scenarios.

Two calculations need to be performed as part of the BIA: the *recovery time objective* (RTO) and the *recovery point objective* (RPO). The RTO is simply the acceptable amount of time required to restore function and is usually measured in hours or days. You could have two RTOs: one for partial capacity and another for full capacity. The RPO is the acceptable amount of recent data loss that would be tolerated. It can also be measured in hours or days, or it may be measured in minutes for critical systems. The RPO can be used to drive the mandatory backup routines for a system. If, for example, you perform backups once a day, then in the event of an incident, you might be able to afford to lose up to a day's worth of data. If the RPO is set to one hour, how are you going to meet that requirement with a once-daily backup at 2 A.M.?

RTO and RPO also determine the costs associated with appropriate recovery and resiliency as a whole. So if you want a very low RTO and RPO of five minutes, you're going to need more systems to support real-time replication (as an example), and it's going to cost you way more than if you required only a two-week recovery. Proper assessment will drive acceptable investments in DR capabilities to meet appropriate recovery times at an acceptable cost. Figure 6-1 shows this process graphically.

Finally, you need to understand the different types of *site recovery options*. In a traditional data center environment, you need to consider the potential loss of the data center itself. Where are you going to rebuild your systems? Although this consideration is completely transformed if you use the cloud, I'll cover the different site recovery options in cold sites, warm sites, and hot sites here, because these have significant cost differences and support the RTO/RPO.

- **Cold site**   Offers the lowest cost and longest downtime. Space in an alternative processing environment is available to host servers, but there is little at this location as far as equipment is concerned. For example, you may have a contract with a co-location provider and have power, cooling, network connectivity, and other core requirements addressed, but there won't be any server hardware immediately available.

- **Warm site**   Offers moderate cost and moderate downtime. In this scenario, the facilities and the hardware are available, and the applications may be installed (but data is re-created from backup media). Obviously, costs are higher than those at a cold site because you need to have multiple hardware systems in place for both production and DR purposes.

- **Hot site**   Offers the highest cost and least downtime. The site has all hardware, software, data, and people ready to cut over at a moment's notice. The trick here is the continuous replication of data from the data center to the hot site.

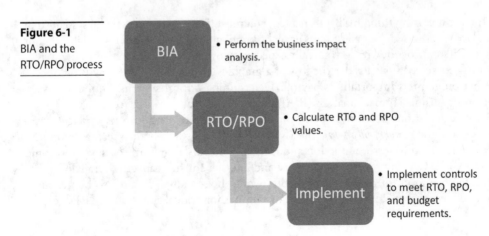

Figure 6-1
BIA and the
RTO/RPO process

BIA
- Perform the business impact analysis.

RTO/RPO
- Calculate RTO and RPO values.

Implement
- Implement controls to meet RTO, RPO, and budget requirements.

Let's apply this information to the cloud environment by looking at how the cloud changes business continuity and disaster recovery plans.

Architecting for Failure

If you fail to plan, you plan to fail. BCP/DR in the cloud is like everything else we've covered in this book, in that it involves a shared responsibility. The provider gives you the tools for DR, but you need to perform the BIA to understand the critical systems and implement appropriately to meet recovery objectives. That's what architecting for failure is all about.

The really fascinating aspect of DR in a cloud environment is that there's no longer the concept of a cold, warm, or hot site to deal with. Some companies refer to DR sites in the cloud (IaaS, most appropriately) as a "pilot light" site. If a site is properly planned and continuously tested, you can go from nothing to a completely available site in minutes through the beauty of *infrastructure as code* (IaC). IaC, which is covered in Chapter 10, is essentially the creation (and maintenance) of a script that uses templates that will build anything you want, ranging from networking to systems. Using IaC, you have the ability not only to rebuild a virtual infrastructure programmatically in minutes instead of hours, but you also remove the potential of human error that is often introduced when people are under pressure and trying to do things as quickly as possible.

Service models do have a significant impact on BCP and DR in the cloud, based on the good old security responsibility sharing model. Let's consider the various service models and how BCP/DR may be impacted:

- **IaaS** DR options in IaaS range from running everything in a single data center, to using IaC to build an infrastructure very quickly and restoring data from snapshots, to building a secondary hot site in a different geographical region while data is continuously copied from one region to another. How do you determine what is appropriate?

- **PaaS** How do you store your data and application code within a provider's environment? Did you bake encryption into your application, or are you relying on the provider for that service? The answer directly impacts your lock-in potential with a provider. (*Vendor lock-in* refers to the inability to move from one environment to another without significant effort on the customer side.) Finally, how do you export this data if a provider goes out of business or is sold to another company?

- **SaaS** In SaaS, your BCP/DR plans may be as simple as exporting data on a regular basis. When considering SaaS, however, consider data availability. Make sure your provider allows you to export data in a common format at acceptable times to support your RTO/RPO requirements. For example, imagine you have an RTO of one hour, but the provider allows you to export data only once a week. How are you going to meet your RTO if the provider goes bankrupt and stops communicating with you, the latest export is five days old, and data is stored in a proprietary format? How portable is data that can be used only with provider tools when those tools are unavailable?

Business Continuity Within the Cloud Provider

I'm going to get this somewhat controversial statement out of the way now: do not use multiple cloud providers as part of your IaaS BCP/DR planning. Before you slam the book shut, let me justify my statement. Building a single IaaS environment properly is hard enough on its own. Securing the metastructure of additional providers to the same level is much harder. First, every provider needs to expose controls (and how they do so will likely differ from how your primary CSP does it, if at all). Then you need the people who are experts in the target CSP to implement required controls. Do you really think there's a mass of people out there who know everything there is to know about the security of a single provider, let alone two or three, and that have the time to double or triple their efforts to secure all of them? It's not just about the data. In fact, I would say copying the data from one provider to another is the easy part; you must consider the entire logical model of the cloud and all the layers to understand what's at stake:

- **Metastructure**   As you know, this is your entire virtual infrastructure. Creating a properly secured environment is a challenge on its own. Why would you want to do it all over again in a different environment that may not even offer the same controls? Oh, and remember you have to manage multiple environments continuously so there's no configuration drift between the two. I think that's just crazy talk. Sure, there's IaC, but as you saw earlier in the API backgrounder section, all the commands are different, so you can't use one script from one vendor in another vendor's environment. The metastructure makes a properly secured and maintained multicloud failover approach to DR unrealistic for most companies. This is a leading reason why the CSA Guidance includes a section specifically dealing with business continuity within the cloud provider. Get that done properly before considering using multiple providers.

- **Software defined infrastructure**   Software defined infrastructure (SDI) enables you to define and implement an infrastructure through software orchestration, which can help greatly with recovery efforts. This capability is leveraged by using IaC, as you will learn in Chapter 10.

- **Infrastructure**   Your provider will likely make multiple regions available for you to leverage as part of your BCP/DR plans. Having geo-redundancy is a very viable approach and may be warranted (or even mandated) depending on the criticality of particular systems and/or data. Even the biggest cloud providers have experienced times when entire regions became unavailable. When considering geo-redundancy, you need to understand what services are available across different portions of the provider's infrastructure (not all services may be available in all regions, for example) and the costs associated with copying data from one region to another. You also need to consider items that must be addressed when moving something from one region to another (such as copying of images and resulting resource IDs changes).

- **Infostructure**   If you plan on implementing real-time replication of data—not just from one server instance to another, but from one side of North America to the other, for example—you must consider latency and continuously test it.

- **Applistructure**   The applistructure includes the full range of everything included in an application. If everything required for an application is self-contained in a single server, it will be much easier to move than if, for example, your application is tied into other services supplied by the cloud provider. Containers, microservices, and serverless computing are great examples of application code leveraging other services.

By taking all of this into account, you can see why accepting the risk of downtime is a viable option according to CSA Guidance. If you determine that downtime is acceptable, you need to make sure that your systems will fail gracefully. For example, if a customer-facing web page is unavailable, it may be a good idea to add DNS redirection to point to a page displaying that you are aware of the issue and are working on it, rather than presenting some generic "server error 500" message.

One last thing to consider is provider guidance on your DR plans. It might be great to say, "We'll just fail over from Region A to Region B in the event of failure, and we test that every month," but I want to highlight a problem with this plan by using a comparison. You know those fire evacuation drills your company has on a quarterly basis? Let's say you work in an office tower with 30 floors and your company occupies a full floor. As you go through your drill, it takes everyone 15 minutes to evacuate the building. Awesome. But what would happen if there were an actual emergency and all 30 floors were evacuating at once? Think it's still going to take 15 minutes to get your people out of the building? Not very likely, right? Well, what if you are located in a region with six data centers and a total capacity of, say, six million virtual CPUs (vCPUs), and your target DR region has two data centers and a total capacity of two million vCPUs. What do you think is going to happen if you experience a failover in one or more regions? It's a game of musical chairs, but the music just stopped, and everyone with the same plans as yours are kicking off their DR processes. It's just a matter of time until capacity is reached and chaos ensues. So talk to your particular vendor about your DR plans. You may have to purchase capacity reservations, have reserved instances, or take other steps as part of DR planning to guarantee space in the target region.

Chaos Engineering

Chaos engineering is the disciplined approach to experimenting on a system to build confidence in its ability to withstand turbulent and unexpected conditions in production. One leading company not only adopted chaos engineering but created an entire suite of chaos engineering tools and open sourced it to the world: Netflix. As part of its continuous testing of business continuity, Netflix will literally degrade portions of its cloud to determine whether systems are recovering and performing as expected. The company does this in production, not in development.

You may be thinking right now that the Netflix technical leadership is crazy, and there's no way you would ever take this approach. When you think hard about it, though, it makes sense. This approach forces Netflix developers and engineers to assume failure and build for it from the start. In any organization, this process can help address DR, because failure is already addressed as part of design. In a way, you can consider chaos engineering as continuous resiliency testing.

Business Continuity for Loss of the Cloud Provider

The potential for a provider's entire environment being unavailable obviously depends on the provider itself. This scenario is extremely rare for leading IaaS providers, however. In fact, the only time I can recall that an entire IaaS provider became unavailable was the Microsoft Azure outage of 2012, when a leap-year bug brought everything down for about nine hours. Amazon and Google have had outages, but these have impacted particular regions, not the entire infrastructure across all regions.

Of course, the minimal risk of a major IaaS failing is one thing, but the failure of PaaS and SaaS are another. In fact, it's not that rare for a PaaS or SaaS provider to go out of business or be sold to another provider that may not meet contractual obligations or that change the terms and conditions on you with little advance notice. With that in mind, you should be aware of a few important terms if you are considering moving data or applications from one cloud provider to another:

- **Interoperability**   The ability for system components to work together to deliver a service.
- **Portability**   The ability to move from one environment to another with minimal changes required.
- **Lock-In**   Providers can lock in clients not just from a contractual perspective but from a technical one as well—for example, by not supporting the exporting of data in a common format (which, as you may recall from our legal discussion, may impact admissibility of evidence as well).

 TIP   When thinking of SaaS portability specifically, remember that this is essentially a custom application. If you've ever been involved with migrating from Lotus Notes to Microsoft Exchange, for instance, you know all too well the difficulties that can be encountered during application migration, and SaaS migration is no different. Before you adopt a particular SaaS vendor for production use, you should understand how you can get your data exported and what format that data will be in.

Continuity for Private Cloud and Providers

If you are responsible for your company's private cloud, all aspects of BCP and DR apply, from the facilities up to the applications and data stored. You could determine that a public cloud is the best secondary site, or you could have a traditional spare site that is cold, warm, or hot. As always, plan and test, test, test.

If you are a cloud service provider, the importance of BCP/DR is highly critical—to the point at which the viability of the company as a whole can depend on proper BCP/DR capabilities. You could, for example, lose your business as a result of inappropriate BCP/DR capabilities. Or, if your system is perceived as being undependable by prospective clients, they won't use your service. If you break service level agreements, you could face penalties. Or if your DR includes failing over to a different jurisdiction, you may be breaking contractual obligations and even potentially data residency laws.

Chapter Review

This chapter covered the importance of APIs, the role of both web consoles and APIs when accessing the management plane, and the use of the IAM functionality supplied by the provider to secure the management plane. This chapter also covered some background information on business continuity planning and disaster recovery and the need for proper planning and architecture of DR in the cloud to meet business requirements.

In preparation for your CCSK exam, you should be comfortable with the following concepts:

- Master accounts should use MFA and be treated as emergency access only.
- Establish accounts using a least-privilege approach.
- All accounts should use MFA when possible to access the management plane.
- Ensure that strong perimeter security exists for API gateways and web consoles.
- BCP and DR are risk-based activities. Remember that not all systems are equally important to business continuity.
- Always architect for failure with regard to BCP and DR.
- Remember that downtime is always an option.
- When considering BCP/DR, consider the entire logical stack.
- Using multiple providers as part of DR can be very difficult, if not impossible, from a metastructure perspective. Strongly consider failover within a single provider before contemplating adding another provider.
- Understand the importance of portability and how it is impacted in BCP/DR.

Questions

1. What level of privileges should be assigned to a user account with access to the metastructure?

   A. Read-only

   B. Administrative access

   C. Least privileges required to perform a job

   D. Administrative access only to the system the user is using

2. How should the master account be used in a cloud environment?

   A. It should be treated as any other privileged account.

   B. The password for the account should be shared only through encrypted e-mail.

   C. It should be used only to terminate instances.

   D. It should have MFA assigned and be locked in a safe.

3. What layers of the logical stack should be considered as part of BCP/DR?

   A. Infostructure

   B. Metastructure

   C. Infrastructure

   D. All layers of the logical model

4. How should BCP/DR be architected in the cloud?

   A. Architect for failure.

   B. Architect using a single cloud provider.

   C. Architect using multiple cloud providers.

   D. Architect using real-time replication for all data.

5. What is meant by "lock-in"?

   A. Lock-in applies when you are contractually unable to export your data.

   B. Exporting data out of a provider would require significant effort.

   C. Data exported can be used only with the original provider's services.

   D. All of the above are correct.

6. Which of the following needs to be part of business continuity planning by the customer?

   A. Determining how to guarantee availability in the DR region by discussing your DR plans with the vendor

   B. Determining how the IaaS provider will fix any availability issues in your application

   C. Using contracts to ensure that DR does not result in a different jurisdiction being used to store and process data

   D. Implementing chaos engineering

7. What is infrastructure as code (IaC)?

   A. IaC uses templates to build your virtual network infrastructure.

   B. IaC uses templates to build an entire virtual infrastructure, ranging from networking through to systems.

   C. IaC is a ticketing system through which additional instances are requested from the provider.

   D. IaC is a ticketing system through which limit increases are requested from the provider.

8. What is the release cycle for new functionality?

   A. API functionality is released first, followed by CLI, followed by web console.

   B. CLI functionality is released first, followed by API, followed by web console.

   C. Web console and API functionality are released first, followed by CLI.

   D. The method used to expose new capabilities is determined by the provider.

9. Alice wants to update, but not replace, a file via a REST API. What method should Alice use?

   A. GET

   B. POST

   C. PUT

   D. PATCH

10. Which of the following introduces the most complexity when considering a multicloud approach to BCP/DR?

   A. Applistructure

   B. Metastructure

   C. Infrastructure

   D. Infostructure

Answers

1. **C.** Least privileges should always be used. None of the other answers is applicable.

2. **D.** The master account should have a hardware MFA device assigned, and the credentials along with the MFA device should be locked in a safe to be used only in the event of an emergency.

3. **D.** All layers of the logical model should be considered for BCP/DR.

4. **A.** You should always architect for failure when dealing with BCP/DR.

5. **D.** Lock-in occurs when you cannot easily change providers and export data. It can be addressed only through strong due diligence processes for adopting cloud service providers.

6. **A.** You need to consult your vendor to determine guaranteed availability in the region. Not all regions have the same amount of capacity and may be over-subscribed in the event of failure in another region. An IaaS provider will not address issues with your own applications. Although data residency regulations may be critical to some companies in certain lines of business, not all companies will face this issue, so C is not the best answer. Chaos engineering may not be for everyone.

7. **B.** The best answer is that IaC uses templates to build an entire virtual infrastructure, ranging from networking through to systems. Using IaC, you can not only build an entire infrastructure, including server instances based off configured images, but some IaaS providers go so far as supporting the configuration of servers at boot time. It is not a ticketing system.

8. **D.** Connection and functionality exposed to customers are always dependent on the provider. They may expose new functionalities in many different ways.

9. **D.** Alice should use the PATCH method to update, but not replace, a file. The PUT method creates a new file. POST is similar to PATCH, but a POST will update and delete the file.

10. **B.** The metastructure introduces the most complexity when considering a multicloud approach to BCP/DR.

Infrastructure Security

This chapter covers the following topics from Domain 7 of the CSA Guidance:
- Cloud Network Virtualization
- Security Changes with Cloud Networking
- Challenges of Virtual Appliances
- SDN Security Benefits
- Microsegmentation and the Software Defined Perimeter
- Hybrid Cloud Considerations
- Cloud Compute and Workload Security

Companies in every industry need to assume that a software revolution is coming.
—Marc Andreessen

Although the title of this chapter is "Infrastructure Security," we need to be aware that the cloud is truly possible only because of the software that is used to automate and orchestrate the customer's use of the underlying physical infrastructure. I'm not sure exactly when Mr. Andreessen made the preceding statement, but I think it's fair to say the software revolution is now officially here. The great news is that you will be a part of it as a cloud security professional. This chapter covers some of the new software-driven technologies that make the cloud possible.

Virtualization isn't exactly new. Some claim that it started back in the 1960s, while others argue the virtualization we know today began in the 1990s. Either way, today's virtualization is very different from what it was when it was essentially a way to run multiple virtual servers on a single physical computer. Workloads in a cloud environment are so much more than just virtual machines. Today's cloud infrastructure uses software defined networking (SDN), containers, immutable instances, serverless computing, and other technologies that are covered in this chapter.

How is this virtual infrastructure protected? How are detection and response performed? Where are your log files being stored? Are they protected in the event of an account compromise? These are just some of the questions that arise with these new forms of virtualized environments. If your plan for protection is based on installing an agent on a server instance and your plan for vulnerability assessments in the cloud is limited to running a scanner against a known IP address, you need to rethink your options in this new environment.

The physical infrastructure is the basis for everything in computing, including the cloud. Infrastructure is the foundation of computers and networks upon which we build everything else, including the layer of abstraction and resource pooling that makes the cloud rapidly scalable, elastic, and, well, everything that it is. Everything covered in this domain applies to all cloud deployment models, from private to public clouds.

I won't cover data center security principles such as the best number of candle watts required for a walkway versus a parking lot, or how rocks should be integrated into the landscape to protect the data center, because such items aren't covered in the CSA Guidance and you won't be tested on them. Although you may be disappointed that I won't cover the merits of boulders versus metal posts as barriers, I will cover workload virtualization, network virtualization, and other virtualization technologies in this chapter.

I'll begin by discussing the two areas (referred to as *macro layers* in the CSA Guidance) of infrastructure. First are the fundamental resources such as physical processors, network interface cards (NICs), routers, switches, storage area networks (SANs), network attached storage (NAS), and other items that form the pools of resources that were covered back in Chapter 1. These items are, of course, fully managed by the provider (or by your company if you choose to build your own private cloud). Next we have the virtual/abstracted infrastructure (aka virtual world, or metastructure) that is created by customers who pick and choose what they want from the resource pools. This virtual world is managed by the cloud user.

Throughout the chapter, we will be taking a look at some networking elements that operate behind the scenes and are managed by the provider. Although the backgrounder information provided here won't be included on your CCSK exam, this information will help you gain an appreciation for some of the new technologies that are being used when you adopt cloud services. I'll call out when subject material is for your information and not on the exam.

By the way, I'm including callouts to relevant requests for comment (RFCs) throughout this chapter. If you are unfamiliar with RFCs, they are formal documents from the Internet Engineering Task Force (IETF) that are usually associated with publishing a standard (such as TCP, UDP, DNS, and so on) or informational RFCs that deal with such things as architectures and implementations. These are included here in case you really want to dive headfirst into a subject. RFCs can always be considered the authoritative source for networking subjects, but you do not need to read the associated RFCs in preparation for your CCSK exam.

Cloud Network Virtualization

Network virtualization abstracts the underlying physical network and is used for the *network resource pool*. How these pools are formed, and their associated capabilities, will vary based on the particular provider. Underneath the virtualization are three networks that are created as part of an Infrastructure as a Service (IaaS) cloud: the management

Figure 7-1
Common
networks
underlying IaaS

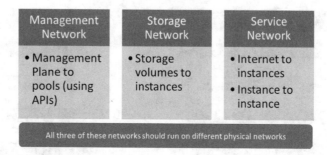

Management Network	Storage Network	Service Network
• Management Plane to pools (using APIs)	• Storage volumes to instances	• Internet to instances • Instance to instance

All three of these networks should run on different physical networks

network, the storage network, and the service network. Figure 7-1 shows the three networks and the traffic that each supports.

TIP These three networks have no functional or traffic overlap so they should run on three separate networks dedicated to associated activity. Yes, this means that the provider needs to implement and maintain three sets of network cables and network infrastructure.

We'll check out the virtualization technologies that run on top of the underlying physical networks that make this whole cloud thing a reality. Before we go there, though, I think a crash review of the famed OSI reference model is required. There's nothing cloud-specific in the following OSI backgrounder, but it is important for you to know about, if for nothing more than understanding what I mean when I say something "operates at layer 2."

OSI Reference Model Backgrounder

The Open Systems Interconnection (OSI) reference model is a pretty ubiquitous model that many people are familiar with. Ever heard the term "layer 7 firewall" or "layer 2 switch"? That's a nod to the OSI reference model layers. You will not be tested on the OSI reference model as part of the CCSK exam because the CSA considers it assumed knowledge. As such, I'm not going to get into every tiny detail of the model but will look at it from a high level.

The OSI stack consists of seven layers (I call it a seven-layer bean dip), ranging from the application layer at the top (layer 7) down to the physical medium layer (layer 1). There's a mnemonic to help us remember the OSI reference model: "All People Should Try New Diet Pepsi" (layer 7 to layer 1), or, alternatively, "Please Do Not Trust Sales People's Advice" (layer 1 to layer 7). Figure 7-2 shows the OSI reference model in all its glory.

The reference model is reflected in how a packet is created. Application data is *encapsulated* (Figure 7-3) by each layer as it goes down the stack. Relevant information is added by each layer and then sent across the network, where it is picked up by the

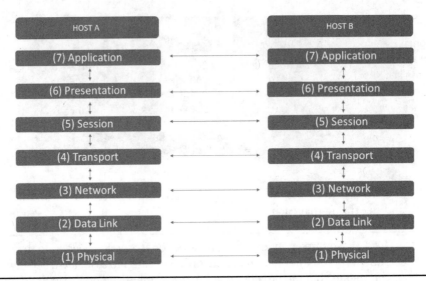

Figure 7-2 OSI reference model

receiving machine (such as the media access control [MAC] hardware address at layer 2) and corresponding layer data is stripped off and sent up the stack.

Table 7-1 highlights what happens at each layer of the OSI reference model.

 NOTE The information in Table 7-1 is not meant to be exhaustive. I'm aiming for a high-level explanation to help support the rest of the networking discussion.

VLANs

Virtual local area networks (VLANs) have been around for a very long time. VLAN technology was standardized in 2003 by the Institute of Electrical and Electronic Engineers as IEEE 802.1Q and operates at layer 2 of the OSI model. VLAN technology essentially uses tagging of network packets (usually at the port on the switch to which a system is connected) to create single broadcast domains. This creates a form of *network segmentation*,

Figure 7-3 Packet encapsulation at each layer on the OSI stack

	OSI Reference Layer	High-Level Layer Information
Table 7-1 What Happens at Each Layer of the OSI Reference Model	Layer 7: Application	Application data (such as HTTP or SQL)
	Layer 6: Presentation	Encryption and decryption
	Layer 5: Session	Session control between hosts
	Layer 4: Transport	End-to-end connections (such as TCP and UDP ports)
	Layer 3: Network	Logical addressing (such as IP addresses)
	Layer 2: Data Link	Physical addressing (such as MAC addresses) and collision/error detection
	Layer 1: Physical	Converts all data received from the higher layers to the format of the physical network

not *isolation*. Segmentation can work in a single-tenant environment like a trusted internal network but isn't optimal in a cloud environment that is multitenant by nature.

NOTE The terms "segmentation" and "isolation" are often used interchangeably but are very different things. In a networking context, *segmentation* refers to partitioning a network into smaller networks (a broadcast domain). In a broadcast domain, all systems that are assigned to that VLAN will receive all broadcast traffic. *Isolation*, on the other hand, restricts communication to the intended destination machine only, as is the case in software defined networking (SDN). Grouping trusted computers together is one thing; doing so in a multitenant environment is another thing altogether.

Another issue when it comes to the use of VLANs in a cloud environment is address space. Per the IEEE 802.1Q standard, a VLAN can support 4096 addresses (it uses 12 bits for addressing, so $2^{12} = 4096$). That's not a whole lot when you consider there are IaaS providers out there with more than a million customers.

NOTE A later IEEE standard (802.1aq) dramatically bumped up this number, but that standard is nowhere close to the level of adoption of 802.1Q, so you can safely ignore its existence for our purposes.

VXLAN

Virtual Extensible LAN (VXLAN) isn't mentioned at all in the CSA Guidance, but core features of VXLAN are discussed as part of SDN, so you should know this material for your exam. (And, as a bonus, it will help you understand how SDN does what it does.) VXLAN is a network virtualization technology standard (RFC 7348, released in August 2014) that was created by VMware and Cisco (along with others) and supported

| IP Addressing for Routing Across Network | UDP Information | VTEP Adds VNI Addressing | Original Frame Sent to VTEP |

Figure 7-4   Example of VXLAN packet encapsulation

by numerous vendors to address the scalability and isolation issues with VLANs. VXLAN encapsulates layer 2 frames within UDP packets by using a *VXLAN Tunnel End Point* (VTEP), essentially creating a tunneling scenario where the layer 2 packets are "hidden" while they traverse a network, using layer 3 (such as IP) addressing and routing capabilities. Inside these UDP packets, a *VXLAN network identifier* (VNI) is used for addressing; this packet encapsulation is shown in Figure 7-4. Unlike the VLAN model discussed earlier, VXLAN uses 24 bits for tagging purposes, meaning approximately 16.7 million addresses, thus addressing the scalability issue faced by normal VLANs.

As you can see in Figure 7-4, the original Ethernet frame is received by the tunnel endpoint, which then adds its own addressing, throws that into a UDP packet, and assigns a routable IP address; then this tunneled information is sent on its merry way to its destination, which is another tunnel endpoint. Using VXLAN to send this tunneled traffic over a standard network composed of routers (such as the Internet) is known as creating an *overlay network* (conversely, the physical network is called an *underlay network*). By encapsulating the long hardware addresses inside a routable protocol, you can extend the typical "virtual network" across office buildings or around the world (as shown in Figure 7-5).

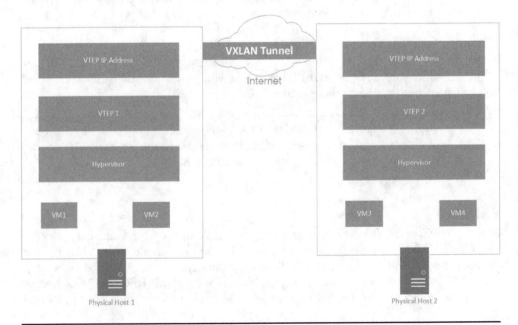

Figure 7-5   Example of VXLAN overlay network

NOTE There's obviously much more to VXLAN than the basics covered here. Check out RFC 7348 for everything there is to know about VXLAN if you are so inclined. Again, though, you don't need to know all this for your CCSK exam.

Networking Planes Backgrounder

Before we get to the SDN portion of this chapter, there's one last area that we should explore regarding the different *planes* associated with networking equipment in general. Every networking appliance (such as a router or switch) contains three planes—management, control, and data—that perform different functions. The following is a quick discussion of each plane:

- **Management plane**   Maybe this term sounds familiar? It should! Just as you manage the metastructure in a cloud via the management plane, you access the management plane to configure and manage a networking device. This plane exposes interfaces such as a CLI, APIs, and graphical web browsers, which administrators connect to so they can manage a device. Long story short, you access the management plane to configure the control plane.

- **Control plane**   This plane establishes how network traffic is controlled, and it deals with initial configuration and is essentially the "brains" of the network device. This is where you configure routing protocols (such as Routing Information Protocol [RIP], Open Shortest Path First [OSPF], and so on), spanning tree algorithms, and other signaling processes. Essentially, you configure the networking logic in the control plane in advance so traffic will be processed properly by the data plane.

- **Data plane**   This is where the magic happens! The data plane carries user traffic and is responsible for forwarding packets from one interface to another based on the configuration created at the control plane. The data plane uses a flow table to send traffic where it's meant to go based on the logic dictated by the control plane.

Understanding the three planes involved is important before we get to the next topic: software defined networking. Just remember that the control plane is the brains and the data plane is like the traffic cop that sends packets to destinations based on what the control plane dictates.

Software Defined Networking

SDN is an architectural concept that enables centralized management and emphasizes the role of software in running networks to dynamically control, change, and manage network behavior. Centralized management is achieved by breaking out the *control plane* (brains) and making this plane part of an SDN controller that manages the *data plane*, which remains on the individual networking components (physical or virtual). Dynamic change and management are supplied through the *application plane*. All three of these planes (mostly) communicate via APIs. Figure 7-6 shows the various planes in an SDN environment.

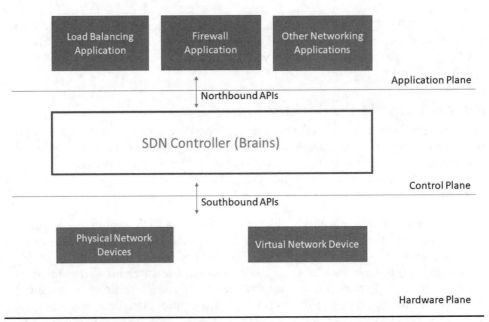

Figure 7-6   Simplified SDN architecture

So SDN separates the control plane from the data plane. Wait…hold on. Those are already separate, right? Exactly so, but as I said in the previous section, in traditional networking gear, all three planes exist in the single hardware appliance. SDN moves the control plane from the actual networking device to an SDN controller. This consolidation and centralization of control result in a more agile and flexible networking environment. Remember that SDN isn't a networking protocol, but VXLAN is a networking protocol. Quite often, as in the CSA Guidance, people will combine the two technologies when talking about SDN, but just remember that SDN is an architectural concept that can be realized by using a protocol such as VXLAN.

You can't spell SDN without OpenFlow. Well, let me rephrase that: OpenFlow is very integral to the whole SDN discussion and is referenced 34 times in informational RFC 7426, "SDN Layers and Architecture Terminology." The OpenFlow protocol was first released in 2011 by the Open Networking Foundation (ONF) and is considered the enabler of SDN. In fact, many people refer to the southbound APIs as the "OpenFlow Specification." OpenFlow is defined in RFC 7426 as "a protocol through which a logically centralized controller can control an OpenFlow switch. Each OpenFlow-compliant switch maintains one or more flow tables, which are used to perform packet lookups."

NOTE   Don't take the term "OpenFlow switch" too literally. Just remember that every network device (physical or virtual) has a data plane that contains a flow table that is managed by the control plane (SDN controller in this case).

There are multiple open source OpenFlow SDN controllers available in the marketplace, such as the OpenDaylight Project and Project Floodlight. In addition to the open source OpenFlow standard, many vendors have seen the power of SDN and have come up with their own proprietary SDN implementations (such as Cisco's Application Centric Infrastructure [ACI] or Juniper Contrail).

The OpenFlow SDN controllers will communicate with the OpenFlow-compliant networking devices using the OpenFlow specification (such as southbound APIs) to configure and manage the flow tables. Communication between the controller and the applications occurs over the northbound interface. There is no standard communication method established for these northbound interfaces, but typically APIs are used.

Through the implementation of SDN (and enabling technologies), cloud providers can offer clients much higher flexibility and isolation. By design, cloud providers offer clients what they are generally accustomed to getting. For example, clients can select whatever IP range they want in the cloud environment, create their own routing tables, and architect the metastructure networking exactly the way they want it. This is all possible through the implementation of SDN (and related technologies). The SDN implementation not only hides all the underlying networking mechanisms from customers, but it also hides the network complexities from the virtual machines running in the provider's network. All the virtual instance sees is the virtual network interface provided by the hypervisor, and nothing more.

 NOTE I cover the security benefits associated with SDN later in this chapter in the section "SDN Security Benefits."

Network Functions Virtualization

Network functions virtualization (NFV) is another area that isn't covered in the CSA Guidance, so it won't be on your test, but it's a technology that I think is worth exploring a little bit. NFV is different from SDN, but the two can work together in a virtualized network, and you'll often see "SDN/NFV" used in multiple publications.

The NFV specification was originally created by the European Telecommunications Standards Institute (ETSI) back in 2013. The goal of NFV is to transform network architectures by replacing physical network equipment that performs network functions (such as a router) with virtual network functions (VNFs) that could be run on industry-standard servers and deliver network functions through software. According to the ETSI, such an approach could decrease costs, improve flexibility, speed innovation through software-based service deployment, improve efficiencies through automation, reduce power consumption, and create open interfaces to enable different vendors to supply decoupled elements.

NFV requires a lot of virtualized resources, and as such, it requires a high degree of orchestration to coordinate, connect, monitor, and manage. I'm sure you can already see how SDN and NFV can work together to drive an open-virtualized networking environment that would benefit a cloud service provider. Remember the distinction between the two in that SDN separates the control plane from the underlying network devices and NFV can replace physical networking appliances with virtualized networking functions.

How Security Changes with Cloud Networking

Back in the good old days of traditional networking, security was a whole lot more straightforward than it is today. Back then, you may have had two physical servers with physical network cards that would send bits over a physical network, and then a firewall, intrusion prevention system (IPS), or another security control would inspect the traffic that traversed the network. Well, those days are gone in a cloud environment. Now, virtual servers use virtual network cards and virtual appliances. Although cloud providers do have physical security appliances in their environments, you're never going to be able to ask your provider to install your own physical appliances in their cloud environment.

Pretty much the only commonality between the old days of physical appliance security controls and today's virtual appliances is that both can be potential bottlenecks and single points of failure. Not only can appliances become potential bottlenecks, but software agents installed in virtual machines can also impact performance. Keep this in mind when architecting your virtual controls in the cloud, be they virtual appliances or software agents.

These new ways of securing network traffic in a cloud environment offer both challenges and benefits.

Challenges of Virtual Appliances

Keep in mind that both physical and virtual appliances can be potential bottlenecks and single points of failure. After all, virtual machines can crash just like their associated physical servers, and an improperly sized virtual appliance may not be able to keep up with the amount of processing that is actually required. Also, remember the costs associated with the virtual appliances that many vendors now offer in many Infrastructure as a Service (IaaS) environments.

Think about the following simplistic scenario for costs associated with these things: Suppose your cloud environment consists of two regions, both with six subnets, and the vendor recommends that their virtual appliance be placed in each subnet. This translates to a total of 12 virtual appliances required. Single point of failure you say? Well, assuming the vendor supports failover (more on this later), you need to double the required virtual firewall appliances to 24. Say the appliance and instance cost a total of $1 an hour. That's $24 an hour. You may be thinking that $24 an hour is not such a big deal. But unlike humans who work 8 hours a day (so I hear), appliances work 24 hours a day, so your super cheap $24 an hour means an annual cost of more than $210,000 (365 days equals 8760 hours, multiplied by $24, comes to $210,240). That's for a super simple scenario! Now imagine your company has fully embraced the cloud, is running 70 accounts (for recommended isolation), and each account has two subnets (public and private) and a failover region as part of the company's business continuity/disaster recovery (BC/DR) planning. That requires 280 (70 accounts × 2 subnets × 2 regions) appliances at $1 an hour, for a grand total of more than $2.4 million a year. Darn. I forgot the single point of failure aspect. Make that $4.8 million a year. This is a great example of how architecture in the cloud can financially impact an organization.

On the other hand, the capabilities offered by virtual appliance vendors are all over the map. Some providers may support high availability and auto-scaling to take advantage of the elasticity of the cloud and offer other features to address potential performance bottleneck scenarios; others may not support these features at all. You must understand exactly what the provider is offering.

The vendors I particularly love (which shall remain nameless) are those that advertise that their "Next Generation Firewall" product offers multiple controls (firewall, intrusion detection system, intrusion prevention system, application control, and other awesome functionalities) and high availability through clustering, but when you actually read the technical documentation, nothing works in a cloud environment other than the core firewall service, and that cannot be deployed in HA mode in a cloud. This forces you into a single point of failure scenario.

It's important that you identify virtual appliances that are designed to take advantage of not only elasticity but also the velocity of change associated with the cloud, such as moving across regions and availability zones. Another area to consider is the workloads being protected by the virtual appliance. Can a virtual appliance handle an auto-scaling group of web servers that suddenly jumps from five servers to fifty and then back to five in a matter of minutes, or can it handle changes to IP addresses associated with particular workloads? If the virtual appliance tracks everything by manually configured IP addresses, you're immediately in trouble, because the IP addresses associated with particular virtual servers can change often, especially in an immutable environment (see the later section "Immutable Workloads Enable Security").

Benefits of SDN Security

I've covered the purpose and basic architecture of SDN, but I didn't specifically call out the security benefits associated with SDN that you will need to know for your CCSK exam. Here, then, are the security benefits associated with SDN according to the CSA Guidance:

- **Isolation**   You know that SDN (through associated technologies) offers isolation by default. You also know that, thanks to SDN, you can run multiple networks in a cloud environment using the same IP range. There is no logical way these networks can directly communicate because of addressing conflicts. Isolation can be a way to segregate applications and services with different security requirements.

- **SDN firewalls**   These may be referred to as "security groups." Different providers may have different capabilities, but SDN firewalls are generally applied to the virtual network card of a virtual server. They are just like a regular firewall in that you make a "policy set" (aka firewall ruleset) that defines acceptable traffic for both inbound (ingress) and outbound (egress) network traffic. This means SDN firewalls have the granularity of host-based firewalls but are managed like a network appliance. As part of the virtual network itself, these firewalls can also be orchestrated. How cool is it that you can create a system that notices a ruleset change and automatically reverts back to the original setting and sends a notification to the cloud administrator? That's the beauty of using provider-supplied controls that can be orchestrated via APIs.

- **Deny by default**   SDN networks are typically deny-by-default-for-everything networks. If you don't establish a rule that explicitly allows something, the packets are simply dropped.

- **Identification tags**   The concept of identifying systems by IP address is dead in a cloud environment; instead, you need to use tagging to identify everything. This isn't a bad thing; in fact, it can be a very powerful resource to increase your security. Using tags, you could automatically apply a security group to every server, where, for example, a tag states that a server is running web services.

- **Network attacks**   Many low-level network attacks against your systems and services are eliminated by default. Network sniffing of an SDN network, for example, doesn't exist because of inherent isolation capabilities. Other attacks, such as ARP spoofing (altering of NIC hardware addresses), can be eliminated by the provider using the control plane to identify and mitigate attacks. Note that this doesn't necessarily stop all attacks immediately, but there are numerous research papers discussing the mitigation of many low-level attacks through the software-driven functionality of SDN.

Microsegmentation and the Software Defined Perimeter

You know that a VLAN segments out networks. You can take that principle to create *zones*, where groupings of systems (based on classification, perhaps) can be placed into their own zones. This moves network architecture from the typical "flat network," where network traffic is inspected in a "north–south" model (once past the perimeter, there is free lateral movement), toward a "zero-trust" network based on zones, and traffic can be inspected in both a "north–south" and "east–west" (or within the network) fashion. That's the same principle behind microsegmentation—except microsegmentation takes advantage of network virtualization to implement a fine-grained approach to creating these zones.

As the networks themselves are defined in software and no additional hardware is required, it is far easier and practical for you to implement smaller zones to create a more fine-grained approach to workload zoning—say, grouping five web servers together in a microsegmented zone rather than creating a single demilitarized zone (DMZ) with hundreds of servers that shouldn't need to access one another. This enables the implementation of fine-grained "blast zones," where if one of the web servers is compromised, the lateral movement of an attacker would be limited to the five web servers, not every server in the DMZ. This fine-grained approach isn't very practical with traditional zoning restrictions associated with using VLANs to group systems together (remember that VLANs have a maximum of 4096 addresses versus 16.7 million for VXLAN).

Now this isn't to say that implementing microsegmentation is a zero-cost effort. There may very well be an increase in operational costs associated with managing all of the networks and their connectivity requirements.

Building on the concepts discussed in SDN and microsegmentation, the CSA has developed a model called the *Software Defined Perimeter* (SDP). The SDP combines both device and user authentication to provision network access to resources dynamically. There are three components in SDP (as shown in Figure 7-7):

- An SDP client (agent) installed on a device
- The SDP controller that authenticates and authorizes SDP clients based on both device and user attributes
- The SDP gateway that serves to terminate SDP client network traffic and enforces policies in communication with the SDP controller

---

 NOTE For more information on SDP, check out the CSA research, such as the "SDP Architecture Guide." You won't need that level of detailed knowledge for your CCSK exam, but it is an excellent resource to read all the same.

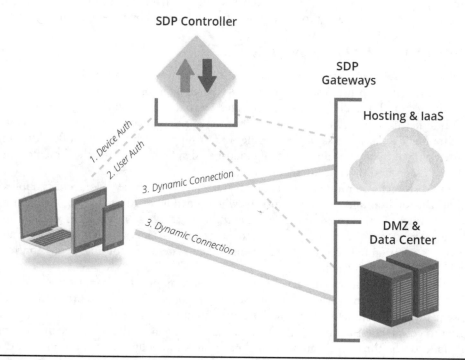

Figure 7-7 Software Defined Perimeter. (Used with permission of Cloud Security Alliance.)

Additional Considerations for CSPs or Private Clouds

Unlike consumers of the cloud, CSPs are required to properly secure the physical aspects of a cloud environment that everything is built upon. A security failure at the physical layer can lead to devastating results, where all customers are impacted. As the consumer, you must always remember to ensure that the provider has acceptable security in place at the physical layer, because other tenants, especially in a public cloud, must be considered as untrusted—and even potentially adversarial. Private clouds should be treated the same way.

As mentioned, SDN offers the ability to maintain segregation and isolation for the multitenant environment. Providers must always consider all tenants as being potentially hostile, and, as such, CSPs must address the additional overhead associated with properly establishing and maintaining SDN security controls. Providers must also expose security controls to cloud consumers so they can appropriately manage their virtual network security.

Perimeter security still matters in a cloud environment. Providers should implement standard perimeter security controls such as distributed denial of service (DDoS) protection, IPS, and other technologies to filter out hostile traffic before it can impact consumers in the cloud environment. This is not to say that consumers should assume that the provider will block any potentially hostile network traffic at the perimeter. Consumers are still required to implement their own network security.

Finally, as far as reuse of hardware is concerned, providers should always be able to properly clean or wipe any resources (such as volumes) that have been released by clients before reintroducing them into the resource pool to be used by other customers.

Hybrid Cloud Considerations

Recall from Chapter 1 an example of a hybrid cloud—when a customer has their own data center and also uses cloud resources. As far as large organizations are concerned, this connection is usually made via a dedicated wide area network (WAN) link or across the Internet using a VPN. In order for your network architects to incorporate a cloud environment (especially IaaS), the provider has to support arbitrary network addressing as determined by the customer, so that cloud-based systems don't use the same network address range used by your internal networks.

As a customer, you must ensure that both areas have the same levels of security applied. Consider, for example, a flat network in which anyone within a company can move laterally (east–west) through the network and can access cloud resources as a result. You should always consider the network link to your cloud systems as potentially hostile and enforce separation between your internal and cloud systems via routing, access controls, and traffic inspection (such as firewalls).

The *bastion* (or transit) virtual network is a network architecture pattern mentioned in the CSA Guidance to provide additional security to a network architecture in the cloud. Essentially, a bastion network can be defined as a network that data must go through in order to get to a destination. With this in mind, creating a bastion network and forcing all cloud traffic through it can act as a chokepoint (hopefully in a good way). You can tightly control this network (as you would with a bastion host) and perform all the

Figure 7-8
Bastion/transit
network between
the cloud and a
data center

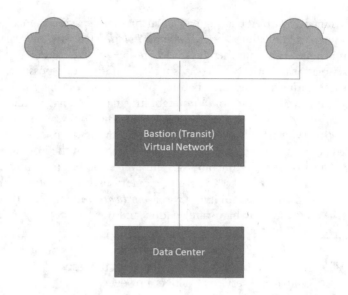

content inspection that is required to protect traffic coming in and out of the data center and cloud environments. Figure 7-8 shows the bastion network integration between a cloud environment and a data center.

Cloud Compute and Workload Security

A *workload* is a unit of processing. It can be executed on a physical server, on a virtual server, in a container, or as a function on someone else's virtual server—you name it. Workloads will always run on some processor and will consume memory, and the security of those items is the responsibility of the provider.

Compute Abstraction Technologies

The CSA Guidance covers four types of "compute abstraction" technologies that you will likely encounter in a cloud environment. I will introduce each of these technologies next, but you'll find more detailed information regarding each technology in later chapters, which I'll point out in each section.

Virtual Machines

These are the traditional virtual machines that you are probably accustomed to. This is the same technology offered by all IaaS providers. A *virtual machine manager* (aka hypervisor) is responsible for creating a virtual environment that "tricks" a guest OS (an *instance* in cloud terminology) into thinking that it is talking directly to the underlying hardware, but in reality, the hypervisor takes any request for underlying hardware (such as memory) and maps it to a dedicated space reserved for that particular guest machine. This shows you the abstraction (the guest OS has no direct access to the hardware) that hypervisors perform. Allocating particular memory spaces assigned to a particular guest environment demonstrates *segregation* and *isolation* (the memory space of one guest OS cannot be accessed by another guest OS on the same machine).

The isolation qualities of a hypervisor make multitenancy possible. If this isolation were to fail, the entire multitenancy nature, and therefore business model, of cloud services would be thrown into question. Vulnerabilities in the past have intended to break memory isolation, such as the Meltdown and Spectre vulnerabilities (and subsequent offshoots). Both of these vulnerabilities had to do with exploiting the manner by which many CPUs handled accessing memory spaces, essentially bypassing the isolation of memory spaces. This meant that if this vulnerability were ever exploited in a multicloud environment, one tenant could be able to access the memory used by another tenant. Note that this was not a *software* vulnerability; it was a *hardware* vulnerability that impacted the way memory was handled by hardware vendors and was leveraged by operating systems.

 NOTE Don't worry about these vulnerabilities being part of your CCSK exam. Knowing about them does highlight the responsibilities a customer shares with cloud service providers, however.

Meltdown and Spectre vulnerabilities needed to be addressed (patched) by the cloud provider because they involved hardware issues, but as many operating systems were also using the same techniques of memory mapping, customers were advised to patch their own operating systems to ensure that one running application could not access the memory space of another application on the same virtual server. (You can read more about the Meltdown vulnerability by checking out CVE-2017-5754.) This example is not meant to say in any way that isolation is a "broken" security control—because it isn't. In fact, I think it goes to show just how quickly cloud vendors can address a "black swan" vulnerability. Mostly used in the financial world, the term *black swan vulnerability* is used when an event is a risk that isn't even considered, yet would have a devastating impact if realized. This hardware vulnerability is by all means a black swan event, so much so that when discovered, researchers dismissed it as an impossibility. Lessons have been learned, and both hardware and software vendors continue to improve isolation capabilities.

 NOTE If you are unfamiliar with the Common Vulnerabilities and Exposures (CVE) database, it is a list of all known vulnerabilities that is maintained by the MITRE Corporation in association with several US organizations.

I cover virtual machine security a bit more in Chapter 8.

Containers

Containers are sort of an evolution of the virtual machines just covered. They are compute virtualization technologies, but they are applied differently. "A picture paints a thousand words" comes to mind here, so take a look at Figure 7-9 to see what containers are and how they differ from the standard virtualized machine running on top of a virtual machine manager.

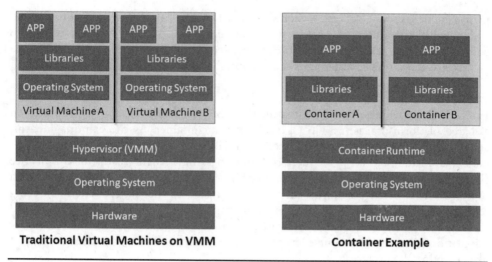

Figure 7-9 Virtual machines versus containers

As you can see in the figure, containers differ from traditional virtual machines in that a container doesn't have all the "bloat" of an operating system to deal with. (I mean, really, does your application require calc.exe in order to run?) Instead of cramming an operating system, required libraries, and the application itself into a 30GB package with a VM, you can place the application and any dependencies (such as libraries) the application requires in a much smaller package, or container if you will. With containers, the application uses a shared kernel and other capabilities of the base OS. The container provides code running inside a restricted environment with access only to the processes and capabilities defined in the container configuration. This technology isn't specific to cloud technologies; containers themselves can run in a virtualized environment or directly on a single server.

 NOTE Containers are just a fancy way of packaging applications and required dependencies.

Because a container is much smaller than a traditional virtual machine, it offers two primary benefits: First, a container can launch incredibly quickly because it involves no OS that needs time to boot up. This aspect can help you with agility. Second, a container can help with portability. Note that I said "help," not "fully address," portability. Moving a container is obviously a quick operation, but the container itself will require a supported shared kernel. But that only addresses the runtime (engine) dependency itself, and many providers will support the Docker Engine, which has become pretty much the default container engine today. Where portability can get derailed is in all of the other elements of containerization technology, such as container hosts, images, and orchestration via management systems (such as Docker Swarm or Kubernetes). You need to consider and address all of the aspects involved with containers if you plan on using containers to address portability across providers, or even between your data center and the cloud.

I discuss the various components of containers in Chapter 8.

Platform-Based Workloads

Platform-based workloads are defined in the CSA Guidance as anything running on a shared platform that isn't a virtual machine or a container. As you can imagine, this encompasses an incredibly wide array of potential services. Examples given in the SCA Guidance include stored procedures running on a multitenant Platform as a Service (PaaS) database and a job running on a machine-learning PaaS. I'm going to stick with those two here, because I don't want to add confusion to the subject. The main thing to remember for your CCSK exam is that although the provider may expose a limited amount of security options and controls, the provider is responsible for the security of the platform itself and, of course, everything else down to the facilities themselves, just like any other PaaS offering.

Serverless Computing

"Serverless," in this context, is essentially a service exposed by the provider, where the customer doesn't manage any of the underlying hardware or virtual machines and simply accesses exposed functions (such as running your Python application) on the provider's servers. It's "serverless" to you, but it absolutely runs on a backend, which could be built using containers, virtual machines, or specialized hardware platforms. The provider is responsible for securing everything about the platform they are exposing, all the way down to the facilities.

Serverless computing is discussed in Chapter 10.

How the Cloud Changes Workload Security

The main item that changes security in a cloud environment is multitenancy. It is up to the provider to implement segregation and isolation between workloads, and this should be one of the provider's top priorities. Some providers may offer a dedicated instance capability, where one workload operates on a single physical server, but this option is usually offered at additional cost. This is true for both public and private cloud environments.

Immutable Workloads Enable Security

Immutable workloads are a key capability that a cloud customer with mature cloud processes will eventually implement. I say this because, in reality, most enterprises take a "like-for-like" approach (aka "We've always done it this way") to cloud adoption at first. When you hear the term "immutable," you should think of *ephemeral*, which means "lasting for a very short time." However, immutable has some incredible security benefits. This section will cover what immutable workloads are and why you want to use them.

I always describe immutable servers as the "Vegas model of compute." Unlike the traditional "pets" model of running servers where you patch them, take care of them, and they are around for years, the immutable model takes a "cattle" approach to server maintenance. The server runs, does its job, and then is terminated and replaced with a new server (some call this the "nuke and pave" approach). Now where does the "Vegas model" come into play? Well, if you've ever been to a casino and you sat at a table for a while, you will eventually see the dealer clap her hands and leave. Why do dealers do this? Because the casinos want to address any possible collusion between a dealer and a customer.

How does this translate to cybersecurity? You know that after an attacker successfully exploits a vulnerability, they'll install a back door for continued access. The attacker knows it's only a matter of time until you get around to patching the vulnerability. The attacker will slowly explore your network and siphon off data. It can take months until they perform their ultimate goal. That said, in the typical approach, your system patch affects the original vulnerability and does nothing to the back door that's been installed. But in an immutable approach, you replace the server with a new instance from a patched server image, thus removing the vulnerability *and* the back door (assuming you do things properly!). You essentially "time out" your servers, just like Vegas times out casino dealers.

How is this done? It depends on how the provider exposes this functionality. Typically, you need to take advantage of the elasticity supplied by the cloud provider through the use of auto-scaling. You would state that you require, say, three identical web server instances running in an auto-scaling group (you can call this a cluster if you like). When the time comes (say, every 45 days), you would update the image with the latest patches (keep in mind that not all patches are security patches) and test the new image. Once you are happy with the image itself, you tell the system to use the new image, which should be used for the auto-scaling group, and blow away (terminate) a server. The auto-scaling group will detect that an instance is missing and will build a new server instance based on that new image. At that point, one of your server instances will be built from the new image. Do your real-life error monitoring, and assuming everything passes, you rinse and repeat until the entire group is running the newly patched image.

EXAM TIP   For the exam, remember that using an immutable approach enables you to perform the bulk of security tests on the images before they go into production.

Sounds simple, right? Well, it is—at the metastructure level. Your applications need to be able to deal with this immutability as well, and that's where things can become very complicated. For example, if you are using a single storage volume to host the operating system, application, and all the data, you're probably going to need to re-architect your applications so that data is written to a location other than the volume used to run the OS.

EXAM TIP   Here's the good news for your CCSK exam—you won't be asked about how this is done at the applistructure layer. You will be asked only about the metastructure (or virtual infrastructure) implementation.

The biggest "gotcha" in using an immutable approach? Manual changes made to instances. When you go immutable, you cannot allow any changes to be made directly to the running instances, because they will be blown away with the instances. Any and all changes must be made to the image, and then you deploy the image. To achieve this, you would disable any remote logins to the server instances.

I've provided an example of the pure definition of immutability. Of course, hybrid approaches can be taken, such as the preceding example, including pushing application updates via some form of a centralized system. In this case, the basic requirement of restricting access to the servers directly is still in place, and the security of the system is still addressed, because everything is performed centrally and people are restricted from making changes directly on the server in question.

There are also other security benefits of an immutable approach. For example, whitelisting applications and processes requires that nothing on the server itself be changed. As such, arming the servers with some form of file integrity monitoring should also be easier, because if anything changes, you know you probably have a security issue on your hands.

Requirements of Immutable Workloads

Now that you understand the immutable approach and its benefits, let's look at some of the requirements of this new approach.

First, you need a provider that supports this approach—but that shouldn't be an issue with larger IaaS providers. You also need a consistent approach to the process of creating images to account for patch and malware signature updates (although those could be performed separately, as discussed with the hybrid approach).

You also need to determine how security testing of the images themselves will be performed as part of the image creation and deployment process. This includes any source code testing and vulnerability assessments, as applicable. (You'll read more about this subject in Chapter 10.)

Logging and log retention will require a new approach as well. In an immutable environment, you need to get the logs off the servers as quickly as possible, because the servers can disappear on a moment's notice. This means you need to make sure that server logs are exported to an external collector as soon as possible.

All of these images need to have appropriate asset management. This may introduce increased complexity and additional management of the service catalog that maintains accurate information on all operational services and those being prepared to be run in production.

Finally, running immutable servers doesn't mean that you don't need to create a disaster recovery plan. You need to determine how you can securely store the images outside of the production environment. Using cross-account permissions, for example, you could copy an image to another account, such as a security account, for safekeeping. If your production environment is compromised by an attacker, they will probably delete not only your running instances but any images as well. But if you have copied these images elsewhere for safekeeping, you can quickly rebuild.

The Impact of the Cloud on Standard Workload Security Controls

With all the new approaches to running workloads beyond standard virtual machines, you'll want to be familiar with some changes to traditional security for your CCSK exam. Here is a list of potential challenges you will face in different scenarios:

- Implementing software agents (such as host-based firewalls) may be impossible, especially in a serverless environment (see Chapter 10).

- Even if running agents is possible, you need to ensure that they are lightweight (meaning they don't have a lot of overhead) and will work properly in a cloud environment (for example, they will keep up with auto-scaling). Remember that any application that relies on IP addresses to track systems (via either the agent side or the central console) is basically useless, especially in an immutable environment. CSA often refers to this as having an "ability to keep up with the rapid velocity of change" in a cloud environment. The bottom line is this: ask your current provider if they have "cloud versions" of their agents.

- By no means a cloud specific, agents shouldn't increase the attack surface of a server. Generally, the more ports that are open on a server, the larger the attack surface. Beyond this, if the agents consume configuration changes and/or signatures, you want to ensure that these are sourced from a trusted authoritative system such as your internal update servers.

- Speaking of using internal update services, there is little reason why these systems shouldn't be leveraged by the systems in a cloud environment. Consider how you do this today in your traditional environment. Do you have centralized management tools in every branch office, or do you have a central management console at the head office and have branch office computers update from that single source? For these update services, you can consider a cloud server instance in the same manner as a server running in a branch office, assuming, of course, you have appropriate network paths established.

Changes to Workload Security Monitoring and Logging

Both security monitoring and logging of virtual machines are impacted by the traditional use of IP addresses to identify machines; this approach doesn't work well in a highly dynamic environment like the cloud. Other technologies such as serverless won't work with traditional approaches at all, because they offer no ability to implement agents. This makes both monitoring and logging more challenging.

Rather than using IP addresses, you must be able to use some other form of unique identifier. This could, for example, involve collecting some form of tagging to track down systems. Such identifiers also need to account for the ephemeral nature of the cloud. Remember that this applies both to the agents and to the centralized console. Speak with your vendors to make sure that they have a cloud version that tracks systems by using something other than IP addresses.

The other big area that involves change is logging. I mentioned that logs should be taken off a server as soon as possible in a virtual server environment, but there's more to the story than just that. Logging in a serverless environment will likely require some form of logging being implemented in the code that you are running on the provider's servers. Also, you need to look at the costs associated with sending back potentially large amounts of traffic to a centralized logging system or security information and event management (SIEM) system. You may want to consider whether your SIEM vendor has a means to minimize the amount of network traffic this generates through the use of some kind of "forwarder" and ask for their recommendations regarding forwarding of log data. For example, does the vendor recommend that network flow logs not be sent to the centralized log system due to overhead? If network traffic costs are a concern (and when is cost of operations not a concern?), you may need to sit down and create a plan on what log data is truly required and what isn't.

Changes to Vulnerability Assessment

There are two approaches to performing vulnerability assessments (VAs). On one hand, some companies prefer to perform a VA from the viewpoint of an outsider, so they will place a scanner on the general Internet and perform their assessment with all controls (such as firewall, IPS, and so on) taken into consideration. Alternatively, some security professionals believe that a VA should be performed without those controls in place so that they can truly see all of the potential vulnerabilities in a system or application without a firewall hiding the vulnerabilities.

The CSA recommends that you perform a VA as close to the actual server as possible, and, specifically, VAs should focus on the image, not just the running instances. With this in mind, here are some specific recommendations from the CSA that you may need to know for your CCSK exam.

Providers will generally request that you notify them of any testing in advance. This is because the provider won't be able to distinguish whether the scanning is being performed by a "good guy" or a "bad guy." They'll want the general information that is normally requested for internal testing, such as where the test is coming from (such as the IP address of the test station, the target of the test, and the start time and end time). The provider may also throw in a clause stating that you are responsible for any damages you cause not just to your system but to the entire cloud environment. (Personally, I think the notion of a scan from a single test station taking out an entire cloud is highly unlikely, but if this is required, you'll probably want someone with authority to sign off on the test request.)

As for testing the cloud environment itself, forget about it. The CSP will limit you to your use of the environment only. A PaaS vendor will let you test your application code but won't let you test their platform. Same thing for SaaS—they won't allow you to test their application. When you think of it, it makes sense after all, because in either example, if you take down the shared component (platform in PaaS or application in SaaS), everyone is impacted, not just you.

Performing assessments with agents installed on the server is best. In the deny-by-default world that is the cloud, controls may be in place (such as SDN firewalls or security groups) that block or hide any vulnerabilities. Having the deny-by-default blocking potentially malicious traffic is great and all, but what if the security group assigned to the instances changes, or if the instances are accidentally opened for all traffic? This is why CSA recommends performing VAs as close to the workload as possible.

 TIP Regarding vulnerability assessments versus penetration testing: Generally, a VA is considered a test to determine whether there's a potential vulnerability, and a pentest will try to exploit any discovered potential vulnerabilities found. Quite often, the provider will not make a distinction between the two as far as approvals are concerned.

Chapter Review

This chapter covered virtualization of both networking and workloads and how security changes for both subjects that are used in a cloud environment. For your CCSK exam, you should be comfortable with the technologies discussed in both the networking (such as SDN) and compute (such as virtual machines and immutable servers) sections. Most importantly, you need to be aware of how security changes as a result of these new technologies. From a more granular perspective, remember the following for your CCSK exam:

- The cloud is always a shared responsibility, and the provider is fully responsible for building the physical aspects of a cloud environment.

- SDN networking should always be implemented by a cloud provider. A lack of a virtualized network means a loss of scalability, elasticity, orchestration, and, most importantly, isolation.

- Remember that the isolation capabilities of SDN allow for the creation of multiple accounts/segments to limit the blast radius of an incident impacting other workloads.

- CSA recommends that providers leverage SDN firewalls to implement a deny-by-default environment. Any activity that is not expressly allowed by a client will be automatically denied.

- Network traffic between workloads in the same virtual subnet should always be restricted by SDN firewalls (security groups) unless communication between systems is required. This is an example of microsegmentation to limit east–west traffic.

- Ensure that virtual appliances can operate in a highly dynamic and elastic environment (aka "keep up with velocity of change"). Just like physical appliances, virtual appliances can be bottlenecks and single points of failure if they're not implemented properly.

- For compute workloads, an immutable environment offers incredible security benefits. This approach should be leveraged by customers whenever possible.

- When using immutable servers, you can increase security by patching and testing images and replacing nonpatched instances with new instances built off the newly patched image.

- If using immutable servers, you should disable remote access and integrate file integrity monitoring because nothing in the running instances should change.

- Security agents should always be "cloud aware" and should be able to keep up with the rapid velocity of change (such as never use IP addresses as system identifiers).

- As a best practice, get logs off servers and on to a centralized location as quickly as possible (especially in an immutable environment), because all servers must be considered ephemeral in the cloud.

- Providers may limit your ability to perform vulnerability assessments and penetration testing, especially if the target of the scans is their platform.

Questions

1. When you're considering security agents for cloud instances, what should be a primary concern?

    A. The vendor has won awards.

    B. The vendor uses heuristic-based detection as opposed to signature-based detection.

    C. The vendor selected for cloud server instances is the same vendor you use for internal instances.

    D. The vendor agent does not use IP addresses to identify systems.

2. Which of the following is/are accurate statement(s) about the differences between SDN and VLAN?

    A. SDN isolates traffic, which can help with microsegmentation. VLANs segment network nodes into broadcast domains.

    B. VLANs have roughly 65,000 IDs, while SDN has more than 16 million.

    C. SDN separates the control plane from the hardware device and allows for applications to communicate with the control plane.

    D. All of the above are accurate statements.

3. When you're using immutable servers, how should administrative access to the applistructure be granted to make changes to running instances?

A. Administrative access should be limited to the operations team. This is in support of the standard separation of duties approach to security.

B. Administrative access should be limited to the development team. This is in support of the new approach to software development, where the developers own the applications they build.

C. Administrative access should be restricted for everyone. Any changes made at the applistructure level should be made to the image, and a new instance is created using that image.

D. Administrative access to the applistructure is limited to the provider in an immutable environment.

4. Which of the following is the main purpose behind microsegmentation?

A. It is a fine-grained approach to grouping machines to make them easier to administer.

B. It is a fine-grained approach to grouping machines that limits blast radius.

C. Microsegmentation can leverage traditional VLAN technology to group machines.

D. Microsegmentation implements a zero-trust network.

5. Which of the following statements is accurate when discussing the differences between a container and a virtual machine?

A. A container contains the application and required dependencies (such as libraries). A virtual machine contains the operating system, application, and any dependencies.

B. A virtual machine can be moved to and from any cloud service provider, while a container is tied to a specific provider.

C. Containers remove the dependency of a specific kernel. Virtual machines can run on any platform.

D. All of the above are accurate statements.

6. What is the main characteristic of the cloud that impacts workload security the most?

A. Software defined networks

B. Elastic nature

C. Multitenancy

D. Shared responsibility model

7. Select two attributes that a virtual appliance should have in a cloud environment.

   A. Auto-scaling

   B. Granular permissions for administrators

   C. Failover

   D. Ability to tie into provider's orchestration capability

8. Wendy wants to add an instance to her cloud implementation. When she attempts to add the instance, she is denied. She checks her permissions and nowhere does it say she is denied the permission to add an instance. What could be wrong?

   A. Wendy is trying to launch a Windows server but has permission to create only Linux instances.

   B. Wendy does not have root access to the Linux server she is trying to run.

   C. This is because of the deny-by-default nature of the cloud. If Wendy is not explicitly allowed to add an instance, she is automatically denied by default.

   D. Wendy is a member of a group that is denied access to add instances.

9. How is management centralized in SDN?

   A. By removing the control plane from the underlying networking appliance and placing it in the SDN controller

   B. By using northbound APIs that allow software to drive actions at the control layer

   C. By using southbound APIs that allow software to drive actions at the control layer

   D. SDN is a decentralized model

10. Before beginning a vulnerability assessment (VA) of one of your running instances, what should be done first?

    A. Select a VA product that works in a cloud environment.

    B. Determine whether a provider allows customers to perform a VA and if any advance notice is required.

    C. Open all SDN firewalls to allow a VA to be performed.

    D. Establish a time and date that you will access the provider's data center so you can run the VA on the physical server your instance is running on.

Answers

1. **D.** The best answer is that the agent does not use IP addressing as an identification mechanism. Server instances in a cloud can be ephemeral in nature, especially when immutable instances are used. All the other answers are optional in nature and not priorities for cloud security agents.

2. **D.** All of the answers are correct.

3. **C.** Administrative access to the servers in an immutable environment should be restricted for everyone. Any required changes should be made to an image, and that image is then used to build a new instance. All of the other answers are incorrect.

4. **B.** The best answer is that the purpose behind implementing microsegmentation is to limit the blast radius if an attacker compromises a resource. Using microsegmentation, you are able to take a very fine-grained approach to grouping machines (such as five web servers in the DMZ, but not every system in the DMZ, can communicate). This answer goes beyond answer D, that microsegmentation creates a "zero-trust" network, so B is the better and more applicable answer.

5. **A.** A container contains the application and required dependencies (such as libraries). A virtual machine contains the operating system, application, and any dependencies.

6. **C.** The best answer is that multitenancy has the greatest impact on cloud security, and for this reason, cloud providers need to make sure they have very tight controls over the isolation capabilities within the environment. Although the other answers have merit, none of them is the best answer.

7. **A, C.** Auto-scaling and failover are the two most important attributes that a virtual appliance should have in a cloud environment. Any appliance can become a single point of failure and/or a performance bottleneck, and these aspects must be addressed by virtual appliances in a cloud environment. Granular permissions are a good thing to have, but they are not cloud specific. Finally, tying into a provider's orchestration would be great, but this is not one of the two best answers. You may be thinking that elasticity is tying into the orchestration, and you would be correct. However, the degree of the integration isn't mentioned. For an example of orchestration, does the virtual appliance have the ability to change a firewall ruleset based on the actions of a user in the cloud or a particular API being called? That's the type of orchestration that would be ideal, but it requires the vendor to have very tight integration with a particular provider. This type of orchestration is usually native with the provider's services (for example, a security group can be automatically changed based on a particular action).

8. **C.** A cloud provider should take a deny-by-default approach to security. Therefore, it is most likely that Wendy is not explicitly allowed to launch an instance. Although it is possible that Wendy is also a member of a group that is explicitly denied access to launch an instance, C is the better answer. Metastructure permissions are completely different from operating system permissions, so A and B are incorrect answers.

9. **A.** SDN is centralized by taking the "brains" out of the underlying networking appliance and placing this functionality in the SDN controller. Answer B is a true statement in that northbound APIs allow applications (or software if you will)

to drive changes, but it does not answer the question posed. I suppose you could argue that C is also a true statement, but again, it doesn't answer the question posed.

10. **B.** You should determine whether your provider allows customers to perform a VA of their systems. If they don't and you haven't checked, you may find yourself blocked, because the provider won't know the source of the scan, which could be coming from a bad actor. An agent installed in the applistructure of a server will function regardless of whether the server is a virtual one in a cloud or a physical server in your data center. Opening all firewalls to perform a VA, answer C, would be a very unfortunate decision, because this may open all traffic to the world if it's done improperly (any IP address on the Internet could have access to any port on the instance, for example). Finally, you are highly unlikely to gain access to a provider's data center, yet alone be given permission to run a VA against any provider-owned and -managed equipment.

Virtualization and Containers

This chapter covers the following topics from Domain 8 of the CSA Guidance:

- Major Virtualization Categories
- Security of Compute Virtualization
- Security of Network Virtualization
- Security of Storage Virtualization
- Container Components
- Security of Containers and Related Components

Companies in every industry need to assume that a software revolution is coming.

—Marc Andreessen

Yes, the opening quote in this chapter is the same quote used in Chapter 7. I did this intentionally to highlight the fact that this chapter builds on the topic of the software revolution introduced in Chapter 7. It expands the discussion to address the security issues surrounding virtualization and the responsibility split between the provider and the customer. The material is presented in this fashion to provide consistency with the CSA Guidance and the CCSK exam. If a subject has been addressed as part of another chapter, however, I'll point you there as a refresher.

 NOTE As always, backgrounder material is included in this chapter to address any subject material that isn't covered as part of the CSA Guidance. This material is presented to improve your understanding of core technologies and concepts that the CSA Guidance assumes you already know; it's not required for the CCSK exam.

As you now know, virtualization is a core enabling technology in the cloud, and it's not just about virtual machines. Virtualization is how compute, network, and storage pools are created and is the enabling technology behind the multitenancy aspect of cloud services. In this chapter, we look at the responsibility split for securing various virtualized technologies—what to look for from the provider and what you need to do as the consumer. You'll also learn about the various components involved with containers and some approaches to securing them.

> **NOTE** Virtualization provides the abstraction needed for resource pools, which are then managed using orchestration. Without virtualization, there is no cloud.

Much of the security we use today in an IT world assumes that we have physical control of the underlying infrastructure. This hasn't changed; what has changed with the cloud is that the provider is responsible for securing the physical infrastructure. In addition, virtualization adds two new layers for security controls:

- Security of the virtualization technology itself, such as hypervisor security. This rests with the provider.
- Security controls for the virtual assets. The responsibility for implementing available controls rests with the customer. Exposing controls for the customers to leverage is the provider's responsibility.

Major Virtualization Categories Relevant to Cloud Computing

The main areas of virtualization that you need to know for your exam are straightforward: Compute, Network, Storage. Each of the three creates its own storage pools, and those pools are possible only as a result of virtualization; it makes sense, then, that these are areas of focus for the CCSK exam. The following sections will refresh your memory on each of these pools. Then I will cover how the CSA splits the security responsibilities of each technology.

Compute Virtualization

You know about virtual machines and hypervisors already, so consider this a refresher. Compute virtualization abstracts the running of code (including operating systems) from the underlying hardware. Instead of running code directly on the hardware, it runs on top of an abstraction layer (such as a hypervisor) that isolates (not just segregation!) one virtual machine (VM) from another. This enables multiple operating systems (guest OSs) to run on the same hardware.

> **EXAM TIP** For the exam, remember that compute virtualization abstracts the running of code (including operating systems) from the underlying hardware.

Although compute virtualization is generally tied to virtual machines, there is more to it than VMs (or, more appropriately, instances, when discussing the cloud). An older form of virtualization that you may be aware of is the Java Virtual Machine (JVM). Rather than go too deeply into JVMs, I'll limit this discussion by simply saying the JVM creates an environment for a Java application to run in. The JVM abstracts the underlying hardware from the application. This allows for more portability across hardware platforms, because the Java app does not need to communicate directly with the underlying hardware, only with the JVM. There are, of course, many other examples of virtualization out there, but the big takeaway is that virtualization performs abstraction.

NOTE Java Virtual Machines are called out in the CSA Guidance as a form of compute virtualization.

The next era of compute virtualization that needs to be addressed is about containers and serverless computing technologies. Both technologies also perform some form of compute abstraction. I cover serverless computing in greater depth in Chapter 14.

Cloud Provider Responsibilities

The primary security responsibilities of the cloud provider in compute virtualization are to enforce isolation and maintain a secure virtualization infrastructure. Isolation ensures that compute processes or memory in one virtual machine/container are not visible to another. This isolation supports a secure multitenant model, where multiple tenants can run processes on the same physical hardware (such as a single server). The cloud provider is also responsible for securing the underlying physical infrastructure and the virtualization technology from external attack or internal misuse. Like any other software, hypervisors need to be properly configured and will require the latest patches installed to address new security issues.

Cloud providers should also have strong security in place for all aspects of virtualization for cloud users. This means creating a secure chain of processes from the image (or other source) used to run the virtual machine all the way through a boot process, with security and integrity being top concerns. This ensures that tenants cannot launch machines based on images that they shouldn't have access to, such as those belonging to another tenant, and that when a customer runs a virtual machine (or another process), it is the one the customer expects to be running.

Finally, cloud providers should also assure customers that volatile memory is safe from unapproved monitoring, since important data could be exposed if another tenant, a malicious employee, or a bad actor is able to access running memory belonging to another tenant.

EXAM TIP Remember that volatile memory contains all kinds of potentially sensitive information (think unencrypted data, credentials, and so on) and must be protected from unapproved access. Volatile memory must also have strong isolation implemented and maintained by the provider.

Cloud Consumer Responsibilities

The primary responsibility of the cloud user is to implement security properly for everything deployed and managed in a cloud environment. Cloud customers should take advantage of the security controls exposed by their providers for managing their virtual infrastructures. Of course, there are no rules or regulations as to what a provider must offer customers, but some controls are usually offered.

Cloud providers offer security settings such as identity and access management (IAM) to manage virtual resources. When you're considering the IAM offered by the provider, remember that this is generally at the management plane, not the applistructure. In other words, we're talking about the ability for your organization's users accessing the management plane to be given the appropriate permissions required to start or stop an instance, for example, not log on to the server itself. For a refresher, review the "Securing the Management Plane" section in Chapter 6.

Cloud providers will also likely offer logging of actions performed at the metastructure layer and monitoring of workloads at the virtualization level. This can include the status of a virtual machine, performance (such as CPU utilization), and other actions and workloads.

IAM is as important in a cloud environment as it is in a traditional data center. Cloud compute deployments are based on master images—a virtual machine, container, or other code—that are then run as an instance in the cloud. Just as you would likely build a server in your data center by using a trusted, preconfigured image, you would do the same in a cloud environment. Some Infrastructure as a Service (IaaS) providers may have "community images" available. But unless they are supplied by a trusted source, I would be very hesitant to use these in a production environment, because they may not be inspected by the provider for malicious software or back doors being installed by a bad actor who's waiting for someone to use them. Managing images used by your organization is one of your most vital security responsibilities.

Another option that providers may offer is that of "dedicated instances" or "dedicated hosting." This usually comes at an increased cost, but it may be a useful option if the perceived risk of running a workload on hardware shared with another tenant is deemed unacceptable, or if there is a compliance requirement to run a workload on a single-tenant server.

TIP Dedicated instances may have various limitations associated with them. For one thing, although the workload may be running on single-tenant hardware, your data is likely stored in a multitenant storage environment. You may also have other technical restrictions in place, such as not all services being supported or available for dedicated instances. This area requires that you fully understand what the provider is really offering when they offer "dedicated" anything.

Finally, the customer is responsible for the security of everything within the workload itself. All the standard stuff applies here, such as starting with a secure configuration of the operating system, securing any applications, updating patches, using agents, and so on. The big difference for the cloud has to do with proper management of the images used to build running server instances as a result of the automation of cloud computing. It is easy to make the mistake of deploying older configurations that may not be patched or properly secured if you don't have strong asset management in place.

Other general compute security concerns include these:

- Virtualized resources tend to be more ephemeral and can change at a more rapid pace. Any corresponding security, such as monitoring, must keep up with the pace.

- Host-level monitoring/logging may not be available, especially for serverless deployments. Alternative log methods such as embedding logging into your applications may be required.

Network Virtualization

This section covers much of what was covered in Chapter 7, so I'm going to make this as brief as possible for you. You know there are multiple network virtualization technologies out there, ranging from virtual LANs (VLANs) to software defined networking (SDN). By now, you understand that "software-driven everything" is the way the industry is going. The software-driven aspect is a key contributor for the resource pooling, elasticity, and all other aspects that make the cloud work at the scale it does.

I'll be touching on a few items regarding security of virtual environments and will then cover the responsibilities of each party (provider and customer). First up is filtering and monitoring of virtual networks.

Filtering and Monitoring

If network traffic between two VMs never leaves a physical computer, is it inspected and filtered by an external physical firewall? It's not, so where does that leave us? We still have a requirement to perform inspection and filtering of network traffic, but we can no longer use the same security controls we have used in the past. Back in the early days of virtualization, some people thought it was a good idea to send all virtual network traffic out of the virtual environment, inspect the traffic using a physical firewall, and then reintroduce it back to the virtual network. Newer virtual approaches to address this problem could include routing the virtual traffic to a virtual inspection machine on the same physical server or routing the network traffic to a virtual appliance on the same virtual network. Both approaches are feasible, but they still introduce bottlenecks and require less efficient routing.

Remember that all is not lost. The provider will most likely offer some form of filtering capability, be it through the use of an SDN firewall or within the hypervisor.

 NOTE Remember that any appliance, virtual or physical, can be a bottleneck and/or a single point of failure.

From a network monitoring perspective, don't be surprised if you can't get the same level of detail about network traffic from the provider that you had in the past in your own environment. This is because the cloud platform/provider may not support access for direct network monitoring. They will state that this is because of complexity and cost. Access to raw packet data will be possible only if you collect it yourself in the host or by using a virtual appliance. This accounts only for network traffic that is directed to, or originates from, a system that you control. In other environments, such as systems managed by the provider, you will not be able to gain access to monitor this network traffic, because this would be a security issue for the provider.

Management Infrastructure

By default, the virtual network management plane is available to the entire world, and if it's accessed by bad actors, they can destroy the entire virtual infrastructure in a matter of seconds via an API or web access. It is therefore paramount that this management plane be properly secured. See "Securing the Management Plane" in Chapter 6 if you need a refresher on this critical subject.

Cloud Provider Responsibilities

As with compute virtualization in a cloud environment, virtual networks have a shared responsibility. I'll begin with the responsibilities of the provider and then move to the customer responsibilities for network virtualization.

The absolute top security priority is segregation and isolation of network traffic to prevent tenants from viewing another tenant's traffic. At no point should one tenant ever be able to see traffic from another tenant unless this is explicitly allowed by both parties (via cross-account permissions, for example). This is the most foundational security control for any multitenant network.

Next, packet sniffing (such as using Wireshark), even within a tenant's own virtual networks, should be disabled to reduce the ability of an attacker to compromise a single node and use it to monitor the network, which is common in traditional networks. This is not to say that customers cannot use some packet-sniffing software on a virtual server, but it means the customers should be able to see traffic sent only to a particular server.

In addition, all virtual networks should offer built-in firewall capabilities for cloud users without the need for host firewalls or external products. The provider is also responsible for detecting and preventing attacks on the underlying physical network and virtualization platform. This includes perimeter security of the cloud itself.

Cloud Consumer Responsibilities

The consumer is ultimately responsible for adhering to their own security requirements. Quite often, this will require consuming and configuring security controls that are created and managed by the cloud provider, especially any virtual firewalls. Here are several recommendations for consumers when it comes to securing network virtualization.

Take advantage of new network architecture possibilities. For example, compartmentalizing application stacks in their own isolated virtual networks to enhance security can be performed at little to no cost (aside from operational costs, which will likely go up). Such an implementation may be cost prohibitive in a traditional physical network environment.

Next, software defined infrastructure (SDI) includes the ability to create templates of network configurations. You can essentially take a known-good network environment and save it as software. This approach enables you to rebuild an entire network environment incredibly quickly if needed. You can also use these templates to ensure that your network settings remain in a known-good configuration.

Finally, when the provider doesn't expose appropriate controls for customers to meet their own security requirements, customers will need to implement additional controls (such as virtual appliances or host-based security controls) to meet their requirements.

Cloud Overlay Networks

I'm including this section because I want to make sure the mappings to the actual CSA Guidance document remain intact. Like much of the content of this chapter, cloud overlay networks were covered in Chapter 7. It's important for you to remember that cloud overlay networks are a function of the Virtual Extensible LAN (VXLAN) technology, and they enable a virtual network to span multiple physical networks across a wide area network (WAN). This is possible because VXLAN encapsulates packets in a routable format. Note that the CSA Guidance specifically states that this technology is beyond the scope of the necessary material and it will therefore not be part of your CCSK exam.

Storage Virtualization

Storage virtualization sounds like new technology, but it really isn't: I present to you, by way of example, the classic redundant array of independent disks (RAID), a storage virtualization method that has been around for many years (since the 1970s) and can be implemented in any operating system today. I'm going to spare you a discussion of the various RAID levels, but I am going to say that RAID 0 (stripe set), for example, enables you to take three 1TB hard drives and make them look like a single 3TB hard drive. What could you call that? How about a pool of storage? Yes, that should work. Using software RAID, you virtualize your storage by joining drives together virtually to form a storage pool. (This example is courtesy of Windows NT in the mid-'90s—look it up if you need to.)

You know that the concept of storage virtualization has been around for quite a while, but how is it done in a cloud environment? Well, chances are pretty good that providers aren't using just a general-purpose server with a handful of drives installed (aka direct attached storage using "just a bunch of drives"). They are likely using network attached storage (NAS) or storage area networks (SANs) to form these pools. As SAN is often a bit of a gray area for many people, the next section is a high-level backgrounder on the subject. If you are familiar with SAN, or you just don't care, you can skip it.

Storage Area Network Backgrounder

Research shows that SANs account for about two-thirds of the network storage market. The key word here is "network." The SAN is a dedicated network of storage devices. It is a combination of hardware and software that offers a block-level storage mechanism.

It doesn't offer a file system, but it stores and send blocks of data as requested by authorized servers. As such, it cannot be accessed directly by a user on a workstation; like most everything virtualized, the access is abstracted, and actions are orchestrated.

From a high-level architectural perspective, the SAN reference architecture can generally be divided into three layers: host layer, fabric layer, and storage layer. Figure 8-1 shows the three layers typically involved in a SAN.

Each layer serves a specific purpose:

- **Host layer** This is where servers (or hosts) take calls from the local area network (LAN) and enable access to/from the underlying SAN fabric.
- **Fabric layer** This is where all the networking components live. SAN network devices include switches, routers, bridges, gateways, and even cables.
- **Storage layer** As you can imagine, this is where the actual storage devices live. Direct physical communication generally (still!) occurs using Small Computer System Interface (SCSI).

SAN uses its own protocols to do its job. These protocols are Fibre Channel, Fibre Channel over Ethernet (FCoE), Internet SCSI (iSCSI), and InfiniBand. All of these are purpose-built to transfer blocks of data at high speeds and have higher throughput than Transmission Control Protocol (TCP) networks do. Fibre Channel is considered the most popular protocol in large SAN environments, with some reports stating that up to 80 percent of the SANs in use today use Fibre Channel, whose speeds can theoretically reach up to 128 Gbps.

As the name might imply, Fibre Channel uses fiber-optic cables. To connect to the SAN, host bus adapters (HBAs) or converged network adapters (CNAs) are used. Both of these network cards will have a fiber-optic connector. The CNA will have both a fiber-optic connector and a standard Ethernet network adapter.

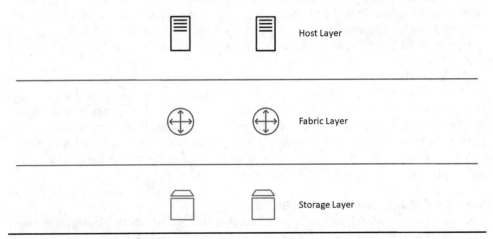

Figure 8-1 Three layers of a SAN

To minimize expense and additional optical network cables from being required, companies may opt to use standard Ethernet to transmit SAN traffic in a *converged network*. The two main protocols that allow for this are FCoE and iSCSI. Both encapsulate SCSI commands in an Ethernet frame and use standard Ethernet cables for transport. iSCSI is generally considered useful in smaller environments, but it's not appropriate for high-volume SANs.

Logical Unit Numbers Now that you know the high-level architecture of a SAN and some of the components and the protocols used in storage virtualization, let's look at another SAN item that you should be aware of: the *logical unit number* (LUN). A LUN is assigned to every drive and partition in a SAN. Let's say, for example, that you have a large SAN that's 1000TB in size. You don't want everyone in your company (or cloud) to have access to a 1000TB drive that everything is just dumped into. Instead, you want to divide that large SAN into smaller 1TB volumes. You would do this by creating the 1TB logical volumes and associating a LUN to them so they can be accessed (and controlled, which you'll see in a little bit). The LUN is used to present a logical drive to a host server, giving the host abstracted access to a reserved space in a pool of storage.

 NOTE LUN is not just a SAN thing. The concept of LUNs goes back to the SCSI technology standard that defines how storage is accessed, so it is applicable in many forms of storage, be it storage arrays from the '90s all the way up to the latest SAN technology.

You may wonder how you would limit access to these virtual drives to appropriate requestors. The answers for restricting access to storage come in zoning and LUN masking.

Zoning allows for a logical grouping of ports or nodes that restricts certain hosts to accessing only specified storage devices. This is usually configured on the Fibre Channel switch in the SAN fabric. In an FCoE implementation, this would be performed in the same manner as a VLAN. There are two different ways to set up zoning, soft zoning and hard zoning:

- Soft zoning is performed in software on the Fibre Channel switches to prevent ports from being seen from outside of their assigned zones. The security issue with soft zoning is that views are filtered and not physically blocked. Therefore, unauthorized ports can be accessed if a Fibre Channel address is spoofed.

- Hard zoning implements restrictions in hardware and physically blocks access to a zone from any unauthorized device. Hard zoning is considered the more secure approach to block communication between devices not in the same zone.

LUN masking is performed in addition to the zoning to provide additional security to the storage environment. Remember that zoning establishes which hosts and storage devices are grouped together, and it restricts access to zone members. However, as you know, a storage device could contain multiple logical drives. LUN masking is used to identify the virtual drives that can be accessed within a zone. LUN masking can be performed at the host bus adapter (HBA) of a host server or on a storage controller. From a security perspective (because of spoofing), it is generally considered that LUN masking should be enforced at the storage controller.

Storage Virtualization Security

Most cloud platforms use highly redundant and durable storage mechanisms that make multiple copies of data and spread those copies across multiple storage locations. This is called *data dispersion*. This approach enables the provider to offer incredible levels of resiliency (some providers even offer "11 9's," or 99.999999999 percent, resiliency SLAs).

NOTE Resiliency and availability aren't the same thing. Data can be inaccessible if the network is down. The data is still there (resiliency), but it cannot be accessed (availability).

Providers will usually encrypt all customer data at the physical level, which doesn't protect data at the virtual level, but does protect data on a drive that is decommissioned and is awaiting destruction (and, of course, it protects the data if the drive is stolen by a rogue administrator).

I will address additional security measures that customers can use (such as encryption, access controls, and more) to protect stored data in Chapter 11.

Containers

In Chapter 7, I mentioned that containers could help address portability but that this technology relies on more than just source code and that all components need to be properly secured. This section covers the various components of a container system and the high-level security recommendations from the CSA. Note that although container technology is fairly mature, it is a rapidly evolving technology.

You know that containers are a compute virtualization technology and that they differ from virtual machines in that only the application and required dependencies are bundled in a container, which is then run in an isolated user space on a shared kernel. Containers can run directly on a physical server (even a laptop), or they can run in a virtual machine.

NOTE A container is an abstraction at the application layer that isolates software from its environment. Containers don't necessarily provide full-stack security isolation, but they do provide task segregation. On the other hand, virtual machines typically do provide security isolation. You can put tasks of equivalent security context on the same set of physical or virtual hosts to provide greater security segregation.

Container systems always have the following components:

- **Container**   This is the execution environment itself. The container provides code running inside a restricted environment with access only to the processes and capabilities defined in the container configuration via a configuration file (covered later in this chapter). While a VM is a full abstraction of an operating system, a container is a constrained place to run segregated processes while still utilizing the kernel and other capabilities of the base OS.

- **Engine**   Also referred to as the *container runtime*, this is the environment on top of which a container is run. A very popular example of a container runtime is Docker Engine. This isn't to say it's the only container runtime, but it is arguably the first container runtime (as we know containers today) and it is the most well-known.

- **Orchestration and scheduling controller**   Container orchestration deals with managing the lifecycle of containers. Orchestration deals with items such as provisioning and deployment of containers, scaling, movement of containers, and container health monitoring. When a container needs to be deployed, the orchestration tool schedules the deployment and identifies an appropriate system to run the container on. It knows how to deploy and manage containers based on a configuration file that tells the orchestration software where to find the container image (repository) and configuration items such as networking, mounting of storage space, and where to store container logs. Examples of container orchestration and scheduling tools include Kubernetes and Docker Swarm.

- **Image repository**   This is where all of the images and code that can be deployed as containers are stored. Docker Hub is a popular example of a container image repository. Image repositories can be public or private.

 EXAM TIP   For image repository, I'm using the naming used in the CSA Guidance, but you should know about two related concepts—image registries and image repositories. An *image registry* is used to host and distribute images. An *image repository* is technically different, because it is defined as a collection of related images. Long story short, this means that an image registry can contain multiple repositories. You'll often see these terms used interchangeably. Your CCSK exam will use the term "image repository."

Keeping all of these elements in mind, I hope you can appreciate how there may be some proprietary dependencies in place that make portability a bit more difficult than you may have expected. For example, what about moving a container from Windows to Linux runtimes (and vice versa)? What if you presently use Kubernetes as the orchestration and scheduling service and then decide to use a cloud provider's orchestration service instead? Are the runtimes backward-compatible? As I said, a container can help with portability, but it isn't a guaranteed magic bullet for portability.

Container Definitions Backgrounder

As you know, containers are built and managed according to a definition file you create. The definition file is passed to a service (daemon) to build an image so it is properly allocated resources and other configuration settings are implemented.

 NOTE Container definition files are not in the CSA Guidance and therefore will not be covered in your CCSK exam. They are covered here to give you a better understanding of how containers are configured and managed.

Following is a list of some of the available options in configuration files used by Amazon Elastic Container Service (Amazon ECS) to build and manage containers:

- **Name** The name of the container
- **Image** The name of the image in the repository that should be used to build the container
- **Memory** The amount of memory to be allocated to the container
- **Port mappings** The required network ports for the container
- **Protocol** The required network protocol (TCP or UDP)
- **Health checks** Monitors the health of the container; if the container is unreachable, it is removed and replaced
- **CPU** The required CPU capacity of the container
- **Working directory** The directory in the container where commands are run
- **Secrets** Credential storage location outside of the container
- **DNS servers** A list of DNS servers for the container to use
- **Mount points** Supplies data volumes
- **Log configuration** Where the container should store logs
- **User** The username to use in the container; the "privileged" user can run everything as root (administrator)

Now you should have a pretty good idea of how containers are built and how the orchestration and scheduling service launches and maintains containers. Again, you won't be tested on any of these items.

Container Security Recommendations

As I mentioned, container technology is maturing, but many products out there have their own security requirements. Following is a list of security recommendations from the CSA as to general security best practices that you should consider when deploying container technology internally or within a cloud environment:

- **Securing the underlying infrastructure**   Security always begins in the container, and in a cloud environment, this is the provider's responsibility. Just as the provider is responsible for security of the physical infrastructure and the hypervisors in a virtual machine world, the provider is responsible for the physical infrastructure and the container platform hosting consumer containers.

- **Securing the orchestration and scheduling service**   You know that orchestration and scheduling are critical components of container deployments and management. CSA Guidance refers to this as the "management plane" for containers.

- **Securing the image repository**   The image repository for containers can be considered in the same way as images for virtual machines. Images need to be stored in a secure location, and appropriate access controls should be configured to ensure that only approved access is granted to modify images or configuration files.

- **Securing the tasks/code in the container**   Containers hold software code. Weak application security will be weak regardless of whether it is run in a container or on a VM. Weak security isn't limited to the code in the container; it can also apply to the definition files you read about in the "Container Definitions Backgrounder." Appropriate network ports, file storage, secrets, and other settings can increase security of the container environment and therefore the application as a whole.

NOTE   These are general best practices. Always consult vendor documentation for the latest product-dependent security recommendations. Check out the Cloud Security Alliance web site for more in-depth container security recommendations, such as the "Best Practices for Implementing a Secure Application Container Architecture." Also, the Center for Internet Security provides industry recommendations on securing specific products such as Docker and Kubernetes.

A final takeaway for security of a container environment is that tools will offer varying degrees of security. At a bare minimum, all products should have strong access controls and authentication capabilities. They should also support secure configurations that isolate file system, process, and network access.

Chapter Review

This chapter expanded on the coverage related to the virtualization of Compute, Network, and Storage. It also included additional information on the security responsibilities split between the providers and customers. As always, backgrounder information was included to address any knowledge gaps that you may have, but that information will not be part of your exam.

When preparing for your CCSK exam, make sure you are comfortable with the following items:

- Cloud providers must make strong isolation of workloads their primary duty.

- Providers are responsible for all physical security and any virtualization technologies that customers use. They must keep hypervisors secured and implement any required security patches.

- Providers must implement all customer-managed virtualization features with a "secure-by-default" (aka deny-by-default) configuration.

- Providers must ensure that any volatile memory is properly secured to prevent unintended access by other tenants or administrators.

- Providers must implement strong networking controls to protect customers at the physical level as well as virtual networking the customers cannot control.

- Providers must isolate virtual network traffic, even when networks are controlled by the same customer.

- Providers must secure the physical storage system in use. This can include encryption at the physical layer to prevent data exposure during drive replacements.

- Consumers always need to know what security is offered by the provider and what they need to do in order to meet their own security requirements.

- For container security, remember that all the various components (engine, orchestration, and repository) need to be properly secured.

- Containers offer application isolation, but not complete isolation. Containers with similar security requirements should be grouped together and run on the same physical or virtual host to provide greater security segregation.

- Proper access controls and strong authentication should be in place for all container components.

- Ensure that only approved, known, and secure container images or code can be deployed.

Questions

1. Why must the provider encrypt hard drives at the physical layer?

   A. It prevents data from being compromised as a result of theft.

   B. It prevents data from being accessed by others via the virtual layer.

   C. It prevents data from being compromised after the drive is replaced.

   D. Answers A and C are correct.

2. How do containers perform isolation?

   A. They perform application layer isolation.

   B. They perform isolation at all layers like a virtual machine does.

   C. They perform isolation of the repository.

   D. All of the above are correct.

3. Which of the following is the number one security priority for a cloud service provider?

   A. Implementing SDN firewalls for customers

   B. Isolating tenant access to pools of resources

   C. Securing the network perimeter

   D. Offering network monitoring capability to customers

4. Which of the following are examples of compute virtualization?

   A. Containers

   B. Cloud overlay networks

   C. Software templates

   D. A and C

5. Nathan is trying to troubleshoot an issue with a packet capture tool on a running instance. He notices clear-text FTP usernames and passwords in the captured network traffic that is intended for another tenant's machine. What should Nathan do?

   A. This is normal behavior in a cloud. He should contact the other tenant and advise them that using clear-text credentials in a cloud is a bad idea.

   B. Nathan should contact the other tenant and submit his finding for a bug bounty.

   C. This is not possible because FTP is prohibited in a cloud environment.

   D. He should contact the provider and advise them that he will be canceling his use of their cloud services because the provider has failed to isolate the network.

6. What is/are benefits of a virtual network compared to physical networks?

   A. You can compartmentalize application stacks in their own isolated virtual networks, which increases security.

   B. An entire virtual network can be managed from a single management plane.

   C. Network filtering in a physical network is easier.

   D. All of the above are true.

7. How is a storage pool created?

   A. The provider uses direct storage with a bunch of hard drives attached to a server.

   B. The provider uses a storage area network.

   C. The provider uses a NAS.

   D. The provider builds the storage pool however they want.

8. A provider wants to ensure that customer data is not lost in the event of drive failure. What should the provider do?

   A. Use a SAN and copy the data across multiple drives in a storage controller.

   B. Replicate the data to an offshore third party.

   C. Make multiple copies of the data and store the copies on multiple storage locations.

   D. Store client data using solid state drives (SSDs).

9. Why is volatile memory a security concern for providers?

   A. It isn't. Volatile memory protection is the customer's responsibility.

   B. Volatile memory may contain unencrypted information.

   C. Volatile memory may contain credentials.

   D. B and C are correct.

10. Which of the following components in a container environment require access control and strong authentication?

    A. Container runtime

    B. Orchestration and scheduling system

    C. Image repository

    D. All of the above

Answers

1. **D.** Answers A and C are correct. Providers encrypt hard drives so that the data cannot be read if the drive is stolen or after it is replaced. Encryption at the physical layer does not protect data that is requested via the virtual layer.

2. **A.** Containers perform isolation only at the application layer. This is unlike a virtual machine that can offer isolation for all layers. Repositories require appropriate controls to be put in place to restrict unauthorized access to the code and configuration files held within.

3. **B.** The top priority for providers is ensuring that they implement strong isolation capabilities. All of the other answers are possible priorities, but B is the best answer.

4. **A.** Of the list presented, only containers can be considered as compute virtualization. Software templates are used to build an entire environment quickly. Although you could use these templates in infrastructure as code (IaC) to build or deploy containers and VMs, this is not considered a compute virtualization. A cloud overlay network enables a virtual network to span multiple physical networks.

5. **D.** Nathan is able to see network traffic destined for other machines, so there has been a failure of network isolation, and this should be the provider's top security priority. If I were Nathan, I would change cloud providers as soon as possible. All the other answers are not applicable (although writing a bunch of screen captures to the other tenant's FTP directory to advise them of their exposure would be pretty funny).

6. **A.** The only accurate answer listed is that virtual networks can be compartmentalized, and this can increase security; this is expensive, if not impossible, in a physical network. SDN can offer a single management plane for physical network appliances, and the "ease" of filtering is quite subjective. Filtering in a virtual network is different, but it may or may not be more difficult.

7. **D.** It is completely up to the provider as to how they build a storage pool. They can use any of the other technologies listed in the answers, or they can use something completely different and proprietary.

8. **C.** To offer increased resiliency, the provider should make multiple copies of customer data and store copies across multiple storage locations. Answer A looks good, but it's not the best answer, because a SAN is not required and, more importantly, writing data to multiple drives in the same controller will not protect against the single point of failure in the controller (or the controller corrupting the data). Finally, we haven't discussed the difference between "normal" magnetic storage drives versus solid state drives, but SSDs can fail just like magnetic ones, so D isn't the best answer either.

9. **D.** The correct answer is that volatile memory can contain sensitive information such as credentials and data that needs to be unencrypted in order to be processed. Both the provider and the customer play a role in ensuring security related to volatile memory. The provider needs to ensure that volatile memory from one tenant is never seen by another tenant (an even better way to think of it is that one workload shouldn't have access to another workload). The customer needs to make sure that volatile memory is wiped from a system prior to it being imaged. This can be achieved by rebooting the instance prior to creating the image.

10. **D.** Yes, all of the above is the right choice this time. But wait! There's a good story here that I'm including for those of you still with me. In February 2018, Tesla (the car company) was breached. Thankfully for Tesla, the attackers only wanted

to use Tesla cloud resources for bitcoin mining. How was Tesla breached? Was it a zero-day attack? Was it advanced state-sponsored agents? Nope! Its container orchestration software (Kubernetes in this case) was accessible from the Internet and didn't require a password to access it! Not only did this give the attackers the ability to launch their own containers, paid for courtesy of Tesla, but inside the Kubernetes system was a secrets area that had Amazon S3 keys stored in it. The keys were used to access nonpublic information from Tesla. Again, container security involves much more than just application security within a container.

Incident Response

This chapter covers the following topics from Domain 9 of the CSA Guidance:
- Incident Response Lifecycle
- How the Cloud Impacts Incident Response

Strategy without tactics is the slowest route to victory. Tactics without strategy is the noise before defeat.

—Sun Tzu

I suppose I could have used the quote, "If you fail to plan, you plan to fail," but the type of strategy Sun Tzu is referring to—military strategy—is close to what we must follow when dealing with incident response (IR). You need to make the plan and then test the plan often in preparation for an incident. Incident response needs to be planned and practiced for when, not if, things go wrong. Have you ever heard of any preventative control that has been 100 percent successful in stopping every attack? You haven't, because it doesn't exist. And there are more incident types to consider than just intentional attacks. How many times have you heard of "human error" being blamed for an incident? Never forget that incidents can be caused accidentally as well as intentionally. Your IR strategy needs to address all of these cases.

Most organizations have IR plans in place, which is great. I wonder, though, how many companies have extended these plans to include their cloud systems and how many are considering the changes in response capabilities, forensics collection, and governance changes. Remember that you need virtual tools (software) for a virtual world in the cloud. You're not plugging in a dongle to a machine to perform a bit-level copy of a hard drive anymore, for example. Your IR plans may be extended to include cloud services, but what about the people and the processes cloud services depend on? Are the people trained in IR with regard to a particular cloud environment? Do the IR processes address cloud-specific opportunities and challenges equal to those addressed in a traditional data center? These are the types of gaps this chapter attempts to address while preparing you for your CCSK exam. A well-prepared and practiced strategy is everything, and without it, your tactics will consist of a bunch of people running around with their hair on fire, probably just making the situation even worse. Be like Sun Tzu and prepare.

This chapter leverages the existing IR lifecycle as promoted by NIST in SP 800-61 Rev 2. You can also check out other standard frameworks, published in ISO/IEC 27035 and the European Network and Information Security Agency (ENISA) publication "Strategies for Incident Response and Cyber Crisis Cooperation," if you're so inclined.

Incident Response Lifecycle

The IR lifecycle in the CSA Guidance is drawn from the document "Computer Security Incident Handling Guide" (NIST 800-61r2). As Figure 9-1 shows, there are four phases of the IR lifecycle: preparation; detection and analysis; containment, eradication, and recovery; and post-incident activity.

Before we get to the CCSK material, I need to define what an incident actually is and why computer security IR is quite different from business IR, with a backgrounder on incidents and events.

NOTE As always, backgrounder material is included in this chapter to address any subject material that isn't covered as part of the CSA Guidance. This material is presented to improve your understanding of core technologies and concepts that the CSA Guidance assumes you already know; it's not required for the CCSK exam.

Incident and Event Backgrounder

Although the rest of the chapter is obviously focused on IR in the cloud, I first need to clearly define a couple of terms with definitions from ITIL.

NOTE If you're unaware of ITIL, it's an organization that focuses on continuous improvement of IT service management. Basically, ITIL describes a framework of best practices for delivering IT services. ITIL provides the language used by many business executives and owners relating to IT. The latest version, ITIL 4, was released in 2019.

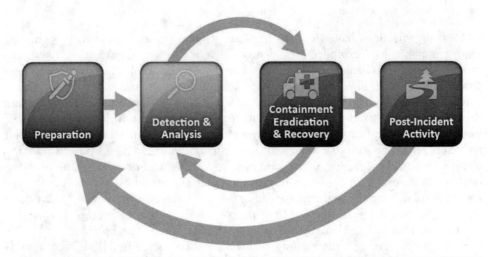

Figure 9-1 NIST incident response lifecycle. (Source: NIST 800-61r2.)

- **Event**   An event is a "change of state that has significance for the management of an IT service or other configuration item (CI)." What's a configuration item? It can be confusing, but a CI is basically anything that needs to be managed in order to deliver an IT service. This includes software, infrastructure, processes, and other things.

- **Incident**   An incident is defined as "an unplanned interruption to an IT service, or a reduction in the quality of service." Failure of a configuration item that has not yet affected service is also an incident. What does that mean? Here's an example: You have multiple read replicas (copies, essentially) of a database, and one of those replicas fails. This is an incident, because even though a service hasn't been interrupted or degraded, you still need to act on the fact that your replicas aren't working as they should, and that may impact availability down the road.

All incidents are events, but not all events are incidents. In other words, if you don't have event management in place, you'll never be able to declare an incident. Incident management analyzes those events. If an event is qualified as an incident, incident response kicks in.

Now what does ITIL say about state-sponsored attackers from the other side of the world stealing corporate intellectual property? Nothing. As security professionals, we look at everything as a security incident, but that's not the case with a standard ITIL definition of IR. Is a physical component failing and thus making a service unavailable an incident? Well, it's an unplanned interruption, so, yes, it's an incident. How about an overseas attacker grabbing 5TB of data from our storage in the cloud? Hmm.... Seems to me that the ITIL definition needs some improvement—or we have to change our focus to computer security incident response and computer security incident response teams (CSIRTs).

So there's a difference between the business world's definition and the security world's definition of "incident" and the different teams and disciplines required for both. Let's get back to our regularly scheduled IR in the cloud discussion now, with a high-level description of each phase in the IR lifecycle, and then we'll move on to how IR in the cloud changes at each phase.

   NOTE   The highlighted activities in the following phases are from the CSA Guidance. The guidance calls out a few items but is not an exhaustive list of activities in each phase. Feel free to consult NIST 800-61r2 for a more extensive list.

Preparation Phase

Preparation is where the battle is won or lost before it begins. In other words, it is in the preparation phase that a company establishes its computer security IR capability and creates a CSIRT so that the company is properly equipped and ready to respond to incidents.

Following are the required elements listed in the CSA Guidance for this phase:

- Process to handle the incidents
- Handler communications and facilities
- Incident analysis hardware and software
- Internal documentation (port lists, asset lists, network diagrams, current baselines of network traffic)
- Training identification
- Evaluation of infrastructure by proactive scanning and network monitoring, vulnerability assessments, and performing risk assessments
- Subscription to third-party threat intelligence services

I'm going to summarize this list with another Sun Tzu quote: "Know yourself and you will win all battles." In other words, know your assets and your weaknesses and have knowledgeable people both internally (CSIRT) and externally (third-party threat intelligence services), and you will be well prepared.

Detection and Analysis Phase

This phase is all about the telemetry (logging, monitoring, metrics, alerts, and other messages) you get from systems and other IT components. As you just learned, there's a difference between ITIL incident response and computer security incident response. Here's an area that highlights the different approaches. Simply looking at CPU usage and other generic telemetry is insufficient to detect attacks. The CSIRT needs security-specific detection and analysis tools.

The following tasks are recommended as part of the CSA Guidance:

- Form a system of alerts, including endpoint protection, network security monitoring, host monitoring, account creation, privilege escalation, other indicators of compromise, SIEM, security analytics (baseline and anomaly detection), and user behavior analytics.
- Validate alerts (reducing false positives) and escalation.
- Estimate the scope of an incident.
- Assign an incident manager who will coordinate further actions.
- Designate a person who will communicate the incident containment and recovery status to senior management.
- Build a timeline of the attack.
- Determine the extent of the potential data loss.
- Set up notification and coordination activities.

Containment, Eradication, and Recovery Phase

This is the battle part of IR. It shows you just how prepared you actually are, not how prepared you assumed you were.

First, you must contain the attack by taking systems offline. Consider data loss versus service availability. Ensure that systems don't destroy themselves upon detection. Next, eradication and recovery involve cleaning up compromised devices and restoring systems to normal operation. Confirm that systems are functioning properly. Deploy controls to prevent similar incidents. Finally, document the incident and gather evidence (chain of custody).

Post-Incident Activity Phase

Did you ever watch the original *Star Trek* series on TV? Remember the guys in the red shirts (security detail) who would beam down to a planet and get crushed by some green alien with a huge rock? That's what comes to mind whenever I think of postmortem meetings. (In fact, I wore a red shirt to one just for fun. Nobody in the meeting got the significance, but that's okay.) These post-incident meetings are meant to help everyone learn about possible IR process improvements; unfortunately, they always seem to wind up being a blame game. Rather than casting blame, ask the following questions:

- What could have been done better?
- Could the attack have been detected sooner?
- What additional data would have been helpful to isolate the attack faster?
- Does the IR process need to change? If so, how?

The Five Whys Backgrounder

Not that this will be on your exam, but have you ever heard of the "Five Whys" approach to getting to the bottom of an incident (aka, finding the root cause)? The following example is taken from an accident that happened at an Amazon fulfillment center, where an employee was hurt (thumb injury) on the job:

Why 1: Why did the associate damage his thumb?
Answer 1: Because his thumb got caught in the conveyor.
Why 2: Why did his thumb get caught in the conveyor?
Answer 2: Because he was chasing his bag, which was on the conveyor.
Why 3: Why was he chasing his bag?
Answer 3: Because he placed his bag on the conveyor and it turned on by surprise.
Why 4: Why was his bag on the conveyor?
Answer 4: Because he used the conveyor as a table.

- **Root Cause:** The associate used the conveyor because he didn't have a table.
- **Solution:** Provide tables at work stations for associates.

Now in this case, it took four whys to get to the root cause, but it should never take more than five whys to get there. Try it next time you're in a postmortem meeting (and wear a red shirt).

How the Cloud Impacts Incident Response

The cloud will introduce change at every phase of the IR lifecycle. It may change by having to contact your provider if the incident impacts something they are responsible for, or it may change the processes used for a configuration item you are responsible for. Either way, you need to prepare for IR in a cloud environment.

Preparation

You know that governance is going to change in a cloud environment. Governance and related service level agreements (SLAs) are the first areas that need to be addressed. What SLAs are in place with your provider(s), and how is communication with the provider achieved? Here are some key questions you should ask about your cloud provider's IR support:

- Who is responsible for IR and in which scenarios? In other words, how are responsibilities allocated between the CSP and its customers?
- What are the points of contact? If an incident occurs, does the CSP know who to contact, can your organization call someone at the CSP, do they offer e-mail support, or do they provide access to a discussion forum? Is a contact available 24×7 or just during business hours?
- How long does the CSP have to respond to you after an incident occurs? Is it ten minutes? Ten hours? Ten days?
- What are the CSP's escalation procedures?
- Is out-of-band communication possible if networks are down?
- How do hand-offs work between the customer IR team and that of the provider?
- Does the customer have access to data and logs to support IR? Which data and logs are included?
- Are logs available in a format that your IR team can easily access using their own tools, or do you require access to the provider's tools to access them?
- Under what circumstances does the CSP alert customers of an ongoing incident? What are their SLA requirements for such notification?
- Does the CSP have a dedicated IR team?

(I have consulted in multibillion-dollar companies that had only basic support [read: discussion forum support] from their IaaS provider. Turned out that paying for a proper support plan, where they could at least e-mail someone at the CSP's offices, was possible, but there was no follow-through and it never happened. Implementing a support agreement simply fell through the cracks.)

Communication, of course, is a two-way street. Here are a few suggestions to ensure that you and your CSP have solid opportunities for communication in the event of an incident:

- Make sure that you have an open access channel to engage with the provider, and also that the provider is able to contact you in the event of a problem.

- Avoid listing a particular employee as a main contact. What if the provider is trying to advise you of an incident, but the contact listed with the provider is no longer with your company? Make sure the contact's e-mail address is monitored and that notifications are integrated into your IR processes.

Testing is also vital to preparing for an incident. If possible, review and test your IR processes with your providers annually or when significant changes are made. Most providers want to have happy clients, and they would much rather work with you to make sure you're ready for an incident than have an upset client on their hands. Your processes will have to change, and the provider may be able to make recommendations on what they have seen from other customers in the past and how you can improve your processes.

You'll probably need new cloud-specific tools (and training) to overcome the fact that you don't have physical access to the provider's server. The CSA Guidance calls this a "cloud jump kit." These tools will need to work for both the metastructure and the applistructure. If it is not already included as part of your regular logging activities, the jump kit will enable you to get information about activities in the cloud platform itself (metastructure) and activities from the systems you're running in the cloud environment (applistructure). This can be performed in many ways, ranging from API calls for metastructure information to using free open source software (FOSS) and commercial off-the-shelf (COTS) software to perform actions such as accessing memory on a running server.

By using immutable workloads, virtual networks, SDN firewalls, and other new options and capabilities to architect your cloud environment, you can dramatically increase your IR capabilities. Following are some highlights from the CSA Guidance regarding architecture and how it works with IR in the cloud:

- Know where your systems and data are stored. The CSA Guidance calls out "Application Stack Maps" as a means to factor in geographic differences in monitoring and data capture. An Application Stack Map essentially identifies all the components of an application (such as instances used, databases, and other services it interacts with).

- Know where your log files are stored. Do investigators have access to them?

- Know how you are isolating your workloads. Rather than dealing with an incident that scales from one system to hundreds, implementing a tight blast radius as part of your architecture can go a very long way in IR. This will reduce how far an incident can spread and make it easier to analyze and contain it.

- Leverage immutable workloads. You can get back up and running very quickly by moving workloads from a compromised instance to a known-good instance. This will also allow for a greater detective capability with file integrity monitoring and configuration management, because no changes should be made on running instances in an immutable model.

- Perform threat modeling (discussed in Chapter 10) and tabletop exercises to determine the most effective means of containment for different types of incidents on different components in the cloud stack.

Cloud Controls Matrix Incident Response Controls

I think it's important to incorporate the controls found in the Cloud Controls Matrix (CCM) and Consensus Assessment Initiative Questionnaire (CAIQ) into this incident response section. Although the CSA Guidance does not address the specific controls found in the CCM, I think that taking a few moments to go over these controls isn't a bad thing at all as part of the preparation phase. (That said, although specific controls are not directly tested as part of your CCSK exam, I'm not calling this a backgrounder because I think there's a big benefit to understanding what the CSA says should be asked of a provider as part of your due diligence activities.)

The following table covers both the CCM and CAIQ (v3.0.1) entries for the various IR controls. I suggest you open a copy of both the CCM and the CAIQ to review these as well. Again, you're not going to be tested on the specifics of the controls themselves, but this exercise will show you what the CSA sees as important aspects of IR and will deliver more exposure to both the CCM and the CAIQ, which you *will* be tested on as part of your CCSK exam.

 EXAM TIP   For the exam, remember that the CCM states the control and the responsible party, whereas the CAIQ provides questions you can ask in plain language.

CCM Control ID	CCM Control Specification	CAIQ Question	Responsibility
BCR-02	Business continuity and security incident response plans shall be subject to testing at planned intervals or upon significant organizational or environmental changes. Incident response plans shall involve impacted customers (tenant) and other business relationships that represent critical intra–supply chain business process dependencies.	Are business continuity plans subject to testing at planned intervals or upon significant organizational or environmental changes to ensure continuing effectiveness?	Customer and provider
SEF-01	Points of contact for applicable regulation authorities, national and local law enforcement, and other legal jurisdictional authorities shall be maintained and regularly updated (e.g., change in impacted scope and/or a change in any compliance obligation) to ensure direct compliance liaisons have been established and to be prepared for a forensic investigation requiring rapid engagement with law enforcement.	Do you maintain liaisons and points of contact with local authorities in accordance with contracts and appropriate regulations?	Customer and provider

SEF-02	Policies and procedures shall be established, and supporting business processes and technical measures implemented, to triage security-related events and ensure timely and thorough incident management, as per established IT service management policies and procedures.	Do you have a documented security incident response plan? Do you integrate customized tenant requirements into your security incident response plans? Do you publish a roles and responsibilities document specifying what you vs. your tenants are responsible for during security incidents? Have you tested your security incident response plans in the last year?	Customer and provider
SEF-03	Workforce personnel and external business relationships shall be informed of their responsibility and, if required, shall consent and/or contractually agree to report all information security events in a timely manner. Information security events shall be reported through predefined communications channels in a timely manner adhering to applicable legal, statutory, or regulatory compliance obligations.	Does your security information and event management (SIEM) system merge data sources (e.g., app logs, firewall logs, IDS logs, physical access logs, etc.) for granular analysis and alerting? Does your logging and monitoring framework allow isolation of an incident to specific tenants?	Customer and provider
SEF-04	Proper forensic procedures, including chain of custody, are required for the presentation of evidence to support potential legal action subject to the relevant jurisdiction after an information security incident. Upon notification, customers and/or other external business partners impacted by a security breach shall be given the opportunity to participate as is legally permissible in the forensic investigation.	Does your incident response plan comply with industry standards for legally admissible chain-of-custody management processes and controls? Does your incident response capability include the use of legally admissible forensic data collection and analysis techniques? Are you capable of supporting litigation holds (freeze of data from a specific point in time) for a specific tenant without freezing other tenant data? Do you enforce and attest to tenant data separation when producing data in response to legal subpoenas?	Customer and provider
SEF-05	Mechanisms shall be put in place to monitor and quantify the types, volumes, and costs of information security incidents.	Do you monitor and quantify the types, volumes, and impacts on all information security incidents? Will you share statistical information for security incident data with your tenants upon request?	Customer and provider

Detection and Analysis

As mentioned in the previous section, you need visibility into both your part of the cloud infrastructure and the workloads that run in that environment. Your provider should offer monitoring and logging of the metastructure, and you should be storing all of that data in a secure location. Even better, you should be able to have automatic event-driven security in place that will kick off automated responses to incidents in the cloud environment. Did a security group change? Why wait for an engineer to get around to investigating it when you can automatically change it back to what it's supposed to be? The CSA Guidance calls this implementing an "automated IR workflow."

Other data feeds the provider generally offers may be more focused on performance metrics. Although not ideal from a security perspective, as "low and slow" attacks that are crafted to be as quiet as possible (that is, not causing CPU spikes or abnormal amounts of network traffic that may cause an alert), these data feeds may be useful in detecting a security incident. There is potential for chain-of-custody questions with data supplied by providers. To date, there are no legal precedents that demonstrate whether provider data can be considered admissible in a court of law.

External threat intelligence remains applicable in a cloud environment, just as it is in a traditional data center environment, to assist with identifying indicators of a compromise of a system and to gain information on adversaries. This is another example of how managing the applistructure (when it is the responsibility of the consumer) is the same in a cloud environment as it is in a traditional data center.

If a provider doesn't offer full logging of APIs (IaaS and PaaS are more likely to offer full logging than SaaS), the console may be a means to identify any environment or configuration changes. If the provider doesn't appear to offer full logging of APIs, talk with them, because they may have internal log data that could be useful if a serious incident occurs.

When considering logging of "regular" instances such as operating system logs, everything you know about those Windows and Linux logs remains the same in a cloud environment. How these logs are collected will need to be determined and implemented. The best practice is to get system logs off of the instance as quickly as possible and into a centralized logging system. Your provider may have the means to collect operating system log data from individual instances, but you should determine whether an agent is required and whether you are willing and able to install the provider's agents on your systems.

As mentioned in Chapter 8, any network logs will likely be limited in comparison to what can be seen in a traditional data center under your control. You may be able to obtain flow logs, but you won't be able to do a full packet capture of all network traffic in the environment. This is a natural consequence of SDN and microsegmentation (aka hypersegregation).

When dealing with PaaS and serverless applications, you're going to need to add custom application-level logging, because the platform that your application is running on belongs to the provider, and you won't necessarily have access to any of the log data generated by systems under their control. The CSA Guidance refers to this as "instrumenting the technology stack."

In addition, performing forensics in a cloud environment will change significantly. You have an incredible opportunity to streamline forensics in an IaaS environment, from the metastructure through to the applistructure, but you have to architect for it. You will want to leverage imaging and snapshots to take advantage of bit-level copies of data accessible for forensics activities at the applistructure layer. You can architect an isolated blast zone for forensics activities and copy images and snapshots to this environment, where they will be fully isolated.

From the applistructure perspective, you likely have access to tools today that enable you to perform some forensic activities in your existing environment. It all boils down to collecting data from a remote machine, and you can do this with virtual machines in either a cloud-based or a traditional data center.

For the metastructure, you will need to have access to all relevant log data that was discussed in the earlier "Detection and Analysis Phase" section. The main thing to keep in mind, for both real life and the exam, is that your forensic activities need to support appropriate chain-of-custody requirements, and this applies to all forensic activities by the customer and the provider. That said, it's important that you work with your legal team to ensure that this critical component of forensics is being properly addressed.

You have an incredible opportunity to streamline forensics and investigations in a cloud environment. This may be seen by many as not just an opportunity, but a requirement, because of the dynamic nature of a cloud environment and its high velocity of change. Consider, for example, an auto-scaling group automatically terminating a workload, or an administrator manually terminating an instance. Following are some recommended automated actions from the CSA Guidance that can support investigations in a cloud environment:

- Snapshot the storage of the virtual machine.
- Capture any metadata at the time of the alert, so the analysis can happen based on what the infrastructure looked like at the time of the incident.
- If supported by the provider, "pausing" an instance will save the volatile memory.

As listed in the CSA Guidance, other capabilities of the cloud platform that may be leveraged to determine the extent of a potential compromise include the following:

- Analyze network flows to check whether isolation held up. API calls may be available to snapshot the network and virtual firewall ruleset, which could give you an accurate picture of the entire stack at the time of the incident.
- Examine configuration data to check whether other similar instances were potentially exposed in the same attack.
- Review data access logs (for cloud-based storage, if available) and management plane logs to see if the incident affected or crossed into the cloud platform.
- Remember that serverless and PaaS-based architectures will require additional correlation across the cloud platform and any self-generated application logs.

Containment, Eradication, and Recovery

Your first action when responding to an incident is ensuring that the attacker is no longer in the cloud management plane to begin with. To ensure that you have complete visibility, this requires accessing the management plane with the master (root) credentials. (Remember that this account is locked away and only to be used in the case of emergency. This is the time to use it!) Using the master account may unmask activities that are hidden from view when you're using a limited privilege administrator account.

In this phase, you can experience massive gains (especially in IaaS), but again, this is possible only if you plan in advance. Items such as software defined infrastructure, auto-scaling groups, and automated API calls to change virtual network or machine configurations can all be leveraged to enhance your recovery times. Again, though, these can be performed only once you are certain the attacker no longer has access to the management plane. (Remember the Code Spaces example I mentioned way back in Chapter 1? Well, they didn't bother taking into account rule number 1 when they kicked off their incident response plan, and the attacker was still in the management plane when Code Spaces started to take action. The attacker saw this, and that was when he decided to terminate everything.)

Through the use of virtual firewalls, there's no longer a need to remove an instance from the network prior to performing an investigation. An instance can be locked down very quickly by changing the virtual firewall ruleset to allow access only from an investigator's system. By using this approach, nothing changes at the applistructure layer, and the chain of custody remains valid as a result. This isolation technique should be leveraged whenever possible. Isolate the system using virtual firewall changes, build a fresh replacement from a trusted image, and then kick off your investigation of the compromised machine.

Of course, most of this capability is exclusively that of IaaS. For PaaS and SaaS service models, you will be much more reliant on your provider to perform many of the activities associated with response, because these models will likely be more restrictive in the IR capabilities exposed to customers.

Post-Incident Activity

This is where you might realize that your IR team didn't quite have the knowledge of a cloud environment that both your leadership and the team itself thought they had. This will most likely include data collection sources and methods.

From a governance perspective, you may need to re-evaluate SLAs, actual response times, data availability, and other items that were found to be suboptimal. It may be hard to change an SLA with a provider, but this is a great time to come to them with experience under your belt and try to renegotiate.

Chapter Review

This chapter addressed incident response recommendations as per the CSA Guidance. The main items to remember for your exam include the following:

- Establishing SLAs and setting expectations around the roles and responsibilities of the customer and the provider are the most important aspects of IR in a cloud environment. These SLAs must cover all phases of IR.

- Practice makes perfect. You have a great opportunity to create an IR practice environment—use it! Know how to handle aspects of IR that belong to you and how hand-offs to the provider are performed.

- You must establish clear communication channels (from customer to provider and vice versa). Remember that the provider may need to contact your organization if they notice something. Don't allow these messages to be sent to an e-mail address that isn't being monitored.

- Customers must understand the content and the format of the data that a provider may supply for analysis. Data that is supplied in a format that you can't use is useless.

- Understand how any data supplied by the provider meets chain-of-custody requirements.

- Use the automation capabilities of the cloud environment to your advantage. Implementing continuous and serverless monitoring may help you detect potential issues much more quickly than what is possible in a traditional data center.

- Understand the tools that are made available to you by the provider. Engage the provider with your plans—they may be able to improve your IR plan.

- What works in one cloud environment may not work in another. Make sure that the approaches you use to detect and handle incidents are planned for each provider as part of your enterprise IR plan.

- Without logging, there is no detection. Without detection, there is no ability to respond. Make sure your logging has as much visibility into your environment as possible.

- Test, test, test. Testing must be performed at least annually or when significant changes are made. Again, consult your provider and make sure they become part of your tests to the greatest extent possible.

Questions

1. Which area of incident response is most impacted by automation of activities?
   A. Preparation
   B. Detection
   C. Containment, eradication, and recovery
   D. Post-incident

2. Upon investigation of a potential incident, what should be performed first?
   A. The master account credentials should be retrieved and used to perform an investigation of the metastructure to ensure that the attacker is no longer in the management plane.
   B. Every account should be logged off and their passwords reset.
   C. Every server should be terminated.
   D. Snapshots of every instance should be performed using APIs.

3. How can a server instance be quickly quarantined in an IaaS environment?
   A. Perform a snapshot.
   B. Log on to the server instance and disable all user accounts.
   C. "Pause" the instance if the vendor allows such action.
   D. Change the virtual firewall ruleset to allow access only from an investigator workstation.

4. Which of the following is a consideration concerning log data supplied by a provider?
   A. It will meet legal chain-of-custody requirements.
   B. It is in a format that can be used by customers.
   C. It is supplied in a timely manner to support investigation.
   D. A and B are correct.

5. How often should incident response plans be tested?
   A. Annually
   B. Monthly
   C. Quarterly
   D. As part of due diligence prior to production use of the system

6. Which phase does proactive scanning and network monitoring, vulnerability assessments, and performing risk assessments fall under?
   A. Preparation
   B. Detection

C. Containment, eradication, and recovery

D. Post-incident

7. What is (are) the most important aspect(s) of incident response in a cloud environment?

A. Obtaining virtual tools to investigate virtual servers

B. Training of incident response staff

C. Setting service level agreements and establishing roles and responsibilities

D. All of the above

8. What is the purpose of an "Application Stack Map"?

A. To understand the various systems that are used as part of an application

B. To understand where data is going to reside

C. To understand the programming languages used in an application

D. To understand the various dependencies associated with an application

9. What is a cloud jump kit?

A. Having an updated resume ready in the event of an RGE (resume-generating event)

B. A kit with required cables, connectors, and hard drives ready for performing investigation of a physical server

C. A collection of tools needed to perform investigations in a remote location

D. Procedures to follow when handing off an investigation to a provider

10. How may logging in PaaS be different from logging in IaaS?

A. PaaS logs must be supplied by the provider upon request.

B. Custom application-level logging will likely be needed.

C. PaaS log formats will be in JSON format and will require special tools to read.

D. All of the above are correct.

Answers

1. **C.** The correct answer is containment, eradication, and recovery. Although tools supplied by the cloud provider can greatly enhance detection as well, the tools available to you in a cloud environment have the most impact on containment, eradication, and recovery efforts.

2. **A.** An investigation should be performed using the master account so there is complete visibility of all activity taking place in the management plane. Snapshots of servers being investigated can be performed, but this should be done only after it is confirmed that the attacker is no longer in the management plane. Logging everyone off may have limited benefits, but, again, confirmation that the attacker

no longer has management plane access is the first step in incident response of the metastructure. Terminating all server instances is not an appropriate answer at all.

3. **D.** The best answer is to change the virtual firewall ruleset to allow access only from the investigator workstation. The steps in the other answers can be performed after the server instance can no longer be reached by an attacker.

4. **D.** The correct answers are A and B. Timely access to any data supplied by the provider is not mentioned in the guidance.

5. **A.** IR plans should be tested annually. Remember, though, that the CSA Guidance specifically states that tests should be performed *annually or when significant changes are made.* Remember both when you take your exam.

6. **A.** Proactive scanning and network monitoring, vulnerability assessments, and performing risk assessments are all under the preparation phase in the CSA Guidance.

7. **C.** Yes, all of the entries are important, but the question specifically states which is (are) the *most* important. The CSA Guidance states that "SLAs and setting expectations around what the customer does versus what the provider does are the most important aspects of incident response for cloud-based resources." You need to do these things before you can work on the tools and training of individuals.

8. **B.** The best answer is that an Application Stack Map can be implemented to understand where data is going to reside. On top of knowing where your data can reside, it will help address geographic differences in monitoring and data capture.

9. **C.** The cloud jump kit is a collection of tools required to perform investigation of remote locations (such as cloud services). This is the set of "virtual tools for a virtual world" if you will. Of course, if you have an incident in a cloud environment and you realize only at that time that you are lacking virtual tools and knowledge of them, this is most likely a resume-generating event. If a provider takes over investigation on their end, they will likely be using their own investigation tools.

10. **B.** PaaS (and serverless application architectures) will likely need custom application-level logging because there will likely be gaps in what the provider offers and what is required for incident response support. PaaS providers may have more detailed logs available, but you will have to determine when these can be shared by the provider. Finally, although the format of data is important, JSON is easily readable and doesn't require special tools.

CHAPTER 10

Application Security

This chapter covers the following topics from Domain 10 of the CSA Guidance:
- Opportunities and Challenges Surrounding Application Security in the Cloud
- Secure Software Development Lifecycle
- How the Cloud Impacts Application Design and Architectures
- The Rise and Role of DevOps

Quality is never an accident; it is always the result of high intention, sincere effort, intelligent direction, and skillful execution....

—John Ruskin

Security isn't easy. Software development isn't easy. What makes application security so challenging is that these two disciplines often work in isolated silos and, quite frankly, neither group really understands what the other does. Getting these two groups working together takes effort and requires a cultural change to allow for adoption of new technologies such as Platform as a Service (PaaS), serverless computing, and DevOps. As Mr. Ruskin said, quality is the result of sincere effort and intelligent direction. This approach will ultimately improve the quality of the software produced by your company.

When you're talking about application security, you're talking about a wide body of knowledge. For the CCSK exam, you will not be tested on any programming whatsoever. You do, however, need to be prepared for security questions on design and development, deployment, and operational defenses of applications in production. Application development and security disciplines themselves are evolving at an incredibly fast pace. Application development teams continue to embrace new technologies, processes, and patterns to meet business requirements, while driving down costs. Meanwhile, security is continuously playing catch-up with advances in application development, new programming languages, and new ways of obtaining compute services.

In this chapter, we'll look at software development and how to build and deploy secure applications in the cloud—specifically in PaaS and Infrastructure as a Service (IaaS) models. Organizations building Software as a Service (SaaS) applications can also use many of these techniques to assist in building secure applications that run in their own data centers or in those of IaaS providers.

Ultimately, because the cloud is a shared responsibility model, you will encounter changes regarding how you address application security. This chapter attempts to discuss the major changes associated with application security in a cloud environment. It covers the following major areas:

- **Secure software development lifecycle (SSDLC)**   Use the SSDLC to determine how cloud computing affects application security from initial design through to deployment.

- **Design and architecture**   Several new trends in designing applications in a cloud environment affect and can improve security.

- **DevOps and continuous integration/continuous deployment (CI/CD)**   DevOps and CI/CD are frequently used in both development and deployment of cloud applications and are becoming a dominant approach to software development, both in the cloud and in traditional data centers. DevOps brings new security considerations and opportunities to improve security from what you do today.

The SSDLC and Cloud Computing

Many different approaches have been taken by multiple groups with regard to SSDLC. Essentially, an SSDLC describes a series of security activities that should be performed during all phases of application design and development, deployment, and operations. Here are some of the more common frameworks used in the industry:

- Microsoft Security Development Lifecycle
- NIST 800-64, "Security Considerations in the System Development Life Cycle"
- ISO/IEC 27034 Application Security Controls Project
- OWASP Open Web Application Security Project (S-SDLC)

Although these frameworks all work toward a common goal of increasing security for applications, they all go about it just a little differently. This is why the Cloud Security Alliance breaks down the SSDLC into three larger phases:

- **Secure design and development**   This phase includes activities ranging from training and developing organizational standards to gathering requirements, performing design review through threat modeling, and writing and testing code.

- **Secure deployment**   This phase addresses security and testing activities that must be performed when you're moving application code from a development environment into production.

- **Secure operations**   This phase concerns the ongoing security of applications as they are in a production environment. It includes additional defenses such as web application firewalls, ongoing vulnerability assessments, penetration tests, and other activities that can be performed once an application is in a production environment.

Cloud computing will impact every phase of the SSDLC, regardless of which particular framework you use. This is a direct result of the abstraction and automation of the cloud, combined with a greater reliance on your cloud provider.

Remember that in the shared responsibility model, change is based on the service model—whether IaaS, PaaS, or SaaS. If you are developing an application that will run in an IaaS service model, you would be responsible for more security than the provider would be with regard to using and leveraging other features and services supplied by a PaaS provider. In addition, the service model affects the visibility and control that you have. For example, in a PaaS model, you may no longer have access to any network logs for troubleshooting or security investigation purposes.

 NOTE   Remember that application security reviews should look at not only the core application functionality but also the management plane and metastructure.

Secure Design and Development

Figure 10-1 shows the CSA-defined five phases involved in secure application design and development, all of which are affected by cloud computing: training, define, design, develop, and test.

Training

Getting team members trained is the first phase. The CSA Guidance calls for three different roles (developers, operational staff, and security teams) and three categories of training (vendor-neutral cloud security training, vendor-specific training, and development tool training), which should all receive vendor-neutral training on cloud security fundamentals (such as the CCSK). These same groups should also undertake vendor-specific training on the cloud providers and platforms that are being used by an organization. Additionally, developers and operation staff who are directly involved in architecting and managing the cloud infrastructure should receive specific training on any development tools that will be used.

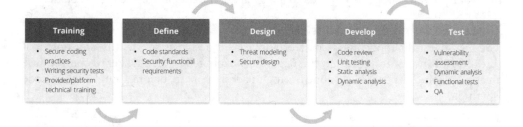

Figure 10-1   Five phases in secure application design and development. (Used with permission of Cloud Security Alliance.)

NOTE In Figure 10-1, notice the inclusion of secure coding practices. The OWASP (Open Web Application Security Project) is one of the leading available resources for web development. You can use the OWASP secure coding practices checklist to address key development items such as input validation, output in coding, authentication and password management, session management, access control, cryptographic practices, error handling and logging, communication security, system configuration, database security, file management, memory management, and general coding practices.

One of the final training elements should deal with how to create security tests. As the old saying goes, the answers you get are only as good as the questions you ask. In fact, some companies tell the developers in advance which security tests will be performed. Because the developers know what will be checked by the security team before a system is accepted, this approach can lead to more secure applications being created in the first place. In a way, this is a way to set up developers for success before they even begin writing code.

Define

In this phase, coding standards are determined (usually based on compliance requirements) and functional requirements are identified. In other words, you determine what this application must do from a security perspective. This is, of course, above and beyond any business requirements that the application needs to address.

Design

During the application design phase, you need to determine whether there are any security issues with the design of the application itself. (Note that this is about design, not actual development.) You need to establish an understanding between the security and software development teams as to how the software application is architected, any modules that are being consumed, and so on. The benefit of going through steps such as threat modeling is that you don't have to take two steps forward and three steps back after the security team starts reviewing the application code itself. This can save you substantial amounts of time in development. Of course, you need to consider cloud providers and provider services as part of this application review. For example, you could ensure that your provider supports required logging capabilities as part of the design phase.

Threat Modeling Backgrounder

The goal of threat modeling as part of application design is to identify any potential threats to an application that may be successfully exploited by an attacker to compromise an application. This should be done during the design phase, before a single line of code is written.

NOTE As always, backgrounders are for your information only. You will not be tested on any backgrounder information.

Threat	Description	Countermeasure
Spoofing	User claiming a false identity	Authentication
Tampering	Malicious modification of data or process	Input validation
Repudiation	Denying an action or event was performed	Audit logging
Information disclosure	Data leakage or breach	Encryption
Denial of service	Causing a service to be unavailable	Rate throttling
Elevation of privilege	Gaining increased access other than intended	Authorization

Table 10-1   STRIDE Threats and Countermeasures

As with everything else, threat modeling can comprise many different variants. In this discussion, I address the STRIDE threat model (which stands for spoofing, tampering, repudiation, information disclosure, denial of service, and elevation of privilege). Table 10-1 gives the lowdown on each of these threats, supplies a high-level description, and offers a common countermeasure.

A threat-modeling exercise can be performed in many ways, ranging from the good-old meeting room with a whiteboard, to tools such as the OWASP Threat Dragon or Microsoft Threat Modeling Tool, to the Elevation of Privilege card game from Microsoft (play a card game using a scoring system!). No matter which method you use to perform threat modeling, at least two teams should always be involved: the security team and the developers themselves. Ideally, you can include business analysts, system owners, and others as part of the threat-modeling exercise. In a way, this is a great form of team-building, and it breaks traditional silos between the security and development teams.

In a threat-modeling exercise, the first step involves diagramming all application components (and where they are located), all users and any other systems that will interact with the application, and the direction of data flows. Once this is done, the security and development teams can work together to identify potential threats to the various components and required countermeasures that need to be in place to stop these threats from being realized. Figure 10-2 presents a high-level example diagram provided by the OWASP Threat Dragon tool.

Having been through the threat-modeling exercise myself, I can tell you firsthand that the benefits are worth the effort. In one particular exercise, threat modeling discovered the following highlights:

- Application was using unencrypted FTP with clear-text credentials
- HTTP without certificates
- No input validation
- No API authentication or rate throttling
- No tracking of successful or unsuccessful logins
- Planned to use an improper identity store
- No Network Time Protocol synchronization for logging

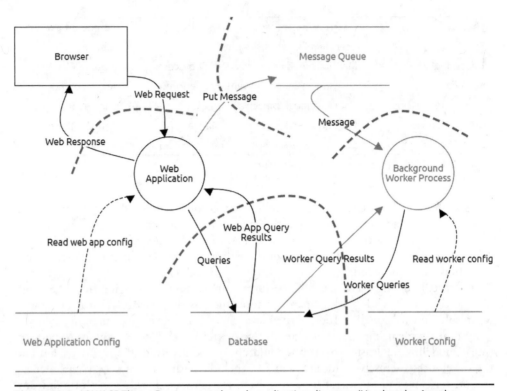

Figure 10-2 OWASP Threat Dragon sample web application diagram. (Used under Apache License 2.0.)

This exercise took approximately three hours. Consider how long it would take to address all of these flaws had the application already been built? A whole lot longer than three hours. In fact, at the end of the exercise, the client CISO declared that every application from that point forward would undergo a STRIDE threat-modeling exercise. The CISO was so impressed with the results of the exercise that the organization changed its policies and processes. I think your company would do the same.

Develop

In the development phase, we finally get to build the application. As with every other system and application ever built in the history of mankind, the development environment should be an exact replica of the production environment. In other words, developers should never create applications in a production environment or hold actual production data as a part of the development phase. Developers will also probably be using some form of CI/CD pipeline, which needs to be properly secured, with a particular focus on the code repository (such as GitHub). In addition, if you will be leveraging PaaS or serverless development, enhanced logging must be baked into an application to compensate for the lack of logging that is usually available in such scenarios.

Test

As mentioned a few times already, testing should be performed while an application is being developed. These tests can include code review, unit testing, static analysis, and dynamic analysis. The next section of this chapter will discuss both static application security testing (SAST) and dynamic application security testing (DAST).

Secure Deployment

The deployment phase marks the transition or handover of code from developers to operations. Traditionally, this has been the point at which a final quality check occurs, including user acceptance testing. The cloud, DevOps, and continuous delivery are changing that, however, and are enabling tests to be automated and performed earlier in the lifecycle. Many types of application security tests can be integrated into both development and deployment phases. Here are some of the application security tests highlighted in the CSA Guidance:

- **Code review**   This process does not change as a result of moving to the cloud. There are, however, specific cloud features and functions that may be leveraged as part of an application, and you need to ensure that least privilege is enabled at all times inside the application code and all dependencies. Not only should user permissions follow least privilege, but services and any roles that may be used to access other services should do so as well. About the worst thing you could do from an application-permission perspective is to have tight access controls for the users who are able to access the application and give the application full control over every aspect of a cloud environment. That said, you need to ensure that anything related to authentication, including the credentials used by an application and any required encryption, are reviewed as part of code review.

 EXAM TIP   You will likely be tested on your understanding that credentials and encryption in an application are the primary differences between applications that run in a cloud versus those that run a traditional data center.

- **Unit testing, regression testing, and functional testing**   These standard tests are used by developers and should address any API calls being used to leverage the functionality provided by a cloud provider.
- **Static application security testing**   SAST analyzes application code offline. SAST is generally a rules-based test that will scan software code for items such as credentials embedded into application code and a test of input validation, both of which are major concerns for application security.
- **Dynamic application security testing**   While SAST looks at code offline, DAST looks at an application while it is running. An example of DAST is fuzz testing, in which you throw garbage at an application and try to generate an error on the server (such as an "error 500" on a web server, which is an internal server error). Because DAST is a live test against a running system, you may need to get approval in advance from your provider prior to starting.

Cloud Impacts on Vulnerability Assessments

Vulnerability assessments (VAs) should always be performed on images before they are used to launch instances. VAs can be integrated into the CI/CD pipeline. Testing images should occur in a special locked-down test environment such as a virtual network or separate account. As with all security tests, however, this must be done after approval for any testing is given by the provider.

With an ongoing VA of running instances, you can use host-based VA tools to get complete visibility into any vulnerabilities on a system. VAs can also be used to test entire virtual infrastructures by leveraging infrastructure as code (IaC) to build this test environment. This enables you to generate an exact replica of a production environment in minutes, so you can properly assess an application and all infrastructure components without the risk of impacting the production environment.

When it comes to performing VAs, there are two schools of thought. One perspective is that a VA should be performed directly on a system itself to provide complete transparency and to allay fears that security controls in front of the system are hiding any exposures that actually exist. This is known as a "host-based" view. The other approach is to take the view of an outsider and perform the VA with all controls, such as virtual firewalls, taken into account. The CSA Guidance suggests that you use a host-based view by leveraging host-based agents. In this case, cloud provider permission will not be required, because the assessment is performed on the server, not across the provider's network.

Cloud Impact on Penetration Testing

As with VAs, penetration tests can also be performed in a cloud environment, and you'll need permission from the provider to perform them. The CSA recommends adapting your current penetration testing for the cloud by using the following guidelines:

- Use testing firms and individuals with experience working with the cloud provider where the application is deployed. Your applications will likely be using services supplied by the cloud service provider (CSP), and a penetration tester who does not understand the CSP's services may miss critical findings.

- The penetration test should address the developers and cloud administrators themselves. This is because many cloud breaches attack those who maintain the cloud, not just the application running in the cloud. Testing should include the cloud management plane.

- If the application you are testing is a multitenant application, ensure that the penetration tests include attempts to break tenant isolation and gain access to another tenant.

Deployment Pipeline Security

It may seem counterintuitive, but automated CI/CD pipelines can actually enhance security through supporting immutable infrastructures, automating security testing, and providing extensive logging of application and infrastructure changes when such changes are performed through the pipeline. The real power here is that there is no opportunity

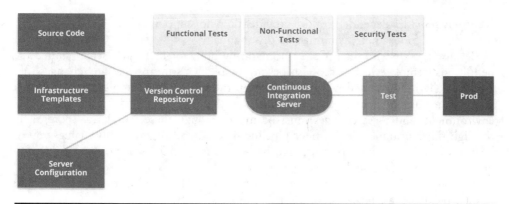

Figure 10-3 Components of a continuous deployment pipeline. (Used with permission of Cloud Security Alliance.)

for human error to occur when it comes to testing—100 percent of the testing is performed 100 percent of the time. Test results can be directed toward a test result bucket so that, in the case of an audit, for example, all testing is easily demonstrated to an auditor. Logs can also be configured to state the person or system that submitted a change, and automated approval can also be implemented in a change management system if all tests were successfully passed.

As with anything else, the pipeline must be tightly secured. Pipelines should be hosted in a dedicated cloud environment with very limited access to production workloads or the infrastructure hosting the pipeline component. Figure 10-3 shows the various components that make up a deployment pipeline.

As you can see in Figure 10-3, there are two central components of the deployment pipeline: The version control repository (such as GitHub) is where code is stored, and the continuous integration server (such as Jenkins) has the ability to use plug-ins in to perform any prebuild, build, and post-build activities. Activities here could include performing security tests or functional tests and sending results to a specified location. Additionally, the continuous integration server can connect to a change management system that will track any approved changes to an environment. You can also set thresholds on test results. For example, if there are any critical findings, the continuous integration server will not even build the application or perform the action that has been requested.

All of these tests are created in advance. From a security perspective, this means that although you still have separation of duties with a CI/CD pipeline, humans are not performing the tests at build time. With this in mind, you can see how some (and, more importantly, the CSA Guidance) consider an automated continuous deployment pipeline as being a more secure approach to deploying software to an environment.

Impact of IaC and Immutable Workloads

You read about IaC in Chapter 6 and immutable workloads in Chapter 7. So you know that IaC uses templates to create everything, from configuration of a particular server instance to building the entire cloud virtual infrastructure. The depth of IaC capabilities is entirely provider-dependent. If the provider does not support API calls to create a new user account, for example, you must do this manually.

Because these environments are automatically built for us from a set of source file definitions (templates), they can also be immutable. This means that any changes that are manually implemented will be overwritten the next time a template is run. When you use an immutable approach, you must always check for any changes made to the environment, and these changes must be made through these templates—potentially through the continuous deployment pipeline if you are using one. This enables you to lock down the entire infrastructure tightly—much more than is normally possible in a non-cloud application deployment.

The bottom line here is that when security is properly engaged, the use of IaC and immutable deployments can significantly improve security.

 EXAM TIP Remember that immutable deployments and IaC can greatly improve security. You will likely be tested on this.

Secure Operations

Once the application is deployed, we can turn our attention to security in the operations phase. Other elements of security, such as infrastructure security (Chapter 7), container security (Chapter 8), data security (Chapter 11), and identity and access management (Chapter 12), are key components in a secure operations phase.

The following is additional guidance that directly applies to application security:

- *Production and development environments should always be separated.* Access to the management plane for production environments should be tightly locked down, compared to that of the development environment. When assessing privileges assigned to an application, you must always be aware of the credentials being used by the application to access other services. These must be assigned on a least-privilege basis, just as you would assign least privilege to user accounts. Multiple sets of credentials for each application service can be implemented to compartmentalize entitlements (permissions) further to support the least-privilege approach.

- *Even when using an immutable infrastructure, you should actively monitor for changes and deviations from approved baselines.* Again, depending on the particular cloud provider, this monitoring can and should be automated whenever possible. You can also use event-driven security (covered in the next section) to revert any changes to the production environment automatically.

- *Application testing and assessment should be considered an ongoing process, even if you are using an immutable infrastructure.* As always, if any testing and/or assessments will be performed across the provider's network, they should be performed with the permission of the CSP to avoid violating any terms of service.

- *Always remember that change management isn't just about application changes.* Any infrastructure and cloud management plane changes should be approved and tracked.

How the Cloud Impacts Application Design and Architectures

Cloud services can offer new design and architecture options that can increase application security. Several traits of the cloud can be used to augment security of applications through application architecture itself.

Cloud services can offer segregation by default. Applications can be run in their own isolated environment. Depending on your provider, you can run applications in separate virtual networks or different accounts. Although operational overhead will be incurred when using a separate account for every application, using separate accounts offers the benefit of enabling management plane segregation, thus minimizing access to the application environment.

If you do have an immutable infrastructure, you can increase security by disabling remote logins to immutable servers and other workloads, adding file integrity monitoring, and integrating immutable techniques into your instant recovery plans, as discussed in Chapter 9.

PaaS and serverless technologies can reduce the scope of your direct security responsibilities, but this comes at the cost of increasing your due-diligence responsibilities. This is because you are leveraging a service from the provider (assuming the provider has done a good job in securing the services they offer customers). The provider is responsible for securing the underlying services and operating systems.

I will cover serverless computing in greater detail in Chapter 14. For now, here are two major concepts that serverless computing can deliver to increase security of our cloud environments:

- **Software-defined security** This concept involves automating security operations and could include automating cloud incident response, changes to entitlements (permissions), and the remediation of unapproved infrastructure changes.

- **Event-driven security** This puts the concept of software-defined security into action. You can have a system monitoring for changes that will call a script to perform an automatic response in the event of a change being discovered. For example, if a security group is changed, a serverless script can be kicked off to undo the change. This interaction is usually performed through some form of notification messaging. Security can define the events to monitor and use event-driven capabilities to trigger automated notification and response.

EXAM TIP If you're asked about the difference between software-defined security and event-driven security, remember that software-defined security is a concept, whereas event-driven security puts that concept into action.

Finally, microservices are a growing trend in application development and are well-suited to cloud environments. Using microservices, you can break down an entire application into its individual components and run those components on separate virtual servers or containers. In this way, you can tightly control access and reduce the attack surface of the individual functions by eliminating all services that are not required for a particular function to operate. Leveraging auto-scaling can also assist with availability, as only functions that require additional compute capacity need to be scaled up. There is additional overhead from a security perspective with microservices, however, because communications between the various functions and components need to be tightly secured. This includes securing any service discovery, scheduling, and routing services.

Microservices Backgrounder

Back in the early 2000s, I worked with a project manager named Ralph. One of Ralph's favorite sayings was, "A system is not a server and a server is not a system." Ralph was pretty ahead of his time! He called microservices before they even existed.

A microservices architecture breaks out the various components of a system and runs them completely separately from one another. When services need to access one another, they do so using APIs (usually REST APIs) to get data. This data is then presented to the requesting system. The gist is that changes to one component don't require a complete system update, which differs from what was required with a monolithic system in which multiple components operate on the same server.

In Chapter 6, I discussed the "API Mandate" from Jeff Bezos at Amazon. The company basically created a microservices architecture, in which every component that was built exposed its APIs. Figure 10-4 shows how various components of an organization like Amazon.com can be broken out into microservices.

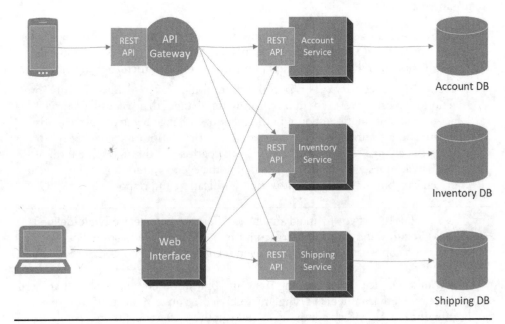

Figure 10-4   Microservices architecture diagram

Major Considerations for Cloud Providers

CSPs of all service models need to pay attention to the following points when it comes to application security:

- All APIs and web services exposed to customers must be tightly secured, and the provider must assume that all customers are potentially hostile.
- API access should be monitored for abuse and any unusual activity detected.
- All services must undergo extensive design and testing to prevent attacks or cross-tenant access.

As you can see, Figure 10-4 includes an account service, an inventory service, and a shipping service. Each of these different services can be written in a language that is appropriate for its particular purpose. For example, the account service could be written in Java, the inventory service in Ruby, and the shipping service in Python. When a change needs to be made to the inventory service, for example, neither the account service nor shipping service is impacted as a result. Also, access to changes can be restricted to the individual developers responsible for an individual service. This enforces a least-privileged approach to access.

In the figure's architecture diagram, notice that an API gateway is being used by the mobile phone application. The API gateway acts as the entry point to all services behind it, so it can handle all aspects of the client accessing a system based on microservices. (I will discuss API gateways and authorizations in Chapter 12.)

The Rise and Role of DevOps

DevOps is a *portmanteau* (a fancy French word that refers to a combination of two words to create a new one) for "development" and "operations." It is a culture, not a tool. Nor is it technology that you can just buy off the shelf and implement. The goal of DevOps is to have a deeper integration of development and operations teams that delivers automation of application deployments and infrastructure operations, resulting in higher-quality code in a faster time frame.

From a technical perspective, DevOps relies on the CI/CD pipeline, covered previously in the section, "Deployment Pipeline Security." It will use programmatic automation tools to improve management of an infrastructure. Although DevOps is a new technology that is often seen in the cloud, it is not exclusively a cloud-based approach to software deployment.

DevOps Backgrounder

In DevOps, the development and operations teams are no longer siloed. Rather, these two teams can be merged into a single team, where software engineers (aka developers) work across the entire application lifecycle, from the development and testing to deployment and finally operations.

DevOps brings significant cultural changes with it, and this is why some companies may be hesitant to adopt it. DevOps can be used to change the way deployments occur, from queuing changes up for weeks and then deploying everything on one weekend, to performing multiple changes throughout the day. You may be wondering how on earth an organization could make multiple changes per day without performing QA testing? That's an excellent question. To address this, many companies will focus on automatic rollback capability and implement a *blue-green deployment* approach to minimize risk even further.

The blue-green deployment approach works much like the immutable deployment approach. Although blue-green deployment can be done with containers and load balancers, I'm going to use an example of immutable virtual machine workloads in an auto-scaling group for our discussion. Consider, then, an auto-scaling group of three web servers. To implement a blue-green deployment approach, you update the web server image with the updated application code. You then terminate one of the running instances. When the auto-scaling group notices that one server is missing, it will automatically deploy the server with the newly patched image as part of that group. Once that is done, 33 percent of the incoming network traffic is directed to this newly patched server. That server is monitored, and if all is good, a subsequent server in that auto-scaling group is deleted or terminated. That now leaves you with 66 percent of network traffic being served by the newly updated application running on the web server pool. You rinse and repeat until all servers have been updated. This is how companies, otherwise known as DevOps unicorns (such as Netflix, Pinterest, Facebook, Amazon, and, well, basically any other global 24×7 web operation), will run to achieve effectively zero downtime.

Another item that concerns some business leaders about DevOps is the fact that developers in a DevOps world basically own what they code. This means that in many DevOps environments, the developers not only create the application, but they are also responsible for management of that application. This, of course, is quite different from a main security principle that states separation of duties must be enforced. However, we want developers to be able to push code quickly, we don't want developers to access production data, and we don't want developers to jeopardize security checks. A modern CI/CD pipeline and its associated automatic security tests enable us to make all of this possible.

In closing this discussion about DevOps, I think it's very important to realize that DevOps is not magic, and it can't happen overnight. It will take some time for business leaders to be convinced, if they aren't already, that performing small and incremental changes can actually improve the security and availability of applications, not to mention provide a significant decrease in time to market.

Security Implications and Advantages of DevOps

To discuss the security implications in advantages of DevOps, look no further than the information presented in the section, "Deployment Pipeline Security," earlier in the chapter. Pipelines will allow only approved code to be deployed. Development, test, and production versions are all based on the exact same source files, which eliminates any deviation from known good standards.

A Few Important CI/CD Terms

Here at the end of the chapter, I want to mention a couple of new terms from the CSA Guidance that you should know about:

- **SecDevOps (aka DevSecOps)**   It doesn't really matter which way you say it, because it means the same thing. Technically, using SecDevOps means you put security first, whereas saying DevSecOps means you do the development, through security, and then hit operations. The main goal either way is that you are integrating security checks into the CI/CD pipeline.

- **Rugged DevOps**   Basically, this refers to integration of security testing throughout the entire application development process to produce more secure (aka rugged) and resilient applications.

The CI/CD pipeline produces master images for virtual machines, containers, and infrastructure stacks very quickly and consistently. This enables automated deployments and immutable infrastructure. How is code approved to be deployed? You integrate security tests into the build process. Of course, manual testing is also possible as a final check prior to the application being launched in a production environment.

Auditing can be supported (and in many cases improved) through this automated testing of application code prior to the application being built. Everything can be tracked down to the individual changes in source files, all the way back to the person who made a change and an entire history of changes, which can be tracked in a single location. This offers considerable audit- and change-tracking benefits.

Speaking of change management, if the change management system you currently use exposes APIs, the CI/CD pipeline can automatically obtain approval for any deployment. Simply put, if a request for deployment comes in through the continuous integration server, the change management system can be set up to approve automatically any change based on the fact that the tests have been successful.

Chapter Review

This chapter discussed application security in a cloud environment. Application security itself does not change as a result of deploying to the cloud, but many new approaches to application architecture and design are possible with the cloud, and these need to be appropriately secured. In addition, the secure software development life cycle (SSDLC) has many different frameworks associated with it, and the CSA divides them into three distinct phases: secure design and development, secure deployment, and secure operations. We also looked at some of the other technologies that are commonly related to (but not exclusive to) the cloud, such as microservices and DevOps.

As for your CCSK exam preparation, you should be comfortable with the following information:

- Understand the security capabilities of your cloud provider and know that every platform and service needs to be inspected prior to adoption.

- Build security into the initial design process. Security is commonly brought into applications when it is too late. Secure applications are a result of a secure design.

- Even if you don't have a formal software development life cycle in your organization, consider moving toward a continuous deployment method and automating security into the deployment pipeline. This still supports separation of duties, but a human is not performing the tests every single time. The security team creates the tests and the automated system runs them 100 percent thoroughly, 100 percent of the time.

- Threat modeling such as STRIDE, static application security testing (SAST), and dynamic application security testing (DAST) should all be integrated into application development.

- Application testing must be created and performed for a particular cloud environment. A major focus of application checks in a cloud environment is that of API credentials that are being used. Simply stated, you want to ensure that any application does not access other services with excessive privileges.

- If you are going to leverage new architectural options and requirements, you will need to update security policies and standards. Don't merely attempt to enforce existing policies and standards in a new environment, where things are created and run differently than in a traditional data center.

- Use software-defined security to automate security controls.

- Event-driven security is a game-changer. Using serverless technology, you can easily kick off a script that will automatically respond to a potential incident.

- Applications can be run in different cloud environments, such as under different accounts, to improve segregation of management plane access.

Questions

1. Prior to developing applications in a cloud, which training(s) should be undertaken by security team members?

    A. Vendor-neutral cloud training

    B. Provider-specific training

    C. Development tool training

    D. A and B

2. Tristan has just been hired as CIO of a company. His first desired action is to implement DevOps. Which of the following is the first item that Tristan should focus on as part of DevOps?

　A. Selecting an appropriate continuous integration server

　B. Choosing a proof-of-concept project that will be the first use of DevOps

　C. Understanding the existing corporate culture and getting leadership buy-in

　D. Choosing the appropriate cloud service for DevOps

3. When you're planning a vulnerability assessment, what is the first action you should take?

　A. Determine the scope of the vulnerability assessment.

　B. Determine the platform to be tested.

　C. Determine whether the vendor needs to be given notification in advance of the assessment.

　D. Determine whether the assessment will be performed as an outsider or on the server instance used by the running application.

4. Better segregation of the management plane can be performed by doing which of the following?

　A. Run all applications in a PaaS.

　B. Run applications in their own cloud account.

　C. Leverage DevOps.

　D. Use immutable workloads.

5. How can security be increased in an immutable environment?

　A. By disabling remote logins

　B. By implementing event-driven security

　C. By leveraging serverless computing if offered by the provider

　D. By increasing the frequency of vulnerability assessments

6. Which of the following CI/CD statements is *false*?

　A. Security tests can be automated.

　B. A CI/CD system can automatically generate audit logs.

　C. A CI/CD system replaces the current change management processes.

　D. A CI/CD leverages a continuous integration server.

7. How does penetration testing change as a result of the cloud?

   A. The penetration tester must understand the various provider services that may be part of the application.

   B. In most cases, server instances used to run applications will have customized kernels, which will not be understood by anyone except the provider.

   C. Because of the nature of virtual networking, penetration tests must be performed by the cloud provider.

   D. Penetration testing is not possible with containers, so many pentest results will be inconclusive.

8. During which phase of the SSDLC should threat modeling be performed by customers?

   A. Design

   B. Development

   C. Deployment

   D. Operations

9. During which phase of the SSDLC should penetration testing first be performed by customers?

   A. Design

   B. Development

   C. Deployment

   D. Operations

10. What is event-driven security?

   A. When a provider will shut down a service for customers in the event of an attack being detected

   B. Automating a response in the event of a notification, as established by the provider

   C. Automating response in the event of a notification, as established by the customer

   D. Automatic notification to a system administrator of an action being performed

Answers

1. **D.** Security team members should take both vendor-neutral training (such as CCSK) and provider-specific training (these are also recommended for developers and operations staff). Tools that are specific to deployments are not listed as required for security team members, only for operations and development staff.

2. C. Remember that DevOps is a culture, not a tool or technology (although a continuous integration service is a key component of the CI/CD pipeline that will be leveraged by DevOps). Understanding the existing corporate culture and getting leadership buy-in should be Tristan's first course of action in implementing DevOps in his new position. DevOps is not a cloud technology.

3. C. You should always determine whether a vendor must be advised of any assessment in advance. If the provider requires advance notice as part of the terms and conditions of your use, not advising them of an assessment may be considered a breach of contract. Answers A and B are standard procedures as part of an assessment and must be performed regardless of the cloud. Answer D is an interesting one, because you are not guaranteed even to have a server instance to log onto as part of your assessment. The application could be built using PaaS, serverless, or some other technology managed by the provider.

4. B. Running applications in their own cloud accounts can lead to tighter segregation of the management plane. None of the other answers is applicable for this question.

5. A. When leveraging immutable workloads, security can be increased by removing the ability to log in remotely. Any changes must be made centrally in immutable environments. File integrity monitoring can also be implemented to enhance security, as any change made to an immutable instance is likely evidence of a security incident.

6. C. The false statement is that a CI/CD system replaces the current change management processes. In fact, a CI/CD system can integrate with your current change management system. All the other statements are true.

7. A. There is a high probability that applications will leverage various cloud provider services. How communication between these services occurs is critical for the penetration tester, so only testers with experience in a particular platform should perform these tests.

8. A. Threat modeling should be performed as part of the application design phase, before a single line of code is actually written during the development phase.

9. C. Penetration testing should be initially performed as part of the deployment phase of the SSDLC. You need to have an actual application to perform penetration testing against, and this testing should be performed before the application runs in a production environment. Of course, periodic penetration testing is a good thing during the operations phase, but the question asked when it should *first* be performed.

10. C. Event-driven security is the implementation of automated responses to notifications. This is created by the customer, who often leverages some form of API monitoring. If an API is used, this will trigger a workflow that may include both sending a message to a system administrator and running a script to address the instance automatically (such as reverting a change, changing virtual firewall rulesets, and so on).

Data Security and Encryption

This chapter covers the following topics from Domain 11 of the CSA Guidance:
- Data Security Controls
- Cloud Data Storage Types
- Managing Data Migrations to the Cloud
- Securing Data in the Cloud

b692bb0826305047a235d7dda55ca2a0

This quote shows encryption (albeit it not very strong) in action. Do yourself and your company a favor and never use MD5 as a way to "encrypt" credentials in code (in a cloud or in a data center). Bonus points if you run this string through an MD5 decryption program online.

This book has previously addressed information risk management from a business perspective. In this chapter, we turn our attention to security controls that are key enforcement tools for implementing information and data governance. We need to be selective with our controls and take a risk-based approach to securing data, because not all data requires the same level of protection.

Data stored in a cloud does not require any changes to your data security approach. That said, there is a natural inclination among many business leaders to apply strong security controls to any data that is to be hosted in a cloud environment instead of sticking with a tried-and-true, risk-based approach, which will be far more secure and cost-effective than a blanket policy that protects all data (even data meant to be publicly consumed) with strong security controls.

Nobody ever said all data must be stored in a cloud. If your company deems that a particular data set is so critically important to the company that improper access by the provider would be devastating, then maybe that data should not be held in the cloud in the first place, encrypted or not.

When considering data security, you need to focus especially on the basics, which still matter. Once you get the basics right, you can move on to more advanced controls such as data encryption both at rest and in transit. After all, how important is "military-grade-strength encryption" when a file is accidentally set up to be accessed by anyone in the world?

Data Security Controls

When considering data security controls in cloud environments, you need to consider three main components:

- Determine which data is allowed to be stored in the cloud, based on data classifications (covered in Chapter 5) that address your legal and regulatory compliance requirements. Pay particular attention to permitted jurisdictions and storage media.

- Protect and manage data security in the cloud. This will involve establishing a secure architecture, proper access controls, encryption, detection capabilities, and other security controls as needed.

- Ensure compliance with proper audit logging established and backups and business continuity in place.

Cloud Data Storage Types

Back in Chapter 8, you learned about the physical and virtual implementations of storage. This chapter dives deeper into the different ways storage technologies are generally exposed to customers. Following are the most common ways storage can be consumed by customers of a cloud provider:

- **Object storage**   This storage type is presented like a file system and is usually accessible via APIs or a front-end interface (such as the Web). Files (such as objects) can be made accessible to multiple systems simultaneously. This storage type can be less secure, as it has often been discovered to be accidentally made available to the public Internet. Examples of common object storage include Amazon S3, Microsoft Azure Block binary large objects (blobs), and Google Cloud Storage service.

 NOTE   Blob storage is used to hold unstructured data such as video, audio, and other file types.

- **Volume storage**   This is a storage medium such as a hard drive that you attach to your server instance. Generally a volume can be attached only to a single server instance at a time.

- **Database**   Cloud service providers may offer customers a wide variety of database types, including commercial and open source options. Quite often, providers will also offer proprietary databases with their own APIs. These databases are hosted by the provider and use existing standards for connectivity. Databases offered can be relational or nonrelational. Examples of nonrelational databases include NoSQL, other key/value storage systems, and file system–based databases such as Hadoop Distributed File System (HDFS).

- **Application/platform** This storage is managed by the provider. Examples of application/platform storage include content delivery networks (CDNs), files stored in Software as a Service (SaaS) applications (such as a customer relationship management [CRM] system), caching services, and other options.

Regardless of the storage model in use, most CSPs employ redundant, durable storage mechanisms that use data dispersion (also called "data fragmentation of bit splitting" in the CSA Guidance). This process takes data (say, an object), breaks it up into smaller fragments, makes multiple copies of these fragments, and stores them across multiple servers and multiple drives to provide high durability (resiliency). In other words, a single file would not be located on a single hard drive, but would be spread across multiple hard drives.

Each of these storage types has different threats and data protection options, which can differ depending on the provider. For example, typically you can give individual users access to individual objects, but a storage volume is allocated to a virtual machine (VM) in its entirety. This means your approach to securing data in a cloud environment will be based on the storage model used.

Managing Data Migrations to the Cloud

Organizations need to have control over data that is stored with private and public cloud providers. This is often driven by the value of data and the laws and regulations that create compliance requirements.

To determine what data is "cloud friendly," you need to have policies in place that state the types of data that can be moved, the acceptable service and deployment models, and the baseline security controls that need to be applied. For example, you may have a policy in place that states that personally identifiable information (PII) is allowed to be stored and processed only on specific CSP platforms in specific jurisdictions that are corporately sanctioned and have appropriate controls over storage of data at rest.

Once acceptable storage locations are determined, you must monitor them for activity using tools such as a database activity monitor (DAM) and file activity monitor (FAM). These controls can be not only detective in nature but may also prevent large data migrations from occurring.

The following tools and technologies can be useful for monitoring cloud usage and any data transfers:

- **Cloud access security broker (CASB)** CASB (pronounced "KAS-bee") systems were originally built to protect SaaS deployments and monitor their usage, but they have recently expanded to address some concerns surrounding Platform as a Service (PaaS) and Infrastructure as a Service (IaaS) deployments as well. You can use CASB to discover your actual usage of cloud services through multiple means such as network monitoring, integration with existing network gateways and monitoring tools, or even monitoring Domain Name System (DNS) queries. This could be considered a form of a discovery service. Once the various services in use are discovered, a CASB can monitor activity on approved services either through an API connection or inline (man-in-the-middle) interception. Quite often, the power of a CASB is dependent on its data loss prevention (DLP) capabilities (which can be either part of the CASB or an external service, depending on the CASB vendor's capabilities).

- **URL filtering**   URL filtering (such as a web gateway) may help you understand which cloud services your users are using (or trying to use). The problem with URL filtering, however, is that generally you are stuck in a game of "whack-a-mole" when trying to control which services are allowed to be used and which ones are not. URL filtering will generally use a whitelist or blacklist to determine whether or not users are permitted to access a particular web site.

- **Data loss prevention**   A DLP tool may help detect data migrations to cloud services. You should, however, consider a couple of issues with DLP technology. First, you need to "train" a DLP to understand what is sensitive data and what is not. Second, a DLP cannot inspect traffic that is encrypted. Some cloud SDKs and APIs may encrypt portions of data and traffic, which will interfere with the success of a DLP implementation.

 EXAM TIP   Anything that you will be tested on as part of your CCSK exam regarding CASB has been covered in this section, but there is much more to know about this technology, which is covered in the backgrounder.

CASB Backgrounder

CASB began as an SaaS security control but has recently moved toward protecting both PaaS and IaaS. The CASB serves multiple purposes, the first of which is performing a discovery scan of currently used SaaS products in your organization. It does this by reading network logs that are taken from an egress (outbound) network appliance. As the network logs are read, a reverse DNS lookup is performed to track the IP addresses to provider domain names. The resulting report can then tell you what services are used and how often. Optionally, if the discovery service supports it, you may be able to see the users who are using particular SaaS services.

 NOTE   Remember that you will not be tested on backgrounder material as part of your CCSK exam. It is provided for your understanding of this important technology.

After the discovery is performed, CASB can be used as a preventative control to block access to SaaS products. This functionality, however, is being quickly replaced through the integration of DLP. Through integration with a DLP service, you can continue to allow access to an SaaS product, but you can control what is being done within that SaaS product. For example, if somebody uses Twitter, you can restrict certain keywords or statements from being sent to the platform. Consider, for example, a financial services company. A disclosure law states that recommendations cannot be made without disclosure regarding the company's and individual's ownership position of the underlying

> ## Is It an SaaS App or Just a Web Site?
>
> Just a final thought on Twitter being used as an example of an SaaS. The line between what is a web site and what is an SaaS is quickly being blurred. I like to consider whether the web site is being used for legitimate business purposes and, if so, whether it is an SaaS application even though it may be free. Many companies offer customer support on Twitter, for example. To me, this makes Twitter a business application and therefore qualifies it as an SaaS application. How about a used car web site? If you are a car dealership, your web site is most likely being used to buy and sell cars and is therefore a business application, not just a time-waster used by employees when they are bored. I mention this because many CASB vendors claim that the average company uses more than 1500 SaaS applications. But in reality, they are counting the number of sites employees access for both business and personal purposes.

stock. In this case, you can allow people to use Twitter for promotion of the brokerage company itself, but you can restrict them from making expressions such as "Apple stock will go up $50 per share."

Now that you know about CASB discovery and inline filtering capabilities, let's move on to the API integration aspect that some CASBs can offer. When you are considering a CASB for API integration, you are looking to determine how people are using that cloud product by being able to see things about the metastructure of the offering. This is where CASB can tell you the amount of logins that have occurred, for example, and other details about the cloud environment itself. You need to pay particular attention to whether the CASB vendor supports the platform APIs that you are actually consuming.

Concerning inline filtering versus API integration of CASBs, most vendors have moved toward a hybrid model that offers both. This is a maturing technology and is experiencing rapid changes. When you're investigating CASB, it is very important that you perform vendor comparisons based on what you actually need versus what the CASB vendors offer. After all, who cares if a CASB supports the most APIs by volume if it doesn't support any of the providers you use or plan to use in the near future? The same can be said for integration being able to leverage external DLP solutions.

Regarding the use of CASB for control of PaaS and IaaS, this is a fairly new introduction to the majority of CASBs in the marketplace. You will get API coverage of only the metastructure for the most part. In other words, you cannot expect the CASB to act as some form of application security testing tool for the applications that you are running in a PaaS, for example, and you cannot expect to use a CASB to act as a centralized location to perform vulnerability assessment of instances in an IaaS environment.

Securing Cloud Data Transfers

To protect data as it is moving to a cloud, you need to focus on the security of data in transit. For example, does your provider support Secure File Transfer Protocol (SFTP), or do they require you to use File Transfer Protocol (FTP) that uses clear-text credentials across the Internet? Your vendor may expose an API to you that has strong security mechanisms in place, so there is no requirement on your behalf to increase security.

As far as encryption of data in transit is concerned, many of the approaches used today are the same approaches that have been used in the past. This includes Transport Layer Security (TLS), Virtual Private Network (VPN) access, and other secure means of transferring data. If your provider doesn't offer these basic security controls, get a different provider—seriously.

Another option for ensuring encryption of data in transit is that of a proxy (aka hybrid storage gateway or cloud storage gateway). The job of the proxy device is to encrypt data using your encryption keys prior to it being sent out on the Internet and to your provider. This technology, while promising, has not achieved the expected rate of adoption that many, including myself, anticipated. Your provider may offer software versions of this technology, however, as a service to its customers.

When you're considering transferring very large amounts of data to a provider, do not overlook shipping of hard drives to the provider if possible. Although data transfers across the Internet are much faster than they were ten years ago, I would bet that shipping 10 petabytes of data would be much faster than copying it over the Internet. Remember, though, that when you're shipping data, your company may have a policy that states all data leaving your data center in physical form must be encrypted. If this is the case, talk with your provider regarding how best to do this. Many providers offer the capability of shipping drives and/or tapes to them. Some even offer proprietary hardware options for such purposes that they will ship to you.

Finally, some data transfers may involve data that you do not own or manage, such as data from public or untrusted sources. You should ensure that you have security mechanisms in place to inspect this data before processing or mixing it in with your existing data.

Securing Data in the Cloud

You need to be aware of only two security controls for your CCSK exam: The core data security controls are *access controls* and *encryption*. Remember that access controls are your number-one controls. If you mess this up, all the other controls fall apart. Once you get the basics right (meaning access controls), then you can move on to implementing appropriate encryption of data at rest using a risk-based approach. Let's look at these controls.

Cloud Data Access Controls

Access controls must be implemented properly in three main areas:

- **Management plane**   These access controls are used to restrict access to the actions that can be taken in the CSP's management plane. Most CSPs have deny-by-default access control policies in place for any new accounts that may be created.

- **Public and internal sharing controls**   These controls must be planned and implemented when data is shared externally to the public or to partners. As you read in Chapter 1, several companies have found themselves on the front pages of national newspapers after getting these access controls wrong by making object storage available to the public.

- **Application-level controls**   Applications themselves must have appropriate controls designed and implemented to manage access. This includes both your own applications built in PaaS as well as any SaaS applications your organization consumes.

With the exception of application-level controls, your options for implementing access controls will vary based on the cloud service model and the provider's specific features. To assist with planning appropriate access controls, you can use an entitlement matrix on platform-specific capabilities. This entitlement matrix is essentially a grid, similar to the following, that lists the users, groups, and roles with access levels for resources and functions:

Entitlement	Super Admin	Service Admin	Storage Admin	Developers	Security Audit	Security Admin
Volume Describe	X	X		X	X	X
Object Describe	X		X	X	X	X
Volume Modify	X	X		X		X
Read Logs	X				X	X

NOTE   I will cover these entitlement matrices in Chapter 12.

After entitlements are established, you must frequently validate that your controls meet requirements, with a particular focus on public-sharing controls. You can establish alerts for all new public shares or for changes in permission that allow public access to quickly identify any overly permissive entitlements.

It is important that you understand the capabilities exposed by the provider to support appropriate access controls on all data under your control and that you build your entitlement matrix and implement these controls in the environment. This spans all data such as databases and all cloud data stores.

NOTE   The primary purpose of an entitlement matrix is to implement application-level operational risk controls. If the provider doesn't offer you the ability to fine-tune permissions (aka granularity) needed to implement your entitlements, you should look for a different provider.

Storage (at Rest) Encryption and Tokenization

Before I discuss model-specific encryption options, I need to address the various ways that data can be protected at rest. The two technologies addressed in the CSA Guidance are *encryption* and *tokenization*. Both of these technologies make data unreadable to unauthorized users or systems that are trying to read your data.

Encryption scrambles the data to make it unreadable for the foreseeable future (well, until quantum computing becomes mainstream, at which point all bets are off—but I digress). Tokenization replaces each element of a data set with a random value. The tokenization system stores both the original data and the randomized version in a secure database for later retrieval.

Tokenization is a method proposed by the payment card industry (PCI) as a means to protect credit card numbers. In a PCI tokenization system, for example, a publicly accessible tokenization server can be used as a front end to protect actual credit card information that is held in a secure database in the back end. When a payment is processed, the vendor receives a token that acts like a reference ID that can be used to perform actions on a transaction such as refunds. At no time does the vendor need to store actual credit card information; rather, they store these tokens.

The CSA Guidance states that tokenization is often used when the format of the data is important. Format-preserving encryption (FPE) encrypts data but keeps the same structural format.

 EXAM TIP Remember for your exam that encryption will often dramatically increase the string of a text, while tokenization and data masking techniques can keep the same length and format of data while rendering it unusable to anyone who may access it.

FPE vs. Standard Encryption

What problem does FPE solve? Let's look at an example of a credit card that goes through MD5, AES-256, and finally tokenization.

- Original credit card number: 4503 7253 6154 9980
- MD5 value: 3f50ae380920a524b260237b2c63fe0d
- AES-256 value: VS3kSTTJc8mNk8NChcfFscekJFUW1UwdT3zwpf0xAsL n+tV4mCKqwMdJp9yrHRgl
- Tokenized value: 4623 5622 9867 5645

In this example, we are using a format-preserving encryption tokenization example (not all tokenization systems need to be format-preserving). Unlike the other examples, the format is the same, but the real card number is "obfuscated," meaning it is useless to anyone who improperly accesses the data.

Another example of format-preserving encryption is data masking. The main difference between the two obfuscation technologies is reversibility. Tokens that use FPE can use a known "alphabet" to change the numbers and can be reversible, whereas data masking is often irreversible. Tokens are often used in payment-processing systems to protect credit card numbers, while data masking is often used for development environments.

In the cloud, there are three components of an encryption system and two locations. The three components are the data itself, the encryption engine, and key management that holds the encryption keys.

Any of these components can be run in any location. For example, your data could be in a cloud environment, and the encryption engine and key-management service that holds the keys could be within your data center. Really, any combination is possible. The combination will often be based on your risk appetite. One organization could be perfectly fine with all three being in a cloud environment, whereas another organization would require that all data be stored in a cloud environment only after being encrypted locally.

These security requirements will drive the overall design of your encryption architecture. When designing an encryption system, you should start with a threat model and answer some basic questions such as these:

- Do you trust the cloud provider to store your keys?

- How could the keys be exposed?

- Where should you locate the encryption engine to manage the threats you are concerned with?

- Which option best meets your risk tolerance requirements: managing the keys yourself or letting the provider do that for you?

- Is there separation of duties between storing the data encryption keys, storing the encrypted data, and storing the master key?

The answers to these and other questions will help guide your encryption system design for cloud services.

Now that you understand the high-level elements of encryption and obfuscation in a cloud environment, let's look at how encryption can be performed in particular service models.

IaaS Encryption

When considering encryption in IaaS, you need to think about the two main storage offerings: volume-storage and object- and file-storage encryption.

Volume-storage encryption involves the following:

- **Instance-managed encryption** The encryption engine runs inside the instance itself. An example of this is the Linux Unified Key Setup. The issue with instance-managed encryption is that the key itself is stored in the instance and protected with a passphrase. In other words, you could have AES-256 encryption secured with a passphrase of 1234.

- **Externally managed encryption** Externally managed encryption stores encryption keys externally, and a key to unlock data is issued to the instance on request.

Object-storage encryption involves the following:

- **Client-side encryption**   In this case, data is encrypted using an encryption engine embedded in the application or client. In this model, you are in control of the encryption keys used to encrypt the data.

- **Server-side encryption**   Server-side encryption is supplied by the CSP, who has access to the encryption key and runs the encryption engine. Although this is the easiest way to encrypt data, this approach requires the highest level of trust in a provider. If the provider holds the encryption keys, they may be forced (compelled) by a government agency to unencrypt and supply your data.

- **Proxy encryption**   This is a hybrid storage gateway. This approach can work well with object and file storage in an IaaS environment, as the provider is not required to access your data in order to deliver services. In this scenario, the proxy handles all cryptography operations, and the encryption keys may be held within the appliance or by an external key-management service.

PaaS Encryption

Unlike IaaS, where there are a few dominant players, there are numerous PaaS providers, all with different capabilities as far as encryption is concerned. The CSA Guidance calls out three areas where encryption can be used in a PaaS environment:

- **Application-layer encryption**   When you're running applications in a PaaS environment, any required encryption services are generally implemented within the application itself or on the client accessing the platform.

- **Database encryption**   PaaS database offerings will generally offer built-in encryption capabilities that are supported by the database platform. Examples of common encryption capabilities include Transparent Database Encryption (TDE), which encrypts the entire database, and field-level encryption, which encrypts only sensitive portions of the database.

- **Other**   PaaS providers may offer encryption for various components that may be used by applications such as message queuing services.

SaaS Encryption

Encryption of SaaS is quite different from that of IaaS and PaaS. Unlike the other models, SaaS generally is used by a business to process data to deliver insightful information (such as a CRM system). The SaaS provider may also use the encryption options available for IaaS and PaaS providers. CSPs are also recommended to implement per-customer keys whenever possible to improve the enforcement of multitenancy isolation.

NOTE   Customers may choose to use the encryption supplied by the provider for many reasons. For example, data that is encrypted by the client (by implementation of an encryption proxy) may not be able to be processed by the provider.

Key Management (Including Customer-Managed Keys)

Strong key management is a critical component of encryption. After all, if you lose your encryption keys, you lose access to any encrypted data, and if a bad actor has access to the keys, they can access the data. The main considerations concerning key-management systems according to the CSA Guidance are the performance, accessibility, latency, and security of the key-management system.

The following four key-management system deployment options are covered in the CSA Guidance:

- **HSM/appliance**   Use a traditional hardware security module (HSM) or appliance-based key manager, which will typically need to be on premises (some vendors offer cloud HSM), and deliver the keys to the cloud over a dedicated connection. Given the size of the key material, many vendors will state that there is very little latency involved with this approach to managing keys for data held in a cloud environment.

- **Virtual appliance/software**   A key-management system does not need to be hardware-based. You can deploy a virtual appliance or software-based key manager in a cloud environment to maintain keys within a provider's environment to reduce potential latency or disruption in network communication between your data center and cloud-based systems. In such a deployment, you still own the encryption keys, and they cannot be used by the provider if legal authorities demand access to your data.

- **Cloud provider service**   This key-management service is offered by the cloud provider. Before selecting this option, make sure you understand the security model and service level agreements (SLAs) to determine whether your key could possibly be exposed. You also need to understand that although this is the most convenient option for key management in a cloud environment, the provider has access to the keys and can be forced by legal authorities to hand over any data upon request.

- **Hybrid**   This is a combination system, such as using an HSM as the root of trust for keys but then delivering application-specific keys to a virtual appliance that's located in the cloud and manages keys only for its particular context.

Many providers (such as storage) may offer encryption by default with some services (such as object storage). In this scenario, the provider owns and manages the encryption keys. Because the provider holding the encryption keys may be seen as a risk, most providers generally implement systems that impose separation of duties. To use keys to gain access to customer data would require collusion among multiple provider employees. Of course, if the provider is able to unencrypt the data (which they can if they manage the key and the engine), they must do so if required to by legal authorities. Customers should determine whether they can replace default provider keys with their own that will work with the provider's encryption engine.

Customer-managed encryption keys are controlled to some extent by the customer. For example, a provider may expose a service that either generates or imports an encryption key. Once in the system, the customer selects the individuals who can administer and/or use the key to encrypt and decrypt data. As the key is integrated with the provider's encryption system, access to encrypted data can be used with the encryption engine created and managed by the provider. As with provider-managed keys, because these keys are accessible to the provider, the provider must use them to deliver data to legal authorities if required to do so.

If the data you are storing is so sensitive that you cannot risk a government accessing it, you have two choices: use your own encryption that you are in complete control of, or don't process this data in a cloud environment.

 NOTE Data that is processed in a cloud environment needs to be unencrypted in order to be processed. This will remain true until homomorphic encryption becomes a valid technology.

Data Security Architecture

You know that cloud providers spend a lot of time and money ensuring strong security in their environments. Using provider-supplied services as part of your architecture can result in an increase of your overall security posture. For example, you can realize large architectural security benefits by something as simple as having cloud instances transfer data through a service supplied by the provider.

Consider, for example, a scenario in which you need to analyze a set of data. Using a secure architecture design (shown in Figure 11-1), you could copy the data to your

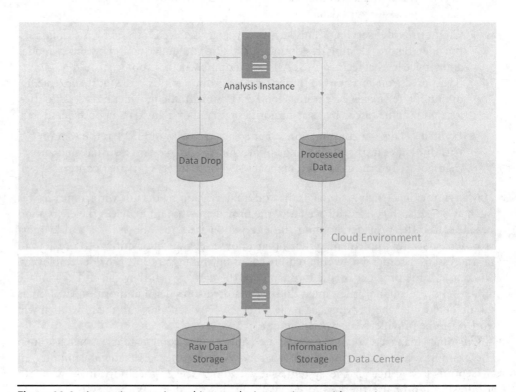

Figure 11-1 Increasing security architecture by integrating provider service

provider's object store. Your cloud analysis instance accesses the object storage, collects the data, and then processes the data. It then sends the processed information to the object storage and sends you a notification that your job is done. To retrieve the information you want, you connect to the storage directly and download the file(s). Your application does what is needed, and there is no path from a server running in a hostile network to your data center. This is just one example of the infinite possibilities regarding new security architecture patterns possible with cloud.

In many cases, you will be able to find opportunities to incorporate provider services into your architecture that will be more scalable, cheaper, and more secure than traditional architecture patterns used in your current computing environment.

Monitoring, Auditing, and Alerting

When considering monitoring of your cloud environment, you need to have access to telemetry data from both the applistructure and metastructure layers. In other words, you need to collect logging from the server and applications (applistructure), as well as from the metastructure itself.

- **Applistructure**   Collect event logs from servers and applications and deliver to security information and event management (SIEM). To collect database activity, consider a DAM solution.
- **Metastructure**   Collect any data from the API activity occurring in your cloud environment, as well as logs from any service you may be consuming, such as any file access in object storage.

Strong monitoring, auditing, and alerting capabilities cannot be seen as optional. Copies of log data should be stored in a safe location, such as a separate logging account. You want to do this for multiple reasons, including chain of custody for legal purposes. Note, however, that log data will likely need to be accessible to administrators and engineers so they can troubleshoot issues. You may want to determine whether the provider offers the ability to replicate this data to the logging account. This way, administrators can access the logs without requiring any access to a centralized logging area.

Additional Data Security Controls

Numerous additional security controls can help augment security. The following sections address some options for securing systems and information in a cloud environment.

Cloud Platform/Provider-Specific Controls

It is essentially impossible to keep up with all of the various controls offered by cloud providers, especially IaaS providers. Providers may offer machine learning–based anomaly detection, intrusion prevention systems, layer 7 firewalls (such as web application firewalls), data classification systems, and more. In fact, provider offerings that are not designed for security can be leveraged to augment security. Examples include increasing security architecture through the implementation of a service that removes direct data paths, or even services that can tell you the various services consumed by an application running in a serverless environment.

 EXAM TIP These additional services and how they can be leveraged are provider-specific, so you won't be tested on them as part of your CCSK exam. The following technologies *are* in the guidance, however, so you do need to understand them prior to attempting the exam.

Data Loss Prevention

A DLP system is both a preventative and detective control that can be used to detect potential breaches or misuse of data based on information it is programmed to identify. It can work with data in use (installed on an endpoint or server, for example), in motion (such as a network device), or at rest (such as scan data in storage). DLP systems need to be configured to understand what is sensitive data and in what context it is considered sensitive. For example, the words "jump" and "roof" themselves are not words to be concerned about, but the phrase, "I'm going to jump off the roof," is a very concerning statement. As with the statement, the individual pieces of information may not be considered sensitive or important, but in certain contexts, they are very much so. DLP can be configured to understand what a credit card number looks like, for example, to perform a test (a Luhn algorithm check) to ensure that it is a valid credit card number, and then to report or block that data from being sent to another system or outside of your network.

DLP is generally considered an SaaS security control. You know that DLP services are often used in a CASB to identify and stop potentially sensitive data from being sent to an SaaS product through integration with inline inspection. DLP functionality in a CASB can either be supplied as part of the CASB itself or it can integrate with an existing DLP platform. When investigating potential CASB solutions, you should be sure to identify the DLP functionality and whether it will integrate with an existing DLP platform you own. The success of your CASB to identify and protect sensitive data will rely heavily on the effectiveness of the DLP solution it is leveraging.

Your CSP may offer DLP capabilities as well. For example, cloud file storage and collaboration products may be able to scan uploaded files using preconfigured keywords and/or regular expressions in their DLP system.

Enterprise Rights Management

Enterprise rights management (ERM, not to be confused with enterprise *risk* management) and digital rights management (DRM) are both security controls that provide control over accessing data. While DRM is more of a mass-consumer control and typically used with media such as books, music, video games, and other consumer offerings, ERM is typically used as an employee security control that can control actions that can be performed on files, such as copy and paste operations, taking screenshots, printing, and other actions. Need to send a sensitive file to a partner but want to ensure the file isn't copied? ERM can be used to protect the file (to a degree).

NOTE Enterprise rights management is also known as information rights management.

Both ERM and DRM technologies are not often offered or applicable in a cloud environment. Both technologies rely on encryption, and as you know, encryption can break capabilities, especially with SaaS.

Data Masking and Test Data Generation

Data masking is an obfuscation technology that alters data while preserving its original format. Data masking can address multiple standards such as the Payment Card Industry Data Security Standard (PCI DSS), personally identifiable information (PII) standards, and protected health information (PHI) standards. Consider a credit card number, for example:

4000 3967 6245 5243

With masking, this is changed to

8276 1625 3736 2820

This example shows a substitution technique, where the credit card numbers are changed to perform the masking. Other data-masking techniques include encryption, scrambling, nulling out, and shuffling.

Data masking is generally performed in one of two ways: *test data generation* (often referred to as static data masking) and *dynamic data masking*:

- **Test data generation**   A data-masking application is used to extract data from a database, transform the data, and then duplicate it to another database in a development or test environment. This is generally performed so production data is not used during development.

- **Dynamic data masking**   Data is held within its original database, but the data stream is altered in real time (on the fly), typically by a proxy, depending on who is accessing the data. Take a payroll database, for example. If a developer accesses the data, salary information would be masked. But if an HR manager accesses the same data, she will see the actual salary data.

Enforcing Lifecycle Management Security

As mentioned, data residency can have significant legal consequences. Understand the methods exposed by your provider to ensure that data and systems are restricted to approved geographies. You will want to establish both preventative controls to prohibit individuals from accessing unapproved regions and detective controls to alert you if the preventative controls fail. Provider encryption can also be used to protect data that is accidentally moved across regions, assuming the encryption key is unavailable in the region to which data was accidentally copied.

All controls need to be documented, tested, and approved. Artifacts of compliance may be required to prove that you are maintaining compliance in your cloud environment.

Chapter Review

This chapter addressed the recommendations for data security and encryption according to the CSA Guidance. You should be comfortable with the following items in preparation for your CCSK exam:

- Access controls are your single most important controls.

- All cloud vendors and platforms are different. You will need to understand the specific capabilities of the platforms and services that your organization is consuming.

- Leveraging cloud provider services can augment overall security. In many cases, a provider will offer controls at a lower cost than controls you would have to build and maintain yourself and that don't have the same scalability or orchestration capabilities.

- Entitlement matrices should be built and agreed upon with a system owner to determine access controls. Once these are finalized, you can implement the access controls. The granularity of potential access controls will be dependent on cloud provider capabilities.

- Cloud access security brokers (CASBs) can be used to monitor and enforce policies on SaaS usage.

- Remember that there are three components involved with encryption (engine, keys, and data), and these components can be located in a cloud or a local environment.

- Customer-managed keys can be managed by a customer but are held by the provider.

- Provider-managed encryption can make encryption as simple as checking a box. This may address compliance, but you need to ensure that your provider's encryption system is acceptable from a security perspective.

- Whenever the provider can access an encryption key, they may be forced to provide data to government authorities if required to do so by law. If this is an unacceptable risk, either encrypt the data locally with your own keys or avoid storing that data in a cloud environment.

- Using your own encryption (such as using an encryption proxy device) will generally break SaaS. Unlike IaaS and PaaS providers, SaaS providers are often used to process data into valuable information.

- Did I mention access controls are your most important controls?

- New architectural patterns are possible with the cloud. Integrating cloud provider services as part of your architecture can improve security.

- Security requires both protective and detective controls. If you can't detect an incident, you can never respond to it. Make sure you are logging both API- and data-level activity and that logs meet compliance and lifecycle policy requirements.

- There are several standards for encryption and key-management techniques and processes. These include NIST SP 800-57, ANSI X9.69, and X9.73. (Note: Just know that these exist; you don't need to study these standards in preparation for your CCSK exam.)

Questions

1. What should be offered by SaaS providers to enforce multitenancy isolation?

   A. Provider-managed keys

   B. Encryption based on AES-256

   C. Per-customer keys

   D. Customer-managed hardware security module

2. If your organization needs to ensure that data stored in a cloud environment will not be accessed without permission by anyone, including the provider, what can you do?

   A. Use a local HSM and import generated keys into the provider's encryption system as a customer-managed key.

   B. Use an encryption key based on a proprietary algorithm.

   C. Do not store the data in a cloud environment.

   D. Use customer-managed keys to allow for encryption while having complete control over the key itself.

3. Which of the following controls can be used to transform data based on the individual accessing the data?

   A. Enterprise rights management

   B. Dynamic data masking

   C. Test data generation

   D. Data loss prevention

4. Why would an SaaS provider require that customers use provider-supplied encryption?

   A. Data encrypted by a customer prior to being sent to the provider application may break functionality.

   B. Customer-managed keys do not exist in SaaS.

   C. SaaS cannot use encryption because it breaks functionality.

   D. All SaaS implementations require that all tenants use the same encryption key.

5. Which of the following storage types is presented like a file system and is usually accessible via APIs or a front-end interface?

   A. Object storage

   B. Volume storage

   C. Database storage

   D. Application/platform storage

6. Which of the following should be considered your primary security control?

   A. Encryption

   B. Logging

   C. Data residency restrictions

   D. Access controls

7. Which of the following deployment models allows for a customer to have complete control over encryption key management when implemented in a provider's cloud environment?

   A. HSM/appliance-based key management

   B. Virtual appliance/software key management

   C. Provider-managed key management

   D. Customer-managed key management

8. Which of the following security controls is listed by the payment card industry as a form of protecting credit card data?

   A. Tokenization

   B. Provider-managed keys

   C. Dynamic data masking

   D. Enterprise rights management

9. Which of the following is a main differentiator between URL filtering and CASB?

   A. DLP

   B. DRM

   C. ERM

   D. Ability to block access based on whitelists and blacklists

10. Which of the following is NOT a main component when considering data security controls in cloud environments?

    A. Controlling data allowed to be sent to a cloud

    B. Protecting and managing data security in the cloud

    C. Performing risk assessment of prospective cloud providers

    D. Enforcing information lifecycle management

Answers

1. **C.** SaaS providers are recommended to implement per-customer keys whenever possible to provide better multitenancy isolation enforcement.

2. **C.** Your only option is not using the cloud. If data is encrypted locally and then copied to a cloud, this would also stop a provider from being able to unencrypt the data if compelled by legal authorities to do so. It is generally not recommended that you create your own encryption algorithms, and they likely wouldn't work in a provider's environment anyway.

3. **B.** Only dynamic data masking will transform data on the fly with a device such as a proxy that can be used to restrict presentation of actual data based on the user accessing the data. Test data generation requires that data be exported and transformed for every user who is accessing the copied database. None of the other answers is applicable.

4. **A.** If a customer encrypts data prior to sending it to the SaaS provider, it may impact functionality. SaaS providers should offer customer-managed keys to enhance multitenancy isolation.

5. **A.** Object storage is presented like a file system and is usually accessible via APIs or a front-end interface. The other answers are incorrect.

6. **D.** Access controls are always your number-one security control.

7. **B.** The only option for an encryption key-management system in a cloud environment is the implementation of a virtual machine or software run on a virtual machine that the customer manages.

8. **A.** Tokenization is a control the payment card industry lists as an option to protect credit card data.

9. **A.** The main difference between URL filtering and CASB is that, unlike traditional whitelisting or blacklisting of domain names, CASB can use DLP when it is performing inline inspection of SaaS connections.

10. **C.** Although risk assessment of cloud providers is critical, this activity is not a data security control.

Identity, Entitlement, and Access Management

This chapter covers the following topics from Domain 12 of the CSA Guidance:
- Identity and Access Management Standards for Cloud Computing
- Managing Users and Identities
- Authentication and Credentials
- Entitlement and Access Management

Don't bore me with basics.

—Undisclosed system engineer

Someone actually said this as I was discussing the importance of proper identity and access management (IAM) for files stored in Amazon Web Services (AWS) S3. Some time later, it was discovered that this engineer's company had leaked millions of customer records via an AWS S3 share that granted access to everyone in the world. Yes, IAM may be "basic," but proper IAM is critical and cannot be dismissed.

As with all other security considerations in the cloud, IAM is a shared responsibility. As the customer, you are dependent on the provider for exposing robust controls not only for an identity service but also for entitlements and access controls (that is, identity, entitlement, and access, or IdEA). The most important concept you need to be familiar with regarding IAM in a cloud environment is *federated identity*. Federation will enable you to keep a consistent identity management approach across the multiple cloud platforms and services you use as a cloud consumer.

The cloud brings with it a need for changes to your existing IAM procedures with each provider, as each will have different controls exposed. You need to adopt these services with least privilege by design. IAM in the cloud requires a trust relationship between the customer and the provider and a clear understanding of the roles and responsibilities of each party.

Federation enables you to maintain control of authentication while delegating authorization to your CSPs based on your requirements. Cloud adoption of any significant size requires federation. Without federation, every user will require a user account in all services your organization uses.

NOTE   Both this book and the CSA Guidance often use the term "federation" in place of the more accurate term "federated identity."

This chapter focuses on the changes to IAM that have occurred as a result of using cloud services. Backgrounder information will take a deep dive into some of the standards covered in the CSA Guidance. As with all other backgrounders in this book, this information is included for your understanding of the technologies mentioned in the CSA Guidance; you won't be tested on backgrounder information in the CCSK exam.

How IAM Works in the Cloud

Let's begin this conversation with what doesn't change with IAM in the cloud. You still have to map an entity (anything interacting with a system, such as a person, a system, or an agent) to an identity that has attributes (such as a group) and then make an access decision based on resulting permissions. You may know this process as *role-based access control* (RBAC). So, a user is a member of a group and therefore gets permission to use a resource.

Working with many providers brings complications with regard to IAM. Without something like federated IAM, you will ultimately have to manage dozens, if not hundreds, of different IAM systems. You may manage the settings in all these different locations to enforce IAM, but you will have to control this in environments that are owned and operated by a cloud provider, and what they expose to you may be limited.

From an operational perspective, you will have to create every user account not just once in your on-premises directory service (such as Active Directory), but dozens or hundreds of times. Who in your company is going to provision all these accounts? Worse yet, who is responsible for deprovisioning all these accounts? Consider a company that uses 100 Software as a Service (SaaS) products and is forced to lay off 1000 users in a cost-cutting measure. That's 100,000 accounts that need to be disabled! How many people do you need to hire to do that?

Now consider the impact on your users in your environment. Your users have enough of a hard time remembering their corporate login details. Do you think they'll be able to handle remembering 100 different passwords? One of two things will inevitably happen—they'll use the same password in every SaaS system (not a great idea), or they'll flood your help desk asking for password resets (also suboptimal).

With these scenarios alone, I'm sure you can see why federation is a must-have technology that is being forced on your company as a result of cloud. This is why the CSA Guidance says that IAM in the cloud is a "forcing function." Wide-scale adoption of the cloud and the challenges faced from an IAM perspective will force companies to take action to address what will be (if it isn't already) a significant pain point. Addressing this will likely require the adoption of federation.

On top of federation, adoption of the cloud gives your organization an opportunity to build new infrastructure and processes on modern architectures and standards used in cloud environments. I'll be exploring some of these advancements and standards as part of this chapter.

IAM Terms

Many terms are associated with IAM, and they are not necessarily universal. Even the term "IAM" itself is not universal and is often referred to as "identity management" (IdM), or even "identity, entitlement, and access management" (IdEA). The following terms are used by the Cloud Security Alliance as part of the Guidance document. Remember them for your CCSK exam:

- **Entity**   Someone or something that has an identity.

- **Identity**   A unique expression of an entity within a given environment. For example, when you log onto a public web site, you usually do so with your e-mail address because this is globally unique. When you log into a work system, your username would be your identity.

- **Identifier**   A cryptographic token in a digital environment that identifies an identity (such as a user) to an application or service. Windows systems, for example, use a security identifier (SID) to identify users. In real life, an identifier could be a passport.

- **Attribute**   A facet (aspect) of an identity; anything about the identity and the connection itself. An attribute could be static (group membership, organizational unit) or highly dynamic (IP address used for your connection, your physical location). For example, if you log on with multifactor authentication, an attribute could be used to determine the permissions granted to your access (attribute-based access control).

- **Persona**   Your identity and attributes in a specific situation. You are you, but your persona will change based on context. For example, at work you may be an IT administrator; that's your work persona. At home, your persona may be the parent of two children. In your hockey league, your persona may be the left winger and captain of your team. Your identity is who you are. Your persona takes context and attributes into account.

- **Role**   1. A temporary credential that is inherited by a system within a cloud environment. 2. A part of federation; how your group membership within your company is granted entitlements in your Infrastructure as a Service (IaaS) provider. 3. The job you perform at work.

- **Authentication (Authn)**   The process of confirming your identity. Want to check into a hotel on a business trip? The first thing the front desk will ask for is your ID so they can authenticate that you are who you say you are. Of course in a digital world, we generally present a username and password to authenticate ourselves.

- **Multifactor authentication (MFA)** The three factors in authentication: something you know, something you have, and something you are. For example, you may be authenticating with your username and password (something you know) and then be prompted for a time-based one-time password (TOTP) generated on your cell phone with Google Authenticator (something you have).

- **Access control** A control that restricts access to a resource. This is the "access management" portion of IAM.

- **Accounting** Logging and monitoring capabilities.

- **Authorization (Authz)** The ability to allow an identity to do something. The hotel key you get after authorization allows you to access your room, the gym, laundry, and so on. In an IT analogy, you are authorized to access a file or system.

- **Entitlement** The permissions you have to something. The CSA uses the term "entitlements" rather than "permissions," but the meaning is the same. Entitlements determine what an identity is allowed to do by mapping an identity to an authorization. These can (and should) be documented as an entitlement matrix.

- **Single-sign-on (SSO)** A token or ticket system used to authorize a user rather than having the user sign on to individual systems in a domain. Kerberos is an example of SSO in a Windows environment.

- **Federated identity management** A key enabler of SSO across different systems that enables the action of authenticating locally and authorizing remotely.

- **Authoritative source** The "root" source of an identity. A common example of this is a directory server (such as Active Directory). Alternatively, the payroll system could be the true authoritative source.

- **Identity provider** The party that manages the identities and creates the identity assertions used in federation.

- **Relying party** The system that consumes identity assertions from the identity provider. This is sometimes referred to as a "service provider."

 EXAM TIP Remember these terms for your exam.

IAM Standards

There are numerous standards in the IAM world that you need to know about. I'm breaking this section into two parts: The first part covers what the CSA Guidance has to say on the standards, and the second part presents a series of backgrounders that will discuss each standard at a deeper level to improve your understanding.

For your CCSK exam, you may be tested on the following information regarding each standard:

- **Security Assertion Markup Language (SAML)**   This OASIS standard for federated identity management supports both authentication and authorization. Assertions are based on XML and are used between an identity provider and a relying party. These assertions can contain authentication, attribute, and authorization statements. SAML is widely supported by many cloud providers and many enterprise tools as a result. SAML is initially complex to configure.

- **OAuth**   This IETF authorization standard is widely used for web and consumer services. OAuth works over HTTP and is currently at version 2.0. There is no backward-compatibility between version 2.0 and its predecessor, OAuth 1.0. In fact, OAuth 2.0 is considered more of a framework and is less rigid than version 1.0. OAuth is most often used for delegating access control and authorization (delegated authorization) between services.

- **OpenID**   This standard for federated authentication is well supported for web services. Like OAuth, it runs over HTTP with URLs to identify identity providers. The current version is OpenID Connect 1.0 and is commonly seen in consumer services such as logging in to web sites.

The CSA Guidance mentions two other standards that aren't as widely adopted. These are not discussed in a backgrounder because they won't be commonly encountered. For your exam, just know that they exist:

- **eXtensible Access Control Markup Language (XACML)**   This is the standard for defining attribute-based access controls and authorizations. XACML is a policy language for defining access controls at a policy decision point (PDP) and passing them to a policy enforcement point (PEP). XACML can work with both SAML and OAuth, as it decides what an entity is allowed to do with a set of attributes as opposed to handling logins or delegation of authority.

- **System for Cross-domain Identity Management (SCIM)**   This standard deals with exchanging identity information between domains. It is used for provisioning and deprovisioning accounts in external systems and exchanging attribute information.

All of these standards can be used in federated identity systems. For the most part, all of them rely on a series of redirects that involve the web browser, the identity provider, and the relying party. Figure 12-1, from the CSA Guidance, denotes these redirections in effect by using OpenID as their example.

Federation involves both an identity provider and a relying party. Both of these components must have a trust relationship established to enable assertions from the identity provider to be consumed by the relying party. These assertions are used to exchange credentials.

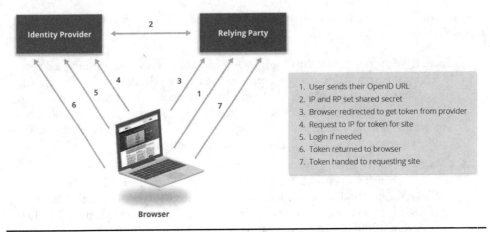

1. User sends their OpenID URL
2. IP and RP set shared secret
3. Browser redirected to get token from provider
4. Request to IP for token for site
5. Login if needed
6. Token returned to browser
7. Token handed to requesting site

Figure 12-1 Federated identity example using OpenID. (Used with permission of Cloud Security Alliance.)

For an example of federation in operation, consider a scenario of a user logging into a workstation and then accessing an internal web server that has a list of SaaS applications the user can log into. The user selects the desired SaaS application and is automatically logged on without having to provide a username and password. This is possible because the user's identity provider will create an assertion and send that assertion to the relying party. The relying party will determine and implement the authorizations for the user based on the assertion that is created only after the trusted identity provider has authenticated the user. In other words, the local directory server authenticates the user and tells the relying party what authorization the user should have in the remote system. (For a more detailed understanding of how federation works, see the "Federation Backgrounder," coming up next.)

Most, if not all, cloud providers will have their own IAM system, which may be referred to as "internal identities." Your ability to have a federated identity relationship with a provider is dependent on the provider exposing some form of a federated identity connector. Although most providers expose some form of federation capability based on standards such as SAML, this is not always guaranteed (just like anything else offered by providers).

Providers may expose access to their IAM functionality using HTTP request signing. Although this was addressed back in Chapter 6, I'll refresh your memory. HTTP request signing can use an access key as an identifier and a secret access key that is used to sign the request cryptographically. In the backend, the cloud provider will use their IAM system to determine the appropriate access controls that apply for the entity requesting to perform an action. This request signing may leverage standards such as SAML and/or OAuth, or it could use its own token mechanism.

As you consider which identity protocols to use, also consider the following from the CSA Guidance:

- There is no "one-size-fits-all" standard when it comes to federation protocols. You have to consider the use case you're trying to solve. Are you looking at users logging in via a web browser? You might want to look at SAML. Are you looking at delegated authorization? Then you might want to consider OAuth instead.

- The key operating assumption should be that your identity is a perimeter in and of itself, and as such, any protocol used must be adequately secured to traverse the hostile network known as the public Internet.

Now that I have covered the basics as far as your CCSK exam is concerned, let's dive a little deeper into federation itself and the protocols used to build federation between your organization and your cloud service providers. Again, as always, backgrounder information is for you, not for your CCSK exam.

Federation Backgrounder

Federated identity (federation) is the connection of two distinct organizations that have different internal structures using an agreed-upon standard. In this case, since we are dealing with identity management exclusively, I'll just use the shorter term, federation. We are creating identity management that connects two distinct organizations using a standard such as SAML, OAuth, or OpenID Connect. The main reason why you would perform federated identity with a cloud service provider is to perform SSO. Wrapping all these key words together, when we talk about "federation," we usually mean federated identity and SSO.

Federation isn't just an option for companies that adopt cloud services; it's a requirement. Without it, you'll have mass confusion among your user base. Managing identities when using cloud services without federation is like herding cats—an impossible situation. And this goes beyond day-to-day identity management. Consider, for example, those times when managers need to confirm that their employees have appropriate privileges in accordance with their job functions. That's already a difficult proposition, especially when you consider all of the locations where identities may exist internally. But what if you want to add dozens, or hundreds, of new identity stores? It's simply an impossible task without federation. And then add in the problems created with various temporary users, such as contractors, who may continue to have access to your cloud services for years until discovered. I can't overstate enough how much you are setting yourself up for massive failure regarding IAM if you don't have federation in place.

As a consumer, the goal of federation is simply to authenticate your users locally and authorize them remotely. You are the identity provider (IP), and you manage all the accounts. The provider is the relying party (RP) (which is sometimes referred to as the service provider and may be denoted as RP/SP). Here's the deal: You create the association between your identity provider and the cloud service provider in advance. How you do this depends on the provider and the protocol. Once that association is made, you can use assertions used by a protocol (usually SAML for users, but we'll get to that later on). You generate the assertion (or token, if you will), and then that is consumed by the cloud provider. Because there is a pre-existing trusted association between you and the provider, the CSP will trust the assertion (assuming security checks within the assertion pass).

You can use internal Active Directory as an example of SSO that is made possible by Kerberos. In an Active Directory domain scenario, you log on (authenticate) in the morning with your username and password. When you successfully log on, your workstation receives a Kerberos ticket (there's a whole bunch of mumbo-jumbo related to Kerberos, like ticket-granting tickets and such, but we don't care about that—we care that we get some form of a ticket). When you go to access another server or any resources in the domain, are you asked for another logon? Nope. This is because your workstation automatically presents a Kerberos ticket on your behalf that says who you are (an identifier) and the groups (an attribute) that you are a member of. The resource server then looks up the access control list and determines what level of access you should have based on what your ticket says about you and your group memberships, or if you should be granted any access at all.

Alright, so now you may be asking yourself, why don't we just use Kerberos instead of a different protocol to do our federation? Awesome question. The answer is that Kerberos doesn't really work very well outside of the domain in which it's set up. It's an SSO solution for use within a domain, not a federation protocol for connectivity between different areas owned by different organizations.

How can federation be established with cloud providers? You can build your own connector (preferably standards-based), or you can use a broker that will make federation a little easier than doing it yourself. In this discussion, I'll begin with the "roll-your-own" federation system then move on to cloud-based identity broker services.

Sticking with the Active Directory scenario, you could build your own federation connector by implementing Active Directory Federation Services (ADFS). ADFS is essentially a service installed on a domain controller. In addition to the ADFS implementation itself, you need to build a web server (such as IIS, Internet Information Services) and SQL servers (MSSQL). This drives up your costs significantly, because MSSQL is a pretty expensive license (and you need two of them to address one being a single point of failure). What's pretty cool about this is that you could actually use ADFS in a cloud environment that supports Windows Server and even use it to connect to the SAML provider used by the IaaS system you're using!

The web server needs to be built so your users can connect to the cloud services you have a federated connection with. Users would simply go to the internal web server, click the service they want to use, and, voila! They are automagically connected. Behind the scenes, the web browser uses an assertion that is in its memory. This assertion is consumed by the provider. Depending on the protocol used (likely SAML, since this is a user logging in with a browser), the identity and groups the user is a member of are read, groups are mapped to permissions on the provider side, and the user is authorized to access resources based on what the assertion says. The big deal here is that user accounts and passwords remain within your environment. An added bonus is that users have to log in to the system that you manage in order to get an assertion. If you disable the user's account, you disable their access to all the cloud services with which you have federation implemented.

As for the usage of a cloud-based identity broker, all of the same principles discussed still exist, with the exception, of course, of having to build up your own infrastructure to support federation. So how, then, does this cloud-based system have access to the list of all of our users in our identity provider such as Active Directory? Well, this depends on the provider, but I've generally seen it happen in two ways: either copy your users from Active Directory to the identity broker, or install an agent in your domain. When someone wants to access a cloud service with which you have federation in place, they will connect to your cloud-based identity broker and log on there. Their username and password will then be sent down to the agent, and the agent in turn will check with your AD server to determine whether it's a valid logon ID or not. If everything checks out, the user is presented with a screen showing the various federated links they can use. If you disable the account in Active Directory, the user cannot log on to the identity broker and can't access any of your services.

NOTE The situation is a little (well much) more complicated than the example I've described. The identity broker is likely using hashes, not the actual credentials. You'll want to discuss how credentials are passed around with potential vendors.

Just a final note on using an identity broker: Always double-check to make sure the domain you're installing this agent into and what risks this carries. If it's implemented improperly, you could suddenly realize that you've accidentally opened up your Active Directory accounts to the outside world for brute-force attacks and other nasty surprises. You might even realize that you accidentally installed it in the production domain when you thought it was installed in development (it happens).

Now that you have a high-level understanding of the implementation of federation, let's look at some of the enabling protocols, starting with the king of federation protocols—Security Assertion Markup Language.

Security Assertion Markup Language Backgrounder

SAML is the open standard protocol to use when you want to enable users to access cloud services using a web browser. Currently at version 2.0, SAML does both authorization and authentication. SAML has built-in security, but this doesn't mean it's a failsafe protocol (again, nothing is failsafe when it comes to security).

There are three components involved in SAML: The identity provider (your organization), aka IdP; the service provider (cloud provider), aka SP; and the principal (usually a human). SAML can be used in either an SP-initiated or an IdP-initiated scenario.

In an SP-initiated scenario, the user connects to the service in question and enters their e-mail address (identity). This is checked, and if there is a known SAML association, the user is redirected back to the IdP to get a token. When the token is passed to the workstation, it is then redirected back to the service and the token is presented. Figure 12-2, from the "OASIS Security Assertion Markup Language (SAML) V2.0 Technical Overview" document, demonstrates the steps involved with SP-initiated connections.

In the IdP-initiated scenario, the user goes to an internal web server, selects the desired service, and then gets a token and presents it to the desired service. Figure 12-3, from the same document, demonstrates the steps involved with IdP-initiated connections.

Figure 12-2
SP-initiated
connection steps.
(Source: OASIS.)

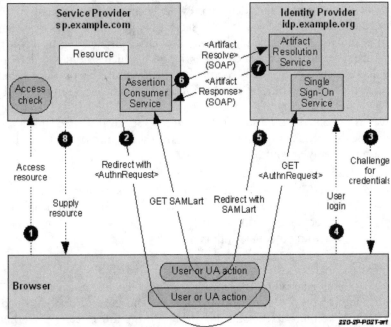

Figure 12-3
IdP-initiated
connection steps.
(Source: OASIS.)

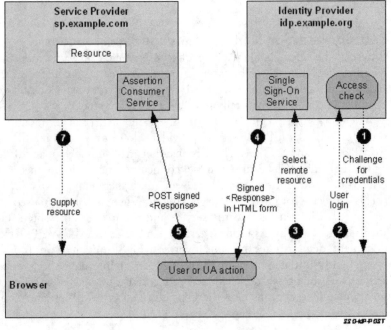

Here's an example of the some of the more interesting contents of a SAML assertion:

```
<saml:Issuer>https://idp.example.org/SAML2</saml:Issuer>
<saml:NameID Format="urn:oasis:names:tc:SAML:2.0:nameid-format:transient">
3f7b3dcf-1674-4ecd-92c8-1544f346baf8
<saml:Conditions NotBefore="2004-12-05T09:17:05" NotOnOrAfter="2004-12-
05T09:27:05">
<saml:AttributeValue xsi:type="xs:string">member</saml:AttributeValue>
```

From these strings, you can see the issuer (IdP) must be known to the relying party, the identity of the requestor (user) is always different (this is an option if so desired so usernames won't be compromised if the assertion is intercepted), timestamps are used, and attributes are exchanged as part of the SAML assertion. Again, this is just some of the information and security within a SAML request. For a much more detailed explanation of SAML and all of its inner workings, consult the "OASIS Security Assertion Markup Language (SAML) V2.0 Technical Overview."

In conclusion, SAML is primarily *the* standard that is used for users accessing a cloud provider with a web browser. So how do systems and mobile apps perform federation and SSO? That's usually where OAuth and OpenID come in. Let's look at those standards.

OAuth Backgrounder

OAuth is for the authorization (remember OAuth stands for AuthOrization) of users and systems. It is very lightweight in comparison to SAML and therefore is ideal for system-to-system communication over APIs using HTTP. Currently, version 2.0 is incompatible with OAuth 1.0.

The term "delegated authorization" has become fairly synonymous with OAuth. What does it mean in real life? Have you ever been to a web site that allows you to log on with Google, or Facebook, or LinkedIn, or myriad of other large web sites? When you do this, you are basically saying you want Google's identity system to be the source from which you'll be authorized to access the target web site. You don't need a separate username and password to access the target site. You'll click the Logon With Google button and you'll be redirected back to Google to verify your wish to log on (and possibly share your information) to the target site. Once you click OK, you are redirected back to the target site and have access.

Here's another example: Say you want to build an app called tweetermaster that schedules tweets for customers on a daily basis as the customer. In order for the tweetermaster app to post tweets on the customer's behalf, it would have to be authorized by the user to be able to access Twitter and post on the user's behalf. This is an example of how you could use OAuth for delegated authorization. In this scenario, you delegate authority to allow something do something on your behalf.

NOTE For more information on the OAuth standard, check out RFC 6749 "OAuth 2.0 Framework," RFC 6750 "The OAuth 2.0 Authorization Framework: Bearer Token Usage," and RFC 8252 "OAuth 2.0 for Native Apps."

Figure 12-4, from the RFC 6749 documentation, demonstrates the delegated authorization flow with OAuth.

Figure 12-4
Delegated
authorization
with OAuth

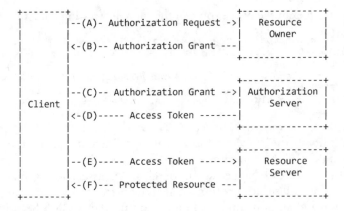

```
+--------+                 +---------------+
|        |--(A)- Authorization Request ->| Resource      |
|        |                 | Owner         |
|        |<-(B)-- Authorization Grant ---|               |
|        |                 +---------------+
|        |
|        |                 +---------------+
|        |--(C)-- Authorization Grant -->| Authorization |
| Client |                 | Server        |
|        |<-(D)----- Access Token -------|               |
|        |                 +---------------+
|        |
|        |                 +---------------+
|        |--(E)----- Access Token ------>| Resource      |
|        |                 | Server        |
|        |<-(F)--- Protected Resource ---|               |
+--------+                 +---------------+
```

OAuth has substantial use cases with APIs in both mobile and microservices implementations. OAuth 2.0 can use JSON Web Tokens (JWTs) as bearer tokens in an API environment. (When thinking of bearer tokens, you can think of the statement "give access to the bearer of this token.") Figure 12-5 shows how JWTs can work with OAuth to allow access to resources.

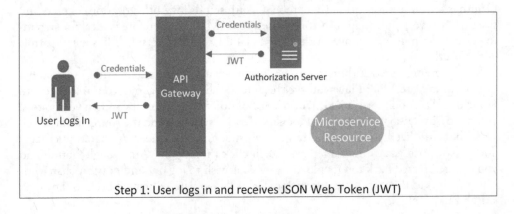

Step 1: User logs in and receives JSON Web Token (JWT)

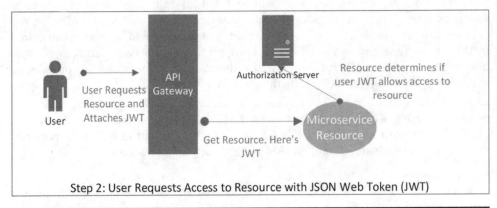

Step 2: User Requests Access to Resource with JSON Web Token (JWT)

Figure 12-5   JWTs usage in microservices

> **NOTE** For a detailed understanding of JWTs, consult RFC 7519.

Finally, OAuth is related to OpenID in that OpenID Connect builds authentication on top of the authorization capability of OAuth. The next backgrounder will discuss OpenID and, more specifically, OpenID Connect (OIDC).

OpenID Connect Backgrounder

The latest version of the OpenID standard (version 3) is OpenID Connect (OIDC). Version 1.0 was released in 2005 and replaced with OpenID 2.0 in 2007. OIDC was released in 2014. As per the OIDC FAQ, the problem that OIDC solves is that it "lets app and site developers authenticate users without taking on the responsibility of storing and managing passwords in the face of an Internet that is well-populated with people trying to compromise your users' accounts for their own gain." In other words, the goal of OIDC is to centralize credentials used on a wide set of web sites to a smaller set of trusted identity providers.

OIDC is an authentication layer built on top of OAuth 2.0. This enables OIDC to address authentication and authorization requirements. OIDC is restricted to HTTP and uses JSON as a data format (OpenID 2.0 used XML). The addition of OIDC's authentication layer on top of OAuth's authorization capabilities allows for verification of the identity of an end user based on the authentication performed by an authorization server.

OIDC is an open identity standard backed by a number of significant companies such as Microsoft and Google, as well as agencies such as the National Institute of Standards and Technology (NIST) and other global governmental and nonprofit organizations. Apple has recently built its Sign In with Apple offering with OIDC.

With the creation of OIDC and its tight integration with OAuth 2.0, the lines are getting blurred as to the functionality that each standard brings. As long as you remember the following points, you'll be able to make sense of all these competing standards:

- SAML 2.0 does authentication and authorization for web users.
- OAuth 2.0 does authorization and is lightweight.
- OIDC 1.0 runs on top of OAuth 2.0 and provides lightweight identity and authentication services.

Managing Users and Identities for Cloud Computing

The *identity* part of identity and access management is all about registering, provisioning, propagating, managing, and finally deprovisioning identities. With those actions in mind, you probably shouldn't be surprised to learn that identity management itself may actually be done outside of a directory service (such as Active Directory). The authoritative source of identities in your network may actually be the payroll system, for example: users are added to the payroll system, and their identities are then propagated to the directory server.

Thanks to these centralized directory services, it is no longer required to add accounts to every individual server and application in a traditional environment. Of course, users still have multiple accounts to support applications that are not integrated with these centralized directory services, so the dream of true SSO remains elusive, but there are, thankfully, fewer of these accounts than there used to be in the past.

In a cloud environment, both providers and consumers need to plan on how they will manage identities:

- Cloud providers need to offer an identity service that supports customers to use their own identities, identifiers, and attributes. They should also offer federation services based on standards to enable customers to minimize the overhead associated with identity management when using their cloud offerings.

 EXAM TIP The identity service offered by the provider may be referred to as the "internal" identity system on the exam.

- Cloud customers need to determine how they want to manage identities moving forward. This will require that customers determine the architecture models to use for identity management and the technologies that should be implemented to support integration with their current and future cloud providers.

As mentioned multiple times in this chapter, federation will be required as an enabling technology for cloud implementations of any substantial size. Without federation, you will lose control of IAM. This isn't to say there won't be any accounts created and managed in a provider's internal IAM system. You will likely still have a limited amount of administrator accounts within the provider's IAM system to support troubleshooting in the event of failure of the federated link, for instance.

To establish a federated link, the customer needs to determine what system will be the "authoritative source" to serve as the identity provider. This is usually a directory server. This identity provider then needs to perform the federation. There are two main approaches to creating this connectivity: use a free-form model that creates a separate connection between the identity provider and the various cloud services (as shown in Figure 12-6), or use the hybrid (hub-and-spoke) model that uses a central identity broker to connect to all the cloud providers (as shown in Figure 12-7).

The free-form model comes with a few disadvantages compared to the hub-and-spoke model. First off, your authoritative source needs to be connected to the Internet to connect with all of the cloud providers. Second, in order to support users outside of your network, these users will need to VPN into the corporate network to access any cloud solution that has a federated link established. Finally, in an environment that may have multiple authoritative servers (such as multiple domains that are not joined for corporate

Figure 12-6
Free-form model.
(Used with
permission of
Cloud Security
Alliance.)

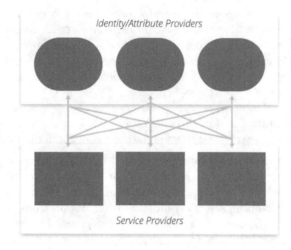

purposes), each of these authoritative servers will need to connect to the providers, which multiplies the amount of connections required.

In the hub-and-spoke model, an identity broker can be cloud-based. Implementation of a cloud-based identity broker can facilitate the establishment of the federation with numerous cloud providers, and external users need not VPN into the corporate network to use federated links to your various providers.

Another option exists in running your directory server in a cloud environment itself (or by consuming a directory service from the provider). In this scenario, you could synchronize your internal directory server with the cloud-based directory server (or service).

Figure 12-7
Hub-and-spoke
model. (Used
with permission
of Cloud Security
Alliance.)

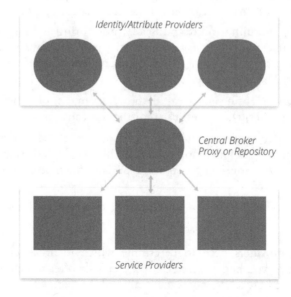

In turn, this cloud-based directory could serve the operating systems and applications (applistructure) in the cloud environment and act as an authoritative server for any federated links with other parties that rely on the cloud provider.

In addition to the big-picture deployment model considerations, the following process and architectural decisions need to be made:

- *How will identities for application code, systems, devices, and other services be managed?* Most of the focus in this chapter has been on users accessing services. Services accessing services and other requirements may call for a different approach.

- *How will identity provisioning processes change when consuming cloud services, if at all?* Identity provisioning is not limited to creating identities only; it also deals with changing permissions and, of course, deprovisioning identities. A provisioning system could take information from an HR database and then be used to provision access to various systems in addition to the directory server, such as web applications, database servers, and, most importantly for our discussion, cloud services. If provisioning systems today are inefficient, adopting cloud services may offer an opportunity to readdress and improve your provisioning systems.

- *Formal processes should be implemented when on-boarding new cloud providers and integrating them into your existing IAM environment.* This includes establishing federation and the following considerations:

  - Building an entitlement matrix that is created using the granularity exposed by the provider. This may vary based on the service model (for example, SaaS versus IaaS).

  - Determining how attributes will be mapped between the identity provider and the relying party. This includes mapping internal groups (roles) to the groups in the provider environment.

  - Determining and enabling any monitoring and logging that need to be implemented to meet your security policies. Newer IAM implementations may offer new services that you may want to include in your policies, such as behavioral analytics.

  - Documenting any break/fix processes in case of failure of any of the federation (or other techniques) used for the relationship.

  - Updating current incident response plans related to identity takeovers to include the process for cloud providers. This may include steps required to engage the provider for their assistance, especially when dealing with a privileged account takeover.

  - Determining how accounts can be deprovisioned (or attributes changed) in the cloud environment.

Finally, providers need to determine which identity standards they will offer to customers. As you know, providers will generally offer some form of identity and access management system. Providers may enhance this with either custom or standards-based federation offerings. In the event of standards-based offerings, SAML will likely be requested by customers.

Authentication and Credentials

Authentication is always the responsibility of the identity provider. If you have federation in place, a system under your control acts as the identity provider. If you don't have a federated link, the CSP acts as the identity provider. Authentication technically occurs any time an identity needs to be confirmed, such as when an entity proves who they are and assumes an identity, not just during logon.

As cloud services, by their very nature, have broad network access, simple usernames and passwords are insufficient to protect accounts. Multifactor authentication should always be offered by a cloud provider to enhance authentication security, especially for privileged accounts. The CSA Guidance calls this "strong authentication using multiple factors."

Being authenticated with MFA can be used as an attribute. That said, using this as part of your access control (access management), you can enhance security by granting entitlements based on this attribute. This would be an example of an attribute-based access control (ABAC). Preferring ABAC over RBAC is generally recommended for cloud environments. Keep in mind, though, that adding attributes to access decisions will introduce complexities.

You know the factors involved with authentication: you know something, have something, or are something. With these in mind, the CSA Guidance calls out the following options for different factors above and beyond the simple factor of knowing a password:

- **Hard token** This physical device shows a one-time password or can be plugged in to a computer. This is the best option when high security is required.

- **Soft token** This serves the same purpose as a hard token in as much as it will display a one-time password, but it runs as software on a phone or computer. Unlike the hard token, any compromise (such as malware) of a user's device may compromise the one-time passwords. This must be considered as part of a threat model. There are a multitude of applications that can offer soft tokens.

- **Out-of-band passwords** These passwords are sent via a separate communication method, such as a text message (SMS). Threat models must consider that messages may be intercepted (especially SMS text messages).

- **Biometrics** Unlike the other options presented that all involve a "something you have" factor, biometrics are a "something you are" factor. For cloud services, the biometric is a local protection and any biometric data is kept on the device, not sent to the provider. Biometric authentication may be an attribute that can be sent to the provider and used as part of ABAC.

Beyond the listed options, you might want to check out the FIDO Alliance for new MFA approaches, such a FIDO Universal 2nd Factor (U2F) authentication that will offer stronger security options in the future. As with all other technologies, it often takes some time between the creation of more secure solutions and industry adoption.

Entitlements and Access Management

The cloud impacts entitlements, authorizations, and access management in multiple ways. Following is a list of changes that you should be comfortable with before taking your CCSK exam:

- Cloud providers will have authorizations specific to them. Some providers will offer more granular authorization options than others. Mapping entities to these authorizations (entitlements) will usually need to be performed by the consumer (unless the provider supports XACML, which is rare).

- The cloud provider is always responsible for enforcing authorizations and access controls. Federation doesn't change this. Federation enables the identity provider to control authentication and instruct the relying party regarding how to enforce authorization.

- Attribute-based access control (ABAC) is the preferred model for cloud services because it offers greater flexibility and security than the role-based access control (RBAC) model. Attribute decisions can be based on anything regarding the user and the connection itself, such as MFA authentication, IP address, geographical location, and so on.

- Cloud providers should offer granular attributes and authorizations to enable ABAC that enable customers to implement more effective security for cloud users.

Privileged User Management

Privileged accounts require the strongest authentication possible. Additionally, all actions taken by a privileged account should be recorded to obtain maximum visibility and therefore accountability for actions performed by these accounts. Having these accounts log on via a bastion host or a "jump box" may allow for tighter control of both authentication and monitoring of actions.

Chapter Review

This chapter addressed the recommendations for identity, entitlement, and access management as per the CSA Guidance. You should be comfortable with the following recommendations from the Guidance in preparation for your CCSK exam:

- Organizations need to plan for IAM changes. This will require the development of plans and processes for managing identities and authorizations.

- Implement federation services to maintain control of the authentication of users. Try to minimize the amount of identities held within individual cloud provider identity services.

- Identity brokers may ease the effort associated with creating federation connections with a large amount of cloud service providers. Consider using them when appropriate.

- Consumers should always retain control of the identity provider role when implementing federation.

- Remember that the authoritative source of identities may not be your directory services. HR systems are often the authoritative source, and these identities are then replicated to a directory server, which can act as an identity provider.

- Distributed organizations can leverage cloud-based directory services. Directory services can be installed on a cloud instance just like any other software. These cloud-based directory services can be used to serve multiple organization locations and support cloud services.

- Because of the very nature of the cloud having broad network access, accounts should have MFA applied as an additional authentication control. This is especially true for privileged user accounts.

- Any attribute about a user or their connection can be used as part of an attribute-based access control (ABAC). This is true for connections that are MFA authenticated as well.

- Creating an entitlement matrix on paper and having the entitlements agreed upon with the business owner before implementing them technically will save everyone time and effort. If your cloud provider supports it, you may be able to copy these entitlements to the cloud provider to implement these settings.

- ABAC is always preferable to RBAC for cloud deployments—use it!

- Cloud providers usually offer internal identity services. They should offer federation using open standards (such as SAML) as well.

- Federation protocols all have their own strengths and weaknesses. Choose your use cases and constraints first to determine appropriate standards to implement.

Questions

1. Which of the following is an example of an attribute that can be used with ABAC?

   A. If the user logged on with MFA

   B. Biometric data

   C. Biometric authentication status

   D. A and C

2. Why should multifactor authentication always be considered?

   A. It is a best practice according to the CSA Guidance.

   B. Cloud services can be accessed by anyone using a web browser.

   C. Cloud services have the essential characteristic of broad network access.

   D. MFA is not recommended because users who lose their phones will require manual effort to reset their accounts.

3. Which of the following is the best federation protocol to implement and support?

   A. SAML

   B. OAuth

   C. OpenID

   D. There is no best protocol. You have to determine your use cases and constraints before selecting a protocol.

4. What is the authoritative source of identity?

   A. The system from which identities are propagated

   B. HR system

   C. Directory services system

   D. Cloud provider's IAM system

5. When creating federated identity with an IaaS provider, which party is the relying party and which is the identity provider?

   A. The organization is the relying party and the IaaS provider is the identity provider.

   B. The organization is the identity provider and the IaaS provider is the relying party.

   C. The organization is both the identity provider and the relying party because it is reliant on the cloud provider to implement federation.

   D. The cloud provider is both the identity provider and the relying party in a federated model.

6. Which standard uses the concepts of policy decision points (PDPs) and policy enforcement points (PEPs)?

   A. SAML

   B. OAuth

   C. XACML

   D. SCIM

7. What is the difference between an identity and a persona?

   A. Your identity is your username; your persona is the group you are a member of.

   B. Your identity is your username; your persona is your identity and all other attributes associated with you in a specific situation.

   C. Your identity is used to authorize you; your persona is used to authenticate you.

   D. Your identity is used to authenticate you; your persona is used to authorize you.

8. What is a role?

    A. A role is a part of federation. It is how your group membership within your company is granted entitlements in your IaaS provider.

    B. A role is the job you perform at work.

    C. A role is a temporary credential that is inherited by a system within a cloud environment.

    D. All of the above are correct.

9. Which of the following is a factor in multifactor authentication?

    A. A secret handshake

    B. The color of your eyes

    C. A one-time password

    D. All of the above

10. Which of the following protocols is XML-based and supports both authentication and authorization?

    A. SAML

    B. OAuth

    C. OpenID

    D. SCIM

Answers

    1. D. Everything about a user and their connection can be used as an attribute to determine access control. However, in the biometric model, actual biometric data is held within the device itself. The fact that biometrics were used is an attribute that can be used.

    2. C. Cloud services have the essential characteristic of broad network access. This is similar to the fact that it can be accessed by any browser (B), but C is the better response because not all access to a cloud service will always require a web browser. Of course, implementing MFA is a CSA best practice, but that alone is not the reason why it should be implemented. While loss of a cell phone with a soft-token MFA device will likely require manual effort to reset the MFA settings, it is not a valid reason to avoid the use of MFA, especially for privileged accounts.

    3. D. There is no "magic bullet" protocol for federation. You must always consider your requirements based on use cases and constraints.

    4. A. The authoritative source of identities can be any system. It is the system in which user accounts are created and then propagated out to others. This could be the directory server in some environments, or it could be the HR system in others. You never want the cloud service with which you are creating a federated link to be the authoritative source or the identity provider.

5. **B.** The organization is the identity provider, and the IaaS provider is the relying party. You always want to retain the role of the identity provider when establishing federation.

6. **C.** XACML uses the concepts of policy decision and policy enforcement points. XACML is used for more fine-grained access control decisions and can work with SAML or OAuth. XACML implementations are rare.

7. **B.** Your identity is your username, and your persona is your identity and all other attributes in a specific situation.

8. **D.** All the answers are correct. This is why the CSA Guidance says that "role is a confusing and abused term used in many ways."

9. **D.** The factors are something you know (secret handshake), something you have (one-time password), and something you are (eye color). Do these make sense from a technical perspective? Probably not, but they meet the criteria of the three factors all the same.

10. **A.** SAML is XML-based and handles both authentication and authorization. OAuth only deals with "AuthOrization" (memory trick), and OpenID only deals with authentication. SCIM is a provisioning language.

Security as a Service

This chapter covers the following topics from Domain 13 of the CSA Guidance:
- Potential Benefits and Concerns of SecaaS
- Major Categories of Security as a Service Offerings

> *Plus ça change, plus c'est la même chose.*
> —Jean-Baptiste Alphonse Karr

The more things change, the more they stay the same. That's what we're looking at when it comes to Security as a Service (SaaS).

Everything I have covered up to now has been focused on understanding the shared responsibilities of the cloud. You've seen the aspects of security that the provider and the customer are responsible for. This chapter looks at how cloud services (typically SaaS and Platform as a Service [PaaS]) can be used to secure assets deployed in both the cloud and traditional environments.

The CSA Guidance refers to these services as "Security as a Service," or SecaaS, but I prefer to use "Security Software as a Service," because, after all, you are procuring a SaaS solution that happens to focus on security. Whether you are procuring cloud-based security services from a dedicated SecaaS vendor or leveraging security services from an Infrastructure as a Service (IaaS) provider, you are considered to be procuring SecaaS services. Whichever way you procure these services, they must meet the following criteria:

- They must be a security product or service delivered as a cloud service.
- They must meet the essential characteristics of cloud computing.

 EXAM TIP Remember that you're procuring security software that meets the essential characteristics of the cloud, and you'll be fine.

Like everything else in IT (especially in the cloud), new offerings are constantly being released. For your exam, focus on the categories covered in the following sections.

Potential Benefits and Concerns of SecaaS

I'm going to make this as simple as possible. You already know about the benefits and constraints associated with procuring cloud services, and most of that applies to SecaaS as well. That said, the following lists provide a summary of the benefits and disadvantages that are specifically associated with SecaaS.

SecaaS offers several potential benefits:

- **Cloud-computing benefits**   The normal potential benefits of cloud computing apply to SecaaS, including reduced capital expenses, more agility, redundancy, high availability, and resiliency. As always, you must do your due diligence to ensure that you are selecting an appropriate provider to meet your requirements.

- **Staffing and experience**   This is a big one, and it may be the biggest reason to adopt SecaaS. Companies around the world are struggling to find qualified cybersecurity professionals. By adopting SecaaS, you can immediately tap into a pool of experts in the area you are procuring. This can enable your staff to focus on your organizational "big picture" of cybersecurity.

- **Intelligence sharing**   Honestly, this is nothing new. Antivirus customers have been benefitting from intelligence sharing for decades. When the provider gets a malware sample from another customer, they make a signature file that can identify and quarantine the virus, and this will be used by all other customers.

- **Deployment flexibility**   This is another core benefit of SecaaS. Think of how you manage multiple locations today. Are all security controls located at your headquarters, or do you purchase hardware for every site you manage? Now how about remote workers? How do you protect them? Do you force everyone to VPN into the corporate network just to impose your controls on their connections? There is a better way: it's called SecaaS.

- **Insulation of clients**   Why would you choose to allow malware into your corporate network so you can inspect it locally? You're congesting the perimeter network for what reason again? With SecaaS, you can create a "clean pipe" coming into your network by having a remote system scan and can clear out malicious traffic before it hits your corporate network.

- **Scaling and cost**   What happens if your 500-person company buys another company with 250 employees? Suddenly, you have to support a 50 percent larger user base. This often requires integration of different technologies and new hardware to meet this demand on resources. With SecaaS, you'd simply procure an additional 250 licenses. This is an example of the "pay-as-you-grow" cost benefits of using SecaaS.

On the other hand, using a SecaaS vendor may result in these issues:

- **Lack of visibility**   We know the nature of outsourcing means that our visibility into what the provider does is hindered. SecaaS is no different. You may have a high-level view of what the provider does, but you won't have detailed knowledge of their operations. The biggest impact is in the telemetry (such as log data) that you receive from the provider. You need to ensure that available sources meet your requirements. Always remember to do your due diligence!

- **Regulation differences**   Where is your provider located, and can they address regulatory issues that your organization faces based on the jurisdictions in which you operate?

- **Handling of regulated data**   Is your provider able to be a partner? With HIPAA, for example, the SecaaS provider must be able to be a business associate if their systems will be exposed to health records. And what about PCI? Along with these standards, the Guidance calls out a scenario about employee monitoring. What is legally allowed in one jurisdiction may be prohibited in another. Again, due diligence should address these questions.

- **Data leakage**   Security-related information (such as logs) often contains sensitive data. This data must be highly protected in a multitenant environment. This requires that the provider implement very strong isolation and segregation. Of course, this type of data may also be required in the event of legal cases. You need to ensure that your data will not be accidentally exposed when another client faces an e-discovery request. Another example of data leakage would be leaking internal IP addresses.

- **Changing providers**   When you procure a SecaaS solution, you are essentially procuring a proprietary application. Changing from one provider to another will likely be a difficult effort, because there may be limited tools available to migrate data from one provider to another. A major item, in real life and for your CCSK exam, is that you must retain historical logs and other data that may be necessary for legal and compliance requirements. Not being able to export this data in a format that you can actually use without access to the provider's tools may lead to vendor lock-in.

- **Migration to SecaaS**   Adoption of cloud services must always be well planned and executed. SecaaS is no different.

Major Categories of SaaS Offerings

New technology is released on an almost daily basis, so you don't need to worry about any category that is not listed in this chapter for your CCSK exam. Notice that many of the technologies in the following sections have been covered previously in this book. That said, don't just skip this section, because you'll see category-specific entries here that you may be tested on as part of the exam.

Identity, Entitlement, and Access Management Services

The major offering in this category of SecaaS services is that of identity brokers. This technology can be used to implement federated identity. The CSA Guidance also presents other offerings in this category, such as Policy Enforcement Points (PEP as a Service), Policy Decision Points (PDP as a Service), Policy Access Points (PAP as a Service), services that provide entities with identities, and services that provide attributes (such as multifactor authentication).

Two other offerings are referenced in this category, including the strong authentication services that use apps and infrastructure to simplify the integration of various strong authentication options, including mobile device apps and tokens for MFA. The other category hosts directory servers in the cloud to serve as an organization's identity provider. You can do this in IaaS by implementing directory services in your own instances, for example.

Cloud Access Security Broker

There is nothing new in the CSA Guidance here that was not covered in the CASB back-grounder back in Chapter 11. Just in case you skipped that backgrounder, you need to be aware of a few things regarding the CASB technology for your exam.

CASB can be used in inline blocking mode that intercepts communications that are directed toward a cloud service, or it can use APIs to monitor activities and enforce policies. Whereas traditional web-filtering tools allow for whitelisting and blacklisting of web sites, you want to be able to allow or restrict based on the content, not just on the web sites being accessed. This is the main differentiator between the two solutions. CASB can enforce the content type of blocking via integration with data loss prevention (DLP) services.

CASB can be deployed as an on-premises control, or it can be deployed in a cloud environment. As mentioned earlier, a cloud deployment allows for greater options when it comes to protecting both multiple locations and remote users.

CASB vendors often support some form of rating system for cloud vendors. They will perform a general risk assessment of providers and may advise you on things such as data center locations, ownership of data used in the provider systems (owned by customer or provider once uploaded), and other items. In some instances, CASB vendors use the Cloud Controls Matrix as the basis for this risk assessment.

Although a vendor may offer both CASB and identity broker solutions, the majority of vendors offer these solutions separately.

Web Security Gateway

This technology provides web filtering, which has been around for quite some time. Web filters can determine what categories of web sites are blocked (for example, hacking sites are restricted from access from endpoints). These solutions can also determine what times of the day sites can be accessed and other web protection solutions.

The power of having a cloud-based solution is the ability to implement your policies on a global basis. For example, imagine your organization has an office in New York City, and a salesperson is working in Singapore for a series of meetings. Rather than forcing this user to connect to the office via VPN so you can inspect their web usage, their workstation would use a local point of presence in Singapore to enforce your policies.

 EXAM TIP Remember that a major benefit of SecaaS is the ability to enforce your policy using someone else's infrastructure.

Application authorization management can provide an extra level of granular and contextual security enforcement for web applications.

E-mail Security

Implementing SecaaS that provides e-mail security is a no-brainer. With more than 90 percent of e-mail being spam these days, why would you bring all of that into your environment just so you can drop it? This is probably the best example of the "insulation of clients" benefit.

Any e-mail security solution should be able to provide control over inbound and outbound e-mail, protect the organization from risks such as phishing and malicious attachments, enforce corporate polices such as acceptable use and spam prevention, and provide business continuity options. Some e-mail security SecaaS solutions may offer functionality such as e-mail encryption and digital signatures to support confidentiality, integrity, and nonrepudiation.

Security Assessment

Security assessment solutions have been around for a good number of years. Companies can use these to support NIST, ISO, PCI, and other compliance activities. The only difference between those mature products and the SecaaS solutions is that one is performed locally and the other is in the cloud.

The CSA Guidance specifically lists three forms of security assessment systems, and you should remember these for your exam:

- Traditional security/vulnerability assessments of cloud-based instances and on-premises servers and workstations

- Application security assessments, including static application security testing (SAST), dynamic application security testing (DAST), and management of runtime application self-protection (RASP).

- Cloud platform assessment tools that connect to a cloud environment via exposed APIs to assess the metastructure configuration and server instances

---

Risk Tolerance and Security Assessments

I'm going to digress here and talk about risk tolerance for a moment. The security assessment SecaaS is a solution that some people love, while others wouldn't touch it with a ten-foot pole. Why? Because some of the security assessment SecaaS solutions take the results of vulnerability scans (cloud and traditional) and place them in a cloud environment. Some people love this because they can "view the vulnerabilities in my network while riding the train" (a real CISO quote). Personally, I don't want to have all the skeletons in my network exposed to anyone who guesses my password. Talk about a roadmap to completely exploiting my network!

Web Application Firewall

The web application firewall (WAF) in SecaaS is a cloud-based firewall that operates at layer 7; it therefore understands HTTP and can block malicious traffic as a result. This SecaaS category is another "no-brainer" as far as I'm concerned. As with e-mail, how much Internet traffic hitting your network today is either junk or malicious? Drop it using someone else's systems according to your policies.

Many cloud WAFs can stop a distributed denial of service (DDoS) attack against your network. Can your network handle a 1.3 Tbps DDoS attack? This is what GitHub was hit with back in 2018. Their services were impacted for about 20 minutes in total (about 10 minutes to identify the attack and 10 minutes for their cloud WAF vendor to fully address the malicious traffic, at which point the attacker gave up).

 NOTE   Just a quick personal note on DDoS. My child, Tristan, came home yesterday from school (he's in grade 8) and told me that a couple of kids hired a bot for free on their cellphones to target some online game during their lunch time. Yes, that's right—13-year-old kids launching a DDoS at lunch for fun! How things have changed (yes, we had a talk about laws). Can your network be taken down by a pack of kids?

Intrusion Detection/Prevention

Intrusion detection systems (IDSs) and intrusion prevention systems (IPSs) are controls that can detect (IDS) and/or prevent (IPS) malicious activity in your network or your hosts. These systems can work based on anomaly detection and/or signature. SecaaS doesn't change anything about what these controls do.

What the SecaaS version of IDS/IPS changes is how data is collected and analyzed. Rather than a company having to analyze data supplied by the agents in-house, this analysis is performed by a provider using their platform. This is an opportunity to discuss another benefit of SecaaS, mentioned earlier—your organization can outsource the analysis of potentially malicious network traffic in your environment to an organization that can potentially bring much deeper expertise and new technology to assist clients, such as using machine learning and artificial intelligence to greatly enhance what is realistically possible for the average organization.

Security Information and Event Management (SIEM)

I don't think it's a secret when I say that SIEM is a challenge to implement properly. We know that SIEM is able to take logs and perform all kinds of advanced analytics against them. As with IDS/IPS, the SecaaS version of SIEM doesn't change the functionality; it eases the implementation of SIEM, turning a potential multimonth project into an outsourced solution that may be possible to implement in the same day.

I also don't think it's a secret to say that SIEM experts are very expensive, and there is a very limited pool of talent available. Again, when you use SecaaS, you benefit from tapping into a pool of product experts. This is turn enables your security teams to focus on the big picture of your security posture.

Encryption and Key Management

You know about encryption and the importance of a strong key management system. You also know that you can't spell "encryption" without "cry." SecaaS providers in this space can encrypt data on your behalf and/or manage encryption keys on your organization's behalf.

 EXAM TIP It's important to remember that whether you are procuring a dedicated "encryption as a service" provider or using customer-managed keys from an IaaS provider, you are procuring a SecaaS.

This category includes encryption proxies for SaaS. Again, recall that, unlike IaaS and PaaS, encryption often breaks SaaS when the SaaS provider can't access the keys to unencrypt data. This is because the SaaS provider likely needs to work with data that you upload to their platform.

 EXAM TIP Remember that encryption breaks SaaS. This may help you answer multiple questions in your CCSK exam.

Business Continuity and Disaster Recovery

This category is one that you might actually be using at home today. BC/DR SecaaS vendors back up data from individual systems (local servers or cloud instances) and copy that data up to a cloud environment.

These systems could use a local gateway to speed up data transfers and perform local recovery. This category of SecaaS can help with a worst-case scenario of having to access stored data in the event of a disaster, or it could be used as an archival solution. Using this as an archival solution gets you away from having to manage backup tapes. It also has the obvious benefit of supplying you with an offsite storage capability.

Security Management

I think this should be called "endpoint security management," because that's what it is all about. The security management SecaaS solution centralizes common endpoint controls such as an endpoint protection platform (EPP), agent management, network security, and mobile device management into a single cloud service. Because the centralized console is cloud-based, there is no need for local management servers, which may be very beneficial for organizations with multiple locations and remote workers.

Distributed Denial of Service Protection

Although cloud WAF does offer DDoS protection, you may be able to procure dedicated DDoS protection solutions. There is really nothing else to add that hasn't already been said in the WAF section of this chapter. Just know for the exam that this can be a separate SecaaS and doesn't need to be part of a WAF solution.

Chapter Review

This chapter addressed the benefits and disadvantages of SecaaS and discussed some of the various offerings available according to the CSA Guidance. You should be comfortable with the following items in preparation for your CCSK exam:

- Selection of any cloud service requires due diligence on your organization's behalf. SecaaS doesn't change this critical activity.

- Data generated by security tools of all types can be highly sensitive, and that remains true when considering SecaaS. You need to have a clear understanding of all requirements for compliance purposes. This will determine requirements for data handling and archival of log data.

- Regulated data needs to be managed appropriately. If SecaaS systems interact with regulated data, they will need to meet or exceed existing controls within your organization.

- Lock-in can happen if your provider doesn't support exporting of data in a readable format.

- Understand your provider's data retention capabilities. If you require a five-year retention period, but your provider supports only six months, you have a gap that you'll need to address (possibly exporting and retaining locally), or you'll need to find another provider.

- Finally, you need to ensure that your SecaaS service is compatible with your current and future plans as much as possible. Does the SecaaS provider support your current or planned cloud providers, operating systems, and mobile platforms, for example?

Questions

1. Which of the following SecaaS solutions can be used to inspect HTTP traffic and can stop DDoS attacks?
   A. BC/DR
   B. WAF
   C. CASB
   D. Web filtering

2. Which of the following SecaaS solutions can be used to enforce your policies using someone else's systems?
   A. WAF
   B. Web filtering
   C. E-mail security
   D. All of the above

3. You ask your SecaaS provider for an export of web filtering log data. They tell you that you can access the data using only their tools. What is the problem with this?

   A. This may be a lock-in scenario.

   B. You need to be able to export data in a CSV format for analytical purposes.

   C. Data cannot be ingested into a SIEM.

   D. All of the above are correct.

4. What criteria must a SecaaS meet?

   A. Must have a security product or service delivered as a cloud service

   B. Must have a SOC 2 report and/or ISO/IEC 27001 certification

   C. Must meet the essential characteristics of cloud computing

   D. A and C

5. What is NOT listed as a benefit of SecaaS?

   A. Insulation of clients

   B. Cost savings

   C. Deployment flexibility

   D. Intelligence sharing

6. Which of the following best defines the IDS/IPS SecaaS?

   A. Local agents are installed on workstations.

   B. Local agents are installed on servers.

   C. Agents feed data to the cloud provider instead of local servers.

   D. All of the above are correct.

7. What can be performed by security assessment SecaaS?

   A. Traditional network assessment

   B. Assessment of server instances in a cloud

   C. Assessment of applications

   D. All of the above

8. What does a web security gateway SecaaS solution do?

   A. Inspects web traffic

   B. Limits web sites that users can access

   C. Encrypts connections

   D. A and B

9. What is NOT a disadvantage associated with SecaaS?

   A. Lack of multitenancy

   B. Handling of regulated data

   C. Migrating to SecaaS

   D. Lack of visibility

10. How can data transfers be sped up when using BC/DR SecaaS?

   A. Using compression supplied by the provider

   B. Implementing a local gateway device

   C. Using de-duplication techniques supplied by the provider

   D. A and C

Answers

1. **B.** Web application firewalls (WAFs) can inspect network traffic at layer 7 and understand HTTP traffic as a result.

2. **D.** All of above is the correct answer. SecaaS generally enables you to enforce your policies using your provider's systems.

3. **A.** If a vendor forces you to use their platform to read log data, this will likely lead to a lock-in scenario. You will be required to maintain the relationship to access data that you will likely need to demonstrate compliance and/or satisfy legal requirements. The other answers may or may not be true.

4. **D.** In order to be considered a SecaaS service, the provider must have a security product or service delivered as a cloud service and must meet the essential characteristics of the cloud. SOC or ISO/IEC is not listed as a requirement.

5. **B.** Yes, this is a tricky answer. Note the "cost" benefit doesn't say you will save money using a SecaaS service. It says you can "pay as you grow." Does this mean SecaaS is cheaper? Not necessarily. In fact, it could be more expensive than internal systems you use today.

6. **C.** IDS/IPS systems ingest data from agents and analyze such data in the provider's environment.

7. **D.** All of the listed activities can be performed as by a security assessment SecaaS.

8. **D.** Web security gateways offer a protective control that can inspect web traffic for malware and limit the web sites that users can access. They do not perform encryption.

9. **A.** Strong multitenancy is something you should check for when performing due diligence of a provider, because a lack of it could cause issues, specifically if other tenant data is compromised as a result of an e-discovery request against another tenant.

10. **B.** The correct answer is to implement a local gateway device. Though a local gateway may speed up data transfers by using the other techniques, they are not identified directly.

CHAPTER 14

Related Technologies

This chapter covers the following topics from Domain 14 of the CSA Guidance:

- Big Data
- Internet of Things
- Mobile
- Serverless Computing

Once a new technology rolls over you, if you're not part of the steamroller,
you're part of the road.

—Stewart Brand

In my opinion, this quote from Mr. Brand perfectly summarizes your career in information technology. There are always new developments that you need to understand to some degree. This is not to say that you need to be an expert in every new technology, but you at the very least need to understand the benefits that new technology brings.

This chapter looks at a few key technologies that, while not cloud-specific by any extent, are frequently found in cloud environments. These technologies often rely on the massive amounts of available resources that can quickly (and even automatically) scale up and down to meet demand.

In preparation for your CCSK exam, remember that the mission of the CSA and its Guidance document is to help organizations determine who is responsible for choosing the best practices that should be adopted and implemented (that is, provider side or customer side) and why these controls are important. This chapter focuses on the security concerns associated with these technologies, rather than on how controls are configured in a particular vendor's implementation.

If you are interested in learning more about one or more of these technologies, check out the Cloud Security Alliance web site for whitepapers and research regarding each of these areas.

Big Data

The term "big data" refers to extremely large data sets from which you can derive valuable information. Big data can handle volumes of data that traditional data-processing tools are simply unable to manage. You can't go to a store and buy a big data solution, and big data isn't a single technology. It refers to a set of distributed collection, storage, and data-processing frameworks. According to Gartner, "Big data is high volume, high velocity, and/or high variety information assets that require new forms of processing to enable enhanced decision making, insight discovery, and process optimization."

The CSA refers to the qualities from the Gartner quote as the "Three Vs." Let's define those now:

- **High Volume**   A large amount of data in terms of the number of records or attributes
- **High Velocity**   Fast generation and processing of data (such as real-time or data stream)
- **High Variety**   Structured, semistructured, or unstructured data

The Three Vs of big data make it very practical for cloud deployments, because of the attributes of elasticity and massive storage capabilities available in Platform as a Service (PaaS) and Infrastructure as a Service (IaaS) deployment models. Additionally, big data technologies can be integrated into cloud-computing applications.

Big data systems typically are typically associated with three common components:

- **Distributed data collection**   This component refers to the system's ability to ingest large volumes of data, often as streamed data. Ingested data could range from simple web clickstream analytics to scientific and sensor data. Not all big data relies on distributed or streaming data collection, but it is a core big data technology. See the "Distributed Data Collection Backgrounder" for further information on the data types mentioned.

- **Distributed storage**   This refers to the system's ability to store the large data sets in distributed file systems (such as Google File System, Hadoop Distributed File System, and so on) or databases (such as NoSQL). NoSQL (Not only SQL) is a nonrelational distributed and scalable database system that works well in big data scenarios and is often required because of the limitations of nondistributed storage technologies.

- **Distributed processing**   Tools and techniques are capable of distributing processing jobs (such as MapReduce, Spark, and so on) for the effective analysis of data sets that are so massive and rapidly changing that single-origin processing can't effectively handle them. See the "Distributed Data Collection Backgrounder" for further information.

 EXAM TIP   Remember the three components listed here: data gets *collected*, *stored*, and *processed*.

A few of the terms used in the preceding bulleted list deserve a bit more of an explanation. They are covered in the following backgrounders.

NOTE As always, information in the backgrounders is for your understanding, not for the CCSK exam.

Distributed Data Collection Backgrounder

Unlike typical distributed data that is often sent in a bulk fashion (such as structured database records from a previous week), streaming data is continuously generated by many data sources, which typically send data records simultaneously and in small sizes (kilobytes). Streaming data can include log files generated by customers using mobile or web applications, information from social networks, and telemetry from connected devices or instrumentation in data centers. Streaming data processing is beneficial in most scenarios where new and dynamic data is generated on a continuous basis.

Web clickstream analytics provide data that is generated when tracking how users interact with your web sites. There are generally two types of web clickstream analytics:

- **Traffic analytics** Operates at the server level and delivers performance data such as tracking the number of pages accessed by a user, page load times, how long it takes each page to load, and other interaction data.

- **E-commerce–based analytics** Uses web clickstream data to determine the effectiveness of e-commerce functionality. It analyzes the web pages on which shoppers linger, shopping cart analytics, items purchased, what the shopper puts in or takes out of a shopping cart, what items the shopper purchases, coupon codes used, and payment methods.

These two use cases demonstrate the potential of vast amounts of data that can be generated in day-to-day operations of a company and the need for tools that can interpret this data into actionable information the company can use to improve revenues.

Hadoop Backgrounder

Hadoop is fairly synonymous with big data. In fact, it is estimated that roughly half of Fortune 500 companies use Hadoop for big data, so it merits its own backgrounder. Believe it or not, what we now know as big data started off with Google trying to create a system they could use to index the Internet (called Google File System). They released the inner workings of their invention to the world as a whitepaper in 2003. In 2005, Doug Cutting and Mike Cafarella leveraged this knowledge to create the open source big data framework called Hadoop. Hadoop is now maintained by the Apache Software Foundation.

The following quote from the Hadoop project itself best explains what Hadoop is:

The Apache Hadoop software library is a framework that allows for the distributed processing of large data sets across clusters of computers using simple programming models. It is designed to scale up from single servers to thousands of machines, each offering local computation and storage.

Notice that Hadoop allows for distributed processing of data in large data sets. To achieve this, Hadoop runs both storage and processing on a number of separate x86 systems in a cluster. Why did they make it so that data and processing are both running on individual x86 systems? Cost and performance. These x86 systems (such as your laptop or work PC) are cheap in comparison to customized hardware. This decentralized approach means you don't need super-costly, powerful, high-performance computers to analyze huge amounts of data.

This storage and processing capability is broken down into two major components:

- **Hadoop Distributed File System (HDFS)**   This is the storage part of Hadoop. When data is stored in an HDFS system, the data is broken down into smaller blocks that are spread out across multiple systems in a cluster. HDFS itself sits on top of the native file system on the operating system you operate (likely Linux, but Windows is supported as well). HDFS allows for multiple data types (structured, unstructured, streaming data) to be used in a cluster. I'm not going to get into the details of the various components (SQOOP for databases and Flume for streaming data) that enable this ingestion to occur, because that's getting way too deep for this brief explanation of Hadoop (and especially HDFS).

- **MapReduce**   This is the processing part of Hadoop. MapReduce is a distributed computation algorithm—its name is actually a combination of *mapping* and *reducing*. The map part filters and sorts data, while the reduce part performs summary operations. Consider, for example, trying to determine the number of pennies in a jar. You could either count these out by yourself, or you could work with a team of four by dividing up the jar into four sets (map function) and having each person count their own and write down their findings (reduce). The four people working together would be considered a cluster. This is the divide-and-conquer approach used by MapReduce. Now let's say that you have a 4TB database you want perform analytics on with a cluster of four Hadoop nodes. The 4TB file would be split into four 1TB files and would be processed on the four individual nodes that would deliver the results you asked for.

To consider a real-life big data scenario, consider a very large retailer that needs to read sales data from all cash registers on a real-time basis from 11,000 stores conducting 500 sales an hour, so they can determine and forecast what needs to be ordered from partners and shipped out on a daily basis. That's a pretty complex computation that needs to be done. This data may very well be streaming data that we discussed earlier. This would be ingested into the Hadoop system, distributed among the nodes in the cluster, and then required orders and deliveries could be processed and sent to the appropriate systems via REST APIs.

These two components were the basis of the original Hadoop framework. Additional components have been added over time to improve functionality, including these:

- **Spark**   Spark is another data processing function that may replace MapReduce. It allows for more in-memory processing options than MapReduce does.

- **YARN**   Yet Another Resource Negotiator, as you can guess, performs a resource management function (cluster resource management specifically) in the Hadoop system.

- **Hadoop Common**   These tools enable the operating system to read data stored in the Hadoop file system.

This completes your 101-level crash course of big data analytics using Hadoop as an example. It's a field that is big today and is only going to become bigger. One last thing: There are commercial big data offerings out there that you can check out. Like most other new areas, mergers and acquisitions are common. For example, two of the larger big data solution providers, Cloudera and Hortonworks, completed their merger in 2019.

Security and Privacy Considerations

You know that big data is a framework that uses multiple modules across multiple nodes to process high volumes of data with a high velocity and high variety of sources. This makes security and privacy challenging when you're using a patchwork of different tools and platforms.

This is a great opportunity to discuss how security basics can be applied to technologies with which you may be unfamiliar, such as big data. At its most basic level, you need to authenticate, authorize, and audit (AAA) least-privilege access to *all* components and modules in the Hadoop environment. This, of course, includes everything from the physical layer all the way up to the modules themselves. For application-level components, your vendor should have their best practices documented (for example, Cloudera's security document is roughly 500 pages long) and should quickly address any vulnerabilities with patches. Only after these AAA basics are addressed should you consider encryption requirements, both in-transit and at-rest as required.

Data Collection

When data is collected, it will likely go through some form of intermediary storage device before it is stored in the big data analytics system. Data in this device (virtual machine, instance, container, and so on) will also need to be secured, as discussed in the previous section. Intermediary storage could be swap space (held in memory). Your provider should have documentation available for customers to address their own security requirements.

EXAM TIP   For your CCSK exam, remember that all components and workloads required of any technology must have secure AAA in place. This remains true when underlying cloud services are consumed to deliver big data analytics for your organization. An example of a cloud-based big data system could consist of processing nodes running in instances that collect data in volume storage.

Key Management

If encryption at rest is required as part of a big data implementation (everything is risk-based, after all), implementation may be complicated by the distributed nature of nodes. As far as the protection of data at rest, encryption capabilities in a cloud environment will likely be defined by a provider's ability to expose appropriate controls to secure data, and this includes key management. Key management systems need to be able to support distribution of keys to multiple storage and analysis tools.

Security Capabilities

CSP controls can be used to address your security requirements as far as the services that may be consumed (such as object storage) as part of your big data implementation. If you need your data to be encrypted, see if your cloud provider can do that for you. If you need very granular access control, see if the provider's service includes it. The details of the security configuration of these services and controls should be included in your security architecture.

Identity and Access Management

As mentioned, authorization and authentication are the most important controls. You must ensure that they are done correctly. In your cloud environment, this means starting with ensuring that every entity that has access to the management plane is restricted based on least-privilege principles. Moving from there, you need to address access to the services that are used as part of your big data architecture. Finally, all application components of the big data system itself need to have appropriate access controls established.

Considering the number of areas where identity and access management (IAM) must be implemented (cloud platform, services, and big data tool level), entitlement matrices can be complicated.

PaaS

Cloud providers may offer big data services as a PaaS. Numerous benefits can be associated with consuming a big data platform instead of building your own. Cloud providers may implement advanced technologies, such as machine learning, as part of their offerings.

You need to have an adequate understanding of potential data exposure, compliance, and privacy implications. Is there a compliance exposure if the PaaS vendor employees can technically access enterprise data? How does the vendor address this insider threat? These are the types of questions that must be addressed before you embrace a big data PaaS service.

Just like everything else covered in this book, risk-based decisions must be made and appropriate security controls implemented to satisfy your organizational requirements.

Internet of Things (IoT)

Internet of Things includes everything in the physical world, ranging from power and water systems to fitness trackers, home assistants, medical devices, and other industrial and retail technologies. Beyond these products, enterprises are adopting IoT for applications such as the following:

- Supply chain management
- Physical logistics management
- Marketing, retail, and customer relationship management
- Connected healthcare and lifestyle applications for employees and consumers

Depending on the deployment (for example, mass consumer use), I'm sure you can appreciate the amount of streaming data these devices can generate. While the cloud is not a requirement to support all of this incoming data and the subsequent processing required, it is often used to support these IoT devices.

The following cloud-specific IoT security elements are identified in the CSA Guidance:

- **Secure data collection and sanitization**   This could include, for example, stripping code of sensitive and/or malicious data.

- **Device registration, authentication, and authorization**   One common issue encountered today is the use of stored credentials to make direct API calls to the backend cloud provider. There are known cases of attackers decompiling applications or device software and then using those credentials for malicious purposes.

- **API security for connections from devices back to the cloud infrastructure**   In addition to the stored credentials issue just mentioned, the APIs themselves could be decoded and used for attacks on the cloud infrastructure.

- **Encrypted communications**   Many current devices use weak, outdated, or nonexistent encryption, which places data and the devices at risk.

- **Ability to patch and update devices so they don't become a point of compromise**   Currently, it is common for devices to be shipped as-is, and they never receive security updates for operating systems or applications. This has already caused multiple significant and highly publicized security incidents, such as massive botnet attacks based on compromised IoT devices.

 NOTE   Check out articles on Mirai and Torii malware for information on how compromised IoT devices can make for very large botnets used in massive DDoS attacks.

Mobile Computing

Mobile computing is, of course, nothing new. Companies don't require cloud services to support mobile applications, but still, many mobile applications are dependent on cloud services for backend processing. Mobile applications leverage the cloud not only because of its processing power capabilities for highly dynamic workloads but also because of its geographic distribution.

The CSA Guidance identifies the following security issues for mobile computing in a cloud environment:

- Device registration, authentication, and authorization are issues for mobile applications, as they are for IoT devices, especially when stored credentials are used to connect directly to provider infrastructure and resources via an API. If an attacker can decompile the application and obtain these stored credentials, they will be able to manipulate or attack the cloud infrastructure.

- Any application APIs that are run within the cloud environment are also listed as a potential source of compromise. If an attacker can run local proxies that intercept these API calls, they may be able to decompile the likely unencrypted information and explore them for security weaknesses. Certificate pinning/ validation inside the application may help mitigate this risk.

 NOTE The Open Web Application Security Project (OWASP) defines pinning as "the process of associating a host with their expected X509 certificate or public key. Once a certificate or public key is known or seen for a host, the certificate or public key is associated or 'pinned' to the host."

Serverless Computing

Serverless computing can be considered an environment in which the customer is not responsible for managing the server. In this model, the provider takes care of the servers upon which customers run workloads. The CSA defines serverless computing as "the extensive use of certain PaaS capabilities to such a degree that all or some of an application stack runs in a cloud provider's environment without any customer-managed operating systems, or even containers."

When most people think of serverless computing, they (incorrectly) think of running a script on the provider's platform (see the "Serverless vs. Function as a Service [FaaS]" sidebar). But serverless is much more than that very limited use case. The following serverless computing examples are provided by the CSA:

- Object storage
- Cloud load balancers
- Cloud databases
- Machine learning

- Message queues
- Notification services
- API gateways
- Web servers

I have no doubt that if your organization is using the cloud today, you are using serverless computing in some capacity. If your organization is planning on using the cloud, you will likely be using serverless offerings. There's nothing inherently wrong with this, because these services can be highly orchestrated (aka event-driven) and have deep integration with IAM services supplied by the provider. Just be aware that the more you leverage services supplied by the provider, the more dependent (locked in) your organization becomes, because you would have to re-create the environment in a new environment.

From a security perspective, the CSA Guidance calls out the following issues that you should be aware of before taking your CCSK exam:

- Serverless places a much higher security burden on the cloud provider. Choosing your provider and understanding security SLAs and capabilities is absolutely critical.

- Using serverless, the cloud user will not have access to commonly used monitoring and logging levels, such as server or network logs. Applications will need to integrate more logging, and cloud providers should provide necessary logging to meet core security and compliance requirements.

- Although the provider's services may be certified or attested for various compliance requirements, not necessarily every service will match every potential regulation. Providers need to keep compliance mappings up-to-date, and customers need to ensure that they use only the services within their compliance scope.

- There will be high levels of access to the cloud provider's management plane because that is the only way to integrate and use the serverless capabilities.

- Serverless can dramatically reduce attack surfaces and pathways, and integrating serverless components may be an excellent way to break links in an attack chain, even if the entire application stack is not serverless.

- Any vulnerability assessment or other security testing must comply with the provider's terms of service. Cloud users may no longer have the ability to test applications directly, or they may test with a reduced scope, since the provider's infrastructure is now hosting everything and can't distinguish between legitimate tests and attacks.

- Incident response may also be complicated and will definitely require changes in process and tooling to manage a serverless-based incident.

As you read through this list from the Guidance, did each point make sense to you? Did it feel like déjà vu? It should, because we have discussed every entry previously, just not directly in reference to serverless. Trust but verify your provider by performing due diligence, and remember that in addition to preventative controls, you need detection.

Since the services are built and managed by the provider with all serverless offerings, you may need to build logging into applications that are run in a serverless environment.

> ## Serverless vs. Function as a Service (FaaS)
>
> Everything in the "Serverless Computing" section remains true to this day. As the consumer, you are leveraging a service built by, and maintained by, the provider. The customer doesn't need to build functionality or run a server to gain access to functionality. Some confusion has recently arisen as a result of new FaaS offerings, such as AWS Lambda and Microsoft Azure Functions. Although these are often called "serverless computing," they are not that.
>
> When using FaaS, you are executing your own applications on a provider's server. In other words, unlike serverless, where the provider runs everything for you—such as the examples provided in the "Serverless Computing" section—in FaaS, the application is the developer's responsibility, just as it is in traditional compute, but the application runs in stateless compute containers that are built and operated by the provider.

Chapter Review

This chapter covered some newer technologies that you will undoubtedly encounter as your organization adopts cloud services. Just remember the highlights of the various technologies and the security issues surrounding them and you'll be prepared for your CCSK exam. Always remember you're taking an exam on cloud security, not these individual related technologies.

You should be comfortable with the following CSA recommendations for each technology covered in this section in preparation for your CCSK exam.

Big Data Recommendations:

- Authorization and authentication for all services and application components need to be locked down on a least-privilege basis.

- Access to the management plane and big data components will be required. Entitlement matrices are required and may be complicated by addressing these various components.

- Follow vendor recommendations for securing big data components. The CSA has whitepapers available regarding the securing of big data (not required reading for the CCSK exam).

- Big data services from a provider should be leveraged wherever possible. When using provider services as part of a big data solution, you should understand the advantages and security risks of adopting such services.

- If encryption of data at rest is required, be sure to address encryption in all locations. Remember that in addition to the primary storage, you must address intermediary and backup storage locations.
- Do not forget to address both security and privacy requirements.
- Ensure that the cloud provider doesn't expose data to employees or administrators by reviewing the provider's technical and process controls.
- Providers should clearly publish any compliance standards that their big data solutions meet. Customers need to ensure that they understand their compliance requirements.
- If security, privacy, or compliance is an issue, customers should consider using some form of data masking or obfuscation.

Internet of Things Recommendations:

- IoT devices must be able to be patched and updated.
- Static credentials should never be used on devices. This may lead to compromise of the cloud infrastructure or components.
- Best practices for device registration and authentication to the cloud should always be followed. Federated identity systems can be used for such purposes.
- Communications should always be encrypted.
- Data collected from devices should be sanitized (input validation best practice).
- Always assume API requests are hostile and build security from that.
- Changes and advances in the IoT space will continue. Keep up-to-date with recent developments by following the CSA Internet of Things working group.

Mobile Computing Recommendations:

- When designing mobile applications, follow CSP recommendations regarding authentication and authorization.
- As with IoT, federated identity can be used to connect mobile applications to cloud-hosted applications and services.
- Never transfer any keys or credentials in an unencrypted fashion.
- When testing APIs, assume all connections are hostile and that attackers will have authenticated unencrypted access.
- Mobile applications should use certificate pinning and validation to mitigate the risk of attackers using proxies to analyze API traffic that may be used to compromise security.
- Perform input validation on data and monitor all incoming data from a security perspective. Trust no one!

- Attackers will have access to your application. Ensure that any data stored on the mobile device is secured and properly encrypted. No data that may lead to a compromise of the cloud side (such as credentials) should be stored in the device.

- Keep up-to-date with the latest industry recommendations regarding mobile security by following the CSA Mobile Security working group.

Serverless Computing Recommendations:

- Remember that "serverless" simply means the customer doesn't have to worry about configuring the base server operating system. Customers still need to securely configure any exposed controls offered by the provider.

- Serverless platforms must meet compliance requirements. Cloud providers should be able to clearly state to customers what certifications have been obtained for every platform.

- Customers should use only platforms that meet compliance requirements.

- Serverless computing can be leveraged to enhance the overall security architecture. By injecting a provider service into your architectures (such as a message queuing service), attackers would need to compromise both the customer and provider services, which will likely be a significant hurdle for them, especially if a service removes any direct network connectivity between components or the cloud and the customer data center.

- Security monitoring will change as a result of serverless, because the provider assumes more responsibility for security and may not expose log data to customers. This may require that more logging be built into applications created for serverless environments.

- Security assessments and penetration testing of applications leveraging provider platforms will change. Use only assessors and testers who are knowledgeable about the provider's environment.

- Incident response will likely change even more dramatically in PaaS platforms than in IaaS. Communication with your provider regarding incident response roles is critical.

- Always remember that even though the provider is managing the platform and underlying servers (and operating systems), there are likely controls that need to be configured and assessed on a regular basis.

Questions

1. What is certificate pinning?
   A. Installing a certificate on a mobile device
   B. Storing a certificate in an open certificate registry that can be used for validation
   C. Associating a host with a certificate
   D. All of the above

2. Where should encryption of data be performed in a big data system?

   A. Primary storage

   B. Intermediary storage

   C. In memory

   D. A and B

3. What is Spark used for in big data?

   A. Spark is a big data storage file system.

   B. Spark is a machine learning module.

   C. Spark is a big data processing module.

   D. Spark is for storing big data.

4. Which of the following has led to IoT device security issues in the past?

   A. Embedding of credentials in the device

   B. Lack of encryption

   C. Lack of update mechanisms for IoT devices

   D. All of the above

5. Why may entitlement matrices be complicated when using them for big data systems?

   A. Multiple components are associated with big data implementations.

   B. Several components do not allow for granular entitlements.

   C. Cloud environment components are being leveraged as part of a big data implementation.

   D. A and C are correct.

6. What are the common components associated with a big data system?

   A. Distributed collection

   B. Distributed storage

   C. Distributed processing

   D. All of the above

7. What are the Three Vs of big data according to the CSA?

   A. High velocity, high volume, high variance

   B. High velocity, high volume, high variety

   C. High validation, high volume, high variety

   D. High value, high variance, high velocity

8. Which of the following is *not* considered a serverless platform according to the CSA?

    A. Load balancer

    B. DNS server

    C. Notification service

    D. Object storage

9. When should input validation be performed?

    A. When using the cloud as the backend for mobile applications

    B. When using the cloud as the backend for IoT devices

    C. When using cloud services to support a big data system

    D. All of the above

10. According to the CSA, what is an/are attribute(s) of the cloud that makes it ideal to support mobile applications?

    A. Cost of running required infrastructure

    B. Distributed geographical nature of cloud

    C. Inherent security associated with cloud services

    D. B and C

Answers

1. **C.** Certificate pinning is associating a certificate with a host. This can be useful to prevent attackers from using a proxy to view unencrypted network activity that may be used to identify security weaknesses. None of the other answers are correct.

2. **D.** Encryption (if required) of big data must be performed at all storage locations, including primary and intermediary locations.

3. **C.** Spark is a processing module for Hadoop that is considered the next generation of MapReduce. Although Hadoop was discussed only as part of a big data backgrounder, it is specifically called out in the core text of this book and CSA Guidance as a big data processing module.

4. **D.** All of the answers listed have led to security issues in the past for IoT devices.

5. **D.** CSA states that entitlement matrices can be complicated by both the number of components in a big data system as well as the cloud resources that may be leveraged as part of a big data implementation.

6. **D.** A big data system consists of distributed collection, distributed storage, and distributed processing.

7. **B.** The Three Vs are high volume, high velocity, and high variety. This means a big data system has to process a high volume of data that is coming in at a high rate of speed and that can be in multiple formats (structured, unstructured, and streamed).

8. **B.** The DNS server is not a serverless option according to CSA. Hold on, because there's a learning lesson to be had here. Providers may very well offer a DNS *service* to customers. That's not what is written here, though. Take your time when reading questions on your exam to make sure you aren't tricked by wording. You can absolutely build your own DNS server in an IaaS environment, or you can consume a DNS service if the provider offers one. The other possible answers are listed as serverless platforms.

9. **D.** It is a security best practice always to perform input validation on any incoming network traffic. This includes all the technologies listed.

10. **B.** The only listed attribute in the CSA Guidance regarding mobile application suitability for the cloud is the geographical nature of cloud. Yes, a cloud environment may be more secure, but this is, of course, a shared responsibility. You are never guaranteed that running in the cloud will be cheaper than running systems in your own data center.

CHAPTER 15

ENISA Cloud Computing: Benefits, Risks, and Recommendations for Information Security

This chapter covers the following topics from the European Network and Information Security Agency (ENISA) Cloud Computing Security, Risk, and Assessment documentation:

- Isolation Failure
- Economic Denial of Service
- Licensing Risks
- VM Hopping
- Five Key Legal Issues Common Across All Scenarios
- Top Security Risks in ENISA Research
- OVF [Open Virtualization Format]
- Underlying Vulnerability in Loss of Governance
- User Provisioning Vulnerability
- Risk Concerns of a Cloud Provider Being Acquired
- Security Benefits of Cloud
- Risks R.1–R.35 and Underlying Vulnerabilities
- Data Controller Versus Data Processor Definitions
- Guest System Monitoring in IaaS Responsibilities

The European Union Agency for Cybersecurity (ENISA) has been working to make Europe cyber secure since 2004.

—ENISA

As the opening quote states, the ENISA is an agency of the European Union that focuses on cybersecurity issues. As part of this, it created the "ENISA Cloud Computing: Benefits, Risks, and Recommendations for Information Security" document to support European member states and European Union stakeholders that adopt cloud services.

The ENISA document remains largely relevant because of its high-level view of the risks and vulnerabilities associated with cloud services. However, this document was written in 2009, so some risks and documented issues have been added since its publication. Additionally, some technologies such as containers didn't even exist at that time. I have made every effort to focus only on aspects of the ENISA that remain applicable today and items that you are likely to be tested on as part of your CCSK exam. This said, I still recommend that you have the ENISA document available during your open-book CCSK exam.

Many of these items have already been covered in previous chapters of this book. This is because the ENISA document was one of the documents used as the basis for the CSA Guidance documentation. I will, however, include information from the ENISA document that has not been previously addressed. Many of the sections are presented in a quick-hit style so that you can digest the information quickly.

Security Benefits of Cloud

After reading the previous chapters, you should understand the incredible benefits that are possible with cloud implementations. You should also understand that these benefits are possible only when they are planned and architected properly. The following list of security benefits was compiled by members of the ENISA to highlight some of the more pertinent benefits of cloud computing.

Security and the Benefits of Scale

Security measures are cheaper when they're implemented on a larger scale. This means that, from a provider's perspective, economies of scale apply to security. Following are some benefits of scale:

- **Multiple locations**   Providers have the economic resources to replicate content and services in multiple locations. This enables customers to benefit from increased levels of disaster recovery (if architected for in advance, of course).

- **Edge networks**   I haven't discussed edge networks previously. Gartner defines edge computing as "a part of a distributed computing topology in which information processing is located close to the edge—where things and people produce or consume that information." With multiple locations available, you have the potential to minimize the physical distance between your branch offices and your processing. This is particularly true when you consider content delivery networks (CDNs) and additional points of presence that may be available with a cloud provider's offerings.

- **Improved timeliness of response**   In Chapter 9, you learned how incident response can be dramatically improved by using infrastructure as code, by quarantining workloads through virtual firewalls (security groups), and by using other offerings possible in the cloud. These options need to be well architected and tested often.

- **Threat management**   Given the economies of scale surrounding security, as well as the potential reputational damages from security incidents, CSPs will often hire specialists in security threats to provide advanced security threat detection. This ultimately leads to customers benefitting from an increased security baseline in which they operate their workloads.

Security as a Market Differentiator

For many cloud providers, security is a selling point for marketing. You will often see this through the number of compliance standards that providers obtain. Not only does increased security certifications and capability enable providers to sell to companies in various industries, but it helps them market their products as well.

Standardized Interfaces for Managed Security Services

Cloud providers can offer standardized open interfaces to managed security service (MSS) providers. This enables these service providers to resell services to their own customers.

Rapid, Smart Scaling of Resources

Providers have a vast amount of scalable compute resources available. These resources can be reallocated to address threats by filtering incoming traffic and performing other defensive measures to protect customers (such as shielding customers from distributed denial of service attacks). The ENISA documentation also points out that providers can respond in a granular fashion, without scaling all types of system resources (for example, increasing CPU, but not memory or storage). This can reduce the costs of responding to sudden (nonmalicious) peaks in demand.

Audit and Evidence Gathering

I have already covered the increased audit capability in a cloud environment in many of the previous chapters (especially Chapter 4). The ENISA document does point to log storage in a cloud environment as being a cost-effective location to store log data to support audits.

Timely, Effective, and Efficient Updates and Defaults

Immutable (Chapter 7), snapshots (Chapter 9), and infrastructure as code (Chapter 10) technologies can be used to standardize and maintain security controls across all virtual machines in an Infrastructure as a Service (IaaS) environment. Of note from the ENISA document is the following statement: "Updates can be rolled out many times more rapidly across a homogeneous platform than in traditional client-based systems that rely on the patching model." A *homogeneous platform* is owned and supplied by a single vendor. This means that using the tools mentioned earlier can deliver quicker update capability than the standard patching done in your data center today.

With Platform as a Service (PaaS) and Security as a Service (SaaS), updates to the platform will likely be performed in a centralized fashion, which minimizes the time window of the vulnerability.

Audit and SLAs Force Better Risk Management

Given the volume of security certifications faced by providers, it is highly likely that any new risks will be quickly identified during the multiple assessments and audits that will probably be performed throughout the year.

Benefits of Resource Concentration

This ties in with the economies of scale previously mentioned as a benefit associated with cloud providers. The cost of controls on a per-unit basis is likely much lower than a customer faces with a traditional data center. For example, spending $1 million on physical security for 1000 servers in a traditional data center equals a cost per unit of $1000 per server. In a cloud data center with 100,000 servers, the cost per unit is $10.

Top Security Risks

The top security risks according to the ENISA are not presented in any particular order of criticality. Because I have addressed these risks in previous chapters, here I provide quick summaries of the information delivered as part of the ENISA documentation. First, though, is a backgrounder on risk itself.

IT Risk Backgrounder

Both the ENISA document and the CSA Guidance assume you have some understanding of IT risk concepts. ENISA actually uses these concepts quite systematically to analyze cloud security. Although these concepts are are not included in the CCSK exam, it is worthwhile for you to be familiar with them, which will help you understand these documents and assist you in applying cloud security knowledge in practice. In my experience, understanding and applying these concepts will give you more options in securing IT and therefore in securing the cloud. It will also make your conversations easier.

Risk analysis should always start with the thing of value to be protected. This is called the *asset*. An example would be capacity on a storage disk or a set of sensitive data. All assets have vulnerabilities. According to ENISA, a *vulnerability* is "any circumstance or event with the potential to adversely impact an asset through unauthorized access, destruction, disclosure, modification of data, and/or denial of service." In our examples, disk capacity can run out, and sensitive data can get leaked. It is important that you understand that vulnerabilities exist, whether they are realized or not.

ENISA then states that a risk is the result of a threat that exploits a vulnerability. You should understand that the threat can be malicious (an intentional act) or otherwise (such as wear and tear or negligence). In either case, the result is a negative impact or an actual bad consequence. In IT, the negative impacts are typically categorized as loss of confidentiality, loss of integrity, or loss of availability. The damage is, in the end, to the business utilizing the IT, and it should therefore be explained in terms that matter to those stakeholders. This may well be a long scenario, but it is important that you create the full story. If you just say, "This machine can be accessed by a bad actor," any stakeholder could answer, "So what?" If you go about saying that sensitive data is on that machine, which will subsequently get into the hands of the data protection authority, which will lead to them getting a fine or worse, you will get a different response.

In our examples, a storage disk filling up may lead, in the end, to a service no longer being available, which therefore means unhappy customers. Data leakage can lead to reputation loss or legal punishment. Risks, therefore, impact assets and, in particular, the assets' value. The more likely or probable the risk and the higher the negative impact, the more important it becomes to do something about it. Risks with low probability and low impact are not the first concern.

Anything that reduces the likelihood and/or impact of a risk is called a *control* or *countermeasure*. For our examples, we could set up disk space monitoring or encryption of data. In reality, many engineering options exist. The cloud makes certain old controls difficult to use, but it also enables new controls, such as dynamic and granular network access controls. It is therefore difficult to say in general whether the cloud makes IT more or less secure.

Loss of Governance

You know there is a shared responsibility in the cloud. When the client cedes control to the provider, there may be a gap in security defenses if there is no commitment from the provider in a service level agreement (SLA). Contractual clauses (such as Terms of Use) may restrict customers from performing compliance activities that support governance.

If a provider uses their own third parties (such as an SaaS provider using an IaaS provider), you may have no governance capabilities whatsoever. If a provider is acquired by a different company, contractual clauses of the service may be changed by the new company. Such loss of control and governance may lead to an organization being unable to meet security requirements; they may suffer from a loss of performance or deterioration of quality of service, or they may experience significant compliance challenges.

Lock-in

The lack of portability leads to vendor lock-in. There are rarely tools available from vendors or other sources (such as open source) to facilitate the movement of systems and/or data from one provider to another. The causes of lock-in can be numerous. It can happen from annual SaaS contracts with very painful cancellation clauses, and it can happen because of technology issues, such as the inability to export data in a format that can be used in a different provider's environment. Even when the core technology is standardized (such as containers and VMs), there may be significant differences in the providers' management plane interfaces.

The ENISA documentation focuses on the lock-in associated with each service model. The following sections list the various types of lock-ins that customers may face when using the various cloud service models.

SaaS Lock-in

Much of the lock-in potential associated with SaaS has to do with the ability to export data in a format that can be used in another location. Providers will often store tenant data in a custom database schema. There is generally no agreement regarding how data is structured, but there are common formats in which data may be exported (such as XML).

Of course, when dealing with SaaS, you are dealing with a custom application. Migrating from one SaaS provider to another will likely impact end users. This will likely require retraining and can result in significant costs in a large enterprise. Additionally, any integration (such as APIs) with internal systems, and your existing SaaS solution will need to be re-created.

 NOTE Migrating from one SaaS application to another is not much different from application migration in your data center. Both will likely be the source of much effort.

PaaS Lock-in

Although your organization's use of PaaS solutions may consist of application development, you need to be aware of some portability aspects. The primary issue with PaaS lock-in has to do with the use of provider services, which are often accessed by an API and used to build complete application functionality. This is referred to as *API lock-in* in the ENISA documentation.

Application code itself may require customization if a provider does not allow particular functions that they may consider "dangerous" (such as functions that may access the underlying shared operating system layer). This may require that your developers understand these potential limitations and work around them by customizing code to work in a particular environment. ENISA refers to this as *runtime lock-in*.

Aside from application development, any data generated by PaaS systems may not be exportable in a format that can be easily consumed. The ENISA documentation refers to this as *data lock-in*.

IaaS Lock-in

When considering IaaS lock-in, you need to consider both workloads and data stored in the provider's environment. The biggest issue to be aware of in either scenario is what the ENISA document refers to as a "run on the banks" scenario. In the event of a major issue with a provider, numerous customers may begin exporting systems and data simultaneously, leading to poor network performance that could drastically increase the time required to export data.

From a virtual machine lock-in perspective, although software and virtual machine metadata is bundled for portability, this is limited for use within the provider's environment. Open Virtualization Format (OVF) is identified as the means to address virtual machine lock-in.

IaaS storage providers' functionality and features can range widely. The main lock-in issue comes down to potential application-level dependence on specific policy features such as access controls. Such dependence may limit the customer's choice of potential provider.

Isolation Failure

Multitenancy is a defining characteristic of the cloud. It requires a robust isolation capability wherever resources are shared, such as memory, storage, and networking. This isolation requirement is not necessarily just hardware-related. An SaaS offering that uses a multitenant database could also be the source of isolation failure. If this isolation fails, security fails. The impact of such a failure could lead to customers losing valuable or sensitive data and/or service interruption if the CSP shuts down access to address the failure. From a provider's perspective, isolation failure could lead to business failure because of potentially devastating reputational failure and a resulting loss of customers.

Compliance Risks

Compliance with the regulations and industry certifications required for your organization may be challenged by procuring cloud services. Compliance risks may include the following:

- A cloud provider cannot provide evidence of their compliance to regulations and/or industry standards your organization must meet.
- A cloud provider does not allow audits and does not otherwise demonstrate compliance with regulations and/or industry standards your organization must meet.

Management Interface Compromise

Because accessing the provider's management interface (aka management plane) is generally performed across the Internet, it can be accessed by anyone, including malicious users. Remember that access controls are your primary controls for securing the management plane and that multifactor authentication (MFA) should always be used for privileged accounts that access the management plane.

Data Protection

Checking how a provider handles data and ensuring that it is done in a lawful manner on behalf of customers may be difficult. This poses a data protection risk to your organization as a result, especially in the case of multiple providers storing information as part of a solution (such as federated clouds). This risk can be mitigated by reviewing any provider's certifications and supplied security documentation.

Insecure or Incomplete Data Deletion

Deletion of data in a shared cloud environment presents a risk to customers. This is because of the nature of shared storage and the inability to confirm that data has been completely deleted from the provider's environment. Additionally, as covered in Chapter 11, data dispersion is often used by providers. This type of storage will make multiple copies of data and spread them across multiple servers and multiple drives. This, along with the previously mentioned issues, leads to a higher risk for customers than they face with dedicated on-premises hardware.

Malicious Insider

Cloud service provider employees and contractors pose a significant risk to your organization when you use cloud services. Although the likelihood of realizing such risks is low, the impacts of doing so can be very high.

 EXAM TIP Keep in mind that malicious insiders aren't limited to administrators. A similar risk is posed by auditors, because they may have intimate knowledge of the inside architecture, processes, and weaknesses of a provider.

Five Key Legal Issues Common Across All Scenarios

Five key legal issues have been identified as common across all the scenarios. This information is found in "Annex 1" of the ENISA documentation. The information in the following sections is not specific to the cloud and is applicable to all forms of computing.

Money talks. Much of an organization's capability to define contractual controls to meet legal obligations is based on the size of the provider and that of the customer. Very large providers will likely have a "take-it-or-leave-it" approach with smaller potential customers, but they may be more open to negotiate with larger potential customers. This is also true with large customers and smaller providers. Smaller providers will be more likely to negotiate terms with large potential customers but may not do so with small- and medium-sized business (SMB) customers.

 NOTE I have condensed the material from the annex in the following sections so you don't spend an incredible amount of time reading about small details that you likely won't be tested on as part of your CCSK exam.

Data Protection

The data protection referred to in the ENISA document is about processing integrity and availability. Much of this section focuses on Directive 95/46/EC (Data Protection Directive), which has since been replaced by the GDPR.

For your general understanding of this section, just remember that data that contains personally identifiable information (PII) needs to be strongly protected, because this type of data, if compromised, will lead to legal issues for your organization.

 NOTE This section includes coverage of the difference between a data controller and a data processor. I have put that information into a separate section, "Additional Items for the Exam," later in this chapter, because this particular subject is listed as a potential area that you may be tested on as part of your CCSK exam.

Confidentiality

You know that confidentiality is a main security principle, and you know that data should be accessed only by authorized individuals. This section of the annex contains a term that has not been previously covered: "know-how." The ENISA defines *know-how* as something similar to documented trade secrets—how the customer does what it does, such as a manufacturing process.

Intellectual Property

Some cloud providers may contractually take ownership of any data that is uploaded to their systems. As a result, customers should ensure that intellectual property rights are regulated through dedicated contractual clauses in the Intellectual Property Clause and Confidentiality/Non-Disclosure Clause. These clauses should include penalties in case a provider does not properly protect such data and the ability for the consumer to terminate the agreement unilaterally.

Professional Negligence

The easiest way to think of lawsuits is to think about who has contracts with whom. The end user has a contract with the data controller, and the data controller has a contract with the provider (or data processor). If the end user's data is compromised, they are suing the data controller, because that is the party to which they are contractually bound.

Limitation of liability and indemnity clauses may help the company directly using the processor to shift liability to the provider; however, the data controller is always legally responsible and accountable for the loss of any end-user data.

Outsourcing Service and Changes in Control

This part of the ENISA document is all about using a provider that outsources some (or all) functionality to another provider. This leaves you, the customer, with third and fourth parties that you need to be aware of.

ENISA recommends that any outsourcing carried out by the provider be clearly understood as part of your due diligence. Providers should offer guarantees or warranties regarding the performance of outsourced services. The ENISA also recommends that you request contractual clauses that state that your organization must approve of any changes the provider makes in their outsourcing agreements, or you have the ability to terminate or renegotiate terms.

Additional Items for the Exam

The following sections contain additional items from the ENISA document that you may be tested on as part of your CCSK exam.

Open Virtualization Format

The only reference to OVF in the ENISA document is the following sentence: "Migrating between providers is non-trivial until open standards, such as OVF, are adopted." Now what, exactly, is this OVF they're talking about? The OVF is an open standard by the Distributed Management Task Force (DMTF) that is intended to assist with portability of virtual machines by easing the ability to migrate server images from one environment to another.

Of note, you may also see open virtualization archive (OVA), which is essentially a ZIP file (actually a TAR file) that contains all of the files associated with OVF.

 EXAM TIP If you're presented with any questions on OVF on the CCSK exam, remember that portability is the most important element of OVF.

VM Hopping

VM hopping is an isolation failure in which an attacker moves from one virtual machine (VM) to another, which they are not intended to access. This would likely be related to a failure or compromise of the underlying hypervisor that should be providing VM isolation.

 NOTE Spectre and Meltdown are two fairly recent examples of vulnerabilities that could have impacted isolation and therefore allowed VM hopping.

Economic Denial of Service

With the incredible scalability of cloud services, particularly IaaS, you have the ability to increase computing power automatically to meet increased demand (generally performed in IaaS through auto-scaling groups). However, when planning such elasticity, you need to consider the following question: What if you're spending vast sums of compute power to respond to a denial of service attack?

Licensing Risks

Licenses still need to be addressed when used in a cloud environment, especially IaaS. Any server instance running commercial software should report back to a centralized license management system to protect against illegal usage of the software.

Risk Concerns of a Cloud Provider Being Acquired

The acquisition of your CSP can have a significant impact on your organization. The ENISA documentation states that this may cause nonbinding agreements with a provider (for example, things the provider is not contractually required to supply) to be at risk.

There have been real-life examples of CSPs having been acquired, when, in some cases, the new owner has decided to pivot the cloud services to serve only particular industries. In other cases, new ownership decided to terminate the offering a few years after acquiring the provider.

A provider being purchased is an example of your needing to monitor relationships continuously with all providers your organization is using. Failure to do this may introduce risk to your organization if a new owner makes substantial changes and/or changes business plans.

Data Controller vs. Data Processor Definitions

Recall from Chapter 3 that the *data controller* is the entity that determines the purposes and means of the processing of personal data in accordance with laws and regulations in an organization's jurisdiction. The data processor is the entity that processes personal data on behalf of the controller.

Guest System Monitoring in IaaS Responsibilities

Guest system monitoring is the responsibility of the customer. In a nutshell, the ENISA document states that the customer must take full responsibility for their cloud-deployed applications. This, of course, includes monitoring of everything the customer is responsible for.

User Provisioning Vulnerability

Multiple vulnerabilities are associated with user provisioning in the ENISA document. So that we're on the same page regarding the vulnerabilities listed in the document, there are several potential weaknesses regarding processes. This, of course, is not to say that all the vulnerabilities listed here exist; it means these are potential areas that need to be considered and protected from being exploited:

- The customer cannot control the provider's provisioning process.
- The identity of the customer may not be adequately verified upon registration.
- There may be delays between cloud system components having identities and profile content synchronized.
- Multiple copies of an identity may be made, and these may not be synchronized.
- Credentials may be vulnerable to interception and replay.

The ENISA document references this vulnerability as being applicable to the following risks:

- Economic denial of service
- Modifying network traffic
- Privilege escalation
- Social-engineering attacks
- Loss or compromise of operational logs

- Loss or compromise of security logs
- Backups lost or stolen

Underlying Vulnerability in Loss of Governance

I addressed the risk of loss of governance in the "Top Security Risks" section earlier in this chapter. The ENISA document lists the following vulnerabilities and quick descriptions associated with a loss of governance:

- **Unclear roles and responsibilities**   This refers to inadequate attribution of roles and responsibilities in the cloud provider organization.
- **Poor enforcement of role definitions**   A failure to segregate roles may lead to excessively privileged roles, which can make extremely large systems vulnerable.
- **Synchronizing responsibilities or contractual obligations external to cloud**   Cloud customers may be unaware of their responsibilities.
- **SLA clauses with conflicting promises to different stakeholders**   SLA clauses may also be in conflict with promises made by other clauses or clauses from other providers.
- **Audit or certification not available to customers**   The CSP cannot provide any assurance to the customer via audit certification.
- **Cross-cloud applications creating hidden dependency**   Hidden dependencies exist in the services supply chain. Cloud provider architecture does not support continued operation from the cloud when the third parties involved, subcontractors, or the customer's company, have been separated (for example, disconnected) from the service provider.
- **Lack of standard technologies and solutions**   A lack of standards means that data may be locked in to a provider. This is a big risk if the provider ceases operation.
- **Storage of data in multiple jurisdictions and lack of transparency**   Mirroring data for delivery by edge networks and redundant storage without real-time information available to the customer of where data is stored introduces a level of vulnerability.
- **No source escrow agreement**   Lack of source escrow means that if a PaaS or an SaaS provider goes into bankruptcy, its customers are not protected. A software escrow agreement may enable the customer to re-create a similar service with another provider.
- **No control on vulnerability assessment process**   Restrictions on port scanning and vulnerability testing are an important vulnerability, which, combined with a Terms of Use that places responsibility on the customer for securing elements of the infrastructure, is a serious security problem.
- **Certification schemes not adapted to cloud infrastructures**   Not all certifications contain cloud-specific controls, which means that cloud-specific security vulnerabilities are likely to be missed.

- **Lack of information on jurisdictions**   Data may be stored and/or processed in high-risk jurisdictions where it is vulnerable to confiscation by forced entry. If this information is not available to the cloud customer, they cannot take steps to avoid it.

- **Lack of completeness and transparency in terms of use**   This occurs when the provider's usage policy is unclear or lacks detail.

- **Unclear asset ownership**   A customer failing to understand asset ownership could result in inadequate application of security baseline and hardening procedures, human error, and untrained administrators.

Risks R.1–R.35 and Underlying Vulnerabilities

For this section, I list the various risks that are identified by the ENISA and the risk rating as identified by the ENISA for each. Many of the more important risks and vulnerabilities have been previously addressed in this chapter. I recommend that you use this chart to gain an understanding of the high-, medium-, and low-level risks according the ENISA before taking your CCSK exam. There is no need to memorize this table, however.

 NOTE   You may notice that none of the risks identified by the ENISA are listed as low-level risks. This is because there isn't a single risk listed that has a low impact associated with it.

Identified Risk	Risk Rating	Underlying Vulnerabilities
Policy and Organizational Risks		
R.1: Lock-in	High	• Lack of standard technologies and solutions • Poor provider selection • Lack of supplier redundancy • Lack of completeness and transparency in Terms of Use
R.2: Loss of governance	High	See underlying vulnerabilities in the "Loss of Governance" section earlier in the chapter.
R.3: Compliance challenges	High	• Audit or certification not available to customers • Lack of standard technologies and solutions • Storage of data in multiple jurisdictions and lack of transparency • Certification schemes not adapted to cloud infrastructures • Lack of information on jurisdictions • Lack of completeness and transparency in terms of use
R.4: Loss of business reputation due to co-tenant activities	Medium	• Lack of resource isolation • Lack of reputational isolation • Hypervisor vulnerabilities
R.5: Cloud service termination or failure	Medium	• Poor provider selection • Lack of supplier redundancy • Lack of completeness and transparency in Terms of Use

Identified Risk	Risk Rating	Underlying Vulnerabilities
Policy and Organizational Risks		
R.6: Cloud provider acquisition	Medium	• Lack of completeness and transparency in Terms of Use
R.7: Supply chain failure	Medium	• Lack of completeness and transparency in Terms of Use • Cross-cloud applications creating hidden dependency • Poor provider selection • Lack of supplier redundancy
Technical Risks		
R.8: Resource exhaustion	Medium	• Inaccurate modeling of resource usage • Inadequate resource provisioning and investments in infrastructure • No policies for resource capping • Lack of supplier redundancy
R.9: Isolation failure	High	• Hypervisor vulnerabilities • Lack of resource isolation • Lack of reputational isolation • Possibility that internal (cloud) network probing will occur • Possibility that co-residence checks will be performed
R.10: Cloud provider malicious insider	High	• Unclear roles and responsibilities • Poor enforcement of role definitions • Need-to-know principle not applied • AAA vulnerabilities • System or OS vulnerabilities • Inadequate physical security procedures • Impossibility of processing data in encrypted form • Application vulnerabilities or poor patch management
R.11: Management interface compromise	Medium	• AAA vulnerabilities • Remote access to management interface • Misconfiguration • System or OS vulnerabilities • Application vulnerabilities or poor patch management
R.12: Intercepting data in transit	Medium	• AAA vulnerabilities • Communication encryption vulnerabilities • Lack of or weak encryption of archives and data in transit • Possibility that internal (cloud) network probing will occur • Possibility that co-residence checks will be performed • Lack of completeness and transparency in terms of use
R.13: Data leakage upon up/download, intra-cloud	Medium	• AAA vulnerabilities • Communication encryption vulnerabilities • Possibility that internal (cloud) network probing will occur • Possibility that co-residence checks will be performed • Impossibility of processing data in encrypted form • Application vulnerabilities or poor patch management

Identified Risk	Risk Rating	Underlying Vulnerabilities
Technical Risks		
R.14: Insecure or ineffective deletion of data	Medium	• Sensitive media sanitization
R.15: Distributed denial of service	Medium	• Misconfiguration • System or OS vulnerabilities • Inadequate or misconfigured filtering resources
R.16: Economic denial of service	Medium	• AAA vulnerabilities • User provisioning vulnerabilities • User deprovisioning vulnerabilities • Remote access to management interface • No policies for resource capping
R.17: Loss of encryption keys	Medium	• Poor key management procedures • Key generation: low entropy for random-number generation
R.18: Undertaking malicious probes or scans	Medium	• Possibility that internal (cloud) network probing will occur • Possibility that co-residence checks will be performed
R.19: Compromise service engine	Medium	• Hypervisor vulnerabilities • Lack of resource isolation
R.20: Conflicts between customer hardening proce-dures and cloud environment	Medium	• Lack of completeness and transparency in Terms of Use • SLA clauses with conflicting promises to different stakeholders • Unclear roles and responsibilities
Legal Risks		
R.21: Subpoena and e-discovery	High	• Lack of resource isolation • Storage of data in multiple jurisdictions and lack of transparency • Lack of information on jurisdictions
R.22: Risk for chang-es of jurisdiction	High	• Lack of information on jurisdictions • Storage of data in multiple jurisdictions and lack of transparency
R.23: Data protection risks	High	• Lack of information on jurisdictions • Storage of data in multiple jurisdictions and lack of transparency
R.24: Licensing risks	Medium	• Lack of completeness and transparency in Terms of Use
Risks Not Specific to Cloud		
R.25: Network breaks	Medium	• Misconfiguration • System or OS vulnerabilities • Lack of resource isolation • Lack of, or a poor and untested, business continuity and disaster recovery plan
R.26: Network management (congestion, non-optimal use)	High	• Misconfiguration • System or OS vulnerabilities • Lack of resource isolation • Lack of, or a poor and untested, business continuity and disaster recovery plan

Identified Risk	Risk Rating	Underlying Vulnerabilities
Risks Not Specific to Cloud		
R.27: Modifying network traffic	Medium	• User provisioning vulnerabilities • User deprovisioning vulnerabilities • Communication encryption vulnerabilities • No control on vulnerability assessment process
R.28: Privilege escalation	Medium	• AAA vulnerabilities • User provisioning vulnerabilities • User deprovisioning vulnerabilities • Hypervisor vulnerabilities • Unclear roles and responsibilities • Poor enforcement of role definitions • Need-to-know principle not applied • Misconfiguration
R.29: Social engineering attack	Medium	• Lack of security awareness • User provisioning vulnerabilities • Lack of resource isolation • Communication encryption vulnerabilities • Inadequate physical security procedures
R.30: Loss or compromise of operational logs	Medium	• Lack of policy or poor procedures for log collection and retention • AAA vulnerabilities • User provisioning vulnerabilities • User deprovisioning vulnerabilities • Lack of forensic readiness • System or OS vulnerabilities
R.31: Loss or compromise of security logs	Medium	• Lack of policy or poor procedures for log collection and retention • AAA vulnerabilities • User provisioning vulnerabilities • User deprovisioning vulnerabilities • Lack of forensic readiness • System or OS vulnerabilities
R.32: Backups lost or stolen	Medium	• Inadequate physical security procedures • AAA vulnerabilities • User provisioning vulnerabilities • User deprovisioning vulnerabilities
R.33: Unauthorized access to premises	Medium	• Inadequate physical security procedures
R.34: Theft of computer equipment	Medium	• Inadequate physical security procedures
R.35: Natural disasters	Medium	• Lack of, or a poor and untested, business continuity and disaster recovery plan

Chapter Review

This chapter covered the key elements of the ENISA document that will form part of your CCSK exam. The ENISA document accounts for 6 percent of the total questions in your CCSK exam (87 percent is based on the CSA Guidance and 7 percent is based on the Cloud Controls Matrix [CCM] and Consensus Assessments Initiative Questionnaire [CAIQ]). In preparation for your CCSK exam, you should be comfortable with the following:

- Understand the listed security benefits of the cloud from a business perspective.
- Understand the top security risks associated with cloud computing.
- Understand the top legal issues your organization faces across all scenarios.
- Understand the listed risks and associated vulnerabilities.

Questions

1. Which of the following is listed by ENISA as a way for SaaS or PaaS providers to protect their customers?

   A. Providers should have redundant storage in place.

   B. Providers should have a source code escrow agreement in place.

   C. Customers should have contractual agreements that list penalties for loss of code.

   D. All of the above are correct.

2. According to the ENISA documentation, which of the following may be used in IaaS to address portability?

   A. OVF

   B. WAF

   C. IAM

   D. DAM

3. Why is data deletion considered a top security risk according to ENISA?

   A. Because of the shared nature of storage

   B. Because of the inability to verify that data is adequately deleted

   C. Because SSD drives cannot reliably wipe data

   D. A and B

4. Which of the following is *not* an example of vendor lock-in?

   A. Contracts with termination penalties

   B. Provider exports data only in a proprietary format

   C. Custom SaaS applications

   D. PaaS platforms that restrict available functions

5. VM hopping is an attack that is possible in the event of what failure?

   A. Virtual storage control failure

   B. Hypervisor segregation failure

   C. Hypervisor isolation failure

   D. Inadequate security controls by the customer

6. Which of the following could be considered a malicious insider as per ENISA "Top Security Risks"?

   A. Customer administrator

   B. Provider's auditor

   C. Customer's auditor

   D. All of the above

7. A company administrator determines that the best approach to dealing with any sudden increases in network traffic is to create an auto-scaling group that will create an unlimited number of web servers to meet increased demand. What has the administrator created?

   A. The administrator has implemented an auto-scaling practice that is commonly performed to take advantage of the elastic nature of the cloud.

   B. The administrator has implemented an application load-balancing system.

   C. The administrator has implemented a network load-balancing system.

   D. The administrator has created an economic denial of service scenario if there is ever a denial of service attack against the company.

8. Which of the following is *not* considered a vulnerability associated with the risk of loss of business reputation due to co-tenant activities?

   A. Lack of resource isolation

   B. Lack of reputational isolation

   C. Hypervisor vulnerabilities

   D. Object storage

9. Which of the following is *not* listed in the ENISA documentation as a potential area that needs to be considered and protected from being exploited with regard to user provisioning?

   A. Credentials that may be vulnerable to interception and replay

   B. If the customer cannot control the provider's provisioning process

   C. If the identity of the customer may not be adequately verified upon registration

   D. The customer's ability to restrict access to the IAM system supplied by the provider to a specific range of IP addresses

10. What should always be done to protect against possible management interface compromise where an attacker gains access to your cloud environment (select the best answer)?

    A. Connect to the management interface via IPSec VPN.

    B. Protect connections through the use of TLS.

    C. Implement MFA on all privileged accounts.

    D. Create separate accounts for administrators with access to the management plane.

Answers

1. **B.** To ensure that SaaS or PaaS software is not orphaned or abandoned in the event of a provider's failure, customers should seek to ensure that providers have a code escrow agreement in place with a third-party escrow agent. Although the other answers are good ideas for protecting customers, only code escrow agreements are listed in the ENISA documentation.

2. **A.** The ENISA document calls open virtualization format (OVF) as potentially beneficial to address portability in an IaaS environment.

3. **D.** Insecure or incomplete data deletion is a risk in cloud because of the shared nature of storage and the inability to verify that data is adequately deleted. Although SSD wiping is possible (only with vendor-supplied tools), this is not listed as a reason in the document. It is also not true that all providers use SSD for storage of customer data.

4. **C.** All SaaS products are customized applications. This fact is not the source of vendor lock-in. What creates a lock-in situation with SaaS is the lack of ability to move data easily from one SaaS provider to another. If tools exist (generally they are limited) to move from one SaaS provider to another, vendor lock-in can be fairly easily dealt with. All the other answers are lock-in scenarios.

5. **C.** Performing VM hopping is a result of hypervisor isolation failure. None of the other answers is correct. Remember that segregation is not the same as isolation.

6. **B.** The ENISA document lists provider employees and contractors as potential malicious insiders. As such, the only possible correct answer is the provider's auditor.

7. **D.** The administrator has created an economic denial of service scenario if there is ever a denial of service attack against the company. This is because of the measured service characteristic of cloud computing, where companies pay for the resources they use. Load balancing will distribute traffic across only an established amount of servers, so B and C do not address what the administrator has established. Finally, although auto-scaling groups are common, there needs to be a set limit to the amount of servers that will be created.

8. **D.** Object storage is the only answer that is not listed as an associated vulnerability to the risk of loss of business reputation due to co-tenant activities.

9. **D.** The only possible answer *not* listed is that the customer can restrict access to the IAM system supplied by the provider to a specific range of IP addresses. This is because the IAM system is part of the management plane that can be accessed from anyone as part of the broad network access characteristic of the cloud. All other entries are listed as areas for consideration and protection.

10. **C.** Privileged accounts should always access the management plane with MFA. The management plane faces increased risk of compromise because it is globally accessible; therefore, implementing a VPN of any sort is not listed as a potential safeguard. All users accessing the management plane should always have separate accounts, but D addresses repudiation, not security of the accounts accessing the management plane. Although all connections should be protected in transit (such as with TLS), B is not the best answer.

Cloud Computing Security Policy Examples

When adopting cloud services, your organization needs to establish appropriate policies to instruct employees on the governance required for cloud services. Existing IT security policies should not be modified to address cloud-specific security policy statements. Rather, these directives should be included in a separate cloud security policy.

The following cloud security policies for the fictitious company ACME Incorporated are included to give you two different examples of cloud security policies. The first example has the CIO office approving all cloud adoption. This is called the *centralized* example. The second example shows a classification model that instructs employees on which classification levels require CIO office adoption and on which levels employees can procure their own cloud services. This one is referred to as the *classification* example.

As you will notice, both of these security policies are quite short and succinct. As opposed to a standard IT security policy that covers a multitude of areas, cloud-specific security policies are generally focused on the procurement of cloud services. These policies can be treated as a form of a template and be modified to suit the format of your particular environment.

Cloud Security Policy: Centralized Example

This example policy has a centralized approach to procurement of any cloud services that will be used at ACME Incorporated.

Purpose

This policy outlines best practices and approval processes for using cloud computing services to support the processing, sharing, storage, and management of institutional data at ACME Incorporated.

Scope

This policy applies to any ACME Incorporated acquisition of cloud computing services. The project manager must coordinate planning with the operating unit CIO early in the planning process to avoid unnecessary problems later in the planning and acquisition lifecycle.

This policy pertains to the acquisition of services from a source outside of ACME Incorporated. Internal cloud computing services are already covered by existing requirements.

Background

Cloud computing is defined by NIST as "a model for enabling ubiquitous, convenient, on demand network access to a shared pool of configurable computing resources (e.g., networks, servers, storage, applications, and services) that can be rapidly provisioned and released with minimal management effort or service provider interaction." It is composed of five essential characteristics: on-demand self-service, broad network access, resource pooling, rapid elasticity or expansion, and measured services. It can be provided at a low level as hosted infrastructure (IaaS), at a mid-tier level as a hosted platform (PaaS), or at a high level as a software service (SaaS). Cloud providers can use private, public, or hybrid models.

Policy

Use of cloud computing services must be formally authorized in accordance with ACME Incorporated risk management processes. Specifically, the following:

- Use of cloud computing services must comply with all current laws, IT security, and risk management policies.

- Use of cloud computing services must comply with all privacy laws and regulations, and appropriate language must be included defining the cloud computing source responsibilities for maintaining privacy requirements.

- For external cloud computing services that require users to agree to terms of service agreements, such agreements must be approved by ACME Incorporated general counsel.

- All use of cloud computing services must be approved in writing by the operating unit CIO. The operating unit CIO will certify that security, privacy, and other IT management requirements have been adequately addressed prior to approving use of cloud computing services.

- The cloud computing services may not be put into production use until the operating unit CIO has provided written approval.

- The project manager must retain the CIO's certification along with other investment documentation.

Approval Date: December 15, 2017
Last Reviewed: November 14, 2019

Cloud Security Policy: Classification Example

In this example, ACME Incorporated has a hybrid approach to cloud service procurement. The classification of data will determine whether cloud services can be procured by the individual operating unit or must be centrally procured.

Purpose

To ensure that the confidentiality, integrity, and availability of ACME Incorporated information is preserved when stored, processed, or transmitted by a third-party cloud computing provider.

Scope

This policy concerns cloud computing resources that provide services, platforms, and infrastructure that provide support for a wide range of activities involving the processing, exchange, storage, or management of institutional data.

Background

Cloud computing services are application and infrastructure resources that are accessible via the Internet. These services, contractually provided by companies such as Amazon, Microsoft, and Google, enable customers to leverage computing resources. Cloud services provide services, platforms, and infrastructure to support a wide range of business activities. These services support processing, sharing, and storage, among other things. Cloud computing services are generally easy for people and organizations to use; they are accessible over the Internet through a variety of platforms (workstations, laptops, tablets, and smart phones); and they may be able to accommodate spikes in demand much more readily and efficiently than in-house computing services.

Policy

ACME Incorporated employees must be cautious about self-provisioning a cloud service to process, share, store, or otherwise manage corporate data. Self-provisioned cloud services may present significant data management risks or be subject to changes in risk with or without notice. Virtually all cloud services require individual users to accept click-through agreements. These agreements do not allow users to negotiate terms, do not provide the opportunity to clarify terms, often provide vague descriptions of services and safeguards, and often change without notice.

Risks associated with self-provisioned cloud services include the following:

- Unclear and potentially poor access control or general security provisions
- Sudden loss of service without notification
- Sudden loss of data without notification

- Data stored, processed, or shared on the cloud service is often mined for resale to third parties that may compromise people's privacy
- The exclusive intellectual rights to the data stored, processed, or shared on cloud service may become compromised

With the benefits and risks of procuring cloud services in mind, ACME Incorporated has implemented a multitier approach that considers the classification of data to centralize procurement of highly classified data while leaving business units to procure cloud services on their own for publicly available data.

Confidentiality Level	Description	Cloud Use
Level A: Restricted Data	All data that is governed by privacy or information protection mandates required by law, regulation, contract, binding agreement, or industry requirements.	• Cannot use self-provisioned cloud services to store, process, share, or otherwise manage restricted data. Employees wishing to procure any cloud service for restricted data must do so through the office of the CIO.
Level B: Moderate Sensitivity	Corporate data that is meant for limited distribution is available only to those who need the institutional data to support their work. This data derives its value for ACME Incorporated in part from not being publicly disclosed.	• Should not use self-provisioned cloud services to store, process, share, or otherwise manage moderate sensitivity data without ensuring that a service's safeguards are appropriate for confidential institutional data. • Should use only a centrally or locally provisioned cloud service once user has confirmed with the office of the CIO that the service is appropriate for sensitive corporate data. Not all contractually provisioned services are designed to handle sensitive corporate data.
Level C: Public Data	This data does not contain confidential information. Data is meant for wide and open distribution to the public at large.	• May use self-provisioned cloud services to store or manage public data with caution. Employees should ensure that using these cloud services does not violate any licensing agreements. • May use contractually provisioned cloud services to store or manage public institutional data.

Approval Date: December 15, 2017
Last Reviewed: November 14, 2019

About the Online Content

This book comes complete with TotalTester Online customizable practice exam software with 200 practice exam questions.

System Requirements

The current and previous major versions of the following desktop browsers are recommended and supported: Chrome, Microsoft Edge, Firefox, and Safari. These browsers update frequently, and sometimes an update may cause compatibility issues with the TotalTester Online or other content hosted on the Training Hub. If you run into a problem using one of these browsers, please try using another until the problem is resolved.

Your Total Seminars Training Hub Account

To get access to the online content, you will need to create an account on the Total Seminars Training Hub. Registration is free, and you will be able to track all your online content using your account. You may also opt in if you wish to receive marketing information from McGraw-Hill Education or Total Seminars, but this is not required for you to gain access to the online content.

Privacy Notice

McGraw-Hill Education values your privacy. Please be sure to read the Privacy Notice available during registration to see how the information you have provided will be used. You may view our Corporate Customer Privacy Policy by visiting the McGraw-Hill Education Privacy Center. Visit the **mheducation.com** site and click **Privacy** at the bottom of the page.

Single User License Terms and Conditions

Online access to the digital content included with this book is governed by the McGraw-Hill Education License Agreement outlined next. By using this digital content you agree to the terms of that license.

Access   To register and activate your Total Seminars Training Hub account, simply follow these easy steps.

1. Go to this URL: **hub.totalsem.com/mheclaim**

2. To register and create a new Training Hub account, enter your e-mail address, name, and password. No further personal information (such as credit card number) is required to create an account.

NOTE   If you already have a Total Seminars Training Hub account, select **Log in** and enter your e-mail and password. Otherwise, follow the remaining steps.

---

3. Enter your Product Key: **f07m-6r9k-0wgf**

4. Click to accept the user license terms.

5. Click **Register and Claim** to create your account. You will be taken to the Training Hub and have access to the content for this book.

Duration of License   Access to your online content through the Total Seminars Training Hub will expire one year from the date the publisher declares the book out of print.

Your purchase of this McGraw-Hill Education product, including its access code, through a retail store is subject to the refund policy of that store.

The Content is a copyrighted work of McGraw-Hill Education, and McGraw-Hill Education reserves all rights in and to the Content. The Work is © 2020 by McGraw Hill LLC.

Restrictions on Transfer   The user is receiving only a limited right to use the Content for the user's own internal and personal use, dependent on purchase and continued ownership of this book. The user may not reproduce, forward, modify, create derivative works based upon, transmit, distribute, disseminate, sell, publish, or sublicense the Content or in any way commingle the Content with other third-party content without McGraw-Hill Education's consent.

Limited Warranty   The McGraw-Hill Education Content is provided on an "as is" basis. Neither McGraw-Hill Education nor its licensors make any guarantees or warranties of any kind, either express or implied, including, but not limited to, implied warranties of merchantability or fitness for a particular purpose or use as to any McGraw-Hill Education Content or the information therein or any warranties as to the accuracy, completeness, correctness, or results to be obtained from, accessing or using the McGraw-Hill Education Content, or any material referenced in such Content or any information entered into licensee's product by users or other persons and/or any material available on or that can be accessed through the licensee's product (including via any hyperlink or otherwise) or as to non-infringement of third-party rights. Any warranties of any kind, whether express or implied, are disclaimed. Any material or data obtained through use of the McGraw-Hill Education Content is at your own discretion and risk and user understands that it will be solely responsible for any resulting damage to its computer system or loss of data.

Neither McGraw-Hill Education nor its licensors shall be liable to any subscriber or to any user or anyone else for any inaccuracy, delay, interruption in service, error or omission, regardless of cause, or for any damage resulting therefrom.

In no event will McGraw-Hill Education or its licensors be liable for any indirect, special or consequential damages, including but not limited to, lost time, lost money, lost profits or good will, whether in contract, tort, strict liability or otherwise, and whether or not such damages are foreseen or unforeseen with respect to any use of the McGraw-Hill Education Content.

TotalTester Online

TotalTester Online provides you with a simulation of the CCSK exam. Exams can be taken in Practice Mode or Exam Mode. Practice Mode provides an assistance window with hints, references to the book, explanations of the correct and incorrect answers, and the option to check your answer as you take the test. Exam Mode provides a simulation of the actual exam. The number of questions, the types of questions, and the time allowed are intended to be an accurate representation of the exam environment. The option to customize your quiz allows you to create custom exams from selected domains or chapters, and you can further customize the number of questions and time allowed.

To take a test, follow the instructions provided in the previous section to register and activate your Total Seminars Training Hub account. When you register, you will be taken to the Total Seminars Training Hub. From the Training Hub Home page, select **CCSK Certificate of Cloud Security Knowledge All-in-One Exam Guide TotalTester** from the Study drop-down menu at the top of the page, or from the list of Your Topics on the Home page. You can then select the option to customize your quiz and begin testing yourself in Practice Mode or Exam Mode. All exams provide an overall grade and a grade broken down by domain.

Technical Support

For questions regarding the TotalTester or operation of the Training Hub, visit **www.totalsem.com** or e-mail **support@totalsem.com**.

For questions regarding book content, visit **www.mheducation.com/customerservice**.

ABAC (attribute-based access control)   An access control scenario that grants users access rights based on policies that combine attributes. It considers the attributes of an entity and the connection in making access control decisions. For example, a user who used multifactor authentication, which requires two or more authentication factors, may be granted additional access, while a user who does not use MFA authentication would be granted less.

Amazon Simple Storage Service (S3)   A form of storage for use on the Web that provides scalability, data availability, security, and performance and enables you to retrieve any amount of data at any time.

API (application programming interface)   A protocol that exposes functionality through an interface to simplify the receipt of requests and delivery of responses. The two major types of APIs are Representational State Transfer (REST) and Simple Object Access Protocol (SOAP).

attestation   A formal statement that is officially claimed to be true. Attestations are legally binding. Provider attestations are part of a Service Organization Control 2 (SOC 2) report, for example, indicating a third-party, independent assessment of the security of a cloud service provider.

auto-scaling   A method used in the cloud, whereby the amount of computational resources in a server farm, typically measured in terms of the number of active servers, scales automatically based on current load.

automation   The processes and tools an organization uses to reduce the manual efforts associated with provisioning and managing cloud computing workloads.

availability zone   An isolated data center within a geographical region from which public cloud services originate and operate.

AWS (Amazon Web Services)   A public cloud service created and maintained by Amazon that offers compute power, database storage, content delivery, and other functionality to help businesses scale and grow.

Azure   A cloud service created by Microsoft for building, testing, deploying, and managing applications and services through a global network of Microsoft-managed data centers.

bastion virtual network   An emerging architecture for hybrid cloud connectivity. It can also be used to manage connectivity across multiple accounts in the same cloud provider environment while maintaining a single network connection back to a data center.

broad network access   Resources hosted in a cloud environment that are available for access from a wide range of locations and devices. It is an essential characteristic of cloud computing.

CAIQ (Consensus Assessments Initiative Questionnaire)   A survey for cloud consumers and auditors provided by the Cloud Security Alliance to assess the security capabilities of a cloud provider.

CASB (cloud access security broker)   A software service or appliance that is deployed between an organization's on-premises infrastructure and a cloud provider's infrastructure. A CASB acts as a control primarily for Software as a Service (SaaS) and enables the organization to extend the reach of their security policies beyond their own infrastructure.

CCM (Cloud Controls Matrix)   A set of security controls created by the CSA that provides fundamental security principles to guide cloud vendors and to assist prospective cloud customers in assessing the overall security risk of a cloud provider.

CCSK (Certificate of Cloud Security Knowledge)   A certification used to validate that a professional has a broad foundation of knowledge about cloud security, with topics such as architecture, governance, compliance, operations, encryption, virtualization, and much more.

CCSP (Certified Cloud Security Professional)   A certification used to validate that cloud security professionals have the required knowledge, skills, and abilities in cloud security design, implementation, architecture, operations, controls, and compliance with regulatory frameworks.

chaos engineering   A testing methodology by which the interrelationships between components in a system are tested by simulating failures in components and studying what knock-on effect occurs throughout the system. It is used to instill the requirement for resiliency in the development phase.

chargeback   Also known as IT chargeback. An accounting strategy that applies the costs of IT services, hardware, or software to the business unit in which they are used.

CI/CD (continuous integration/continuous deployment)   A set of tools often used with DevOps to establish a consistent and automated way to build, package, and test applications. Also referred to as continuous integration/continuous delivery, depending on the target environment (development or production).

cloud account   Any type of account, personal or business, with a cloud service provider.

cloud broker   An entity that manages the use, performance, and delivery of cloud services and that negotiates relationships between cloud providers and cloud consumers.

cloud bursting   An application deployment model in which an application runs in a private cloud or data center and bursts into a public cloud when the demand for computing capacity spikes.

cloud firewall   Also known as a security group. Policy sets that define ingress and egress rules that can apply to single assets or groups of assets, regardless of network location. Additionally, a cloud firewall can apply to assets based on more flexible criteria than hardware-based firewalls, because they aren't limited to physical topology.

community cloud   A cloud service deployment model that provides a cloud computing solution to a limited number of individuals or organizations and that is governed, managed, and secured commonly by all the participating organizations or a third-party managed service provider. All members of a community cloud share similar security and compliance requirements.

configuration management tool   A tool used to establish and maintain consistency of a product's performance, functional, and physical attributes with its requirements, design, and operational information throughout its life.

container   A logical packaging mechanism in which applications can be abstracted from the environment in which they run. This decoupling enables container-based applications to be deployed easily and consistently, regardless of whether the target environment is a private data center, the public cloud, or even a developer's personal laptop. Containers can help address portability in cloud environments.

continuous integration server   A tool used to support the practice of integrating software very often, typically with any change to an artifact in the source repository. Any time a team member commits a change to the repository, continuous integration can be used to ensure that any change passes a series of tests and that the software can be successfully built, tested, and deployed.

controller   Also known as cloud controller. A service that helps manage or orchestrate cloud operations. For instance, if a user were to make a request (for example, request an instance), the cloud controller processes the request and sends it to the appropriate destination, overseeing the process to completion.

CSA (Cloud Security Alliance)   The world's leading organization dedicated to defining and raising awareness of best practices to help ensure a secure cloud computing environment.

CSP (cloud service provider)   A company that offers some component of cloud computing—typically Infrastructure as a Service (IaaS), Software as a Service (SaaS), or Platform as a Service (PaaS)—to other businesses or individuals.

custodian   Also known as a data custodian. In IT, an entity that is responsible for the safe custody, transport, and storage of data and implementation of business rules. In other words, a custodian is in charge of the technical environment and database structure to protect end-user data.

customer managed key   An encryption key that is managed by a cloud customer, while the cloud provider manages the encryption engine.

DAM (database activity monitor) A suite of tools that can be used to support the ability to identify and report on fraudulent, illegal, or other undesirable behavior, with minimal impact on user operations and productivity. It performs this activity via inspection of SQL code and can therefore be considered a layer 7 firewall for SQL.

DAST (dynamic application security testing) A process of testing an application or software product in an operating state. This kind of testing is helpful for industry-standard compliance and general security protections for evolving projects.

data Information processed or stored by a computing device, which may be in the form of text documents, images, audio clips, software programs, or other types of media.

data dispersion A process that permits data to be replicated throughout a distributed storage infrastructure. It enables a service provider to offer storage services based on the level of the user's subscription or the popularity of the item. Can be thought of as a form of redundant array of independent disks (RAID), but multiple servers are involved.

dedicated hosting A type of Internet hosting in which the client leases an entire server that is not shared with anyone else. This is more flexible than shared hosting, as organizations have full control over the server(s), including the choice of operating system, hardware, and more.

deployment model A model that represents a specific type of cloud environment, primarily distinguished by ownership, size, and access. Four common cloud deployment models are public cloud, community cloud, private cloud, and hybrid cloud.

DevOps A software engineering culture and practice that aims at unifying software development (Dev) and software operation (Ops). The main characteristic of the DevOps movement is to advocate automation and monitoring at all steps of software construction, from integration, testing, and releasing, to deployment and infrastructure management.

DevSecOps A practice that strives to automate core security tasks by embedding security controls and processes into the DevOps workflow.

Direct Connect A service offered by AWS that enables private connectivity between AWS and your data center, office, or colocation environment, which in many cases can reduce your network costs, increase bandwidth throughput, and provide a more consistent network experience than Internet-based connections. Microsoft Azure ExpressRoute and Google Cloud Dedicated Interconnect products are similar.

DLP (data loss prevention) A strategy for ensuring that end users do not send sensitive or critical information outside the corporate network. Also used to describe software products that help a network administrator control what data end users can transfer.

EC2 (Elastic Compute Cloud) A web service offered by Amazon that provides secure and resizable compute capacity in the cloud. It is designed to make web-scale cloud computing easier for developers.

e-discovery   The electronic aspect of identifying, collecting, and producing electronically stored information (ESI) in response to a request for production in a lawsuit or investigation. ESI includes, but is not limited to, e-mails, documents, databases, voicemail, social media, and web sites.

elasticity   The ability of a cloud service provider to provide on-demand offerings by nimbly switching resources when demand goes up or down. It is often an immediate reaction to clients' dropping or adding services in real time.

ENISA (European Network and Information Security Agency)   An organization that enhances the cybersecurity prevention work and capability of the European Union and its member states and, as a consequence, the entire business community, to prevent, address, and respond to network and information security challenges.

entitlement   The mapping of an identity (such as roles, personas, and attributes) to an authorization. In other words, an entitlement indicates what a unique user identity is allowed (and not allowed) to do with specific resources or systems. For documentation purposes, we keep these in an entitlement matrix.

entitlement matrix   A document that outlines the various resources and functions allowed to be used by specific users, groups, and roles.

ephemeral   Describes something that will change rapidly or last for a very short amount of time. For instance, ephemeral storage is not written to disk for long-term storage.

essential characteristics   The characteristics that make a cloud a cloud: the essential characteristics are resource pooling, on-demand self-service, a broad network, rapid elasticity, and measured service. If something has these characteristics, we consider it cloud computing, and if it lacks any of them, it is likely not a cloud.

event-driven security   A type of security system that triggers actions automatically in response to a security event. This type of security can define events that will generate security actions and use the event-driven capabilities to trigger automated notification, assessment, remediation, or other security processes. Certain cloud providers support event-driven code execution. In these cases, the management plane detects various activities that can in turn trigger code execution through a notification message or via serverless hosted code.

federated identity   Also known as federation. The practice of interconnecting the cloud computing environments of two or more service providers for the purpose of load balancing traffic and accommodating spikes in demand.

FedRAMP (Federal Risk and Authorization Management Program)   An assessment and authorization process that US agencies have been directed to use by the Office of Management and Budget to ensure that security is in place when accessing cloud computing products and services.

GDPR (General Data Protection Regulation)   A regulation in EU law on data protection and privacy for all individuals within the European Union. It also addresses the export of personal data outside the EU. The GDPR aims to give control to citizens and residents over their personal data and to simplify the regulatory environment for international business by unifying the regulation within the EU.

HSM (hardware security module) A physical computing device that safeguards and manages digital keys for strong authentication and provides cryptoprocessing. An HSM traditionally comes in the form of a plug-in card or an external device that attaches directly to a computer or network server.

hybrid cloud A composition of two or more clouds (such as private and public) that remain distinct entities but are bound together, offering the benefits of multiple deployment models. It can also be used to refer to a traditional data center and a public cloud.

hypervisor Computer software, firmware, or hardware that creates and runs virtual machines.

IaaS (Infrastructure as a Service) A cloud computing service model. An IaaS cloud provider will host the infrastructure components traditionally found in an on-premises data center, including servers, storage, and networking hardware, as well as the virtualization or hypervisor layer. In this service model, the customer assumes the most responsibility for security.

IAM (identity and access management) The security and business discipline that addresses the need to ensure appropriate access to resources across increasingly heterogeneous technology environments and to meet increasingly rigorous compliance requirements.

IAST (interactive application security testing) A testing process that analyzes the behavior of an application in the testing phase, using a combination of RASP (runtime application self-protection) and DAST (dynamic application security testing), to aid in identifying vulnerabilities within an application, enabling developers to reduce risk during the development process.

IdEA (identity, entitlement, and access) management A solution that leverages directory services to provide access control, giving the right users access to the resources they are allowed to access at a particular time.

identity provider (IdP) A system entity that enables organizations to create and maintain identity information for individuals across a wide range of online services or applications that require user identification.

image A copy made available to a consumer supplied by a provider, or a previously created image used to build server instances.

immutable An object whose state cannot be changed after it is created. In the cloud, an immutable infrastructure means that servers are not altered after they are deployed. If anything needs to be changed, a new server instance will be made from a similar image and the changes will be applied accordingly and then redeployed.

infostructure Any structured or unstructured data that is stored in a cloud environment.

infrastructure   The moving parts that serve as the foundation of a computing system, often consisting of compute, network, and storage; it is owned by the provider in a public cloud.

instance   A server running an image of your server, for which you have complete responsibility with regard to maintenance and ensuring secure operation.

interoperability   The ability for multiple instances to work at the same time without any restrictions.

ISO/IEC (International Standards Organization/International Electrotechnical Commission)   A technical committee that develops, maintains, and promotes a series of IT standards, such as ISO/IEC 27001 and ISO/IEC 27017.

isolation   A practice that ensures that processes in one virtual machine or container cannot be visible to another. It allows for multiple tenants to reside on the same infrastructure.

jump kit   A set of software tools used for incident response in cloud environments.

jurisdiction   Determines applicable laws based on geographic location.

KMS (key management system)   A system that manages keys within a cryptosystem; it deals with the generation, exchange, storage, replacement, use, and destruction of cryptographic keys.

Lambda   A platform offered by Amazon Web Services as an event-driven, serverless computing platform. Microsoft Azure and Google Cloud Functions are competing serverless computing products.

load balancing   A process that distributes workloads across multiple computing resources. Often available as an application or network load balancer service.

management plane   The element of a system that controls the management of infrastructure, platforms, applications, and resources though the use of API calls and web consoles.

measured service   A process by which the cloud provider measures and monitors a system to ensure that users consume only what they are allowed to consume and, if required, are billed for it.

metadata   Information about other data, typically used for discovery and identification.

metastructure   Protocols and mechanisms that provide the interface between the infrastructure and other layers within the system.

MFA (multifactor authentication)   A process whereby the user needs to confirm their identity through the use of two or more authentication factors, such as something you know (password), something you have (smart ID card), or something you are (biometrics).

microservices   Also known as microservice architecture. A method of developing software applications as a suite of individual and independent services.

migration   The process of moving from one system to another—for example, moving processes from a data center to the cloud.

multitenancy   A mode of operation in which multiple individual tenants (such as companies in a public cloud) are operating in a shared environment. The tenants are logically isolated but physically integrated.

NIST 800-53   A guideline created by the National Institute of Standards and Technology (NIST) regarding the security and privacy controls for federal information systems and organizations.

NIST 800-61   A guideline created by the National Institute of Standards and Technology (NIST) regarding computer security incident handling (incident response).

NIST 800-145   A document in which the National Institute of Standards and Technology (NIST) defines cloud computing.

OAuth protocol   An industry standard for authorization, which handles authorization for web, desktop, mobile, and Internet of Things (IoT) devices.

on-demand   The ability to provision computing capabilities automatically and unilaterally without any human interaction.

OpenFlow   A software defined networking (SDN) communications protocol that enables network controllers to determine the path of network packets across a network of switches.

OpenID   An open source standard that enables users to sign into multiple web sites using a single existing account, without requiring new passwords. It can provide authentication on top of OAuth authorization capabilities. The latest version is OpenID Connect (OIDC).

orchestration   The ability to automatically arrange, coordinate, and manage computer systems.

PaaS (Platform as a Service)   A cloud computing service model. This complete development and deployment environment in the cloud is designed to support the complete web application lifecycle: building, testing, deploying, managing, and updating. It enables you to deliver everything from simple cloud-based apps to sophisticated, cloud-enabled enterprise applications.

packet encapsulation   A method for designing modular communication protocols in which logically separate functions in a network are abstracted from their underlying structures by inclusion or hiding information within higher-level objects.

pools   A set of resources ready to be used at any time. In cloud computing, resource pools usually focus on compute, network, storage, and container pools.

portability   The ability to reuse or move applications and/or systems from one environment to another.

private cloud   A cloud infrastructure operated solely for one organization that is managed either by the organization or by a third party and is either on or off premises.

public cloud   A cloud infrastructure owned by an organization selling cloud services to a large number of users.

RASP (runtime application self-protection)   A security technology that works to detect and protect against application attacks in real time.

raw storage   Storage directly connected to a virtual machine that is generally not available in the public cloud.

RBAC (role-based access control)   A method of access security that determines the access an individual is granted based on their role in the organization.

region   The jurisdiction in which the workload will operate, which is typically user-defined within your cloud provider's settings.

relying party   The system that relies on an identity assertion from an identity provider.

resiliency   The ability for a cloud provider to maintain operations while facing challenges. This is done through the use of another redundant set of IT resources in the same cloud.

RESTful (Representational State Transfer) API   An application program interface that uses HTTP requests to GET, PUT, POST, and DELETE data.

SaaS (Software as a Service)   A cloud-based software solution and service model in which the provider assumes the most responsibility for security.

SAML (Security Assertion Markup Language)   An OASIS open standard that defines an SML framework supported by both enterprise tools and cloud providers to federate identity management. It supports both authentication and authorization and creates assertions between an identity provider and a relying party.

SAST (static application security testing)   A white-box testing tool that determines security vulnerabilities from the inside-out by examining the source code of an application. SAST can be used at all points of the software development lifecycle (SDLC).

SCIM (System for Cross-domain Identity)   A standard that allows for the automations of user provisioning, communicating user identity data between identity providers and service providers, and requiring user identity information. Note that SCIM is used for provisioning, not for federation.

SDI (software defined infrastructure)   Also known as infrastructure as code (IaC). A process for automating deployment of a virtual infrastructure using templates.

SDLC (software development lifecycle)   A framework that outlines the tasks and responsibilities that must take place during software development.

SDN (software defined networking)   The process of disassociating network packets from the control plane, improving network performance and monitoring. Serves as the foundation of an automated network environment.

SDN firewall   Also known as a security group in an IaaS environment. A software defined networking (SDN)–based firewall that works as a packet filter and a policy checker. Firewall rules can be applied to a single asset or a group of assets—for example, firewall rules may apply to any asset with a particular tag.

SDP (Software Defined Perimeter)   An approach that combines a device and user authentication to dynamically enable network access to resources and to enhance security.

SecaaS (Security as a Service)   A security-focused SaaS product that can be used to protect cloud and traditional IT assets. It enables you to enforce your policy on all desired systems, regardless of their physical locations.

security group   Defines network rules regarding how an instance handles incoming and outgoing traffic, with rules applied similarly to an SDN firewall.

segmentation   The division of a server's memory into different parts to separate systems and applications from one another.

segregation   A process by which a cloud provider divides up resources among different groups.

self-service   A process that enables access to physical or virtual resources as needed without having to interact with a human.

serverless computing   A model in which the cloud provider runs and manages the server, enabling users to run all or some of an application stack within a cloud provider's environment without the users having to manage any operating systems or containers.

service model   The different fundamental categories of cloud services: Software as a Service (SaaS), Platform as a Service (PaaS), and Infrastructure as a Service (IaaS).

SIEM (security information and event management)   An approach to system log and event data management from virtual and real networks as well as applications and systems, which analyzes the system or network to provide real-time reporting and alerting on information or events that require action.

SOAP (Simple Object Access Protocol)   A web-based API based on a lightweight XML-based protocol for exchanging information.

SOC (Service Organizational Control)   An attestation engagement standard by the American Institute of CPAs (AICPA) that is used by many providers to demonstrate controls in place. Multiple SOC reports include SOC 1 (Internal Controls over Financial Reporting), SOC 2 (Trust Services Criteria), and SOC 3 (redacted SOC 2). Note that SOC is undergoing a name change to System and Organizational Controls.

software defined security   A security model in which security processes are working in an automated fashion.

SOX (Sarbanes-Oxley)   An auditing law passed by the US Congress that is used for publicly traded companies in the United States. Its main focus is to protect investors from fraudulent financial reporting by maintaining internal control over financial reporting from a cloud perspective. Many of the SOX compliance activities relate to application security controls (applistructure).

SSAE 16/18   An audit standard by the American Institute of CPAs that is used to perform SOC attestation engagements.

SSO (single-sign-on)   An access control system that allows for the use of a single ID and password to gain access to a service. Examples of SSOs include Kerberos and Security Assertion Markup Language (SAML), used to perform federation with cloud service providers.

STAR (Security Trust Assurance and Risk)   A Cloud Security Alliance (CSA) repository that can be used to perform due diligence of potential cloud service providers (CSPs). Entries include self-assessments, which are vendor-supplied responses to the CSA's Consensus Assessment Initiative Questionnaire (CAIQ). CSPs may also list third-party assessment–based certifications based on ISO standards and attestations based on AICPA SOC reports.

storage gateway   Also known as hybrid storage gateway. An on-premises storage appliance (virtual or physical) that can interconnect local and cloud storage. A gateway can perform actions such as de-duplication, compression, encryption, and so on.

tag   Also known as resource tag. Consists of a name/value pair and is used in cloud services to identify and perform actions on individual resources or a collection of resources.

TDE (Transparent Database Encryption)   A database encryption system that encrypts a whole database at the file level as a means to support encryption-at-rest compliance for database files.

treaties   A formally concluded and ratified agreement between countries. Applicable treaties for cloud discussion include US/EU Safe Harbor and its replacement, EU/US Privacy Shield, which provides companies with a mechanism to comply with data protection requirements when transferring personal data from the European Union and Switzerland to the United States in support of transatlantic commerce.

version control repository   A storage location for software projects that supports multiple versions of software to facilitate easy rollback and other functionality. Often available in both public and private deployment models. Public repositories have been used to uncover corporate credential files (such as access keys).

virtualization   A system that abstracts hardware from guest operating systems. Virtualization allows for multiple virtual machines (aka guest operating systems) to run in an isolated fashion on the same physical server.

VLAN (virtual local area network)   A group of devices on one or more LANs that are configured to communicate as if they were attached to the same wire (such as the same broadcast domain), when in fact they are located on a number of different LAN segments. Because VLANs are based on logical instead of physical connections, they are extremely flexible.

VM (virtual machine)   A software program or an operating system that not only exhibits the behavior of a separate computer but is also capable of performing tasks such as running applications and programs like a separate computer. A VM, usually known as a guest, is created within another computing environment, referred as a host. Multiple VMs can exist within a single host at one time. In a cloud environment such as AWS, these VMs are referred to as instances.

volatile memory   Computer storage that maintains its data only while the device is powered on. Of most significance from a security perspective, volatile memory can hold cryptographic keys and unencrypted data.

VPC (virtual private cloud)   A pool of shared resources in the cloud that lets you provision a logically isolated section, where you can launch resources in a virtual network that you define. You have complete control over your virtual networking environment, including selection of your own IP address range, creation of subnets, and configuration of route tables and network gateways.

WAF (web application firewall)   A firewall that filters, monitors, and blocks HTTP traffic to and from a web application. A WAF is differentiated from a regular firewall in that a WAF is able to filter based on the content of HTTP traffic, while regular firewalls restrict traffic based on IP and port. A WEF can be traditional or cloud based.

workload   In computing, the amount of processing that the computer has been given to do at a given time. The workload consists of some amount of application programming running in the computer and usually some number of users connected to and interacting with the computer's applications.

XACML (eXtensible Access Control Markup Language)   A standard that defines a declarative fine-grained, attribute-based access control policy language; an architecture; and a processing model describing how to evaluate access requests according to the rules defined in policies.

INDEX

A

acceptable use policy, 34, 104–105

access controls, 220–221, 238

access keys, 121

accounting, 238

Act on the Protection of Personal Information (Japan), 55

Active Directory, 242–243

Active Directory Federation Services (ADFS), 242

ADFS. *See* Active Directory Federation Services (ADFS)

AICPA, 36, 85

Amazon, 115, 128, 206

Amazon Elastic Container Service (Amazon ECS), 172

Amazon S3, 5, 216, 235

Amazon Web Services (AWS), 118, 235

American Institute of Certified Public Accountants. *See* AICPA

Anglo-American model, 31

Apache Software Foundation, 269

API gateway, 118, 207

API lock-in, 288

API Mandate, 115, 206

APIs, 2, 10

 background, 115–118

 external, 115–116

 internal, 115–116

 open, 115–116

 private, 115–116

 REST APIs, 2, 10, 13, 116–118

 SOAP APIs, 2, 13, 116, 118

application design and architectures, how the cloud impacts, 205–207

application plane, 139–140

application programming interfaces. *See* APIs

application security, 195

 DevOps and continuous integration/continuous deployment, 196, 207–209

 how the cloud impacts application design and architectures, 196, 205–207

 secure software development lifecycle (SSDLC), 196–204

Application Stack Maps, 185

application-level controls, 221

application/platform storage, 217

applistructure, 6, 127, 227

"Architectural Styles and the Design of Network-based Software Architectures" (Fielding), 117

attestations, 65, 88

attribute-based access control (ABAC), 251, 252

attributes, 237

audit management

 in the cloud, 83–84

 how the cloud changes audits, 88–90

auditors, 37

 requirements, 90

audits

 background, 82

 computer-assisted audit techniques, 81

 continuous monitoring vs. continuous auditing, 80–81

 defined, 82

 and ENISA, 285, 286

 first-party, 78

 how the cloud changes audits, 88–90

 pass-through, 80